P9-CRW-760

KENNEDY
AND
ROOSEVELT

MICHAEL R. BESCHLOSS

KENNEDY *AND* ROOSEVELT

The Uneasy Alliance

Foreword by James MacGregor Burns

W · W · NORTON & COMPANY · *NEW YORK · LONDON*

 Published simultaneously in Canada by George J. McLeod Limited, Toronto. Printed in the United States of America.

THE TEXT *of this book is composed in photocomposition Caledonia. The display type used is hand set Monotype Garamont. Composition, printing and binding are by the Maple-Vail Book Manufacturing Group. Book design is by Marjorie J. Flock.*

Library of Congress Cataloging in Publication Data

Beschloss, Michael R. 1955–

Kennedy and Roosevelt: the uneasy alliance.

Bibliography: pp. 281–285

Includes index.

1. Roosevelt, Franklin Delano, Pres. U.S., 1882–1945 —Friends and associates. 2. Kennedy, Joseph Patrick, 1888–1969—Friends and associates. 3. United States—Politics and government—1933–1945. 4. United States Foreign relations—1933–1945. I. Title.

E807.B47 1980 973.917'092'2 79–24548

ISBN 0–393–01335–9

FOR MY PARENTS

CONTENTS

Photographs appear following page 130.
Cartoons and illustrations are interspersed throughout the book.

FOREWORD

THE CONFIDENTIAL RELATIONSHIPS among ambitious and competitive leaders are always fascinating and usually revealing. Their letters and messages enable us to penetrate beyond the banalities of "teamwork" to the fierce jockeying for position and the conflicts that rage among the entourage.

Franklin Roosevelt had the knack of making memorable friends and enemies. The galaxy of remarkable people who worked with him—Ickes and Wallace, Cohen and Corcoran, Tugwell and Hopkins, Eleanor Roosevelt and Frances Perkins—is matched only by his assortment of adversaries. In the early days, these ranged from Tammany sachems to Warren G. Harding; later, they included a string of demolished Republican candidates from Hoover to Dewey; and in between, they numbered such personalities as Father Coughlin, Huey Long, Hearst, Lindbergh, and sadly, Al Smith. Only FDR could have pulled the Democrats into a crazy-quilt coalition, but only FDR could have generated such an exquisite array of ill-assorted enemies.

As Michael Beschloss demonstrates in this volume, the relationship between Franklin Roosevelt and Joseph Kennedy combined elements of love and hate more intensely than most of the other well-known connections. The two men present an arresting study in leadership. Not only did they pursue careers in both the business and political arenas—with mixed results—but their political relationship threaded through the central controversies of a pivotal age. The issues of the nineteen-thirties and nineteen-forties were not just another act in the great game of politics. The nation and the world faced momentous challenges whose resolution set the boundaries of human hope and action for generations to come.

Kennedy and Roosevelt resembled each other in many ways—they were both ambitious, energetic, manipulative, activist, proud, and vulnerable—but each was ultimately devoted to his own vision of the public good. At a time when the political establishment recognized the need for far-reaching domestic reforms and the inevitability of a showdown with Hitler, Kennedy listened to a different drummer. Occasionally sycophantic, ordinarily candid, he was willing to confront his boss in a manner that other presidential associates dream about but would not dare. Franklin Roosevelt, despite all his twists and turns, his deceptions and evasions, his concessions and compromises, proved to be everlastingly right in the direction he led the American people. Yet if Joseph Kennedy was the lesser partner in this awkward embrace, he left a special legacy in four sons who were trained in public service.

Placing Joseph Kennedy and Franklin Roosevelt in contrasting political traditions, Michael Beschloss brilliantly illuminates their political leadership and the historical forces that impelled it. In these days of contentious but superficial politics, it is refreshing to turn back to a time when politicians fought each other, heart and soul, because they were committed to conflicting visions of public purpose.

JAMES MACGREGOR BURNS

PREFACE

JOSEPH KENNEDY AND FRANKLIN ROOSEVELT were the sons of fathers who combined business interests with political activism. They studied at Harvard; helped to mobilize American shipbuilding during the First World War; threw themselves into the business civilization of the nineteen-twenties; enjoyed the idea of political dynasty; coveted the presidency; and joined in an uneasy alliance in national and international politics.

Still, the lives played out not in unison, but in counterpoint. Kennedy compiled an almost unbroken series of business triumphs, yet his political dreams ended in frustration. Roosevelt won four terms as president of the United States, yet, as businessman, he lost several small fortunes. A political partnership waxed and waned from intimate collaboration to mutual suspicion and painfully concealed hostility. How explain such grand triumphs and grand frustrations? What brought these two men together; what rent them apart?

This book examines Kennedy and Roosevelt in the context of leadership. It views the two men and their relationship in terms of the human dilemma confronting every leader: the uneasy alliance between the quest for power and the quest for purpose.

Since the earliest days of the Republic, the American tradition has sanctioned two vital definitions of public service. The visionary tradition, with roots in such varied thinkers as Rousseau and John Adams, ordained that individual ambitions be subordinated to a more universal conception of the public interest. The pragmatic tradition of Locke and Adam Smith commanded citizens instead to follow the pull of their own interests; from the large-scale engagement of contending ambitions, the common good would prevail.

Neither ethic exists in purity, of course, but Franklin Roosevelt and

Joseph Kennedy matured in environments that were almost seedbeds of the two traditions—Roosevelt among Hyde Park standards of *noblesse oblige,* Kennedy in the toughminded code of East Boston politics. What made these men exceptional was that each perceived his birthright as an imperfect legacy. Roosevelt grew to seek ideals through a welter of short-run goals and compromises. Kennedy allied his fierce commitment to family advancement, time and time again, with elements of broader principle.

The proposition of this book is that Kennedy and Roosevelt were governed nonetheless by opposing visions of public service and, hence, of leadership. This contest of leadership styles influenced the two men's contrasting performances in commerce and government; it accounted not only for the breakdown in the Kennedy-Roosevelt alliance, but also for its accomplishments.

Francis Biddle once wrote that the main reward for toilers in the New Deal lay "in some deep sense of giving and sharing, far below any surface pleasure of work well done, but rooted in the relief of escaping the loneliness and boredom of oneself, and the unreality of personal ambition." Yet there was also the other side of the Roosevelt government, of disorder and competition, of exuberant energies channeled into new ideas and ventures.

Great leadership emerges from great conflict as well as cooperation. In their uneasy alliance, Joseph Kennedy and Franklin Roosevelt were finally more effective men—both in league and in confrontation—than they would have been on their own.

MICHAEL R. BESCHLOSS

Williamstown, Massachusetts
July 1979

KENNEDY
AND
ROOSEVELT

Prologue

OCTOBER 1940

SUNDAY AFTERNOON, October 27, 1940. Engines roaring, the great blue and silver seaplane hurtled toward New York. An unruly gathering of newspapermen watched at La Guardia Field. At the White House, Franklin Roosevelt discussed politics over lunch with the Speaker of the House, Sam Rayburn, and a young Texas congressman, Lyndon Johnson, as he waited for the *Atlantic Clipper* to arrive from Europe.

Aboard the aircraft was the American ambassador to the Court of St. James's, Joseph Patrick Kennedy. For months, the president had contrived to keep his unhappy envoy in London, away from the presidential campaign, but now Joseph Kennedy was returning to America, promising friends an election-eve "bombshell" that would tip the scales of victory to Wendell Willkie. The balloting was only ten days ahead.

October had seen a lull in the European fighting that seemed to mock the president's warnings against the danger of German might. Fear of Hitler gave way to a more passionate fear of war. "A subsurface anti-war psychology seems to be taking hold generally and almost suddenly," observed a *New York Times* reporter. Wendell Willkie transformed his campaign into a peace crusade against the warrior in the Oval Room. "If his promise to keep our boys out of foreign wars is no better than his promise to balance the budget," he cried in his hoarse and urgent fashion, "they're already almost on the transports!" Other Republican orators cautioned American mothers against the "secret Roosevelt pact" that would consign their sons to Britain's war after election day. As proof, they pointed to the imminent muster of nearly a million young men. The Republican "peace strategy" was working, said Dr. George Gallup. He pronounced Wendell Willkie "within easy striking distance of victory."

No one could confirm or deny secret collaboration between Washington and London with more authority than the American ambassador to Great Britain. Since his installation in March 1938, Joseph Kennedy had steadfastly opposed American intervention in Europe, assuring a visitor that he would "resist to the bitter end." Franklin Roosevelt, inching toward aid to Britain through 1939 and 1940, quietly shifted his major diplomatic transactions from Kennedy to a succession of personal envoys and to the British ambassador in Washington. Indignant at being bypassed, skeptical of the president's professed noninterventionism, Kennedy excoriated his chief before London friends, predicting that he could "put twenty-five million Catholic votes behind Wendell Willkie to throw Roosevelt out."

White House and Whitehall had indeed maintained secret contacts since the outbreak of war, although never to the extent claimed by the most alarmed isolationists. Joseph Kennedy was unaware of many of these negotiations—he would never discover how fully he had actually been circumvented—yet he knew enough of the details to endanger the president's reelection. Now Kennedy stood at the epicenter of the controversy. Would he aid Franklin Roosevelt by calming the widespread fears of Anglo-American collaboration or would he resign in protest, revealing what he knew, creating momentum that could possibly carry Wendell Willkie into the presidency?

Henry Luce, publisher of *Time* and *Life*, who entertained the notion of his own appointment as Willkie's secretary of state, concluded after a telephone call from London that Kennedy was prepared to abandon the president. At the London embassy the previous spring, Clare Boothe Luce had been assured by the ambassador that "I'm going to come back home, get off the plane, and endorse the Republican candidate for president." The publisher was planning to send a delegation to meet Kennedy at La Guardia, one story had it. The delegation would take the ambassador to the Luces' home in Manhattan. Later, Kennedy would deliver a radio address that would be the crowning stroke of Wendell Willkie's campaign.

To Roosevelt, keeping Kennedy out of harm's way in London seemed all the more imperative. But Kennedy would not be restrained; he informed Cordell Hull, secretary of state, that if permission to return were withheld, he would release a blistering indictment of Franklin Roosevelt to appear in American newspapers five days before the election. The president relented, but ensured that he—not Henry Luce or any other Willkie confederate—would be the first to see Kennedy when he arrived.

In late October Joseph Kennedy left London. At every stop along the five-day air journey, he received a message from the president asking for discretion. A letter waiting at Lisbon asked Kennedy "not to make any statement to the press on your way over, nor when you arrive in New York, until you and I have had a chance to agree upon what should be said. Come straight to Washington as I want to talk to you as soon as you get here." When reporters pressed the envoy on rumors he would resign to endorse Willkie, he said, "I have nothing to tell you, boys."

Now the *Atlantic Clipper* approached New York. It was the final day of the World's Fair, and fairgoers saw the whalelike craft pass over the Trylon and Perisphere before it coasted onto the bay.

Kennedy stepped from the forward hatch. He was intercepted by a presidential delegation, whose members presented him with a handwritten invitation from Roosevelt to the White House. As if to underscore the invitation, a Jeep idled nearby to deliver Kennedy to an airplane poised for flight to the Capital.

That evening, the ambassador had dinner and a long conversation with the president. Two nights later, in a national radio broadcast, Joseph Kennedy endorsed Franklin Roosevelt for a third term.

Speculation over the bargaining between Roosevelt and Kennedy that evening would not end. Scores of people in Washington and London believed they knew the genuine story. Some insisted that Joseph Kennedy exacted a presidential pledge of nonintervention as the price of his support. Others were certain that the meeting was an old-fashioned political horsetrade in which Roosevelt offered some political advantage to win Kennedy's endorsement—from a major post in national defense to the president's support as his successor in 1944.

The bargaining of October 1940 echoed the first encounter between Franklin Roosevelt and Joseph Kennedy twenty-three years earlier. Roosevelt, the thirty-five-year-old assistant secretary of the navy, was managing ship production for America's part in the First World War. Kennedy, twenty-nine in 1917, was assistant manager of Bethlehem Steel's Fore River shipyard at Quincy, Massachusetts. Roosevelt had negotiated a contract with Kennedy's yard to produce two battleships for Argentina. The vessels were finished, but Buenos Aires had yet to pay the bill. Kennedy refused to release the ships without cash on the barrelhead.

In a conversation at the Navy Department, the assistant secretary presented a double appeal to Kennedy. First, withholding the ships would damage American foreign relations and hemispheric unity during wartime. Second, if Kennedy did not deliver the ships immediately, Roosevelt would simply command navy tugboats to tow the vessels away. Kennedy resisted both arguments. The ships were towed the following afternoon.

The two transactions between president and ambassador, navy man and businessman, offered brief glimpses of the instincts at work in Kennedy and Roosevelt. What forged the contradictions and the complexities in each man?

One

CONTEST OF TRADITIONS

THE ELEVEN YEARS between the Revolution and the Constitutional Convention were a time for rumination. Publicans, laborers, farmers, scholars, the proprietors of city gazettes, and other political thinkers pondered the form of government that would best promote the public interest. They debated the nature of the American character and how individual ambitions could be most wisely enlisted for the common good. The dialogue was shaped by two emerging views of human nature and public service.

One body of opinion saw an American blessed with a special capacity for rational thought—a New Man, in the phrase of Crèvecoeur. Private ambitions could be expected to give way to the public spirit. Businessmen would make transactions on the basis of community responsibility; in the political realm, issues would be resolved by reason. Americans would seek happiness not in the mere life of private advancement, but in the good life of Aristotle's commonwealth.

The other school of thought questioned this vision, citing instances of greed and selfishness during the century before Independence. It was misguided, they argued, to expect a merchant or politician to "quit the line which interest marks out for him" in the service of an amorphous public good. The survival of liberty could not depend on the willingness of citizens and statesmen to overcome their own ambitions. Government must be structured instead to derive strength from the pursuit of private interests. This conception was fortified in 1776 by the publication of Adam Smith's *The Wealth of Nations*, with its famous argument that the citizen following personal interest "frequently promotes that of the society more effectively than when he really intends to promote it." Citizens would therefore serve the nation most faithfully by competing to the fullest; the engagement of factions would not only prevent a single group from gaining inordinate power but lead to business prosperity and the selection of the finest public servants and public laws.

The Founding period yielded little support for the visionary notion of the virtuous American. State legislatures were filling with men who, James Madison believed, were "without reading, experience, or principle." Journalists lamented the corruption that seemed to sprawl throughout the provinces. So dispirited was George Washington that he concluded in 1782, "It is not the public, but the private interest which influences the generality of mankind, nor can the Americans any longer boast an exception."

The pragmatic vision prevailed at Philadelphia. The new Constitution sought to promote the general welfare less through appeals for public-spirited behavior than by counteracting ambition with ambition. Nevertheless, unwritten law kept alive the more demanding ethic of citizenship. Preachers exhorted their flocks to heed the doctrine of community. Schoolmasters pursued their earnest business of moral education in a system of free schools. The language and literature of the early nineteenth century rang with the music of the commonweal.

The decade after the Civil War was a forcing house of change. Henry Adams, returning from abroad, was astonished by what he saw. Factory towns were springing up across the landscape, the frontier vanishing, immigrants arriving in legions. Strange, unlearned men like Jay Gould and Cornelius Vanderbilt mocked old Yankee notions of austerity and disinterested service, amassing and spending unprecedented fortunes. Cities, swelled with newcomers, elected unusual new figures to office—frank political operators who pledged not Good Government, but a good meal, a municipal job, or a barrel of coal.

A dialogue that had been primarily an intellectual disagreement among the elite took on the lines of a conflict between cultures. Embracing the visionary ethic were the old families and their allies, generally comfortable, Protestant, wary. Against them, a newer group was riding the pragmatic vision into power; largely immigrant, urban, Catholic, they were eager for opportunity and unashamed of competing strenuously. These groups were loose amalgamations, cross-cut by a score of other issues, yet their opposing views of public service stimulated conflicts that were vehement and long-lived.

Perhaps the most characteristic figure of the new epoch was the city boss. His political credo was not oriented toward abstract principle, but toward goals more immediate and palpable. "When a man works in politics," declared George Washington Plunkitt, the artful Tammany man, "he should get something out of it." What bosses like Patrick Kennedy of East Boston got out of politics was the joy of authority and the physical necessities for their constituents—clothing, food, housing, as well as a sympathetic ear, and sometimes, relief from the law. In the stark reality of the wards, national issues frequently meant little more than a distraction from the more serious matters of patronage and party regularity. By 1880, in Philadelphia, New York, Chicago, and Boston, the newcomers outnumbered the old-stock Americans. The most formidable machines were in place.

The heirs to the visionary tradition, like James Roosevelt of Hyde Park, looked on all of this with dismay. But, believing politics had grown too soiled for gentlemen, most patricians remained aloof from the political arena, leaving the banner to be shouldered by a generation of reformers. Newspapermen bared the links between money and votes; cartoonists lampooned the city machines. E. L. Godkin, in the pages of *The Nation*, reproached American intellectuals for failing to teach civic duty to their brethren. Their ranks were diverse and their programs sometimes contradictory, but the reformers were united by their passion to restore the public-minded ideal to the national spirit.

The culprits themselves reacted with petulance. "What do I care about the law?" asked Commodore Vanderbilt. "Hain't I got the power?" Boss Tweed was defiant too. Confronted in 1871 with a complaint against him, he snapped, "What are you going to do about it?" So incongruent was reform with their aspirations, the boss and his disciples found the reformer almost an apparition. Political ideals like women's suffrage, temperance, Sunday laws, and Good Government found few points of reference in their thinking. They were perplexed by a politics not aimed for victory, in which the attainment of some overriding principle was more crucial than winning elections. They ridiculed the reformers and their patrons as "do-gooders," self-appointed to change society against the will of its denizens.

The Roosevelts of Hyde Park

James Roosevelt was born in 1828 to a family securely anchored in the American past. The paterfamilias was Claes Martenszen van Rosenvelt, who left Holland in the middle seventeenth century to establish a farm at New Amsterdam. Two Roosevelt lines came to settle at Oyster Bay, Long Island, and at Hyde Park on the Hudson, leading tranquil lives in commerce and farming.

James J. Roosevelt, of the Oyster Bay branch, startled his family by campaigning for the hero of the common man, Andrew Jackson, and then scandalized them by joining forces with Tammany Hall. Appreciating the young man's social and financial connections, the braves engineered Roosevelt's ascent to the New York assembly and the U.S. House of Representatives. Philip Hone, the diarist who lavishly admired others in the family, called this Roosevelt "the leader of the blackguards." The errant man was also branded a traitor to his class.

Theodore Roosevelt, Sr., better illustrated the family's political code. Born in 1831, he was remembered by a friend as one who "literally went about doing good," backing causes from the Metropolitan Museum of Art to an immigrant welfare society called Miss Slattery's Night School for Little Italians. Roosevelt's nomination by President Hayes as customs collector for the port of New York caused a sensation; the city had long known the post as a wellspring of patronage and unsavory politics. The prospect of the Long Island philanthropist controlling the appointments appalled the men of the machine, and the bosses blocked the nomination.

Mindful perhaps of his father's frustrations, the younger Theodore Roosevelt entered politics not through his social position but through the front door of the Jake Hess Republican Club. Under the puzzled gaze of the men in derbies, he announced that he was ready to begin his political career. An ambitious Hess lieutenant saw the newcomer in pince-nez and three-piece suit as the lever with which to topple the boss. Teddy campaigned among the rich while the lieutenant turned out the votes of the poor. The palace coup succeeded and Roosevelt went to Albany. His political philosophy was germinal, limited mainly to replacing graft and dishonesty with an unspecified kind of right-minded behavior, but even this stance was so striking in the political culture of the eighties that T.R. attracted the admiration of many reformers: "He has a refreshing habit of calling men and things by their right names, and in these days of subserviency to the robber barons of the Street, it takes some courage in a public man to characterize them and their acts in fitting terms."

Although the Hyde Park Roosevelts were Democrats, more from tradition than forethought, James Roosevelt admired the political attainments of the Oyster Bay cousin. His father, Isaac Roosevelt, was a fearful man who studied medicine at Columbia, but refused to practice because he could not bear the sight of human pain. A demanding father, the doctor continually warned his son against the temptations of the city and the evils of idleness: "You know you were created for better things. We live for God—for the good of our fellow men—for duty—for usefulness."

After graduation from New York University, James embarked on a young man's tour of Britain, France, Germany, Greece, Italy, and a continent aflame with the revolutions of 1848. Roosevelt tradition held that James even donned a red shirt to march with Garibaldi's army, but this would have been an unsober act for an eminently sober young gentleman. He returned to attend Harvard Law School and accepted a place with a distinguished New York firm. Roosevelt married his second cousin, Rebecca Howland; they had a son, James Roosevelt Roosevelt, and took up residence on the Hudson. James commuted to the city to practice law, but he was more eager to raise superior horses and to make his farm pay.

He left the law within a year to try his hand at a variety of business propositions. Roosevelt founded a trust company, purchased Wisconsin real estate, ran paddle wheelers on Lake Champlain and Lake George. Three of his plunges might have made James Roosevelt one of the wealthiest men in America. He became a director of the Consolidation Coal Company, the nation's largest bituminous combination, which claimed a near-monopoly over the rich lodes of the Cumberlands; managed the Southern Railways Securities Company, which was drawing the railroads of the Southeast into an exclusive network; joined a partnership to dig a canal across Nicaragua. Each of these ambitious enterprises was ruined by a national recession. Such failures would have exasperated a titan like Vanderbilt, but James and his wife continued the annual cycle of calls on friends along the Hudson, excursions to New York City, summer voyages to Europe.

He showed the same diffidence to politics. If politics for James Roosevelt's contemporaries was "pollution," summoning images of Tammany Hall and the spoilsmen of Washington, he looked on the office-seekers and ward leaders with more amusement than indignation. Yet James's conception of political life was hardly the ebullient enterprise of the Irish bosses downriver at Poughkeepsie. It meant instead the standard of community stewardship set by the early Hudson patroons, of meeting local obligations and setting an example. Roosevelt served as vestryman and warden of the Hyde Park Episcopal church, village supervisor, trustee of school and hospital, discharging his responsibilities with an imperious if kindly air.

"Integrity of work and deed is the very cornerstone of all business transactions," James reminded villagers in a lecture to the St. James's Guild of Hyde Park, the text of which has come to light after more than a century. "No man successed in any undertaking who is dishonest—the store-keeper who gives short weight, short measure or sands his sugar, the mechanic who charges for material not given his employer, the laborer who does not fairly and honestly give his time, all are dishonest and sooner or later will be found out and will not succeed in their work."

What was the prevailing sin of the day? Extravagance! Roosevelt asked his audience to remember their childhoods, when people lived within their means. "No man has any business to live in a style which his income cannot support or to mortgage his earnings of next week or of next year in order to live luxuriously today. The whole system of debt is wrong, when we anticipate or forestall the future." The townspeople should all set aside ten cents a day. "Try it—begin tomorrow. . . . The curtailment of any selfish enjoyment will do it, a cigar, a paper of tobacco, a glass of beer daily. . . . Accumulation of money has become the great desire and passion of the age. Do not save and hoard for the mere sake of saving and hoarding. But I do say aim at accumulating a *sufficiency*. . . .

"Work is full of pleasure and materials for self improvement, it is the strongly marked feature of the American people. . . . There is not so much to *luck* as some people profess to believe. Indeed most people *fail*, because they do not deserve to succeed." Still, the race was not always won by the swift or the strong. James invited his listeners to "go with me to the Tenement houses of New York or London or Paris, many of them containing more people than this whole village." He had once climbed down a ladder "several feet below the sewage and gas pipes" to visit a dwelling beneath a London street. "These homes possess no window and the only way in which light and ventilation can be conveyed to the wretched inhabitants below is through a hole in the pavement." There he saw "half a dozen people nearly nude and hideously dirty children—a man writing by the flame of a tallow candle—a women lying ill abed. . . ." Even worse was the day when "there is no work—nothing laid by—nothing saved—and standing in the corner is that terrible skeleton—starvation." Were there three more fearful words in the English language than "I am starving"?

"Here is *work* for every man, woman, and child in this audience tonight. The poorest man, the daily worker, the obscurest individual, shares the gift and the blessing for doing good. It is not necessary that men should be rich to be helpful to others, money may help, but money does not do all. It requires honest purpose, honest self-devotion, and hard work. Help the poor, the widow, the orphan, help the sick, the fallen man or woman, for the sake of our common humanity, help all who are suffering. Work . . . for your daily support, work for your wives and children, work for fame and honor, work for your Lord and Master."

Rebecca Howland Roosevelt died in 1876. Four years later the widower met the winsome daughter of a fellow clubman at a dinner given by

Mrs. Theodore Roosevelt, Sr. "Did you notice how James Roosevelt kept looking at Sallie Delano?" the hostess asked her daughter. James Roosevelt and Sara Delano were married in October 1880.

That fall a delegation of Democrats, seeking a candidate who would cover his own expenses, offered Roosevelt their congressional nomination. He declined. James knew that the cause of a Democrat was nearly hopeless in Dutchess County, but it is doubtful that he would have accepted even if assured of victory. Two years thereafter, his new wife proudly reported in her diary, "James went to Hudson to a Democratic convention to *prevent* their nominating him."

The Kennedys of East Boston

Little such reluctance held back Patrick Kennedy. The ward boss customarily departed early from the colonial house on the finest street in East Boston. His neighbors included a congressman, an alderman, the consul of the imperial Russian czar; but on the sidewalk, men and women waited under horse chestnuts to bring him their problems. They knew they could depend on Pat to help. In the evenings the big house on Webster Street brimmed with talk of parish, politics, and Ireland. The Boston Democracy of the 1880s was an array of political fiefs, as fragmented and combative as feudal Ireland. Patrick Kennedy ruled his small kingdom so surely that he earned the affectionate style of "mayor of East Boston."

His political creed owed little to British rationalism or the Protestant tradition; it looked instead to the teachings of the Catholic church and the Irish way of politics. Although born in Boston, Patrick Kennedy inherited the zeal and bitterness that was the legacy of the Irish as their people endured conquest and calamity. From the seventeenth century forward, the decrees of the British had swept over the green island like tempests. Irishmen were forbidden to attend school, enter the professions, vote, trade, purchase land, attend Catholic worship, fail to attend Protestant worship. Ireland was rendered a land of struggling tenant farmers, vulnerable to the size of the harvest and the mercies of the British landlord. Magistrates and policemen arrived from England to enforce a system of Anglo-Saxon justice. But the British courts never seemed to find against the British landlords. Irishmen came to look upon the law as a rationalization for the harsh tactics of the oppressor. They saw the Anglo-Saxon code as a weapon not of morality but of naked power, under which might made right.

The Irish developed a countervailing code: to preserve what little they had left, Irishmen must seek power through almost any means available. Bribery, favors, influence—anything to jar the hand of the British. As the farmers and townspeople closed ranks, loyalty to family and friends assumed supreme importance. When a cousin got into trouble with the law, relatives would present a heart-rending plea to the landlord, a gift of eggs to the judge. Sometimes, they took to the streets, and criminals became local heroes by defying the British constables. The Irish political code had little to do with the British allegiance to Commonwealth and Crown. It was improvised, intensely personalistic, and linked inextricably to survival. Bitter experience taught the Irish to think of politics as the struggle between those with power and those without.

The trickle of Irishmen who departed for America during the eighteenth century grew into a stream. With the Great Famine the stream became a flood. Between 1847 and 1851, while their kinsmen starved, one out of eight million Irishmen boarded the "Cunarders" for passage to the new land, exhilarated by the prospect of the "ready-made republic" across the seas. The rancor against the British, nevertheless, died hard. Over a century later Robert Kennedy was said to have confronted the British ambassador to the United States at an embassy dinner: "Why are we, the Kennedys, here in America? Why are we here at all? It is because you, the British, drove us out of Ireland!"

In October 1848 a young Irishman from Dunganstown took the blessing of his priest, bade farewell to his sister and brothers, allowed himself a final longing look at his thatch-roofed birthplace, and started down the dirt road to the seaport at New Ross. Menaced by rising rents and cropland gone barren, the first Patrick Kennedy paid his steerage fare and boarded one of the "coffin ships" for Boston. His dreams may have been similar to those of the Roosevelt founder, but the civilization awaiting him was a distant cry from the fresh land of two hundred years before. Back in Ireland, few had trusted the heady letters from America boasting that all a body had to do to earn a fortune was to stoop, yet the cramped figures in the holds of the Cunarders anticipated an abundance of opportunity in the New World.

Disillusionment lay beyond the Boston wharves. Patrick Kennedy encountered a city out of Hogarth—of three-deck walk-ups, primitive sewers, warehouses converted into pest-ridden tenements, shanty villages along the harborfront. This Boston was not the storied eighteenth-century Athens of Beacon Hill brownstones and Bulfinch state house. It was the other Boston, in Oscar Handlin's term, a society within a society. Too depleted to continue their journeys, hundreds of thousands of Irish men and women crowded into a despairing ghetto. Typhoid and cholera devastated the population. Jobs were often nothing but a mirage. Irish immigrants competed for the most menial labor against one another—and against the increasing sentiment that no Irish need apply. Mayor Theodore Lyman, a forebear of Sara Delano Roosevelt, warned Bostonians against a "race that will never be infused into our own but, on the contrary, will always remain distinct and hostile."

A proud immigrant from Dublin once wrote, "In worn-out, king-ridden Europe, men must stay where they are born. But in America, a man is accounted a failure, and certainly ought to be, who has not risen above his father's station in life." Upward mobility was central to the creed of the American Irish. Although Patrick Kennedy was more resourceful than most, landing a cooper's job and marrying a colleen, his fondest hopes were vested in his children. He died in his early thirties, leaving three daughters and a son and namesake.

Patrick, born in 1858, grew up frail and taciturn. He attended public and parochial schools for various periods, and then gave up his formal education for a job near the harborside. The ambitious young man wed Mary Hickey, of a more established family, and opened a saloon. Throughout the Northeast and Middle West, these poor-man's clubs challenged the parish church as the meetingplace of the Irish community. Weary men assembled at the end of the day to argue, to joke, to listen to an epistle from the Auld Sod and raise a glass to a free Ireland. Here Mr. Dooley inaugurated Mr. Hennessy into the protocols of American politics. The canniest publicans, such as Hinky Dink Kenna of Chicago and the Bowery's Big Tim Sullivan, inducted their regulars into political armies. Turned away by so much of American society, the Irish made their stand in the political arena.

The establishment of Patrick Joseph Kennedy drew a brawny patronage from the docks, but he was an oddly ungarrulous saloonkeeper: P.J. seldom drank or raised his voice. His customers made up for this reserve; emboldened by whisky or ale, the dialogue wandered from jobs and families to a contest of harangues against the British oppression of the Irish and the Yankee oppression of the Boston Irish. Beneath the rodomontade were the persistent fears of unemployment and disease.

Slowly, the charity and advice of a tavernkeeper became the ritual of a ward boss. Pat Kennedy was drawn ineluctably into politics. As his stature rose, he declined to affect the roguery of a Martin Lomasney, the "Boston Mahatma" who received petitioners in a "throne room." The Irish were "great levelers," as Kennedy would say, "If you're up, they'll pull you down, and if you're down, they'll pull you up." Yet the social vision of Patrick Kennedy and every city boss of his era embraced Lomasney's political motto. The masses, said the Mahatma, were interested in only three things: food, clothing, and shelter.

By 1884 Kennedy was a ward Democratic committeeman. Then came nomination to the Massachusetts House of Representatives, to which he was elected by a landslide. After five one-year terms in the House, Pat moved up to the state senate. Leaving the oratory to more silver-tongued colleagues, he voted for virtually every bill that could be construed as a boost to the Irishman, immigrant, or working man. Despite this orthodox voting record, Pat was an extraordinary ward leader. Unlike the other bosses who baited the Yankees and flaunted their electoral shenanigans, he worked for a reputation as a ward boss without taint; he won appointments from Yankee and Irish mayors as Boston wire, fire and election commissioner.

Yet Kennedy saw the rascality of the ward heelers as a necessary cog in the system. A favored method in East Boston was the employment of "repeaters" who voted early and often on election day to secure the victory of the "approved" candidate. As chairman of the Ward Two Democratic Committee, Pat dictated the party's choice for offices ranging from alderman to state senator. He joined other local heroes on Boston's fabled Board of Strategy, the "mayor-makers" who granted patronage, nominated candidates beholden to them, and marshaled the Irish voting bloc over luncheons at the Quincy House. They included South Boston's Smiling Jim Donovan, Joseph Corbett of Charlestown, the North End's John F. Fitzgerald, whom everyone called "Honey Fitz" (and whom Pat called "an insufferable clown"). Party loyalty was valued over statesmanship; a rival, James Michael Curley, complained that the Board's appointments were no more distinguished than Caligula's horse.

Although less disciplined than the rigid hierarchy of Tammany Hall, the Board claimed close cooperation from some Boston businessmen, permitting its members to pursue secondary careers in business. Patrick Kennedy, while running his ward and serving in the state legislature, added another saloon to his original establishment, invested in wholesale liquor houses and a coal company, took fliers in real estate and mining stocks, and purchased a share in the neighborhood bank. These financial successes enabled him to move his family from a modest dwelling near the docks to the white colonial house on Jeffries Point, overlooking Boston Harbor.

Prevented for so long from political participation, the Irish savored the chance to use their skills. So defeated in Ireland, they now yearned desperately to win. The system of rural landlords, constables, and magistrates in the old country translated into a system of urban landlords, policemen, and judges in the new. Taught by hardship to band together in Ireland, they combined to build the American political machines. The Irish offered their numbers to the Democratic party and, as the party recruited them for jobs, they increased their share of patronage and power.

The anguish of Ireland and the American ghetto sensitized them to Catholic ideas about the dark side of human nature, original sin, and the unexplainable influences on human behavior. The code of the American Irish took its shape as a counterpart to the notion of man as rational and perfectable being. Writers for Catholic journals in nineteenth-century Boston considered Hume a "liar and infidel" and found only "philosophical ignorance" in the writings of Emerson.

At their best, the visionary tradition harnessed great careers to great causes and the pragmatic tradition elicited praiseworthy results from spirited competition. At their worst, the visionary tradition degenerated into the powerless pursuit of purpose, the pragmatic tradition into the purposeless pursuit of power. By the late nineteenth century the contest for the American mind had polarized large segments of the electorate—and particularly the Democratic party—with overblown rhetoric and ethnic hostilities. Some of the Boston mugwumps questioned the idea of universal suffrage and wondered whether Catholics could subjugate their papal to their American loyalties. Others lamented the Irish "conquest" of the cities: "Philadelphia, Boston, and New York were once governed by the Quaker, the Puritan, and the Knickerbocker. Are they better governed now, since from the turbulence of municipal politics the Irish American has plucked both wealth and power?"

For their part, the Irish suspected that the reformers were less interested in elevating public morality than in sweeping the Irish from office. They saw reform as an inherently Protestant movement; some saw the reformer as a proselytizer in a new disguise. Surely the boss was the genuine friend of the needy, rather than some Miss Slattery's Night School for Little Italians. Temperance organizations seemed bent on denying the Irish one of their few social pleasures, Good Government groups of the political pleasures they had been denied for centuries. John F. Fitzgerald scaled a platform to reveal that the Good Government people were composed, "in the main, of a band of hypocrites." Jim Curley bested the enemy by forming a *Better* Government Association—and promptly claiming its endorsement. Patrick Kennedy, less bombastic, simply recognized the legitimacy of an ethic that enabled his people to rise: perhaps it offended some of the moralists, but the system fed, housed, and clothed the needy and rewarded important values like gratitude and loyalty. The ward leader from East Boston and his followers plunged all the more vigorously into politics.

Two

APPRENTICES IN BUSINESS AND POLITICS

FOR A MOMENT, the visionaries and the pragmatists gathered under a single banner. In July 1884 the Democrats streamed jubilantly into Chicago. After twenty-four years of exile from the White House, their nomination had at last become a prize; one month earlier, James G. Blaine had been anointed by the Republicans. The prospect of the Plumed Knight, burdened by an old reputation for chicanery, drove reform elements away from the G.O.P. in large numbers. Now they awaited the selection of the Democrats.

James Roosevelt had joined a group of New York lawyers and financiers to raise funds for Grover Cleveland. He knew and liked the governor and admired his record of cautious reform. Predictably, the sachems of Tammany lit into Cleveland's indifference to their patronage demands as a method of "governing without reference to the party which put him in office." Honest John Kelly denounced the governor as an enemy of the Irish and warned that Cleveland's nomination would be political suicide.

Patrick Kennedy followed his fellow ward leaders on such matters. All jealously guarded their domains, but all accorded respect to the unofficial leader of the city Democracy, Patrick A. Collins. "P.A." had the makings of legend. Born in County Cork, he spent his boyhood in the coalfields of Ohio, learned the upholstering trade in Boston, worked his way through Harvard Law School. His ability, mild demeanor, and reverence for Yankee pieties won him a place in a State Street law firm and the esteem of many in old Boston; he was the Booker T. Washington of the Irish. In 1882 Collins became the first Irishman to represent the city in the U.S. House of Representatives.

Collins's choice for president in 1884 was an equally legendary figure,

General Benjamin Franklin Butler, whose perambulations through the hustings were a career in quest of a theme. He left a law practice in Lowell, Massachusetts, to win a seat as a Democrat in the state legislature. At the outbreak of the Civil War Butler rounded up volunteers for the Union army and won appointment as military governor of New Orleans. He surfaced after Appomattox as a Radical Republican in Congress, demanding Andrew Johnson's impeachment. Then followed reelection to Congress on the Greenback ticket and a triumphal return to Massachusetts to run for governor—as a Democrat. The Irish accepted allies where they could find them; they joined up with Butler to aid his election. By 1884 the general was ready for the greatest laurel of all. P. A. Collins and the Irish Democrats of Boston supported him loyally, if without enthusiasm.

Cleveland won the presidential nomination at Chicago. Endorsement by Republican reformers quickly followed. Tammany Hall was silent, but Collins hitched the fortunes of the Boston Irish to the Cleveland star: far better to swallow pride than be left out of power. Contemplating a cabinet post, P.A. exhorted the ward leaders to pull out the stops.

No sooner was Cleveland elected than the alliance began to break apart. The reformers issued their usual complaints that the machines were grasping for spoils. The bosses retorted that the reformers seemed to be no less eager for office—"not any of your petty offices, be it understood, but a foreign mission or consulate, which would enable them to air their aristocratic manners and show their silk stockings to the wondering gaze of European society." Indeed, James Roosevelt was offered such a position. "President Cleveland, Secretary Fairchild, Secretary Whitney and others told James they would any and all do *anything* for him and *begged* him to take a foreign appointment," Sara Roosevelt wrote in her diary. James declined for himself, but consented to send the son of his first marriage, whom they called "Rosy," to Vienna as first secretary of the American embassy.

The Boston Irish were incensed to receive the same short shrift Cleveland had once reserved for Tammany. A delegation of Yankees arrived from Boston to ask the president for a high post for Collins, but no offer came from the White House. After a decent interval, P.A. threw down the gauntlet: let the president's choice for customs collector of Boston reveal whether Irish support was to be properly recognized. Combative reformers took the challenge; they advanced the name of Leverett Saltonstall and declared that Cleveland's decision would decide whether "after all, the politicians are still to rule." When the president seemed to be leaning toward Saltonstall, P.A.'s lieutenants contemplated losing the plentiful patronage of the Customs House; they deserted their leader and backed the reformers' man. Collins, stung by the heretical ingratitude of his own men, resigned his seat in Congress.

Cleveland, with a careful eye on the Irish vote, tried to placate Collins with appointment as chairman of the Democratic Convention in 1888. According to local legend (although unnoted in the official record), Patrick Kennedy seconded the renomination of the president at Baltimore. Cleveland was defeated that fall, but the awkward coalition of the reformers and the machines persisted through the president's return to the White House four years later. It was during this decade that sons were born to James Roosevelt and Patrick Kennedy.

Patrician in the Arena

One of the boy's earliest memories was the band of Hyde Park villagers marching up the Roosevelt carriageway by torchlight to celebrate the first election of Grover Cleveland. The brilliant, flickering procession symbolized a rare intrusion of great events into the Hudson Valley setting where, on January 30, 1882, Franklin Delano Roosevelt was born.

It was a complacent world. The memories that followed the scene on election night 1884 were not of uncertainty and struggle but of sunny family gatherings, voyages to Europe, pony rides and walks through the fields of Hyde Park, the attentions of an adoring mother and father. A sense of permanence was embodied in the clapboard house that crowned the property, the plowfields packed in snow, the evergreens and palisades along the river. Looking back, Franklin Roosevelt remembered, above all, "the peacefulness and regularity of things."

Yet toward this world he would evince an abiding ambivalence. Sara Roosevelt insisted that she and James never tried to influence the boy against his own inclinations, but they did decree a relatively ordered existence. The daily routine of lessons, meals, and play was unrelenting, and even Sara admitted that she was a rather harsh disciplinarian. James accused her of nagging the boy. One day when the three were on holiday at Campobello, the five-year-old Franklin appeared so dispirited that his mother could do nothing to cheer him. Why was he so unhappy? "Oh, for freedom!" was the plaintive reply. Sara detected a "desperate note" in his voice "that made me realize how seriously he meant it." After a conference with James she told Franklin he could do whatever he pleased the following day—"and, I must say, he proved his desire for freedom by ignoring us."

The strict attention of his boyhood may have motivated Franklin Roosevelt to exercise his own authority later; the atmosphere also instilled an undeniable self-confidence. His most ambitious enterprises set aside now, James Roosevelt's life was oriented toward home; he took his son riding, fishing, and sailing, taught him the arts of raising trees and livestock. Sara devoted herself to Franklin with uncommon ardor. He was not a Roosevelt at all, she boasted, but a Delano. Franklin's air of sureness sometimes manifested itself in a peremptory attitude toward playmates. "But Mummie," he replied to his mother's reproach, "if I didn't give the orders, nothing would happen!"

Asked later if she had ever dreamed Franklin might become president, Sara Roosevelt said that public life was the last thing she would have imagined for him. "What was my ambition for him? Very simple . . . to grow to be like his father, straight and honorable, just and kind, an upstanding American." The house at Hyde Park was a near-shrine to his forebears, with its family portraits, objects his Delano grandfather had brought back from the China trade, and leatherbound genealogies dating back centuries. He delighted later in teasing his mother with the news that a Roosevelt ancestor had been a horse thief or that the Delanos had smuggled everything out of China from opium to immigrants, but the family attitude toward public service had meaning for him. In an essay on the colonial Roosevelts, Franklin attributed the vitality of his ancestors to their "very democratic spirit. They have never felt that because they were born in a good position, they could put their hands in their pockets and succeed. They have felt, rather, that being born in a good position, there is no excuse for them if they do not do their duty by the community, and it is because this idea was instilled into them from birth that they have in nearly every case proved good citizens."

From this environment Franklin Roosevelt was sent at age fourteen to Groton School. Like the Oxbridge schools that prepared young Britons for public careers, Groton was essentially a training ground in the visionary ethic of public service. Its rector, Endicott Peabody, had little patience with parents whose aspirations for their sons were as passive as Sara Roosevelt's. "How distressing the political outlook seems to be!" he lamented in 1894. "One looks almost in vain for men who are willing to serve their country. If some boys do not enter political life and do something for our land, it won't be because they have been urged."

The Groton that Franklin Roosevelt attended bore Peabody's ineffable stamp of unquestioning Christian faith and service to church and nation, inculcated through sermons, a spartan regimen, and a parade of missionaries, reformers, and other visitors who came to speak to the boys.

Roosevelt's parents, reluctant to give him up, had postponed his departure so that he arrived at school two years after most classmates. He sought his classmates' approval by earning himself a few black marks and plodding through athletics—notably the high kick—but Franklin prized more the approval of the man whose presence loomed over Groton. Roosevelt said many years later that Peabody's influence had meant more to him than anyone's but that of his mother and father. "More than forty years ago you said, in a sermon in the Old Chapel, something about not losing boyhood ideals in later life," the president would write the rector. "Those were Groton ideals—I try not to forget—and your words are still with me."

Yet in the rough-and-tumble politics of that era, Peabody's exhortations were an imperfect legacy. The rector offered no advice to those who found persistently highminded means inadequate to achieve highminded goals. A more instructive example was Theodore Roosevelt, whose rising fortunes Franklin watched raptly from Groton. Teddy had gone from Albany to Washington as civil service commissioner, a splendid post for an aspiring reformer. The spoils system turned out to be far better entrenched than the merit system, but Republican Roosevelt performed admirably enough to earn reappointment by the Democratic Grover Cleveland. It was Theodore Roosevelt who resisted the patronage claims of men like P. A. Collins and Honest John Kelly. Teddy returned to New York as police commissioner, departed to join the Rough Riders at San Juan Hill, served as assistant secretary of the navy and received a visit from the leader of the New York Republican machine, Boss Platt. Platt offered his support for the governorship—on the condition that Roosevelt clear all decisions with the machine and publicly request Platt's endorsement. Roosevelt's admirers were grieved to see him journey to the Fifth Avenue saloon where the boss held court. But T.R. promptly turned against his sponsor and pushed a civil service law through the New York legislature. The fuming Platt told cronies he was going to "get rid of the bastard." At the Republican Convention of 1900, the boss conspired with other G.O.P. leaders to have his ungrateful protégé kicked upstairs into the vice-presidency.

That fall Franklin Roosevelt went to Harvard. In a burst of enthusiasm for his cousin and fellow Harvard man, he put on a red cap and gown to march with other supporters of McKinley and Roosevelt in a rain-spattered eight-mile procession through the streets of Boston. A year later, after McKinley's assassination, Franklin greeted the new president when he visited Cambridge. With Peabodian energy, he urged students to be active in politics and government, and wondered why the Harvard Political Club did not cross the Charles to examine conditions in the exotic political culture of Boston: "It would be easy to send in parties, under the guidance of some experienced man, which in one day could learn more than through the means of lectures."

During his final year in Cambridge, Franklin Roosevelt became engaged to the cousin who was the president's favorite niece yet eschewed the cascade of tea dances and balls to work with the poor of the Lower East Side. He once accompanied Eleanor to visit a sick child in a home not unlike the flat James Roosevelt had seen in London. "He was absolutely shaken when he saw the cold-water tenement where the child lived," she remembered, "and kept saying he simply could not believe human beings lived that way." The wedding was held on Saint Patrick's Day 1905 so that Uncle Ted could march with the Irish of New York before giving the bride away.

In spite of the marriage, Franklin's mother refused to relinquish her son. James Roosevelt had died during Franklin's first year at Harvard and Sara had looked forward to the day her son would return to live at Hyde Park. Now this was not to be. She presented the couple with a New York brownstone, staffed and furnished it, built an adjoining house of her own, and continued to preside over the home at Hyde Park. Franklin brushed off his mother's efforts to run their lives: he seemed unable or unwilling to comprehend his new wife's frustrations. Eleanor was fast discovering that he would venture only so far from the secure boundaries of Hyde Park.

Roosevelt attended Columbia Law School but found the work so tedious that he failed two courses and took the bar examinations without receiving his degree. In the fall of 1907 he joined the New York firm of Carter, Ledyard and Milburn as an unsalaried clerk. Among its clients were some of the greatest industrial combinations in the United States; one of the firm's duties was to resist the trust-busting assaults of the administration of Theodore Roosevelt. Franklin complained to his mother that he was nothing but "a full-fledged office boy" arguing minor cases against "ninth-rate" lawyers. He confided to a fellow clerk that he planned to seek public office at the earliest opportunity. Like T.R. he would begin with the state assembly, become assistant secretary of the navy, run for governor. "Once you're elected Governor of New York, if you do well enough in that job, you have a good show to be President. . . ."

In 1910 a delegation of Democrats offered Franklin Roosevelt the nomination for assemblyman from Dutchess County. Unlike his father thirty years earlier, he accepted with alacrity. The incumbent was moving up to the state senate, leaving Roosevelt a clear shot at the office. But then the assemblyman changed his mind and announced his candidacy for reelection. Roosevelt gamely shifted his sights to the Senate. "As you know, I accept this nomination with absolute independence," he told party leaders at Poughkeepsie. "I am pledged to no man. I am influenced by no special interests, and so I shall remain." Roving the countryside in a gleaming red Maxwell, he stressed his independence from the state ticket, reminded voters of his ties to Theodore Roosevelt, and endorsed the reform platform of the Republican governor of New York, Charles Evans Hughes.

Only a few weeks after entering the state senate in January 1911, the newly elected legislator proposed to take on the Tammany tiger. At stake was the U.S. Senate seat from New York, to be filled by the legislature. Tammany's candidate was William Sheehan, nicknamed "Blue-eyed Billy," a one-time Buffalo politician who had made his fortune in New York City and presciently contributed to Democratic candidates across the state. Opposing Sheehan for the job was a Brooklyn lawyer named Edward Shepard, a faithful Good Government man. The two sides squared off for a classic confrontation. The issue was "bossism," declared Roosevelt; he led an insurgent group to keep Sheehan from winning the votes he required from the Democratic caucus. A war of nerves ensued. Some of the regular Democrats tried to pressure the rebels by using financial connections to foreclose mortgages and call in loans. Roosevelt announced that he would aid insurgents who were thus aggrieved. "How poor and mean by comparison are the egotistical 'donations' of a Carnegie or the Pharisaical 'philanthropy' of a Rockefeller!" exulted a newspaper writer. "A man of wealth like Senator Roosevelt, who interposes his financial power to bulwark the interests of the state, to uphold civic righteousness, and to protect public men from all the evils of corrupt coercion, recalls an earlier day of patriotism, when rich men were the defense and not the menace of the state." The regulars struck back by charging prejudice against Irish Catholics; the bishop of Syracuse warned of reviving the "old spirit of Know-Nothingism."

After an exhausting deadlock of two months, Charles Murphy, the reigning boss of Tammany, withdrew Sheehan's name in favor of James O'Gorman. As a former Grand Sachem O'Gorman was more of a Tammany man than Sheehan, but he lacked the financial involvements on which many of the insurgents had grounded their opposition to Sheehan. After winning a promise of no reprisals, Roosevelt endorsed O'Gorman.

He later considered the battle a victory for reform—he received a note from an old Groton master congratulating him on setting an example the boys could follow—but the exchange of Sheehan for O'Gorman was a dubious triumph at best.

The two years in the New York Senate were a pivotal time in Franklin Roosevelt's political development. At the time he came to Albany, the supercilious young legislator seemed to welcome the hatred of the Tammany men: "From the ruins of the political machines, we will reconstruct something more nearly conforming to a democratic conception of government." One of his Tammany colleagues referred to Roosevelt as "a political prig"; another reminded Democrats that "disloyalty and party treachery is the political cult of a few souls in our party. Mr. Roosevelt admits that he is the best informed man in the party in this state on obsolete and remote questions of government. . . . My leadership here in Albany depends absolutely upon human sympathy, human interests and human ties among those with whom I was born and bred."

But in the camaraderie of the cloakroom and the heat of debate, Roosevelt began to see the machine men as something other than the caricatures of Thomas Nast. Tammany senators like Alfred E. Smith and Robert Wagner, as well as the reformers, supported progressive legislation such as factory laws and workmen's compensation. Roosevelt was beginning to recognize that the art of compromise could be as noble as digging in his heels on a particular issue.

The gulf between him and the regulars remained, however: in 1912 Roosevelt joined the presidential campaign of the reform governor of New Jersey. From the Baltimore convention, he cabled Eleanor, WILSON NOMINATED THIS AFTERNOON ALL MY PLANS VAGUE SPLENDID TRIUMPH. At the inauguration, Roosevelt ran into Josephus Daniels, the wry North Carolina newspaper editor who was to head the Navy Department. How would Roosevelt like to serve as assistant secretary? Daniels asked. "I'd like it bully well," was the T.R.-like reply, "It would please me better than anything in the world."

"There is a Roosevelt on the job today," the new navy man told reporters on entering office. His name, his ambition, and his persistent demands for a big navy caused friction with the milder Daniels but, in time, Roosevelt's impatience changed to affectionate respect. Roosevelt moved his growing family to Washington and befriended admirals, congressman, diplomats; but the thought of returning to New York to run for office apparently never left his mind. In 1914 he entered the Democratic primary for the U.S. Senate; his old adversary Boss Murphy outwitted him by supporting James Gerard, Wilson's ambassador to Germany. With the president unable to endorse him, Roosevelt lost the election. He finally made his peace with the sachems in 1915 by supporting Al Smith for sheriff. Although wrangling over patronage continued between Roosevelt and the Wigwam, there was a signal of the lifting of the pox—an invitation to deliver the Independence Day speech at Tammany two years later. Old differences were papered over as Murphy, in top hat and regalia, stepped forward to be photographed with the squire of Hyde Park.

At the Navy Department, one of Franklin Roosevelt's principal duties was to negotiate contracts and speed up ship production. Striving for "economy to the last cent," he continually appealed to industrialists to lower their bids. On the eve of American entry into World War One, Roosevelt asked the president of Bethlehem Steel to reduce an estimate for work at the Fore River shipyard. "Navy appeals to you to do your share," he wired. "What reduction will you accept over your quotation to Fore River if Navy buys the material and gives you contract for all." Bethlehem pledged further reductions. The war dramatically accelerated navy work at Fore River. Roosevelt negotiated contracts, wage rates, construction deadlines, labor conditions. The pressure of armament needs sometimes moved him to interpret his own mandate in the widest possible fashion. Battleships were often constructed on no authority but Roosevelt's fiat. He joked later that the sleight of hand he performed at the Navy Department during wartime might have landed him in prison. The transactions with Fore River brought Franklin Roosevelt increasingly into contact with a fellow Harvard man, whose business apprenticeship had been as meteoric as his counterpart's rise in politics.

Rise of a Businessman

Like Roosevelt, one of the earliest glimmers in Joseph Kennedy's memory was an election night—Grover Cleveland's return to the presidency in 1892. Kennedy, age four, remembered the sight of his father's retainers coming to announce, "Pat, we voted a hundred and twenty-eight times today."

Joseph Patrick Kennedy was born on September 6, 1888, followed by a brother who died in infancy, and two sisters, Margaret and Loretta. He matured among the nightly congregations of petitioners, friends, and hangers-on in the family parlor occupied with breathless reports of Masonic parades and the latest indignities inflicted upon the Irish. Quietly dominating the proceedings was the ward boss, wearing rimless spectacles and a full mustache. Joseph Kennedy "worshipped his father," a friend remembered. "He venerated him."

The father and mother carefully schooled the son in his obligations to advance himself and his family. One who knew the family felt that Mary Kennedy regarded herself as "a preliminary antecedent to a dynasty which she co-established." It was during the nineties that Patrick Kennedy rose to the state senate and achieved the business gains that enabled his family to move up to Jeffries Point—successes founded on the ethic of family loyalty, a touch of rascality and personal allegiances that were considered inviolable. Joseph Kennedy never forgot his father's credo: "Be grateful and be loyal at whatever cost."

In 1893 President Cleveland occasioned a celebration in the Kennedy home by doing the unthinkable: he appointed a Boston Irishman to represent the United States in London. P. A. Collins was the nominee, finally collecting his political reward by sailing to Britain as American consul general. For the few Bostonians who could still remember their voyages in the hulls of the Cunarders, Collins became a household god. Patrick Kennedy held up the immigrant from County Cork as a shining example of how a man could honor his family and his people. The lesson was not far from Joseph Kennedy's mind when he departed for London forty-five years later.

The East Boston boyhood was almost a parable of luck and pluck. A ringleader for a group of neighborhood boys, Tom Sawyer–fashion, Joe formed a Decoration Day marching company that paraded in uniform alongside veterans of the Grand Army of the Republic. On the Fourth of July he orchestrated a pageant in the Kennedy barn; Joe shouted instructions from the hayloft. The production culminated when one of his sisters, attired as the Statue of Liberty, unfurled an array of American flags and the entire neighborhood cheered. The young Kennedy read Mark Twain and Horatio Alger and so prized these volumes that he canvassed the district selling soap to earn a suitable bookcase. Before long, his liegemen learned to expect Joe's greeting: "How can we make some money?" He sold newspapers, repaired clocks, aided a haberdasher, ran errands, raised pigeons, sold candy and tickets on a rubberneck boat when Admiral Dewey's fleet entered Boston Harbor. When Joe noticed the crowds that gathered to watch the baseball team he captained, he said, "If we're giving them a show, they ought to pay for it," and passed the hat after the fourth inning.

Joe attended the parochial Assumption School until the eighth grade, when Patrick Kennedy enrolled him in Boston Latin. Many of Boston's most distinguished sons had attended this oldest of American schools since its founding in 1635—Benjamin Franklin, John Hancock, Ralph Waldo Emerson, Henry Adams. Boston Latin was as much of an academy for public service as Groton. "The real thing which has lived through 275 years is an intellectual and moral conception," said alumnus Charles W. Eliot. "It is a steady purpose, well carried out by nine generations of Boston citizens." Unlike Groton, whose student body in Franklin Roosevelt's time was still exclusive, Boston Latin's enrollment was sprinkled with Irish, German, Scandinavian, Jewish, and Italian names. This might have made Kennedy more comfortable on the first day he arrived on the penny ferry from East Boston, but the transition from parochial school to Boston Latin was as novel a journey as Franklin Roosevelt's move from the world of Hyde Park and Groton to the New York State Senate.

He made the transition smoothly. By senior year, Kennedy was captain of the baseball team, manager of basketball, class president. His baseball coach said the trouble with him was that his father held political office: "Everyone's been toadying to you for years and you think you're better than the other boys." Kennedy's scholarship was less inspired, however, and he remained at Boston Latin an extra year to remedy deficiencies. This did nothing to diminish his fondness for the school. "To strangers, I could not possibly convey the reasons for the powerful and sweet hold which the school has on my affections," he later told a reunion dinner audience. "It would be like trying to explain to strangers why I love my family."

It was long the practice of Boston archbishops and ward bosses to talk down Harvard and urge young Catholic men to enroll at fine schools like Boston College and Notre Dame. But Patrick and Mary Kennedy were intent on sending their son to "that place across the river." Kennedy concentrated in history and economics in Cambridge, but the future financier had such difficulty passing one economics course that the professor sighed, "Kennedy, you'll never be able to make a dollar at the rate you're going." (Retelling the story later, Kennedy added, "Today I'm sure I could pay him more in one year than he's made in a lifetime.") On advice of his baseball coach he ultimately majored in music—"because I wanted to make sure I would graduate."

The Harvard of 1908 was a college divided. Endicott Peabody spoke woefully to Grotonians of "the gap between Mount Auburn Street and the Yard." Franklin Roosevelt had tried to bridge the gap somewhat by joining college activities, but the world of the better final clubs was as separate from Harvard Yard as the Back Bay from East Boston. When Joseph Kennedy became prominent later, a Harvard classmate and member of Porcellian said, "They tell me that fellow was in my class, but I never knew anything about him." Kennedy seemed to seek out wellborn Harvard men, one of whom told him that he was being watched for signs of the behavior commonly thought of as Irish. Perhaps to escape the Irish stereotype, Kennedy neither smoked, drank, nor gambled. One evening he and his roommates were invited to dine with Charles Townsend Copeland, the beloved, acerbic Harvard professor who made a tradition of inviting students to his popular readings and to dinner at the Harvard Union. After the meal they repaired to Copey's living room. When Kennedy refused the master's offers of coffee and cigarettes, Copeland pointed his finger and declared, "Young man, I suspect you of some great crime!"

Harvard never received the allegiance Kennedy paid Boston Latin. "I guess I have the old Boston prejudice against it," he confessed later. Some classmates believed his indifference was the result of failure to meet absolute social success in Cambridge. Like Franklin Roosevelt, Kennedy was elected to Hasty Pudding, but his final club was Delta Upsilon, and to this he was evidently admitted late. Kennedy later said that his sense of self-respect depended on his ability to make a great deal of money quickly; he observed that the key to earning money was not intellectual ability but enterprise, bravado, originality.

Invited to play semiprofessional baseball in New Hampshire one summer, Kennedy was asked by the *Boston Globe* if he was interested in reporting social news in the area. He approached a Harvard classmate who was planning to become a journalist, offering to join forces on the column: the friend would write the articles and Kennedy would receive the fee. The column, published under Kennedy's byline, so impressed the *Globe* that they invited "Kennedy" to join the permanent staff. Over three summers Kennedy and a friend conducted sightseeing tours of Boston that earned almost ten thousand dollars. On graduation from Harvard in June 1912, Kennedy set for himself the goal of making a million dollars before reaching the age of thirty-six.

A variety of paths lay open to him. Kennedy might have entered politics in the Boston Democracy that was growing ever more favorable to the Irish, but this would have frustrated the loftier ambitions of both Kennedy and his father. Banking was another possibility, but Boston finance was still marked by discrimination. John F. Fitzgerald often boasted of questioning a Boston banker on why he did not hire more Irish employees; told that a few of the tellers were Irish, Honey Fitz retorted, "Yes, and I suppose the charwomen are too." After applying for a position with a Boston investment firm, Kennedy found the company was not hiring Irish Catholics. (Cardinal O'Connell of Boston reputedly withdrew the archdiocese accounts after hearing this news.) Kennedy once told a friend of being turned down for a loan by a Boston bank for reasons he attributed to his background. "They tell me it's better now," he said long afterwards, "but at that time, the social and economic discrimination was shocking."

Kennedy landed a position—no doubt aided by his father's political influence—as a Massachusetts bank examiner. The hours were long and the salary unimposing, but inspecting banks across the eastern half of the state offered him an unexcelled education in the ways of finance. "I found the work fascinating—too fascinating," he recalled. "In the three years devoted to it, I passed up several chances of good jobs with sizable banks, which would have given me an earlier start in my life work." An opportunity beckoned.

A Boston firm was bidding to take over the Columbia Trust Company in East Boston, of which Patrick Kennedy was part owner. Invited by his father to ward off the attack, the bank examiner gathered enough money from relatives and friends to win control. At twenty-five, Joseph Kennedy became the nation's youngest bank president. The creed of the neighborhood banker was much the same as the creed of the ward boss. Kennedy was known for helping his customers, many of them immigrants, with loans and other impulsive acts of kindness. "He made everyone's problems disappear," recalled Kennedy's secretary at Columbia Trust, "Everyone felt that way about him."

Joseph Kennedy also won a wife. The daughter of Pat Kennedy's sometimes ally, sometimes rival, Rose Fitzgerald was one of the belles of Irish Boston. Honey Fitz was determined to raise his daughter above the difficult social climate of Boston. He tried to discourage her interest in Kennedy, but the couple met in secret—at the homes of friends, across the street from a Boston hospital, in the rear pews of the Christian Science church. Fitzgerald finally relented and the ceremony was performed by Cardinal O'Connell in October 1914.

Kennedy's new father-in-law offered him a peculiar dowry—appointment to the Collateral Loan Company, a quasi-public institution established to protect poor Bostonians from loan sharks. The position had the patina of public service and was of a kind that Patrick Kennedy might have appreciated in an earlier day. But shortly after taking office, Kennedy discovered massive embezzlements, resulting in a crossfire of charges and countercharges. Five months later he resigned. Memories of the experience moved Kennedy to keep out of politics for years. He sought to advance his career in less dangerous ways, forming a real estate partnership and pursuing a place on the board of the Massachusetts Electric Company, the largest utility in New England, whose board included some of the region's most prominent financiers. After several rebuffs, the young bank president from East Boston was elected the first Irishman to serve as a company director. Asked by a friend why the post meant so much to him, Kennedy replied by asking whether there was any better way to meet people like the Saltonstalls.

In the spring of 1917 Kennedy was invited to be assistant manager of the Fore River shipyard. He leaped at the opportunity. With American intervention in Europe, Fore River was undergoing a large expansion program under the legendary chairman of Bethlehem Steel, Charles Schwab. Some of Kennedy's Harvard classmates resented his failure to enlist, but Franklin Roosevelt had wired shipbuilders from the Navy Department that it was their "real patriotic duty" to remain at their posts. Kennedy's duty was the housing, feeding, and transportation of thousands of workers. He established a company town and a lunchroom, the Victory Cafeteria, and negotiated with trolley companies to carry laborers over the eight-mile route from Boston to Quincy. When Kennedy heard that Schwab was arriving from Pittsburgh for an inspection tour, he paved the way for a memorable introduction. He made hotel reservations, met Schwab at the railroad station, whisked him to his suite and a luncheon of Schwab's favorite chicken liver, led the magnate through the shipyard, escorted him to dinner and theater, and later had Schwab alone for two hours of conversation. Fore River broke a sheaf of production records, building thirty-six destroyers in a little over two years. Kennedy worked himself into an ulcer and such an obvious state of exhaustion that Schwab insisted he leave Fore River to convalesce for three months at a health farm. Kennedy also settled an old family score: when James Michael Curley, Pat Kennedy's old political foe, asked the assistant manager to provide draft-exempt shipbuilding jobs to a band of Curley's retainers, Kennedy courteously refused.

The young businessman from East Boston had watched from afar the young politician's progress from Hyde Park to state senate to the Navy Department. Joseph Kennedy was unimpressed. *He's just another rich man's son,* he remembered thinking of Franklin Roosevelt, *with nothing else to do but dabble in politics.*

But many of Fore River's government contracts were assigned by the rich man's son at the navy. Of his earliest encounters with Roosevelt, Kennedy recalled, "We never got along then. He would laugh and smile and give me the needle, but I could not help but admire the man. We had great confidence in him . . . and we made millions of dollars worth of supplies for the government with no more authority than a telephone call from him."

The battle of the Argentine battleships was foreshadowed by an imbroglio between Fore River and navy in 1915. A dispute over alteration charges had induced Bethlehem to refuse delivery of an earlier vessel to Buenos Aires. On that occasion, Franklin Roosevelt was able to overcome Schwab's objections by noting that "if the Argentine government can be made to feel secure in this country, I have no doubt that there will be many opportunities given us for increased business." President Wilson dined aboard ship before Argentine crewmen sailed it southward.

Now, in wartime, the prospects for increased business from Argentina were diminished. The new ships remained at Quincy. Franklin Roosevelt appealed to Schwab for an arbitration session, but the old titan deigned only to send his stripling assistant manager to Roosevelt's office in the State-War-Navy Building across from the White House.

"Don't worry about this matter . . ." the assistant secretary said brusquely to Kennedy. "The State Department will collect the money for you."

"Sorry, Mr. Secretary, but Mr. Schwab refuses to let the ships go until they are paid for."

"Absurd," Roosevelt laughed.

"Not at all absurd, sir," Kennedy replied. "Positively no ship will be delivered until it is paid for."

Roosevelt was unintimidated. With an arm around Kennedy's shoulder, he walked his visitor to the door. He had been happy to meet Kennedy, he said, and hoped that Kennedy would look in on him whenever he came to Washington. But the navy would not be defied: if the ships were not delivered immediately, he would dispatch a fleet of tugboats to Fore River to produce the vessels himself.

This evoked another protest from Kennedy. Roosevelt merely smiled: "Hope to see you very soon again."

Kennedy left Washington to report to Schwab his estimation of the assistant secretary of the navy: "a smiling four-flusher." Schwab agreed: he and Kennedy would call "this youngster's bluff." The battleships remained in their berths.

Then four navy tugboats arrived, manned to the gills with armed marines. As the Fore River workers watched, aghast, the battalions climbed onto the dock, took over the designated vessels, cast off their lines, and towed them into the harbor. Kennedy's shipbuilders were little match for Roosevelt's marines and their bayonets. An Argentine crew waiting nearby was instructed to take over the new addition to its fleet.

A chastened Kennedy was compelled to admit that he had underestimated the opposition. "Roosevelt was the hardest trader I'd ever run up against," he said years later. "When I left his office, I was so disappointed and angry that I broke down and cried."

The Businessman and the Politician

Until now, their careers had unfolded in a curious tandem. Roosevelt was propelled from Hyde Park, Groton, and Harvard into the knockabout worlds of Empire State politics and war production. Yet many politicians made similar journeys without perceptible change. How did Roosevelt, so convincing in the role of unyielding reformer in 1911, so comfortably embrace certain of the dubious compromises of the pragmatic ethic? The answer might lie in the ambivalence of his early years. If Roosevelt loved his parents and the tranquility of Hyde Park, he also chafed at his mother's tendency to domineer and the predictability of their lives along the Hudson. If he revered Endicott Peabody and boosted Harvard, he also felt slightly alienated from his peers at both schools. A relative thought his failure to make Porcellian was "the bitterest moment of Franklin Roosevelt's life." Was he less than fully committed to the society of his birth and the maxims it embraced? His ambivalence, as well as the requisite flexibility of a man eager to win power, might have made Roosevelt more open to experimenting with Tammany and using "blarney, boodle and bludgeon" to persuade war contractors to subjugate profit-making to national needs.

Joseph Kennedy had traveled from the competitive world of Irish Boston to Boston Latin and Harvard. Kennedy too might have made this flight without conspicuous acceptance of the visionary tradition. Still, he was raised at a deliberate distance from the skulduggery of the Boston ward heelers. Patrick Kennedy prided himself on his good name and the esteem of the Yankee political establishment; it was an unorthodox boss who insisted on sending his son to Boston Latin and Harvard. Joseph Kennedy strove for the acceptance of the Yankees by trying for the board of Massachusetts Electric and concealing his vigorous ambitions in copybook principles such as "the office seeks the man." Another businessman would have gloried in his conquest of the Columbia Trust, but Kennedy stretched the truth to tell an interviewer that the offer of the presidency had been "a pleasant surprise."

The dualities in both men would be further tested in the coming decade, for with the signing of the armistice, the temper of the nation seemed to change. Franklin Roosevelt ran for vice-president in 1920; he and his running mate, James Cox of Ohio, were defeated in a landslide. The end of war production at Fore River moved Joseph Kennedy to look for opportunities in finance. Both the businessman and the politician were confronted with the new realities of a business civilization.

Three

MEN OF THE NEW ERA

"IT IS ONLY ONCE in a generation that a people can be lifted above material things," Woodrow Wilson observed early in his term to his assistant secretary of the navy. America's part in the World War had required a leap of imagination to distant ideals on a distant continent. Now the pendulum was swinging back. "Every war brings after it a period of materialism and caution," Franklin Roosevelt wrote after his defeat in 1920. "People tire quickly of ideals. . . ." Could he have been thinking of himself? In public speeches Roosevelt began to substitute the word "realism" for "idealism." By the spring of 1921 the once-proud reformer stopped using the term reform altogether, confessing that it had come to conjure "visions of pink tea artists who dabbled in politics one day a week for perhaps two months in the year."

Cast aside by a war-weary nation, the disciples of Wilson and Theodore Roosevelt were in disarray. Many Americans now sought leadership from Wall Street and the American Chamber of Commerce. An advertising man extolled Jesus Christ as the forerunner of the American businessman. John J. Raskob evangelized in a well-circulated piece that "Everybody Ought to Be Rich." Scores of other executives, brokers, hucksters, and salesmen issued pronouncements at once so blindly optimistic and so unabashedly self-centered that they became weapons of cruel irony after 1929.

Yet the ethic of rugged individualism had also more articulate spokesmen, reviving within the business realm the old tension between the optimistic and pessimistic visions of human nature. Human beings, wrote Charles Fay of the National Association of Manufacturers, were not cooperative but individualistic—"not altruists, but self-seekers, if we tell the honest truth." A Harding man told another business council that the pleasure of achievement, advancement, and acquisition was the God-given reward of human effort. "This individualistic motive and power has driven mankind onward and upward along the highway of social and industrial progress." *Nation's Business* agreed: "The one hundred percent American believes in the doctrine of selfishness, although he is often ashamed to admit it, a fact that leads him into bleary sentiment when he undertakes to define service. The American idea is that every man is out to promote his own interest, and he has discovered that the best way to do this is to make himself useful to others."

Counterpart to the rugged individualist, in the context of the New Era of business, was the business statesman. "What underlies ruthless competitive methods?" asked George Perkins of the Morgan Bank in 1911, "The desire to supply the public with better goods at a lower price?" Perkins believed not: competition was merely a brazen bid for power at the expense of the public interest. "Cooperation must be the order of the day." Herbert Hoover, as secretary of commerce from 1921 to 1929, gave the concept of business statesmanship its meaning for the nineteen-twenties. In *American Individualism*, published in 1922, Hoover argued that the selfish kind of individualism had given way to a new kind, based on values such as service and equal opportunity. Now that large business organizations were owned by thousands of shareholders, businessmen would no longer be moved by the arbitrary considerations of the nineteenth century. America was passing "from a period of extremely individualistic action into a period of associational activities." American individualism, Hoover argued, would no longer represent "the acquisition and preservation of private property—the selfish snatching and hoarding of the common product." The new business statesman would operate under an ethic of cooperation and a vision of commerce as a public trust.

Franklin Roosevelt finished Hoover's book and wrote, "I have taken great pleasure in reading it. . . ."

Business Statesman

On the evening of January 7, 1921 a goodly number of the New York financial community welcomed Franklin Roosevelt to Wall Street. Among the men gathered over a bounteous dinner at Delmonico's to honor Roosevelt were Edward Stettinius of United States Steel; Owen D. Young of General Electric; Adolph Ochs, publisher of the *New York Times;* and Daniel Willard of the Pennsylvania Railroad. After dessert, the guest of honor remarked on his experiences in Albany and in Washington and expressed his gratification at returning to the business world after a decade's absence. In a flippant letter to an old friend, he identified himself as "Franklin D. Roosevelt, Ex V.P., Canned (Erroneously reported dead)" and put politics aside for an expedition into business.

Roosevelt appealed as strenuously for acceptance by Wall Street as he had to American voters in the campaign just ended. In the early months of 1921 he delivered himself of opinions as orthodox as the most orthodox of businessmen. Despite the hardship created by the thousands of foreclosures and firings, the postwar decline was a "natural readjustment." Savings and investment were "the path to real progress." Roosevelt characterized himself to an interviewer as "one of the younger capitalists." Foreseeing an exile from power for himself and his party that might last as long as a decade, Roosevelt was concerned with keeping the embers of his political career glowing and earning some money from the law and business.

From his home on East Sixty-fifth Street, the young capitalist traveled mornings to the Broadway offices of the Fidelity and Deposit Company of Maryland. Van Lear Black, the company's president, had been impressed by young Roosevelt on their first meeting at the 1912 Democratic Convention. After the defeat for vice-president, Black offered him a vice-presidency at Fidelity and the chance to use his wide acquaintanceship in politics, finance, and labor to bring in surety bond customers. Black was certain that Roosevelt would achieve "world-beating" results—"if you can hold expenses."

As a goodwill ambassador for Fidelity, Roosevelt's office hours ran from ten-thirty in the morning until one-thirty in the afternoon—and this included the lunch hour. Throughout the week he maintained an active social schedule in quest of new clients and salesmen for Fidelity. One Boston man had "the right connections, Somerset Club, etc., etc., is generally liked and can make the work pay if he gets out and hustles," Roosevelt reported to Black. "I am convinced of the fact that Boston business cannot be built up by the usual 'Hurrah Boys' method."

At his side was Louis Howe. The musical-comedylike pairing of the debonair young politician and the wizened newspaperman had begun when Howe watched the state senator's battle against Tammany, admired what he saw, and followed Roosevelt to the Navy Department. As assistant to the assistant secretary, Howe was constantly on the telephone with shipbuilders like Joseph Kennedy, issuing blunt commands to hurry up navy work. As assistant to the aspiring politician, Howe charged himself with the long-term plans of Franklin Roosevelt. "Beloved and Revered Future President," he addressed a letter to his protégé—only half in jest.

"Can't you get anything into that Dutch skull of yours?" the little man would bark, or "I hope to God you drown!"

On the Fidelity payroll, Howe searched for bond customers by combing their long list of political contacts, crossing the dividing line between business and politics with the agility of a Boss Murphy. If Franklin buttonholed the mayor of New York on a labor matter or intervened with Governor Al Smith on "a cunning little pardon case," Louis could return to Fidelity with an armload of surety bond orders. Roosevelt mentioned to an executive that "a casual reference in a letter from one of my old friends in the Navy Department to the award of some eight-inch gun forgings to your company brought to my mind the very pleasant relations we had during my term as Assistant Secretary of the Navy, and I wondered if you would feel like letting my company write some of the contract bonds that you are obliged to give the government from time to time." Through the efforts of Roosevelt and Howe, Fidelity and Deposit's New York business increased by three million dollars within five years. Much of this increase was owed to a sudden and mystifying increase in business done with the state of New York.

In the afternoon the surety bond salesman became a lawyer. Before leaving Washington Roosevelt had formed a law partnership with two old friends as a place to settle after the navy. But before long he concluded that forming Emmet, Marvin and Roosevelt had been a mistake. Emmet and Marvin were "dear, delightful people," he acknowledged, but estates and wills were no more fascinating now than they had been when he was a law clerk. Further, Roosevelt complained, he was not receiving "one red cent out of my association with them, whereas, if I were with some real live people working along other lines, I could be of material assistance on reorganizations, receiverships, etc., pulling my weight in the boat and incidentally making some money out of it." In late 1924 Roosevelt departed to enter practice with a young lawyer from Taunton, Massachusetts, via Dartmouth and the Harvard Law School, Basil O'Connor. Roosevelt and O'Connor were full of ideas for new business, but as Roosevelt wrote, "I shall have to spend the greater part of the next four or five years in devoting my primary attention to my legs."

At the end of the summer of 1921 he had accepted Van Lear Black's invitation to sail his yacht to the family retreat at Campobello. The navy man had taken the wheel himself to steer the craft through treacherous seas and fog. Then came the icy plunge into the Bay of Fundy, the numbness and fever, the slow realization that his legs had become useless. Sara Roosevelt insisted that Franklin return to Hyde Park, Eleanor and Louis Howe that he return as quickly as possible to his business and political interests. Roosevelt was back at work in January 1922.

His primary responsibilities lay at Fidelity and Deposit and his law practice, but Roosevelt also raised money for charity, served as trustee of Vassar College and president of the Navy Club, helped to establish the Woodrow Wilson Foundation, worked with the National Crime Commission. In the hours that remained, Franklin Roosevelt set out on a trail of speculative ventures—some as risky, some as comical as any of the jungle of "get-rich-quick" enterprises that flourished through the Dollar Decade.

A promoter named Pat Homer had approached Louis Howe while Roosevelt was still at the navy. (For some reason, Howe succumbed to Homer's wiles; he kidded him about his weakness for chorus girls: "If I were your Missus, I would keep you tied up around the house for a week.") Homer had a proposition to make: a refinery that would be constructed to provide the navy with an oil supply that would be immune from the peaks and valleys of the market. Coyly, he suggested that the plant be built at Fall River, Massachusetts, which just happened to be Mrs. Howe's home town. The idea caught Roosevelt's fancy and he pushed the refinery through the opposition of Josephus Daniels and some skeptical admirals. But after the refinery's completion, market prices for oil fell unexpectedly, and the navy was burdened with a millstone. Roosevelt sold his small holdings in the company and later did not care to be reminded of the episode.

A few years later, Pat Homer was back to invite Howe to take advantage of rising lobster prices. They formed a company and gave Roosevelt majority control. The three men purchased a lobster-packing plant in Rockland, Maine, expecting to sell their catch to hotels and restaurants at a tidy profit as soon as prices went up. But prices never did go up and the three brothers who managed the plant resigned in a quarrel with the owners. Roosevelt was left with pens full of lobsters and a debt totaling over twenty-six thousand dollars. When a women's group in Texas asked Roosevelt for a donation to a white elephant sale, Howe suggested, "Why not send them your stock in the lobster company?"

Another brainstorm consisted of purchasing surplus vessels from the navy—not a difficult proposition for the former assistant secretary—and hauling cargo to the West Coast through the Panama Canal. Roosevelt tried to raise seed money by holding luncheons and teas at his Manhattan home. "I should gladly do this underwriting myself if I did not have so many unusual demands to meet just now," he assured a skeptical investor. Shipping was a perilous business, however, and Twin Coast Navigation was unable to divert cargo orders from larger and older competitors. The only profit Roosevelt ever saw was the result of a peripheral venture, netting him a check in the sum of $633.33.

Still another venture Roosevelt described as a business enterprise serving a social purpose. The Compo Thrift Bond Corporation was created to furnish bonds to individuals through savings banks and private businesses. These institutions were encouraged to set up Compo Clubs, whose members would make weekly deposits toward the purchase of bond certificates. "I feel very strongly that this company is on the right track and that it will not only prove a stimulus to saving on the part of the public in general, but that it is a mighty good proposition for the banks which handle it," testified Roosevelt, a Compo director. Al Smith was lassoed to inaugurate the sale of Compo bonds at a New York bank, but Pat Homer knew a losing venture when he saw one. "What is Compo doing besides catching suckers?" he taunted Howe. Although Compo had no official connection with the U.S. Government, the certificates carried the legend "United States of America." Someone suggested in court that this was a deliberate deception and Roosevelt and Howe were immensely relieved when a judge concluded that it was not. Yet Roosevelt resigned his directorship at a loss of twenty-five hundred dollars, evidently worried about damaging his reputation. Compo liquidated the following year.

Many American investors saw opportunities in the skyrocketing inflation of Weimar Germany. Roosevelt became president of United European Investors, Ltd., infusing money into nineteen German companies, including German Edison and the Nobel Dynamite Company. When a Harvard classmate became interested in the enterprise, Roosevelt explained, "Practically all the company does on this side is to act as a clearing house for German marks. . . . Our German committee is in charge of the investments." But the company's American directors engaged in internecine warfare. Laboring to untangle the mess, Howe sent Roosevelt one of his dope-filled "Dear Boss" letters: "Gould and Roberts have had an awful fight and Gould cannot say enough mean things about him. There is no evidence of any crookedness on Gould's part except the statement of the crooks that Gould was constantly in their office. . . . My recommendations are as follows: That Gould and Roberts be directed to immediately find new offices, preferably in a church or some other respectable place. . . ." When the quarrels were settled, United Investors declared a profit of two hundred percent. Later, political rivals would charge Roosevelt with exploiting Germany's economic distress, but he would point out that one hundred thousand marks had been injected into a shaky economy. His personal gain was five thousand dollars.

Roosevelt was intrigued by the airships that were beginning to appear in American skies. He was certain that the Zeppelin would supplant the airplane as the standard method of American transport. "Wait until my dirigibles are running," he bade a friend, "and then you will be able to take a form of transportation which is absolutely safe." The General Air Service was announced in 1923, with a board of directors divided between New York and Chicago. Airship service would begin with flights between the two cities before expanding into a nationwide network. But investors were more captivated by the airplane, and General Air dispersed after a few years. (Still Roosevelt clung to his idea. As president he directed the Navy Department to design a new dirigible, although three military airships had already crashed. Money was allocated and planning begun, but a year later the *Hindenburg* exploded at Lakehurst.)

Roosevelt invested in one enterprise of which he did not even know the name. Henry Morgenthau, Jr., devised a scheme to market quarter-in-the-slot portraiture machines. Like Roosevelt, Morgenthau was a progressive Democrat and Dutchess County farmer and a lover of the Hudson country and lore. Photomaton caught on and its stock rose sharply in the bull market of 1928. Roosevelt and Morgenthau expanded the concept to postage stamps; their Sanitary Postage Service Corporation installed vending machines in pharmacies and cigar stores. Aiding the cause was a story someone planted in a New York newspaper, entitled "18 Billion Stamps Sold Each Year; One Enough for Myriads of Germs," and lauding the firm for its public-mindedness in providing germ-free stamps to the populace. "I don't need to tell you how delighted I am with the whole proposition," Morgenthau wrote his partner, "and what fun we will have together working it out."

Merging five companies they created the Consolidated Automatic Merchandising Corporation. Camco robots would perform the work of a retail clerk, "releasing human labor for more constructive purposes." The directors prophesied a two-thousand-percent increase in Camco's stock value. They established three prototype "clerkless" stores in New York City. The robots not only sold Smith Brothers cough drops, Gillette razor blades and Lucky Strikes, but said "thank you" and recited advertising jingles. "A NEW INDUSTRY HAS ARRIVED!" proclaimed the prospectus. But customers found they could obtain merchandise by feeding slugs to the machines; when the machines broke down, customers wrecked them. Soon Camco had to hire back the clerks whose labor had been "released" to guard the machines against the wreckers. And when millions of Americans later lost their jobs in the depression, the promise to free workers "from the deadening monotony of a mechanical job" seemed ridiculous. One wag noted that "nothing was said about what they would substitute for the deadening monotony of drawing their paycheck every Saturday." The company lost over three million dollars and died in a blaze of angry lawsuits. Labor foes would resurrect the affair as evidence of Roosevelt's hostility to the working man.

The ventures ranged as widely as Franklin Roosevelt's imagination. He watched the land boom while cruising off Florida and contemplated starting a resort at Boca Chica, but could not interest Morgenthau in the idea before it vanished into the Florida hurricane of 1926. Roosevelt ordered seedlings for a projected experimental tree farm at Hyde Park, but again was unable to find a partner. He considered plans to sell a coffee substitute and advertising space in taxicabs, and took still another flier with Pat Homer—this time an oil deal in Wyoming. It ended when wildcatters could find nothing but sulfur. "Why not go into the sulfur bath industry?" Howe gibed, "Look at Hot Springs!" Roosevelt looked at sugar land in Louisiana, other projects in cotton and radio, a plan to harness electrical power from the tides of Passamaquoddy Bay. None of these ideas came to fruition, though, and Roosevelt laughingly ended his forays into the wilds of speculation. After reading one of the endless, empty forecasts of success for a venture he knew had long ago failed, he scrawled, "Hope springs eternal in the human heart!"

Another speculator who invested in a variety of propositions sensed a fine distinction between speculation and gambling. "I think the primary motive back of most gambling is the excitement of it. While gamblers naturally want to win, the majority of them derive pleasure even if they lose. The desire to win, rather than the excitement involved, seems to me to be the compelling force behind speculation." By this standard of Joseph Kennedy, Franklin Roosevelt was a gambler in business. The jerry-built edifice of dirigibles, lobsters, German marks, and talking robots not only took time and exhausted political capital but it might have damaged Roosevelt's reputation. He received a letter of concern from the director of the Society for Promoting Financial Knowledge about "the use of your name to further the sale of stocks in new promotions that . . . are business risks of the more hazardous type and I am wondering if your attention has been called to the fact that these securities are being offered for public subscription as safe investments." The sender regretted that "a distinguished and honored name should be commercialized in this manner, when there are so many opportunities for employing the prestige that it carries in activities designed to promote some public good." Roosevelt replied that his name had been used, in this instance, without his permission.

Roosevelt's daring mirrored the need he felt to make money. Government salaries over a decade were incapable of covering the expenses of three homes, boats, travel, clubs, political and charitable contributions, the education of five children. At the end of his term at the navy, Roosevelt lamented that he was "honestly a fit candidate for a receiver." But he knew it would never come to that, because his mother usually came to his aid when he was caught short by financial pressures. Sara Roosevelt never offered her son financial independence, preferring to "help out" when needed. One Roosevelt son thought his grandmother used money to purchase her grandchildren's loyalty, to circumvent Eleanor, to keep the up-and-coming politician dependent on his mother. Still, if Roosevelt's speculative plunges represented an effort to assert himself against Sara, this was carried out with more affection than rebelliousness.

After such mastery of politics and government, it was strange that this man would operate with such seemingly little forethought in business. How account for the almost perfect series of failures? The key to the contradiction might lie in Roosevelt's attitude toward ends and means. He was willing to use means such as deception, but only when able to rationalize them—if only to himself—in terms of a greater goal. In politics Roosevelt could deceive in good conscience because he was able to justify the deception in the context of a worthy objective such as stimulating war production. But Roosevelt could grasp no worthy public goal from the world of speculation. In business, although tempted, he was unwilling to use the Machiavellian methods or devote the total commitment that a Pat Homer, or in an earlier age, a Vanderbilt might to serve a purpose as narrow as personal fortune-building. Roosevelt's need to *think* of himself as doing good explains the efforts to characterize the enterprises he did undertake as gifts to progress—from launching a new form of transportation to relieving men and women from tedious jobs. It is doubtful that he fully succeeded in convincing himself. In a toughminded business culture Franklin Roosevelt was little match for the lone wolves.

To another element of his business career Roosevelt was far better suited. In 1922 he became the charter president of the American Construction Council. The Council was one of the "associational activities" that Herbert Hoover advocated in his brief for American individualism. Franklin and Eleanor Roosevelt had frequently dined with the Hoovers during the years both men served under Wilson; Roosevelt had even considered booming Hoover for the Democratic presidential nomination in 1920. The associations Hoover advocated from his platform at the Commerce Department were intended to promote industry cooperation and a vision of public service; implicit was the notion that voluntary self-regulation would preclude the need for regulation by government. The leaders of these associations soon became known as business statesmen. Men like Will Hays in motion pictures and Kenesaw Mountain Landis in baseball, these "autocrats of the business table" were given the mandate to reign over their industries, providing exhortation and information, but not to rule.

Concurrent with the publication of Hoover's volume was a probe of the New York construction industry, revealing rampant corruption and sending a flock of labor and management leaders to prison. To clean up the industry, the American Construction Council was formed. "The tremendous possibilities of such an organization," noted the Council's prospectus, "induced Mr. Herbert Hoover to consent to preside at the formal organization meeting and Mr. Franklin D. Roosevelt to accept the presidency of the organization." Hoover told Council members at the founding meeting that they were taking "one of the most important steps ever taken in the history of the nation." Roosevelt declared that government regulation was unwieldy and expensive. "It means employment of men to carry on this phase of the work; it means higher taxes. The public doesn't want it; the industry doesn't want it."

The job was unsalaried, but it offered the sense of public service he missed in speculation. "Our aim is solely to further the public good," Roosevelt declared somewhat pretentiously in a letter. One of the worst banes of the industry was the problem of seasonality, the yearly cycle in which the number of construction projects fluctuated wildly, often resulting in layoffs. Roosevelt proposed that "if the men of one district are being drained to carry on construction in a second district, number one should hold off until the job is finished, then employ the men who are ready to undertake a new job. This is a patriotic duty as well as an economic one." When a business journal balked at the idea, Roosevelt sent off a forceful reply: ". . . You deliberately insist that no organization or individuals, whether of capital or labor or both combined, should ever suggest a course of action to its individual members. Yours is a creed of 'Every man for himself and the devil take the hindmost.' "

The Council ran into reefs and shoals. Hoover declined to provide Commerce Department services without charge. Louis Howe was annoyed at the need to spend two mornings a week on Council matters. Few of the Council's members took it as seriously as did companies in other industries, such as motion pictures. At a meeting in his Sixty-fifth Street parlor, Roosevelt complained that Council members had not done "one darned thing" but collect dues. The role of business statesman, urging competing interests to heed transcendent purposes, appealed to Franklin Roosevelt, but the failure of the American Construction Council—added to his experience in speculation—cast doubt in his mind that businessmen would set aside their own concerns under anything but compulsory government regulation. Roosevelt's exposure to the dominant ethic of the twenties was the source of much of the antipathy toward "economic royalists" and "the forces of greed and selfishness" that would spring to life in the president a decade later.

Throughout his sundry careers as bond salesman, speculator, lawyer, and business statesman, Roosevelt never really left the political arena. He kept his name before the public, corresponded with Democrats up the length of the Hudson and across the United States. In 1924 Roosevelt hobbled to the podium of the Democratic Convention at Madison Square Garden to nominate Al Smith. He took on the role of spokesman for his party during its years in the political wilderness: "Since the war ended, with its compelling activity and its heights of emotions, American voters everywhere have been passing through a period of preference for the quiet of reaction and material things. . . . Whether the change back to the well-tried principles of the Republic's founders will come back slowly and normally, or whether it will be caused by some sudden happening which expresses the falsity of the existing economic system, no one can tell. . . ."

A friend waxed enthusiastic over the polio clinic at Warm Springs, Georgia. Roosevelt went to see for himself. He purchased a parcel of land there in hopes of developing a nationally recognized polio treatment center. Howe solicited "victims" for financial backing and mobilized the Fidelity and law firm staffs for fundraising duties. "As every patent medicine faker knows," he wrote the Boss, "nothing lures the 'come on' like a before and after photograph . . . showing them doing a hundred yard dash or shoveling coal or something . . . after treatment together with the statement that when they arrived, it required two stretchers and an ambulance to get them down to the pool." Roosevelt bought land for farm experiments, financed a scenic drive along Pine Mountain, and considered expanding the Georgia hamlet into a chain of resorts stretching north to Lake Placid. The villagers called him "Doctor Roosevelt," and he listened attentively to local stories, attended barbecues, wrote a newspaper column called "Roosevelt Says."

After renominating Al Smith at Houston in 1928 Roosevelt contemplated four more years of developing the Warm Springs idea, continuing his law practice and Fidelity work, and learning to walk again. Assuming that the Happy Warrior would lose in 1928, Louis Howe planned for Roosevelt to run for governor of New York in 1932, win reelection by a landslide in 1934, and command the field for president in 1936 to succeed Herbert Hoover's two terms in the White House. Then Smith threw a wrench into the apparatus. In a frantic stream of telephone calls to Warm Springs he warned Roosevelt that unless a strong candidate ran for governor that year, the Democrats would lose New York. "You're asking me to run, Al, but I can't even walk!" he replied. But Smith persisted.

If the postwar American was cautious and weary of idealism, as Franklin Roosevelt wrote at the beginning of the decade, so had he been. Despite the creative impulses in some of his investments and the work for the Construction Council, the animation of higher purpose had been largely absent for eight years. Roosevelt was therefore more receptive to Al Smith's pleas than his response betrayed. Howe told him not to listen. But when the governor asked "Frank" what he would do if the Empire State Democracy drafted him, Roosevelt said he didn't know. "I won't ask any more questions!" cried Smith in triumph.

Resisting the national Republican avalanche, he won the governorship by a hairbreadth. A national journal predicted that "many of those Democrats who look for progressive policies from their party pin their hopes on Governor-elect Roosevelt." A few weeks later, neighbors from six counties crowded into a church near Warm Springs to welcome back "our own great hero whom we worship as our adopted son" and hail Franklin Roosevelt as the next president.

Rugged Individualist

In a hotel room redolent of cigar smoke and ticker tape, Joseph Kennedy lay in bed, telephoning orders to buy and sell. It was April 1924. A Boston friend owned stock in the Yellow Cab Company that was being driven down by bear raiders; he had requested Kennedy's help. "If ever I was scared it was then," Kennedy said later. "After two days' discussion with my wife, I took the assignment." In spite of a severe case of neuritis, he caught a train to New York City and set up shop at the Waldorf-Astoria, orchestrating a series of manipulations so inscrutable that it confounded the raiders. "I woke up one morning, exhausted, and I realized that I hadn't been out of that hotel room in seven weeks. My baby Pat had been born and was almost a month old, and I hadn't even seen her." Kennedy finished the battle thirty pounds lighter but with a victory in hand. "Several of us emerged wealthy men."

He had become manager of the Boston office of Hayden, Stone and Company in June 1919. The salary was less than half the amount he earned at Fore River, but Kennedy gained the tutelage of one of the cleverest speculators of the era, Galen Stone. At Stone's side, Kennedy learned the techniques that were making millionaires on Wall Street. After three years he established his own firm in Boston. "It's easy to make money in this market," he exclaimed to a Harvard classmate. "We'd better get in before they pass a law against it."

There was an enigmatic interlude. In the summer of 1924, Joseph Kennedy cast a line into national politics. Democrat by heritage, he might have been expected to aid John W. Davis, the Wall Street lawyer whose nomination ended the 104-ballot deadlock between William McAdoo and Al Smith. As an aspiring financier, Kennedy might as easily have supported Calvin Coolidge. Kennedy contributed to neither Davis nor Coolidge, but to the campaign of the Progressive party.

Insurgents from both of the major parties had gathered in August to nominate Senators Robert La Follette of Wisconsin and Burton Wheeler of Montana. The Progressive platform opposed internationalism and assailed the New York financial ascendancy. "When the Democratic party goes to Wall Street for its candidate, I must refuse to go with it," declared Wheeler in taking his walk. A native of Massachusetts before going West to practice law in the copper fields, the Montana senator took a place at Wellfleet near his birthplace on Cape Cod to rest for the autumn campaign. He was greeted by a stream of family friends and wellwishers. One of the visitors was Edward Moore, confidential assistant of Joseph Kennedy, who informed Wheeler that his boss would like to see him. "We discussed the political situation," Wheeler remembered of the visit with Kennedy, "and I outlined the philosophy by which La Follette and I intended to save the world." Shortly thereafter, Kennedy joined Wheeler and his family for dinner at the home of Galen Stone. To the candidate's surprise, the two speculators listened sympathetically to his campaign pitch. "We can't take much more of Cal Coolidge," Kennedy said.

Kennedy offered a contribution of one thousand dollars and his limousine and driver to carry Wheeler through New England. "So here was the Progressive candidate for Vice President, who was regarded by some as a radical and had been accused by one labor leader of being financed by Russian Communists," Wheeler marveled years later, "campaigning in a Rolls furnished by a rising investment banker." Kennedy complicated the mystery when he ran into the senator in Washington shortly before the election and confessed his apprehension that the Progressives would carry Massachusetts. Before Wheeler could ask why, Kennedy outlined the steps taken by the Democrats to foil the Progressive cause. "We scared hell out of them. We told them that a Progressive party victory would close the mills and factories. And in South Boston, we told the Irish that the La Follette program would destroy their church." Wheeler never did find out whom Kennedy genuinely favored, but concluded later that his intention was to undermine the Progressive campaign, enjoying "the irony of the spectacle as . . . I denounced Wall Street often from the back seat of a Wall Street speculator." Kennedy's only public explanation was that he had known Senator Wheeler and always liked him.

In 1926, frustrated by the lingering sentiment in Boston against Irish Catholics and yearning to be closer to Wall Street, Joseph Kennedy boarded his family on a private railroad car to New York. Like Franklin Roosevelt, he searched for investments that he could enter on the ground floor. Kennedy considered Florida real estate but, on counsel that the boom would not last, stayed away until the hurricanes ended the land rush; he made small bargains amid the debris. He looked next to the West Coast, where motion pictures had become the fourth largest industry in the United States. As early as 1919 Kennedy had seen the trend, purchasing a theater chain and the New England franchise for Universal Pictures.

Hollywood in the nineteen-twenties was a frenetic colony of starlets, scriptwriters, production engineers, extras, and flamboyant studio moguls. Louis B. Mayer, David O. Selznick, Marcus Loew, and others were renowned for their lavish enterprises, but Kennedy believed the studio system was wasteful and inefficient. "Look at that bunch of pants pressers in Hollywood making themselves millionaires!" he said, "I could take the business away from them." Kennedy purchased a flagging film company called Film Booking Offices. "A banker!" Marcus Loew exclaimed in a line Kennedy often repeated with delight, "I thought this business was only for furriers!"

Kennedy's standard was not artistic distinction but economy. At FBO he cut salaries and budgets, cranking the production schedule up to one picture per week. One film starred Red Grange; another opened under the credit, "Joseph P. Kennedy Presents a Walt Disney Comic." But most of the pictures were as forgettable as they were cheap to produce.

A Poor Girl's Romance, Rose of the Tenements, The Dude Cowboy, and *The Flame of the Argentine* graced Kennedy's catalogue. When an ingratiating Hollywood reporter mentioned that Kennedy had produced some good films that year, the banker brought him up short by inquiring, "What were they?"

One of the first to recommend the film business to Kennedy was the "autocrat" of the industry, Will Hays. A Hoosier lawyer, former Republican national chairman and postmaster general, Hays was brought to Hollywood to improve its reputation after the disastrous revelations of the Fatty Arbuckle scandal. Nervous over threats by religious groups to boycott the box offices, the moguls formed the trade organization that became known as the Hays Office. Hays saw Joseph Kennedy as "a man who, in his business ideals and concepts as in the fine character of his home life, would bring to the industry much that it has lacked in the past." Kennedy pledged that Film Booking Offices would make nothing but clean pictures. "One director, a high-priced man, put in what is known as the sex punch. One of his pictures went before my first board of review—Mrs. Kennedy and the seven Kennedys." The board did not approve. "The director objected to veto, but he was given the alternative of changing his picture or his job." Closely identified with the Catholic church, Kennedy was reluctant to offend such groups as the Legion of Decency, but he also enjoyed the role of the businessman who heeded loftier considerations than mere profit. (This did not prevent him from seeing the humor in his role. Greeting a young woman who called once at the Kennedy apartment in New York to see one of his daughters, Kennedy winked and asked her to leave her coat in the foyer. "Will Hays is coming by in a little while, and I want him to think I've got a girl in the bedroom.")

In 1927 Kennedy proposed that the Harvard Business School study the industry that had sprung up so rapidly in the past decade. It was a fine opportunity for Kennedy to assume the role of public-spirited businessman. He invited some of the leading directors and magnates in Hollywood, including Adolph Zukor, Cecil B. De Mille, Harry Warner, and Will Hays. Not only were many of the guests unused to public speaking, but several were suing one another at the time and had to be assured that process servers would be kept out of the lecture hall. Acting as moderator, Kennedy told the students that their questions after each lecture would "lead in the long run to a mighty searching of consciences, in which our industry and every other must justify itself as a ministry to human needs. In the last analysis, every merchant and every manufacturer is a public servant, and all our works are, or should be, public utilities, even though we operate under a private charter." He edited the talks for publication under the title *The Story of the Films.*

Later that year Kennedy helped to launch a wave of consolidations and mergers that changed the face of Hollywood. Over lunch in a Manhattan oyster bar, he sold a large portion of Film Booking Offices to David Sarnoff, founder of the Radio Corporation of America. Al Jolson's *The Jazz Singer* was playing to packed houses and film executives were scrambling to wire their studios for sound. The union of Kennedy's production facility with the new Photophone system devised by RCA was hailed as one of the first examples of vertical integration in the industry.

Next Kennedy choreographed an intricate minuet of companies that earned him millions of dollars. In February 1928 he sold another segment of FBO stock to the vaudeville chain, Keith-Albee-Orpheum; several months after, he gained control of Keith to become its board chairman. In turn, RCA purchased a large share of Keith, paving the way for a major reorganization. Radio-Keith-Orpheum was created to manage Keith and Film Booking Offices on behalf of RCA, linking film, sound, and theater outlets in one operation. Not only did Kennedy receive large profits from the sale of his stock, but he also accepted a considerable consulting fee for his services in the merger. To his manifold duties Kennedy soon added the chairmanship of Pathé Pictures, but he left most administrative duties to subordinates in order to concentrate on corporate pyramid-building. He earned the sobriquet of "Financial Wizard of Hollywood."

By May 1930 Kennedy gave up his corporate titles, installed functionaries at the helms of Pathé and Radio-Keith-Orpheum, and prepared the greatest merger of all. Rumors of a union between the two companies caused Pathé's stock value to surge. RKO purchased Pathé stock at the inflated price but after winning control, bought the firm's physical assets for but a fraction of their appraised value. The result was that Kennedy's circle realized millions while independent shareholders in Pathé received only a fraction of their stock's assessed value; a number brought suit against Kennedy and other executives charging a conspiracy to sell the firm at an unreasonably low price. The suits were dismissed for lack of conclusive evidence of fraud. Outside owners of RKO were equally indignant because the Pathé purchase so exhausted their corporate treasury that the company had to be refinanced. On the floor of the House, Congressman William Sirovich of New York castigated the inside circle who "emptied the RKO treasury." Another member attacked the motion picture interests who "defrauded and fleeced thousands upon thousands of investors, widows and orphans of nearly two thousands of millions of dollars." Kennedy himself later acknowledged that the American corporation of the twenties was operated not for the benefit of the corporate body, but for its management.

This was a complex and elusive man, this banker who donated to the Progressives, this independent operator who worked with Will Hays and brought the magnates to Harvard, things that more unashamedly pragmatic men might have failed to do. He operated under the competitive ethic yet wished to be thought of as a public-minded businessman. In a rare moment of introspection, Kennedy seemed to recognize this dichotomy in himself. He once quoted Bacon to the effect that every progenitor of a great family possesses qualities of both good and evil. Henry Luce believed it would take an exceptional dramatist or novelist to portray the emotions of Joseph Kennedy—"the rhythm of earthy selfishness and higher loyalties."

Kennedy's loyalties were directed ultimately toward the advancement of his family. "Our opponents became his opponents," Robert Kennedy remembered, "our problems became his problems. . . . His interest in life has been his children—not his business, not his friends, but his children." Toward this interest the patriarch was a driven man, his single-minded fervor sometimes bordering on the compulsive. Time and again, Kennedy would lose an alarming amount of weight, smoke feverishly, live voraciously, and then lapse into periods of inactivity at home in Hyannis Port or Palm Beach. Patrick Kennedy, shortly before his death in 1929, was concerned about his son. "His ulcers are giving him trouble," said the old ward leader, "I'm afraid he's bitten off more than he can chew." So long as Joseph Kennedy was immersed in a task, little else seemed to matter. "I can't expect to live out the ordinary span of life because I've been living too hard," he lamented, "I know I'll die young." So certain of this was Kennedy that he asked William Randolph Hearst for advice on establishing a trust fund for his children. The publisher warned him to prevent his sons and daughters from achieving financial independence because they would then be free to leave him. "Well, if that's the only way to hold them," Kennedy replied, "I've been a lousy father."

He seemed to divide his world between his family and a vanguard of trusted friends and associates, on one side, and the group of men with whom he fenced and allied in Boston, Wall Street, and Hollywood on the other. Schooled in the trickery of ward politics, Kennedy was careful to keep other businessmen from positions in which they could best him; his wife felt there were few people he genuinely liked. His independence enabled Kennedy to enter most of the major fortune-building enterprises of the New Era, from the stock market to motion pictures, Florida land, and radio. He could forge partnerships with men as different as Galen Stone and Marcus Loew and still denounce Yankees, Jews, Italians, and other competitors—real and imagined. Kennedy relished the effectiveness of his toughminded image in scaring away rivals. "I used to eat guys like you for breakfast," he boasted to a friend.

Yet beneath this bravado was a profoundly pessimistic and insecure man. Something lodged deep in Joseph Kennedy's psyche prevented him from ever achieving absolute confidence that his world would not come crashing down. It was this apprehension that moved him to pull almost entirely out of the stock market by October 1929. He was puzzled that speculators as capable as he actually believed that the market would rise endlessly. Big businessmen were the most overrated men in the country, Kennedy told his sons. "Here I am, a boy from East Boston, and I took 'em." With millions of dollars available after the crash, Kennedy further increased his fortune, but he was deeply shaken by the collapse of the culture in which he had established himself. It was a time, Kennedy wrote later, "when seemingly all values were disappearing and ruin threatened." Kennedy said he would have been willing "to part with half of what I had if I could be sure of keeping, under law and order, the other half. Then it seemed that I should be able to hold nothing for the protection of my family."

In ten years Joseph Kennedy had amassed a fortune and a broad acquaintanceship in business, politics, entertainment, journalism—men like Hearst, Burton Wheeler, Bernard Baruch, Herbert Bayard Swope of the *New York World,* Owen D. Young of General Electric. He seemed to one magazine writer "at once the hero of a Frank Merriwell captain-of-the-nine adventure, a Horatio Alger success story, an E. Phillips Oppenheim tale of intrigue, and a John Dos Passos disillusioning report on the search for the big money." The era that enshrined Henry Ford put the story of Joseph Kennedy into a host of popular journals. But Black Tuesday turned the public reverence for the Wall Street speculator into public antipathy.

Through a keen sense of timing, Kennedy had remained abreast of such trends as war production, the advent of the bull market, the rise of Hollywood. Now he sensed that as the money changers fled the temple, the era of Wall Street would give way to a new epoch in which Washington would predominate. One day in 1930 Joseph Kennedy telephoned a friend; in a jocular mood, he bade him to write down the name of the next president. "You're not hearing much about him now, but you will in 1932. It's Franklin D. Roosevelt. And don't forget who told you."

Citizens in a Business Civilization

In light of the differences in background, temperament, and ambition, Roosevelt and Kennedy followed remarkably similar courses through the New Era. Both engaged in speculation, served on company boards, became involved in the trade association movement. In their visions of business, they were business statesman and rugged individualist, but neither man could be wholly confined by these categories.

Franklin Roosevelt was agile enough and sufficiently sensitive to the public mood to move smoothly into the business world after denouncing "Wall Street gamblers" in the campaign of 1920. He gingerly crossed the demarcation lines the old reformers had tried to maintain between the arenas of commerce and politics. For Roosevelt, speculation was, finally, a hobby; he was happy to make money, just as he enjoyed winning at poker or finding a rare stamp for his collection, but was seldom dismayed when he did not.

He harbored few illusions about finding disinterested motives among speculators and promoters, but he was perceptibly disappointed by the failure of the American Construction Council. Roosevelt was raised and educated in the belief that businessmen would lay aside private considerations for the benefit of the community. This confidence was fortified during the war years, when the majority of ship and armament makers acceded to government requests for lowered bids and quickened production. Against the issues of world war, problems like reviving confidence in the construction industry and combating seasonality seemed immediate and easily dramatized. The decade that found Roosevelt in close agreement with Herbert Hoover's view of a business culture operating on principles of public-mindedness left him with a bleak vision of the business community. This shattered faith would be revealed not only in the antibusiness flavor of the Second New Deal but in the president's delight in finding disinterested businessmen like Henry Kaiser and Donald Nelson during his war administration. At the end of the nineteen-twenties, Roosevelt concluded that "while a nation goes speculation crazy and everybody is employed, the average citizen simply declines to think of fundamental principles."

For Joseph Kennedy, business was less an arena of public service—although he disdained to say so—than a means of earning security and stature for his family in a contest based on contending interests and personal alliances. Kennedy wanted to get into the stock market before a law was passed against it; this was the essence of unbridled competition within the limits of the law. "He created new rules as he went along," his daughter Eunice wrote, "his own rules, based on an innate wisdom—because in those days there were little or no regulations." Speculation for Kennedy was hardly the hobby it was for Roosevelt; he would never have accepted losses so complacently or invested in a stock whose name he did not know. One test of his mettle was Kennedy's willingness to place short orders in the months after the crash, knowing that they might damage the national economy by driving down values and further shaking public confidence in the market system.

The two men demonstrated the tension between the two visions of business leadership in the twenties. Roosevelt believed in business statesmanship, although he did not always practice it; by the end of the decade he came to feel that the idea was something of a contradiction in terms. Kennedy practiced rugged individualism but was reluctant to represent that picture of the business world.

They had pursued challenging careers, moving from local business and local politics through the crucible of war production and the frenzy of the business epoch. But these years were only a prelude to power; relatively little was at stake beyond individual careers. The years that followed were the most illuminating test of vision, projecting Joseph Kennedy and Franklin Roosevelt first on a national and finally on a world stage.

Four

SPRINGTIME OF AN ALLIANCE

IN THE SPRING of 1930 Franklin Roosevelt's circle accepted the dual task of winning for the governor a reelection landslide that fall and election to the presidency two years hence. If events conformed to Louis Howe's strategy, one goal would lead to the other. With one eye on Albany and another on Washington, James A. Farley, Frank Walker, Henry Morgenthau, and others in the Roosevelt orbit quietly recruited supporters. Morgenthau invited Joseph Kennedy to lunch with Franklin Roosevelt at the executive mansion.

"Joe had never been directly concerned with politics and was not particularly interested in the political processes except as, from time to time, they directly affected his own interests," Rose Kennedy remembered, "But with the same analytical intelligence that had enabled him to see through the pronouncements of 'a new era of prosperity,' he now saw that the country was heading toward a potential explosion." To stem the chaos, Kennedy sought "a leader who would lead." He consulted figures in business, politics, and journalism ranging from Bernard Baruch to John F. Fitzgerald to William Randolph Hearst. Then came the call from Morgenthau.

The long afternoon of conversation between the wartime counterparts moved from politics to shipbuilding to the economic crisis. Roosevelt favored Kennedy by listening carefully to his views. Underlying the hours of mutual reappraisal was the prospect of political partnership. Kennedy offered the governor a valuable conduit to Wall Street, financial support, and counsel on practical economics and the folkways of the urban machines. Roosevelt offered Kennedy an entree into national politics and a style of leadership that would quell his fears of social upheaval. "I was really worried," Kennedy later confessed, "I knew that big, drastic changes had to be made in our economic system and I felt that Roosevelt was the one who could make those changes. I wanted him in the White House for my own security and the security of our kids—and I was ready to do anything to help elect him." By the end of the afternoon a political alliance had been forged.

Joseph Kennedy told his wife that evening that Franklin Roosevelt was the man who could save the country.

Nomination at Chicago

New Yorkers returned Franklin Roosevelt to Albany that November in the first Roosevelt landslide. The Democratic party, Will Rogers declared, had just nominated its candidate for president. Jim Farley confided to reporters that he could not see how the governor could escape being the nominee in 1932. Roosevelt later laughed, "Whatever you said, Jim, is all right with me."

Early in 1931 Louis Howe established a campaign headquarters on Madison Avenue and began assembling card files on potential convention delegates and rivals. "For himself first, last and all the time," cautioned a typical entry, "Ambitious—Promises everybody everything—Double-crosser." (The victim of this appraisal was Jesse Jones of Texas.) On rare occasions, Louis emerged from the back room to stir up the faithful. Their names and faces meant nothing, he admonished the workers. All they had to worry about, night and day, day and night, was this man Roosevelt—and get him to the White House, no matter what. Farley toured the country, rosters of Democratic luminaries in hand. Frank Walker, treasurer of the campaign, canvassed wealthy Democrats with the aid of a vaudeville performer, Eddie Dowling.

One day, Walker and Dowling called on Joseph Kennedy at his office up the avenue from Roosevelt headquarters. After offering his tithe, Kennedy asked how the campaign was coming along. Walker invited him to come and see for himself. But after leaving Kennedy's office, he began to have second thoughts. Louis Howe, ever vigilant over his precious relationship with the Boss, had alienated more important men than Kennedy. And Louis nurtured an especial dislike for Wall Street speculators. "As a special favor," Walker asked Howe to please be nice to Mr. Kennedy when he came in. "Oh, sure, sure, Walker. You needn't worry about me. Bring him right in," Louis reassured him. On the appointed day, Walker once again asked Howe to please make sure to be polite. "Don't worry, don't worry, I'll put on my best company manners for him."

Walker ushered a beaming Kennedy in for his introduction to the top man in the campaign. When the door opened, Howe was slumped over his desktop, feigning sleep. Walker cleared his throat. There was no response. As Walker hastened to keep the conversation alive, Louis merely arched an eyebrow at Kennedy before joining the dialogue in a desultory fashion. Kennedy left headquarters fuming, but he did not allow Howe's impudence to extinguish his zeal for the campaign.

Borrowing an airplane and pilot from William Danforth, a fellow Boston speculator, Kennedy traversed New England in quest of funds for Roosevelt. Many donors, among them Republicans with few illusions about Herbert Hoover's reelection chances, demanded anonymity, enabling Kennedy to increase his own beneficence by forwarding the money with his own personal check. In April 1932 Kennedy supplied much of the war chest for Roosevelt's campaign in the Massachusetts primary. Most of the Irish vowed they would die with Smith, but James Michael Curley, old foe of Patrick Kennedy and now mayor of Boston, jumped ship for Roosevelt. Neither Curley nor Kennedy could sway the Irish, however, and the Happy Warrior swept the Bay State.

Another prospect for Kennedy's persuasion was a crucial constituency of one, William Randolph Hearst. Years earlier, the combustible publisher had come east in hopes of making a place for himself in New York politics. The Hearst campaigns were royally financed and publicized, but the press lord finally withdrew in defeat to manage his empire from the castle at San Simeon. Tangles in Empire State politics had instilled in Franklin Roosevelt a distaste for Hearst and his artless methods, but the presidential candidate could not ignore the publisher's influence. Hearst dailies reached sixteen million Americans, Hearst magazines over thirty million.

Passionately opposed to internationalism, Hearst dispatched lieutenants to interview each of the 1932 presidential candidates on his attitude toward the League of Nations. After examining the results, he announced his selection. Franklin Roosevelt, Al Smith, Owen D. Young, Albert Ritchie of Maryland, and Newton D. Baker of Ohio were "all good men in their way"—but they were all internationalists. Hearst anointed the Speaker of the House, John Nance Garner. A glowing biography of the Texan was cabled to Hearst outlets and the publisher donated heavily to the Garner cause.

Yet Roosevelt knew that Hearst's support—or at least his neutrality—might be important at a critical juncture. He trimmed his position on the League and sent Joseph Kennedy to California to press his case. Kennedy had grown friendly with Hearst during the Hollywood years and often attended the lavish evenings at San Simeon. In May 1932 he returned from a pilgrimage to Hearst to share a picnic lunch with Roosevelt under the wisteria and oaks in bloom at Warm Springs. Despite Hearst's preference for Garner or Ritchie, Kennedy reported, the publisher was not unfriendly toward Roosevelt. At a meeting with the governor at the executive mansion the following month, Kennedy promised that he would keep in touch with "W.R." on a day-and-night basis.

Chicago in the final week of June was steamy and somnolent. Wheezing, Louis Howe lay half-naked on a dampened mattress at the Congress Hotel, firing off commands by telephone. Jim Farley, in another room on the seventeenth floor, beckoned delegates to a long-distance hookup from Albany, over which the candidate greeted them by name. Joseph Kennedy shuttled between the downtown hotels, delivering confidential messages and short speeches on Roosevelt's behalf.

According to Farley's count, Franklin Roosevelt controlled a majority of the delegates but lacked the two-thirds required by convention rules. At the first assembly of the Roosevelt forces, Huey Long sprang to his feet, demanding that the candidate lead an assault on the two-thirds requirement. Farley was worried the tactic might backfire; he tried to calm the delegates. But by then the supporters were in mutinous spirit and the session adjourned in turmoil. Joseph Kennedy rushed away to telephone the governor, warning that challenging the two-thirds rule might cost them the nomination. He took his case to a meeting of key Roosevelt supporters; a feverish debate ended in deadlock; the principals called the governor to present both sides of the issue. When the delegates streamed into the Chicago Stadium on Monday, June 27, they received an announcement from Roosevelt headquarters: although the governor believed in majority rule, he would not press the issue at this convention.

Now the problem of making up the rest of the two-thirds remained. Howe and Farley decided that the best chance lay in dislodging the Garner forces from the opposition. Telephone calls descended on San Simeon—from Farley, Curley, Kennedy, and many others, urging William Randolph Hearst to pressure Garner to release his delegates. But Hearst insisted that he would remain with the Speaker for at least seven ballots. The Roosevelt men groped for a deal, any deal, that would put the governor over the top. After four days of convention ritual and a sweat-soaked night of oratory, they still lacked the necessary votes. Jim Farley called Albany to ask Roosevelt whether they should not purchase time by delaying the balloting. The candidate told him not to interfere.

It was Friday morning, the first of July. Dawn was breaking. The call of the states began. From Roosevelt headquarters, more frantic telephone calls went to Hearst, but the publisher had retired for the night. Somehow, Joseph Kennedy's call succeeded in getting through, and Hearst was summoned to talk to his friend. The fat was going to be in the fire, Kennedy warned, unless Hearst pressed Garner to release his bloc immediately. If the publisher refused, the convention would probably break the stalemate by choosing Newton Baker, the dark horse who was Wilson's secretary of war, a convinced internationalist, and therefore anathema to Hearst. Was there any chance for Albert Ritchie? the publisher inquired. "No, I don't think so," Kennedy replied. "I think if Roosevelt cracks on the next ballot, it'll be Baker."

Hearst waited through three ballots. The convention recessed without decision at nine o'clock on Friday morning. The publisher dictated a message for his Washington representative to carry to Garner: "Mr. Hearst is fearful that when Roosevelt's strength crumbles it will bring about either the election of Smith or Baker." Nothing could save the country now but for Garner to throw his delegates behind Roosevelt. After reading the message, the pink-faced Texan said, "Say to Mr. Hearst that I fully agree with him." Later in the day Garner delegates from Texas and California caucused amid rumors that their man had been offered the vice-presidency. The fourth ballot began that evening. When California announced its tally, a great cry went up, and the rockslide began. Franklin Roosevelt arranged to fly to Chicago.

Years afterward Joseph Kennedy insisted that it was he who "brought Hearst around for Roosevelt" and lamented that "you can't find any mention of it in the history books." As proof he offered that when Hearst made his contribution to the Roosevelt campaign, he presented the check to Kennedy. "I'm the one who got the Hearst check and gave it directly to Roosevelt—and in politics that meant that I was the one who had delivered Hearst at the convention." Kennedy's persistent courtship and his early-hour telephone call were a persuasive influence on the publisher, but there was a network of forces at work. Hearst men at Chicago were telephoning their chief just as excitedly as the Roosevelt lieutenants, cautioning against the possibility of Smith or Baker. And only when convinced by events that continued allegiance to Garner would nominate one of these pariahs did Hearst send his message to the Speaker. The nomination of Roosevelt depended too on other incidents besides Hearst's consent. Garner and his backers had to be persuaded to switch to the governor, and the Roosevelt forces had to remain firm on the fourth ballot. Joseph Kennedy was nevertheless an important flywheel in this machinery. As the man in the Roosevelt entourage closest to the mercurial publisher, he earned a share of the credit.

On Saturday morning Kennedy awaited the candidate's arrival over breakfast with Herbert Swope. Raymond Moley came into the hotel suite. The poker-faced Ohioan, Columbia professor and chief of the group of academic advisers that was soon known as Roosevelt's "brain trust," had labored over a draft of the acceptance speech, but Louis Howe was threatening to replace it with a version of his own. Anxious to gain support for his draft, Moley read the speech aloud to the two men. Kennedy praised the address as "very bullish."

Late in the afternoon Franklin Roosevelt's airplane landed at Chicago. After a tumultuous ride into the city, as Joseph Kennedy took his seat at the Chicago Stadium, the Democratic nominee stepped before the convention to proclaim "a New Deal for the American people."

The Man of Mystery

Several days after Chicago, Franklin Roosevelt and three of his sons boarded a yawl for a week of fishing up the New England coast. Following behind was a chartered yacht bearing campaign contributors and advisers who would meet with the governor each night in port. Joseph Kennedy planned to remain on shore during the daytime and join the convoy only for the evening strategy sessions.

On a sparkling summer morning the crew prepared to lift anchor off Long Island. A seaplane came into view and landed on the water. Kennedy climbed out and disappeared into the cabin of the Roosevelt yawl for a private word with the governor before departure. Grinning, the candidate took the helm, posing for photographers as the boat was towed away from the dock. Kennedy boarded his plane, took off and hovered overhead. There was a burst of wind. Jib, mainsail and jigger set full, the yawl picked up speed and moved safely through the mouth of the harbor. Kennedy's plane dipped its wings, wheeled around and headed for New York City.

He had an appointment on Park Avenue with the publisher of the Scripps-Howard newspapers. As a prominent man in journalism and a close friend of Newton Baker, Roy Howard assumed that Kennedy's mission was to do "a little selling work" for Roosevelt. But he found Kennedy's discourse so curious that he reconstructed the conversation for Baker in a letter. "I had, in my previous talks with him, voiced my lack of confidence in Roosevelt," Howard wrote. "He himself is quite frank in his very low estimate of Roosevelt's ability, as evidenced by his statement to me yesterday that he intends to keep constant contact with Roosevelt during the cruise on which the latter embarked yesterday. Kennedy expects to fly to whatever port Roosevelt is in for the night, to be present at the evening conferences because he knew that if he were not present, the other men—notably Louis Howe and Jim Farley—would 'unmake' Roosevelt's mind on some of the points which Kennedy had made it up for Roosevelt."

Howard found Kennedy so "very frank in his expressions of understanding of Roosevelt's immaturity, vacillation, and general weak-kneed character" that he asked why Kennedy had been so desperately interested in nominating Roosevelt instead of a man like Newton Baker. "His only excuse was that he did not know you or have any idea as to what, if any, opposition you would have to the existing set-up in Wall Street, to which he claims to have developed a deep-seated enmity."

The publisher figured that the real explanation was that Kennedy had succeeded in ingratiating himself with Roosevelt and therefore believed he would "be able to go a long way toward molding Roosevelt's thought processes and policies along lines agreeable to him." Howard asked Kennedy if he were not worried that "keeping his protege in line" would wear him out by the end of Roosevelt's term. Kennedy shook his head and shrugged. "I think he fully understands the nature of the job he has taken on for himself," Howard concluded, "but having made a great deal of money and being a very energetic Irishman of about forty years, he is, I believe, enjoying his Warwick role."

Kennedy was wont to tailor his conversation to persuade listeners but his vivid portrayal for Howard of a pliable Roosevelt bore the ring of conviction; it echoed Kennedy's perception of the "smiling four-flusher" at the Navy Department fifteen years earlier. He was scarcely the first to be beguiled by Roosevelt's air of agreeable inconsequence. But it was striking that Kennedy, who so burnished his image as tough guy, could be so easily lured into expecting that he would be the power behind Franklin Roosevelt's throne. There was something about Roosevelt, the quality that moved men to lower their guard and overestimate their importance to him, that would confound Joseph Kennedy again and again.

True to his word, Kennedy joined the Roosevelt party every evening as the boats reached port. John Roosevelt, the governor's youngest son, remembered the small swath Kennedy cut with his twilight seaplane landings. When the boats reached Cuttyhunk, Kennedy departed to join his family at Hyannis Port—but not without installing Eddie Moore in his place, no doubt to pick up small bits of conversation and keep his boss apprised. Moore, once secretary to Honey Fitz and two other mutually hostile Boston mayors, employed his considerable Gaelic charm to make friends for Kennedy in his absence. "It was like a litany," Eddie Dowling remembered. "He never stopped telling me, and anybody that would listen, about the greatness of Joseph P. Kennedy." Several times on the cruise, Moore declared, to the laughter of the others, "If we live long enough and he is spared, the first Irish Catholic in the White House will be one of this man's sons."

In August Roosevelt invited Kennedy to join the executive committee of the campaign, but Kennedy shrewdly demurred: there should be no dissenting voices in Louis Howe's office. By the end of the campaign, according to his own accounting, Kennedy contributed twenty-five thousand dollars of his own money, lent fifty thousand more to the Democratic National Committee and funneled more than a hundred thousand dollars of anonymous donations into the Roosevelt coffers. During a visit to Hyannis Port, Herbert Swope warned Kennedy that the Roosevelt campaign would fail in New England without the aid of Al Smith, who had departed bitterly from the convention at Chicago. A long-time supporter of the Happy Warrior, Swope wanted to work on persuading Smith to endorse Roosevelt. With the wiliness of a professional, Kennedy cautioned him to wait for Roosevelt to ask; a favor requested and granted would strengthen Swope's standing with the new administration.

The candidate was scheduled to speak on securities reform on August 20 at Columbus, Ohio; he asked Kennedy for his ideas. Later Kennedy claimed he was one of the first men in the United States to discuss the need for securities regulation with Franklin Roosevelt. The speech (drafted mainly by Adolf Berle) blended whimsy and sternness. The previous decade, Roosevelt declared, had been a "heyday of promoters, sloganeers, mushroom millionaries, opportunists, adventurers of all kinds." The American people had been cast as Alices in Wonderland. "The poorhouse was to vanish like the Cheshire cat. A mad hatter invited everyone to have some more profits. . . . A cynical Father William in the lower district of Manhattan balanced the sinuous evil of a poolridden stock market on the end of his nose." Proposing legislation for truth in securities and regulation of exchanges and holding companies, Roosevelt outlined the task that, two years later, would give Joseph Kennedy his first opportunity for national service.

In September 1932 the Roosevelt campaign embarked on a whistle-stop journey to the Pacific Coast. Invited to accompany the caravan, Kennedy joined Raymond Moley in the Pullman car preceding Roosevelt's. "In the friendly intimacy of the campaign train, the man from Boston became one of the inner circle," Moley recalled. "I permitted him to read the speeches before their delivery and welcomed his shrewd suggestions. His political inheritance from his father and his understanding of very practical economic affairs was valuable." Some of the newspapermen impishly tagged Kennedy "the Little Bernard Baruch."

As the train forged westward, Franklin Roosevelt was increasingly confined by what Arthur Schlesinger, Jr., described as a triangle of advice. One side, whose proponents included Albert Ritchie and Carter Glass of Virginia, advocated retrenchment, laissez-faire economics, and sound money. Another side, embracing men as disparate as Felix Frankfurter and Bernard Baruch, advanced the old Progressive creed of low tariffs, trust-busting, and inflation. The third side of the triangle, including Rexford G. Tugwell and Adolf Berle, envisioned large-scale economic planning and big government to countervail the power of big business.

Like the candidate himself, Kennedy had no ideological axe to grind. He was disturbed by the chaos of laissez-faire competition but was equally hesitant to support deficit spending. He approved moderate inflation, but not the extreme kind favored by some of the western Progressives and the radio priest and Roosevelt supporter, Father Charles Coughlin of Michigan. He thought economic planning might be the answer to the national dilemma, but doubted that it would ever go over in the utopian style of Berle and Tugwell. Roosevelt and Kennedy shared an aversion to dogma and a taste for the novel, but Kennedy's principal influence on the candidate's platform was indirect, exerted mainly through the collaboration with Moley on speeches. He had a hand in the Pittsburgh address in which Roosevelt committed himself to a balanced budget; he inserted some New York slang into a farm speech for Topeka. (Moley removed this, explaining that it would be incomprehensible to Kansans.) When the Roosevelt Special arrived in the Northwest, Key Pittman of Nevada, Thomas Walsh of Montana, and other senators beseeched the governor to approve silver as the legal basis for American currency. Kennedy was for sidestepping the issue, arguing that voters won over by a bimetalist position in the western silver states would be more than offset by losses in the Northeast. After an all-night argument at Butte, Roosevelt blandly announced that, if elected, he would convene a presidential conference on silver.

The governor appreciated Kennedy's mordant sense of humor and his frank counsel. After the train pulled into a station, Kennedy would leave the campaign party to buttonhole local officials and flatter them with requests for their thinking on national affairs. He also carried out confidential missions for Roosevelt. When the train arrived in Chicago during the World Series, "Joe somehow managed to corral tickets for everybody on the train, that is, everybody except Roosevelt," recalled Harold Brayman, who covered the campaign. "I have often wondered what Roosevelt did during that two-and-a-half hour period that he didn't want the newspapermen to know about."

In San Francisco Kennedy arranged a secret meeting between the candidate and A. P. Giannini, president of the Bank of America. Afterwards, Giannini wired his New York representative to "phone Joe Kennedy my congratulations on splendid way he and Farley are running campaign." In Los Angeles Kennedy's Hollywood cronies staged a vast electrical pageant; a hundred thousand Californians awaited the arrival of Roosevelt. Kennedy spied an old Hollywood friend, Jack Warner, and asked if he was counting the house. "No," replied the film magnate, "I was just wondering who's in the theaters tonight."

Kennedy befriended the candidate's flaxen-haired daughter, Anna Roosevelt Dall, and his eldest son James, on whose arm Roosevelt made his way to the train's rear platform at campaign stops. James remembered the speculator from Boston as "a rather fabulous figure to a very young fellow on his father's first campaign train." Kennedy also found chums among the newspapermen who followed Roosevelt. "He liked being with the press more than he liked being with the politicians," thought Ernest Lindley, the Albany correspondent who two years earlier had written Roosevelt's first biography. "He liked the repartee."

Competing with the candidate for publicity, however, would do little to aid his cause. Kennedy was a model of self-effacement. To a Boston reporter sent to interview the home-town boy, Kennedy declared, "There is nothing I want. There is no public office that would interest me. Governor Roosevelt asked me to go with him on this trip and I agreed to accompany him." He went on, "I have heard it said that Roosevelt is indecisive. I certainly have never seen anything indecisive about him. Roosevelt is a glutton for work, but he is one of the easiest men in the world to advise with. He keeps his mind open so well that it is a pleasure to work with him. I do not think he is the greatest man in the world, but I do know he would accomplish things." Kennedy maintained his low profile when Al Smith finally appeared with Roosevelt in Boston at the end of the campaign; a Boston journalist observed that Kennedy "lived up to his reputation as a man of mystery."

On election night, Kennedy permitted himself a moment in the spotlight; he took over two floors of the Waldorf-Astoria to await the returns with friends and family in New York. When news of Franklin Roosevelt's election arrived, the guests clustered around Joseph Kennedy and an orchestra issued the strains of "Happy Days are Here Again."

The Ways of Providence

Kennedy had aided Roosevelt with large sums of money (Rex Tugwell thought Kennedy "bought" his way into the entourage), access to prominent friends like Hearst and Giannini, yeoman work at the convention and on the campaign express. Most important for this man who viewed politics through the prism of personal relationships, Kennedy believed he had won Roosevelt's friendship. When Raymond Moley received his Washington assignment in mid-November, Kennedy wired his campaign roommate that the president-elect was fortunate to have him—"not only for your standards but your clear thinking and ability to get things done. Good luck to you, boy, and may this be just the beginning of a further great career." Settling at Palm Beach for the Christmas holidays, Kennedy confided to intimates that he expected to be tapped for secretary of the treasury.

But Roosevelt's telephone call never came. The president-elect was crafting his government in a fashion that, for Roosevelt, was uncharacteristically systematic, writing out lists of candidates for cabinet and agency jobs to be circulated to Howe, Moley, and the other chief counselors. Joseph Kennedy's name indeed appeared on the treasury list—but not for secretary. Instead Roosevelt had Kennedy in mind, along with two others, for the ceremonial position of treasurer of the United States. Appointing Kennedy to this office would accord him his reward without providing him the authority to shape policy. Roosevelt was a master at depriving ambitious allies of the honors they expected while also depriving them of the cause to complain of ingratitude by offering positions he knew they would decline. The new chief executive infuriated James Michael Curley with an offer of the American embassy in Warsaw when he knew that Rome was his heart's desire.

As it turned out, Kennedy was not even offered the chance for his signature to appear on American currency. Louis Howe's suspicions, intensified by reports of Kennedy's amity with Roosevelt aboard the autumn train, had hardened into implacable opposition. Kennedy might have taken some comfort from the fact that even Jim Farley suffered from the jealousies of Howe, who tried to engineer Farley's exile to a job at the port of New York before Farley uncovered the plot and foiled it. Sharing his frustrations with Curley and Farley, however, did not mitigate Kennedy's disappointment. In February Moley left the Roosevelt party at Jacksonville to spend a few days with Kennedy at Palm Beach. "There I heard plenty of Kennedy's excoriation of Roosevelt, of his criticisms of the President-elect who, according to Kennedy, had no program—and what ideas he had were unworthy of note," Moley recalled. "There must have been hundreds of dollars in telephone calls to provide an exchange of abuse of Roosevelt between Kennedy and W. R. Hearst. The latter by this time was wondering why he had ever supported Roosevelt in the final hours before the nomination."

By inauguration day Joseph Kennedy received exactly one reward. An elderly uncle of his wife, James Fitzgerald, was appointed to the federal alcohol tax office in Boston, a small favor requiring the old man to deceive the civil service about his age.

Puzzled, hurt, angry, Kennedy told Burton Wheeler he was considering a suit against the Democratic National Committee for repayment of his campaign loan. Yet he continued to seek a path into Washington through others close to the president such as Bernard Baruch, Herbert Swope, the investment banker Forbes Morgan, and Raymond Moley. During the Hundred Days, Kennedy invited the man who was singled out as one of the president's chief advisers to lunch in Manhattan. He reminded Moley that his new status in Washington required a standard of living that a government salary could not support; would he allow Kennedy to solicit friends to provide a fund enabling Moley to live as he should? Moley gently demurred by saying he had no elaborate tastes but if he ever needed a loan he would come to Kennedy. But Kennedy persisted, observing that there was no moral stigma attached to supplementing the income of a public man. John W. Davis had employed such a fund while serving as ambassador to Great Britain. Moley refused again; he later wished he had been astute enough to realize that if he finally succeeded in getting Kennedy into the administration, the revelation of such an arrangement would elicit damaging comment in the press, but this did not cross his mind over lunch. He pondered keeping his distance from Kennedy, but finally decided that friends were too valuable to abandon merely because he disagreed with their standard of morality.

Kennedy also pursued a formal correspondence with Franklin Roosevelt through the spring of 1933. While fulminating in private against the president, he sent a florid telegram of congratulations after the inaugural. He had been to a convent, Kennedy wired, and found that "the nuns were praying for you." The Mother Superior had declared that "since your Inaugural, peace seemed to come on the earth; in fact, it seemed like another resurrection. Mortal man can pay you no higher compliment."

Roosevelt replied with thanks for Kennedy's "awfully nice telegram." He reported airily that "we are all keeping our fingers crossed and hoping to get in some real work while the temper of the country and the Congress is so pleasant. Do be sure to let us know when you are going through Washington and stop off and see us."

To another flattering letter, Kennedy received another standoffish response. "I have been meaning for some time to write you and tell you of my real appreciation of all that you did during the campaign," the president wrote, adding that he "need not tell you how helpful you were"—especially "the joy you added when things were most difficult." He invited Kennedy for a cruise one weekend on the presidential yacht.

This time, Kennedy replied with a hint of sarcasm. "It is pleasant to any of us to know that we are remembered in high places." He would always remember the campaign period as "one of the most satisfactory in my life." Kennedy appreciated the sailing invitation but reminded Roosevelt that he was rarely in Washington. "If I am, however, I shall certainly join you. Thanks anyway."

Swope informed Kennedy of a meeting in which Moley, Forbes Morgan, and Frank Walker "all began talking of you and what a damn shame it was that nothing had been done." Swope was particularly sympathetic to Kennedy since his own hopes of appointment as ambassador to Berlin had been dashed. "My view was that the lot of them had been running after you while they needed you, but I had not discerned much running after the need had passed. All agreed and thought it was a damned outrage. They are going to send for you and have the Great White Father hold your hand." The newspaperman relayed reports that there was some mention of Kennedy's installation as undersecretary of war. "I am told that Howe is actually quite friendly, except he wants to keep you away from finance. That's his method, I suppose, of separating the Administration from Wall Street." Swope concluded, "Well anyway you have them in a stew. They really are concerned, even though nothing happens. Probably the thing to do is to wait and then plump hard for a specific request in your own behalf. . . ."

In May the Great White Father summoned Kennedy for his session of hand-holding. "Hello, Joe, where have you been all these months?" Roosevelt asked with arm outstretched, "I thought you'd gotten lost." Overwhelmed by his first visit to the Oval Room, Kennedy was uncommonly subdued. There was an instinctive and almost childlike respect for institutions underneath the layers of plain-spoken man and Wall Street operator; Kennedy once admitted that he tried to reduce men who intimidated him by imagining them in suits of red underclothing. As he exchanged amenities with the president this spring day, his mind kept returning to the freewheeling atmosphere of the campaign, when he had filled his talk with epithets. On one occasion he had told the candidate that his speech was "the stupidest thing I ever heard." Now Kennedy was closemouthed: "It had been permissable then. But in the presence of the power and majesty of the Presidency, it seemed unforgivable." He finally discussed with Roosevelt what was on his mind, but the president suggested no suitable place in the administration. "I told him that I did not desire a position with the Government unless it really meant some prestige to my family," Kennedy wrote his eldest son.

There were rumors that Kennedy would be the New York director of the National Recovery Administration or minister to Ireland. That summer Roosevelt casually suggested his appointment to a commission drafting reciprocal trade agreements with South American nations. Raymond Moley tried to arrange Kennedy's nomination to the American delegation to the London Economic Conference, but its chairman, James P. Warburg, complained of being saddled with "political hacks" for whom he would have to apologize to the Europeans. Moley reassured Warburg that Kennedy was "a decent fellow" whom the president owed a political debt, and proposed his appointment instead to an auxiliary group that would go to London to advise the delegation. Warburg would have none of it; from another source he had discovered that Kennedy was "a completely irresponsible speculator who has been spreading malicious stories about the President." The delegation should be renamed "Patronesses of the Democratic Campaign," Warburg told Moley, adding a threat to resign. Kennedy was not appointed.

The June night before Moley departed for the London conference, Kennedy came to his New York hotel room. "He said, in the spirit of a bird of ill omen, that he had come to warn me," Moley remembered, "He said that he had reason to believe that Roosevelt was growing 'jealous' because of the prominence I had 'enjoyed' as an adviser and assistant of the President. Also that I had better 'watch out for him.' " Moley never quite understood either Kennedy's meaning or his intentions and attributed the visit to some kind of political infighting.

Hopes for a government post receding, Joseph Kennedy returned to

Wall Street. He joined other speculators, including Elisha Walker and Henry Mason Day, in a pool trading shares of Libbey-Owens-Ford. Repeal was imminent and baseless rumors arose that the glass manufacturer was preparing to produce liquor bottles. In the method of the New Era, the pool operators traded shares back and forth; outsiders bought in and the speculators sold short at a handsome profit. Kennedy's part in the operation was discreet, but the Libbey-Owens-Ford pool was precisely the kind of manipulation that the Democratic nominee had proposed to outlaw a year earlier. Within a year, Joseph Kennedy would declare that "a revival of the national conscience" had made practices that were condoned before 1929 unthinkable.

Late in the summer of 1933 Kennedy invited the president's eldest son and his wife to spend a few days at Hyannis Port. James Roosevelt, after graduation from Harvard, had settled in Boston to establish an insurance and investment firm. He also hoped one day to run for governor of Massachusetts; the young Roosevelt had managed his father's Bay State headquarters the previous year. With his intimate knowledge of Boston finance and politics, Kennedy took an interest in James and Betsey Roosevelt. The senior man interrupted one of the sun-washed days in Hyannis Port to telephone a fellow campaigner, Eddie Dowling, requesting a favor for the president's son.

Twenty-six of thirty-two Ford Motor Company assembly plants had been stilled by depression. Henry Ford had launched a broadside against the Democratic candidate during the final days of the 1932 campaign; now he lay ill. As Dowling remembered the episode, Kennedy had learned from Ford's assistant, Harry Bennett, that the founder was eager to bury the hatchet. If the president could be importuned to inquire after Mr. Ford's health, the old man might be better inclined to reopen the factories and provide an important signal of national economic recovery. There might also be an added benefit: James Roosevelt's agency would gain a good crack at a contract for the company's workmen's compensation program. Dowling agreed to the mission. He arranged to call on the president, on holiday at Warm Springs.

Dowling greeted the president and his secretary, Missy Le Hand, at poolside; he mentioned his talk with Kennedy. "Oh, old Joe," the president nodded amiably. "What's Joe up to now?" Dowling delivered the message. "Now let's take Jimmy and that fellow he's teamed up with out of this," said Roosevelt, in Dowling's recollection. "Let's not make this a conditional thing. It strikes me—and I think it does you too, Missy—that the big thing here is a hundred thousand men going back to work, if this man means what he says. It isn't going to take much effort on our part to do this thing, is it?" The president reminded them that Edsel Ford had donated the money to build the pool at Warm Springs; he was "kind of obligated" to do a kindness for the father. He dictated a warm telegram to Henry Ford. Whether influenced by the wire or not, Ford started the assembly lines rolling again. James Roosevelt held long afterwards that his firm received no business from the company.

A month after the visit at Hyannis Port, the Kennedys and the younger Roosevelts sailed for Great Britain. Joseph Kennedy anticipated the end of Prohibition as eagerly as he had the rise of motion pictures and the stock market. He hoped to parlay some of the most coveted franchises for British liquor into a profitable importing business after Repeal. Accompanied by James, Kennedy called on the leading distillery men in London. No doubt impressed by the presence of the president's son, they offered Kennedy his franchises. Later there was talk—denied by James—that the young Roosevelt had expected a share in the enterprise and had been refused by Kennedy.

He and his wife stayed with the Kennedys at Palm Beach that Christmas. "When I am going to hear from the White House?" Kennedy asked. "Don't worry," Roosevelt replied. "You haven't been forgotten." On his return to Washington James asked members of the president's circle what was being planned for Kennedy. "He's getting restless." Kennedy renewed the private criticism of the president's performance that he had earlier rendered to Moley. "If I were to send you a short summary of the whole situation in the country," he wrote Felix Frankfurter at Oxford, "I would just say 'confusion'."

When William Woodin resigned as secretary of the treasury in January 1934, Kennedy's hopes revived, but Henry Morgenthau was appointed. Mrs. Kennedy observed that her husband was more disappointed by this than by the president's initial rebuff. Still he was encouraged by a letter from Raymond Moley: "I had a talk with Jimmy at the White House a week ago and he intimated to me some of the things that have been happening recently and I want to assure you that I very genuinely regret the drift of things. The ways of providence and some other things are inscrutable, however. . . ."

"Set a Thief to Catch a Thief"

In the Senate Caucus Room, a battle was in the offing. Washington was investigating Wall Street. One by one the toppled idols of the New

Era came before the Committee on Banking and Currency and its pugnacious counsel, Ferdinand Pecora. Richard Whitney, president of the New York Stock Exchange, the younger J. P. Morgan, Charles Mitchell of the National City Bank, and other financiers answered and parried queries about misleading stock offerings, oversize bonuses, market pools, and the battery of other practices that were the underside of prosperity.

"For month after month, the country was treated to a series of amazing revelations which involved practically all the important names in the financial community in practices which, to say the least, were highly unethical," Joseph Kennedy wrote later. "The belief that those in control of the corporate life in America were motivated by honesty and ideals of honorable conduct was completely shattered."

The Pecora investigation was both product and cause of a groundswell for financial reform. The most observant financiers noted that the loudest applause during Franklin Roosevelt's inaugural address was reserved for the call to "an end to a conduct in banking and in business which too often has given to a sacred trust the likeness of callous and selfish wrongdoing." The new president fulfilled the promise at Columbus by proposing federal supervision of securities traded over state boundaries. Added to the ancient law of *caveat emptor,* Roosevelt proclaimed, would now be the doctrine of "let the seller also beware." The whirlwind of the Hundred Days carried the bill through Congress by the end of May. At the White House signing ceremony the president observed that the Securities Act of 1933 "at last translates some elementary standards of right and wrong into law"—the first step in "a program to restore some old-fashioned standards of rectitude."

The second step was in the spring of 1934. Thomas Corcoran, Benjamin Cohen, and James Landis were assigned by Moley to draft a bill regulating the stock exchanges themselves. The three lawyers drew up a forceful measure; it proposed federal supervision of trading practices, registration of securities, and strict control over the amount of money speculators could borrow.

Richard Whitney moved to steal the bill's thunder by promising that the New York Exchange would act against stock pools and trading based on inside information. But the lurid incidents revealed in the Pecora probe suggested that the time for self-regulation had passed. Whitney's forces took a house in Georgetown to orchestrate the attack of the Old Guard; it quickly gained the appellation of the "Wall Street Embassy." They warned that federal regulation would render Wall Street "a deserted village." Some cultivated a Red Scare, charging that the bill was the beachhead of a conspiracy to push America toward communism. The New Deal cabal, they warned, was plotting to retard recovery to prepare the way for new social order; in this scenario the president was cast as a Kerensky, playing to a less misguided and more diabolical Lenin. Sam Rayburn read aloud letters from brokerage employees who backed the aims of the bill but were constrained to sign petitions and give money to the opposition. With only some hyperbole, the Texan complained of "the most powerful lobby ever organized against any bill." But not even this pressure could stem public opinion. On June 6 Franklin Roosevelt enacted the Securities Exchange Act of 1934.

Centerpiece of the legislation was the establishment of a Securities and Exchange Commission to enforce the regulations. The president asked Moley for a list of names to fill the five places on the new commission. At the top of Moley's list was the Wall Street financier whom Moley had been trying to bring into the New Deal for over a year. Joseph Kennedy was "the best bet for chairman because of executive ability, knowledge of habits and customs of business to be regulated, and ability to moderate different points of view on Commission." Moley pointed out that Kennedy's wealth would prevent him from taking advantage of the confidential information to which he would be privy—plus "the ethics of politics" required Roosevelt to reward Kennedy's campaign aid with substantial recognition. Bernard Baruch and Herbert Swope also sounded the klaxons for Kennedy at the White House. In mid-June the president assured Moley that he had virtually decided on Kennedy as chairman.

As word of the appointment drifted out, however, Roosevelt began to waver. Louis Howe complained that assigning Kennedy to police Wall Street was like setting a cat to guard the pigeons. Jim Farley, always a bit competitive toward this fellow Irishman, worried that the nomination of a man with Kennedy's Wall Street background would hurt the administration politically.

Kennedy arrived in Washington after hearing of his prospective nomination. The president asked Frank Walker to talk Kennedy out of the chairmanship. Night after night, during walks through the deserted streets of the capital, the president's man reasoned with Kennedy, but to no avail. "You go back and tell him I don't want to be a member of the commission," Kennedy ordered, "I'm going to be chairman—or else." Further clouding the scene, booms were launched from Capitol Hill and newspaper offices for the nominations of Ferdinand Pecora and James Landis.

A few days before the end of June Raymond Moley flew from New

York to Washington. Also aboard the flight was Roy Howard. The publisher was vehemently opposed to the notion of Kennedy as chairman of the SEC. The two men argued for the greater portion of the flight until Moley finally suggested that if Howard felt so strongly, he should present his case to the president. Howard did, but he departed from the White House still unsatisfied. He telephoned Kennedy at his Washington hotel, cautioning him to decline the nomination or endure an attack by the Scripps-Howard newspapers. Kennedy refused, and Howard's *Washington News* issued an impassioned editorial: the president "cannot with impunity administer such a slap in the face to his most loyal and effective supporters as that reported to be contemplated in the appointment of Joseph P. Kennedy."

On the evening of June 28 Roosevelt brought the dispute to a head. He directed Moley to send for Kennedy. Bernard Baruch, an overnight guest at the White House, was summoned as well. The capital was in the throes of a heat wave. At the Shoreham Hotel Kennedy answered Moley's telephoned invitation with "Nuts!" But he agreed to see the president. The conversation of the four men fastened on the membership of the Securities Commission. "What's the matter with that redhead over there?" asked Baruch, pointing to Kennedy.

Roosevelt pulled Moley's memorandum from the stack of papers in his desk basket. "Kennedy is first on the list here. I propose to give him the five-year appointment and the chairmanship."

Kennedy was unwilling to plead for the job; he rose to his feet. "Mr. President, I don't think you ought to do this. I think it will bring down injurious criticism."

"Joe, I know darned well you want this job," Moley interjected. "But if anything in your career in business could injure the President, this is the time to spill it. Let's forget the general criticism that you've made money on Wall Street."

Kennedy reacted precisely as Moley anticipated. Sprinkling his reply liberally with epithets, he defied anyone to question his dedication to the public interest or to point to a single shady act in his life. The president didn't need to worry about that. What was more, Kennedy would offer his critics an administration of the SEC that would be a credit to his country, the president, himself, and his family—down to two-year-old Teddy.

The next day, after a late night, Roosevelt told newspapermen, "All I need is some sleep. I sat up and drank beer with Barney Baruch and Joe Kennedy. I did not do any work at all. It was awful—two o'clock and I have no excuse for it." The following afternoon, on June 30, before leaving for a Caribbean cruise, the president announced Kennedy's nomination.

The prospective chairman of the Securities and Exchange Commission was not content simply to bask in the glory of his selection. Kennedy went to great lengths to create the public appearance that the president had "drafted" him for the post. An article written by a *Boston Post* reporter after an exclusive interview with Kennedy was headlined, "Big Sacrifice for Children's Sake / Joseph P. Kennedy Accepts Securities Exchange Control Job Against Will, But Seeks Public Service Legacy." According to the article, Kennedy believed that when his children grew up, "they will be pleased to know that their father held one of the most important positions in the country at a time when the future of the land was in doubt. Having almost everything else, he wants to leave a name known for public service as well as business success. This is what made him accept a position he did not want. Of course, he was at the mercy of the world's super-salesman, Franklin D. Roosevelt, but even at that, he resisted one call but succumbed to the next when the President pointed out the need for his services. That desire to leave an honorable, unselfish name, which has been the moving force behind so many men of unusual abilities, was what made him give in and agree to go to Washington to take over the job which, at its best, looks like a thankless task."

Kennedy's version of his appointment illuminated the divided man. The operational Kennedy befriended Roosevelt and his family, employed a combination of pleas and threats to secure a Washington job, insisted on his nomination as chairman rather than member of the SEC. But the Kennedy who strove for a public-minded image cautioned the president against making the appointment because of "injurious criticism" and let it be known that Roosevelt had overcome Kennedy's objections to demand that he accept the "thankless task." The duality separated Kennedy from the more purely power-minded politicians; one of the reasons why Jim Curley so resented being denied the embassy in Rome was that his hangers-on might wonder about the degree of his clout at the White House.

After the cabinet meeting at which Franklin Roosevelt announced Kennedy's choice, Harold Ickes, the old progressive Republican and bellicose secretary of the interior, grumbled into his diary. The president seemed to have great confidence in Kennedy, Ickes wrote, "because he has made his pile, has invested all his money in government securities, and knows all the tricks of the trade. Apparently he is going on the assumption that Kennedy would now like to make a name for himself for the sake of his family, but I have never known many of these cases to work out as expected." Roosevelt defended Kennedy's selection in a note to Herbert Swope: "Joe is able, loyal and will make good. What more can one ask?" When advisers, family, and friends complained about the incursion of a Wall Street operator into the New Deal, Roosevelt invoked the smiling smokescreen of nonchalance: "Set a thief to catch a thief."

Business journals welcomed the news. The Kiplinger Newsletter noted that Kennedy's background made him an "object of suspicion, but his personal zeal, energy and integrity may overcome the handicap." The liberal press was scandalized. John T. Flynn, financial editor of the *New Republic,* let out a volley against the nomination. Never in his wildest dreams had Flynn imagined that Roosevelt would permit a Wall Street speculator to chair the Securities Commission. As recently as the previous summer, Kennedy had participated in "one of the pools that produced the squalid little boom of 1933, and when these poolsters withdrew and the boom collapsed, the Administration denounced the men who had operated them." Kennedy, "we are told, succeeds in everything he undertakes. But he has succeeded in one thing and that performance must make the admirers of great acrobatic feats gasp with wonder and admiration. He has gone from a desk in a broker's office to the headship of the commission that will manage Wall Street for the New Deal. . . . I say it isn't true. It is impossible. It could not happen."

Alarmed senators flocked to Burton Wheeler for word of Kennedy's good intentions. The Montanan assured them that Kennedy would never dishonor his family, but Duncan Fletcher of Florida, chairman of the Banking and Currency Committee, postponed the nominee's confirmation until Congress reconvened in January 1935. Then senators could appraise Kennedy's performance in office.

Many around the president were reluctant to accept the Wall Street man into their coterie. Thomas Corcoran first exploded when Ray Moley told him the news; after calming down, he observed, "Oh well, we've got four out of five anyhow." Weren't all five commissioners satisfactory appointments? Moley inquired. "What I mean is that four are for us and one is for business." Moley snapped that neither he nor the president considered themselves as warriors in a battle against business. "Kennedy—as well as other members of the commission—was appointed to work for the people of the United States," he lectured, "not to direct class struggles."

Nonetheless, Kennedy's installation as chairman of the SEC was not foreordained. Despite the obvious preference of the president, the five commissioners were authorized by law to select a chairman from among their number. Confident they would abide by his wishes, Roosevelt asked them to "take a good look at Kennedy." Raymond Moley cautiously asked the president to write out his choice in longhand—just in case. The note was given to James Roosevelt, who handed it to Kennedy before the commisison's first meeting on Monday, July 2.

Moley's fears were justified. Commissioner Ferdinand Pecora arrived at commission headquarters in the wake of rumors he would resign with a blazing attack on the president if Kennedy were elected chairman. With Kennedy in one office and Pecora in another, James Landis shuttled back and forth, trying to reconcile their differences. Finally the two men joined their colleagues and the meeting began two hours late. Kennedy was confirmed as chairman. As photographers snapped pictures of the commission members after the session, Kennedy immediately began working to win over Pecora and the other skeptics. "I'm no sucker," he confessed, "They know more about this law than I ever hope to know." Sitting at a sidewalk cafe with Thomas Corcoran and Benjamin Cohen the next morning, he asked, "Why do you fellows hate me?"

No journalist could claim a more influential readership in the capital than the chief correspondent of the *New York Times* Washington bureau, Arthur Krock. Born in Glasgow, Kentucky, he matriculated at Princeton but low finances compelled him to withdraw after a year; rather than wait on tables in the Princeton Commons he finished his education at a small college in Chicago. Krock arrived in Washington in 1909 as reporter for the *Louisville Times*. He went abroad to cover the Versailles Conference, worked briefly for the Hays Office, wrote for Herbert Swope at the *New York World* before returning to Washington for the *Times*. Colleagues of decades were admonished from addressing Krock by his first name: "I'm sorry, but that's the way I am." Annoyed by Krock's formality and his differences with the New Deal, Franklin Roosevelt rarely tired of telling friends of the columnist's fascination with the wealthy and powerful; he regaled them with the tale of how, shortly after the inauguration, a letter had arrived at the White House from Krock, listing the special privileges he expected to be granted. Yet, as in the case of a different style of journalist, William Randolph Hearst, this did not prevent the president from appreciating the audience of Krock's "In the Nation" column from Washington. Roosevelt, echoed by calls from Krock's friends Swope and Baruch, asked the *Times* correspondent to write a piece that would give Joseph Kennedy a good start in his new job.

Immensely impressed after a candid exchange with the new chairman

The president's note to Moley, June 30, 1934: "Memo. for R.M. I have no objection to your telling Landis & Matthews [sic] *that it is my best considered judgment that even if no decision is now arrived at as to the* permanency *of the Chairmanship, the situation today calls for selection of* Kennedy *as Chairman—F.D.R."*

of the Securities Commission, Krock delivered a glowing report. "J. P. Kennedy Has Excelled in Varied Endeavors" was the title of his Independence Day offering. The column examined Kennedy's career with such enthusiasm that it fell wide of the mark. According to Krock, Kennedy had been a "famous ballplayer" at Harvard, "resolved" the warring interests of Hollywood, and then "became Mr. Roosevelt's campaign, business and financial manager, with amazing success." The incoming New Dealer had "never been in a bear pool in his life or participated in any outside move to trim the limbs. He has been a member of but two pools of any kind. His Wall Street operations have been with his own money, in the interest of his own holdings." Krock attested that Kennedy could be "counted on to make it easy for honest issues and very, very difficult for the other kind." Kennedy was deeply grateful. Krock's article was the beginning of the closest friendship Joseph Kennedy would have in Washington.

The piece drew a jeering letter from a Wall Street broker. "The unrestrained amusement of brokers and investment bankers over the attempt you and Joseph Kennedy are making to build Mr. Kennedy up to the stature of a big man shows that Wall Street, in spite of all its tribulations, has not yet lost its sense of humor." She asked Krock to "look at all Mr. Kennedy's mergers and manipulations today. What happened to the poor suckers who invested their savings in his movie bonanzas?" The general impression in the financial district was that Kennedy would "play ball" with the money changers, the broker reported. "His record in Wall Street being common knowledge, it seems incredible that Mr. Kennedy would attempt a Judas on the men who made him, despite Mr. Roosevelt's attitude toward the stock market."

Kennedy was given the letter by Krock for his response. "I resent very much the fact that anybody made me in Wall Street," he replied, "I have never been a director of any corporation or bank in the country except the ones I personally managed. I have yet to be indebted to anybody or Wall Street for any hand-out. . . . As to whether I will play ball with the moneychangers, time alone will prove whether I will to the detriment of the public interest."

Krock mailed a copy of Kennedy's reply to his Wall Street reader, with the challenge, "How does it impress you?"

New Dealer in Finance

On the afternoon of July 25 trading at the New York Stock Exchange grew slack. Brokers gathered around loudspeakers to hear the broadcast of Joseph Kennedy's maiden speech from Washington. Wall Street was to receive its first clue on how the new SEC chairman intended to wield his powers. Some anticipated a slashing attack on the financial community to affirm Kennedy's New Deal credentials; others reassured one another that this speculator would not turn against the world in which he had made his millions. Neither group knew its man.

At three o'clock Kennedy's words drifted into the trading room. "We of the SEC do not regard ourselves as coroners sitting on the corpse of free enterprise. On the contrary, we think of ourselves as the means of bringing new life into the body of the securities business." The commissioners had "no grudges to satisfy, no venom which needs victims," no passion to "push business around." Their mission, Kennedy declared, was to hasten recovery by restoring faith in the honesty of American business.

"Everybody says that what business needs is confidence. I agree. Confidence that if business does the right thing, it will be protected and given a chance to live, make profits and grow, helping itself and helping the country." If the business community would cooperate with government, "the New Deal in finance will be found to be a better deal for all."

American capital investment was stagnant in the summer of 1934. Kennedy's mandate was to help break the logjam through deft administration of the new securities acts. The legislation was itself potent but vague, offering broad guidelines rather than specific regulations. By their drafting of the regulations, Kennedy and his colleagues exercised extraordinary influence over the future of Wall Street. The battle that was previously waged in Congress now moved to the offices of the Securities and Exchange Commission. The job placed Kennedy on a precarious tightrope between the most adamant of his old colleagues and the most adamant of his new ones.

Few of the Old Guard of Wall Street still argued for complete restoration of unlimited competition in the stock market. Most financiers, particularly the most visible like Richard Whitney, acknowledged that businessmen had sometimes to subjugate their ambitions to the good of the system. Still they believed these sacrifices could be evoked by voluntary regulation and social custom. Whitney himself pointed to the days before the crash when, on behalf of the Morgan group, he invested hundreds of millions of dollars in key stocks in a vain effort to end the wave of panic-selling.

Franklin Roosevelt considered the problem preeminently a matter of moral education. "The fundamental trouble with this whole stock exchange crowd," he wrote Adolf Berle, was "a complete lack of elementary education . . . just an inability to understand the country or the public or their obligation to their fellow men." But the president knew that censoriousness would be only an obstacle to gaining acceptance for federal regulation of finance. Influenced by Moley and others of similar mind, Roosevelt intended the first chairman of the Securities Commission to be more an ambassador to Wall Street than its scourge.

Kennedy walked the tightrope by presenting government supervision as the path of enlightened self-interest. Restoring legitimacy to business through regulation would restore public confidence and encourage new investment. Adolf Berle, one of the authors of the legislation, wrote Kennedy to praise his maiden address. "I hope we struck a compromise with those who would prefer violent methods in cleaning up the exchanges," Kennedy replied. "At any rate, they will have to be patient and give us a chance at peaceful methods." Walter Lippmann also admired the address and told Kennedy "if you can persuade the President himself to speak along those lines, you will do him the greatest possible service. There isn't any conceivable reason why these things shouldn't be said, for if he believes what he is doing, he must believe them."

Bringing the New Deal to Wall Street was, for Kennedy, less a moral crusade than an acceptance of changed realities. "The days of stock manipulation are over," he acknowledged. "Things that seemed all right a few years ago find no place in our present-day philosophy." James Landis admired Kennedy's ability to speak to financiers in their own language and observed that they accepted things from him that they would never have accepted from the reformers. One journalist sized up Kennedy's method: "The victim who gets in the way of a fast one will be greeted with a slap on the back and a loud blast of laughter as over a good joke." Other Washington reporters traded rumors that the securities regulator used information gained from wiretapping to ride herd over his domain.

Characteristically, Roosevelt balanced Kennedy with more reform-spirited commissioners such as Landis and Pecora to ensure that the practical problems of enforcement did not eclipse the central issue of remaking the ethic of Wall Street. Emblematic of Kennedy's disagreements with colleagues for whom reform was paramount was his difference with Ferdinand Pecora. The former Senate counsel, after years spent drawing the accounts of misdeeds out of financiers, insisted that the commission compel companies to reveal their full financial histories. Implicit in this proposal was the expectation that the further discrediting of business would provide a springboard for more reforms. In the suggestion Kennedy saw only a hindrance to investment; he proposed that firms disclose only that information that enabled investors to choose their holdings wisely. Kennedy's will prevailed. Although the two men bore their differences without malice, Pecora departed after six months to accept a place on the New York Supreme Court.

New Dealers who expected Kennedy to show deference to Wall Street, however, were startled by his militant rhetoric taking business elements to task for failure to support the aims of the administration. Financiers were acting in "cowardly" fashion, he complained, when they should be "getting out and fighting for prosperity." The increasing accusations of radicalism in Washington and excessive government interference were the product of "unthinking reactionaries." Kennedy's boldness won him allies among suspicious cohorts in Washington.

His primary duty was to build the administrative machinery that would permit the SEC to regulate securities trading and supervise the exchanges. Kennedy hired a staff that quickly gained respect in Washington, including John Burns, who had resigned from the Massachusetts Superior Court to become commission counsel, and William O. Douglas, recently a Yale Law School professor. Branch headquarters were created across the country: Adlai Stevenson declined Kennedy's invitation to manage the Securities Commission office in Chicago. At a press conference in August 1934 Kennedy unveiled the rules that would govern the registration of individual exchanges, emphasizing the intention to protect rather than harass honest businessmen. The following January he went to the White House to inform the president that securities registration rules had been drawn up. "This is where we hope to get private capital back into industry," he told reporters. The new registration forms eliminated requests for information not specifically required by law or essential to protect investors. "The charge has been made that the act has been holding back the flotations. Well, this is our answer."

In March 1935 the logjam was broken. Swift and Company submitted registration forms for a major refinancing issue. Delighted, Kennedy said it was "a marvelous step in the right direction." Swift's initiative loosed a flood of new investment reaching almost two billion dollars by the end of the year. In April Kennedy completed the final stage by announcing SEC rules against stock manipulation; exchanges would be asked to revise their bylaws to conform with Washington's guidelines. Only if they delayed would the rules be enforced by federal statute. Preventing abuses such as bear raiding, manipulating stock to create the illusion of activity, trading by exchange members to a degree exceeding their personal resources, the rules were immediately endorsed by the New York Stock Exchange. A *Wall Street Journal* survey indicated wide acceptance by financiers.

By establishing a place for the Securities and Exchange Commission in Wall Street and Washington, Joseph Kennedy overcame the doubts of people in both business and government. Reforms reaching beyond the provisions of the original legislation were left for subsequent chairmen and commissioners, but Kennedy could claim much of the responsibility for turning intentions into reality. He won almost universal praise for the salesmanship, political acumen, and ability to moderate conflicting sides that encouraged capital investment and economic recovery. The Senate, after Kennedy's six-month trial period, confirmed his nomination in less than a minute, without debate. The *Washington Post* observed in a news article that "Kennedy has done one of the best jobs of anyone connected with the New Deal and has done it without bluster or publicity seeking and without leaving anyone angry at him." The *New Republic*'s John T. Flynn ate crow and confessed that the chairman was the most useful member of the Securities Commission. Walter Lippmann, who rarely dealt with personalities in his *New York Herald-Tribune* column, noted that Kennedy had been "as suspect by the warriors as a pacifist by triumphant generals," but "in a short time, by sheer political and administrative wisdom, he made the new financial system a practicable reality and then insured its survival."

Few were more impressed by Kennedy's accomplishment than the man who hired him. It was the time of the First New Deal and, pursuing conciliation toward business, the president appreciated the value of the Wall Street financier being seen at his side. Joseph Kennedy increasingly became a familiar figure at the White House. Roosevelt began to enlist him as a troubleshooter on other projects, such as public works, and assigned him to help keep potential adversaries of the New Deal, such as William Randolph Hearst and Father Coughlin, at bay. His delight in the candid repartee Kennedy had provided aboard the campaign train was kindled again. The president ventured out of the White House from time to time to call on Kennedy at the rented estate thirteen miles up the Potomac where Kennedy installed an elevator to make it easier for Roosevelt's visits.

Kennedy's increasing stature was indicated by the surest barometer of presidential favor—the rising suspicions of other New Dealers. The mildly mysterious man of Franklin Roosevelt's campaign was becoming a Washington insider. The *New York Times* reported that Joseph Kennedy was being summoned to the presidential audience as frequently as three and four evenings a week.

Five

MEN OF THE NEW DEAL

Two presidential limousines threaded through an arched gatehouse and down a tree-lined roadway, past herds of Guernsey cattle grazing on the river bank. At the end of a mile, behind a fringe of trees, stood a French Renaissance chateau. Built in the early part of the century by a merchant and his chorus-girl wife, the house was named Marwood.

There were twelve bedrooms inside, a cavernous cinema, an exact replica of the dining room of King James the First. Joseph Kennedy had leased the estate on his arrival in Washington but departed most weekends to join his family in Palm Beach, Bronxville, or Hyannis Port. The opulence provoked the ribbing of Washington friends: the lord of Marwood was presented to a dinner of correspondents as "a man who lives in true Rooseveltian frugality." Kennedy referred whimsically to the house as "the Hindenburg palace."

On this final weekend in June of 1935 he had invited Arthur Krock as his guest. That week, the journalist had taken Franklin Roosevelt to task for his manner of dealing with Congress. Once when Kennedy defended his friend with the reminder that Krock supported ninety-five percent of his program, the president rejoined, "Oh, but that other five percent!"

The lazy hours of sun and rest in Maryland were interrupted at Sunday noon by a telephone call. It was the president, inquiring if he could drive out that evening for cocktails and dinner. Kennedy consented immediately. He replaced the receiver before realizing the embarrassing scene to occur when Roosevelt discovered that Krock was part of the company. Krock courteously alleviated the problem. "The day being intensely hot," he recorded, "I decided, instead of returning to town, to stay in my quarters upstairs, a voluntary prisoner."

The White House cars drew up at seven o'clock, and Krock fled up the staircase. Kennedy greeted the president and his party, which included Missy Le Hand; her assistant, Grace Tully; John Burns of the Securities Commission; and Thomas Corcoran, the adroit and beguiling presidential assistant, who arrived with his famous accordion in hand. Curiously, the men and women Roosevelt had invited to accompany him to Kennedy's home that evening were all Catholics.

Followed by a cordon of Secret Service agents, they gathered by the side of the house. The sun was vanishing into the Potomac, the afternoon heat being dissipated by the river breezes. Would they like mint juleps? Kennedy asked. "Swell," replied the president. After several rounds of cocktails, they sat down to dinner, snippets of laughter and conversation floating up to Arthur Krock's window. "If I could, the way I'd handle Huey Long would be physically," sounded the unmistakable voice of Franklin Roosevelt. "He's a physical coward. I've told my fellows up there that the way to deal with him is to frighten him. But they're more afraid of him than he is of them."

After dessert, Kennedy had a projector and screen set up on the lawn. The film was *Ginger;* Kennedy had arranged the picture to be flown in from Hollywood. It was a sentimental story featuring the child actress Jane Withers. When the last reel ended, the president pronounced her performance "excellent," and graciously added that the motion picture was "one of the best in years."

Tom Corcoran took out his accordion and the real merriment began. Roosevelt had a rather nice tenor-baritone, Krock observed, and the president himself took over the accordion to accompany one of the numbers. "The night after the Chicago convention, we decided we needed some campaign songs," he reminisced. "After working all evening, the only thing we turned out went, 'The old G.O.P., it ain't what it uster be. . . .' " The accordion started up and they sounded the refrain.

Corcoran next chimed in with "Old George Huddleston, he ain't what he uster be . . ." lampooning one of the week's foes in Congress.

Not to be outdone, Roosevelt came back with "Old Carter Glass, he ain't what he uster be . . ." and the others convulsed in laughter.

Someone asked if they had heard that a congressman they knew had once posted his wife for debt. The ladies cried out in mock horror. The president entertained his courtiers with stories of Down East sailors and fisherfolk, told in authentic dialect, and sailing tales of Harvard classmates who were less than brilliant. Kennedy took the opening for a gibe against Roosevelt's annual fishing party aboard Vincent Astor's yacht, men the president had known for years whom reporters labeled "the *Nourmahal* gang." With just a twinge of jealousy, Kennedy said, "Your taste in dumb cruisemates doesn't seem to have changed very much." Roosevelt responded with a laugh.

He asked Corcoran to play "Tim Toolan," the ballad of the Irish lad who had made good in politics. It was one of the president's favorites. When they came to the refrain, Roosevelt's voice rang out:

The majority was more
Than it h'd ever been b'fore
And our hero h'd carried the day!

"The singing and talk went on well after midnight," wrote the eavesdropper in the upper-floor bedroom. "About that time, I fell asleep, pondering the paradoxes of the men who occupy the highest office in the land."

Kennedy and the New Deal

By 1935 the United States was inching toward recovery. The reforms of the First New Deal were law; national income and employment were rising. As his wry piece of evidence of the success of the Roosevelt program, Joseph Kennedy mailed the president a copy of the ledger of the Colony Restaurant in New York, citing a notable increase in profits.

Still, a problem of followership faced Franklin Roosevelt. Income lagged well behind that of 1929 and a fifth of the American labor force remained out of work. The president who had so boldly raised expectations in 1933 was confronted by a promise yet unfulfilled.

The midterm elections had filled the House and Senate with self-styled New Dealers but Congress was in a rebellious spirit. Although investment was resuming and the president still laboring for cooperation, many businessmen and financiers aligned themselves with forces of reaction like the Liberty League. Awakened to the potential in innovative leadership, great numbers of other Americans now looked beyond Franklin Roosevelt to more daring and strident voices like Huey Long and Father Coughlin.

On a visit to the United States H. G. Wells sensed a "widespread discontent and discomfort," an "impatient preparedness for sweeping changes in the great masses of the American population. . . . The actual New Deal has not gone far enough and fast enough for them, and that is what the shouting is about."

In February 1935 the entire monetary policy of the Roosevelt administration was endangered. The Supreme Court was to rule on the constitutionality of the repeal of the "gold clause" statute enacted during the Hundred Days. Repeal had released the treasury from redeeming obligations in gold. If the justices decided against the administration, the public debt would swell instantly by ten billion dollars, the entire national debt by seventy billion. Congress would lose the power to regulate American currency.

Bracing himself for a defeat, Roosevelt drew up his battle plan. If there was bad news, he would nullify the unfavorable ruling by an executive order directing the chairman of the Securities Commission to close the stock exchanges. The president gave Kennedy an advance look at the speech he planned to deliver: "To stand idly by and to permit the decision of the Supreme Court to be carried through to its logical, inescapable conclusion would so imperil the economic and political security of this nation that the legislative and executive officers of the Government look beyond the narrow letter of contractual obligations so they may maintain the substance."

Kennedy thought the statement so strong that he predicted the American people would burn the Court in effigy.

On February 18, at noonday, they awaited the momentous decision, Kennedy at his commission office, Roosevelt at the White House. Chatting with Kennedy by telephone a few minutes before the announcement, Missy Le Hand tried to break the tension with a facetious report that the president had just departed for a carefree automobile ride. Shortly after noon, Kennedy phoned in a surprise to Roosevelt, Henry Morgenthau, and the others waiting anxiously in the Cabinet Room: the justices had found in favor of the New Deal. Gaily the president replied that his only regret was his inability to deliver the belligerent speech. He should include it in his memoirs instead, Kennedy shot back. His adrenaline flowing from the excitement of the day, Kennedy recorded the events in a memorandum, "because I feel the occasion is a historical one and I feel the opportunity of being the person to relay this information to the President would be of value historically to my family."

Roosevelt replied, "How fortunate it is that his exchanges will never know how close they came to being closed by the stroke of the pen of one 'J.P.K.' Likewise, the Nation will never know what a great treat it missed in not hearing the marvelous radio address the 'Pres' had prepared for delivery to the Nation Monday night if the cases had gone the other way. . . .

"In view of the sleepless nights and hectic days of the chairman of the Securities and Exchange Commission, in view of his shrunken frame, falling hair and fallen arches, he is hereby directed to proceed to Palm Beach and return to Washington six hours after he gets there"—here Kennedy was to turn the page—"AND AFTER TEN INTERVENING DAYS HAVE PASSED BY (FOOLED AGAIN!)"

Roosevelt encouraged Kennedy to rove beyond the Securities Commission into other provinces of the New Deal. He asked for independent estimates of the financing of various New Deal programs, knowing that Kennedy would be a more discerning critic than officials who had personal stakes in these enterprises. He appointed his man-of-all-work to the rump National Emergency Council and consulted with Kennedy on monetary policy and the national budget.

Faced with the mocking ten million unemployed, the president was struggling for a new approach to public relief. In October 1934 he called Harold Ickes, Henry Morgenthau, Harry Hopkins, and Kennedy to the White House to discuss a fresh departure. His proposal was a five billion dollar public works program that would shift the emphasis from relief payments to actual jobs. Kennedy argued that there was no need for the program; the nation was already on the threshold of recovery. The others remembered that prosperity had been spotted just around the corner every year since 1929. By the next session a week later, Kennedy swung around to the president's point of view. Roosevelt signed the congressional allocation for his program in April 1935.

Hopkins and Ickes, whose rivalry was already Washington legend, were both intent on being appointed to manage the new arrangement. Morgenthau brought a Solomonic solution to the president. "Please remember, Franklin, that I cannot get anything more out of politics in this life, so what I am going to say to you is motivated by the desire to serve my country and you and nothing else." If either Ickes or Hopkins were chosen, the other would be disgruntled. Without enlisting the talents of both men, the program would surely fail; if it did, the president would not be reelected. Morgenthau's solution: put Kennedy in charge over both of them. His record was outstanding, he could handle people, and he was popular with Congress and the press.

But Roosevelt was doubtful: "The trouble with Kennedy is you always have to hold his hand." After pondering the notion, he came up with a brainstorm. Why not an assistant to the president in charge of public works, who would "really run the show?" For that, Kennedy would be all right. Within the week, the president's idea had grown into a proposed small committee that would supervise public works spending on his behalf; Kennedy would act as the board's secretary. "I can't yet tell either

Hopkins or Ickes that Kennedy is going to be over them," Roosevelt confided to his treasury secretary. "They will have to learn that gradually." Sensing a hornet's nest, however, Kennedy declined the president's offer on grounds that he could not work with Harold Ickes, but he agreed to review financing of public works projects.

Kennedy was turning out to be a more committed New Dealer than almost anyone had expected. An acid test of his allegiance to the president and his policies was the shift from the First to the Second New Deal in 1935, spawn of the continuing problem of recovery and the continuing momentum of reform. Conservative Democrats like Bernard Baruch vainly reminded the president of his pledge to balance the budget; some, including Al Smith and Newton Baker, joined the Liberty League. Raymond Moley prepared to depart from the administration and join the Republican party.

With the exception of disagreements over tax policy, however, Kennedy continued to support Roosevelt down the line. Although he believed in the balanced budget, he would brook continued deficits to speed economic revival. For the time being, balancing the federal accounts was impractical, Kennedy wrote Walter Lippmann, because of "the hesitancy on the part of business to plunge forward with any degree of courage." Continued appropriations by Congress were essential, if disagreeable, to take care of this relief situation in some form. "After all, you and I know that we must take care of people. . . ."

On accepting the chairmanship of the Securities Commission, Kennedy had arranged with the president to resign as soon as the foundations of financial reform and renewed investment were laid. That task complete, he wrote out his letter of resignation in May 1935 and started for the White House. But, as Kennedy later recalled, he glimpsed a newspaper headline on the sidewalk: the Supreme Court had declared the National Recovery Administration unconstitutional, throwing the economic program of the New Deal into confusion. Kennedy returned to his office and agreed to remain in government until the smoke cleared.

His extended Washington tour pulled him into the warfare raging on Capitol Hill over the issue of public utilities. Something in this issue, Raymond Clapper observed, touched a raw nerve in Franklin Roosevelt. The president had long held a Progressive's distrust of concentrated private economic power; as governor of New York, he had carried the fight against the large utilities over the heads of legislators to the people of the Empire State. The bill now proposed by the White House would tame the combinations through an array of devices, especially taxation. At the heart of the measure was a clause, dubbed the "death sentence," that would authorize the SEC within five years to dissolve any holding company that could not provide an economic justification for its existence. Like securities reform, the bill was advanced as a recovery measure, reviving public goodwill toward the utilities industry.

The men of the utilities gathered in the capital en masse. "You talk about a labor lobby. Well, it is a child compared to this utility lobby," Roosevelt said. Testifying against the bill were utilities executives like the president of the Commonwealth and Southern, Wendell Willkie. This was not surprising, but the people at the White House were startled when Joseph Kennedy made known his opposition. In a letter to Senator Burton Wheeler, sponsor of the bill, Kennedy protested the authority granted the Securities and Exchange Commission to decide which holding companies should live. His reasons: "the limits on the human capacity to achieve results" and "my conception of what is wisdom in government." Kennedy complained that the measure offered no definition of the public interest for guidance; it was "not a wise policy to vest in any one group of men the tremendous responsibility involved in this grant of power."

Friends were puzzled because not only had Kennedy never before raised major public objections to big government, but he frequently and energetically boosted the idea of centralized authority. Criticism of the death sentence by the man who would legally administer it dealt a blow to passage of the bill. The death sentence was rejected by Congress and the final Utility Companies Holding Act was but a shadow of the president's proposal. Franklin Roosevelt's defeat on this was perhaps his most frustrating congressional setback since assuming the presidency. He was perturbed by Kennedy's confederation with the utilities lobby.

One note of comic relief sounded in the thick of the fight. Rose Kennedy's uncle, the man for whom Kennedy had wangled a plum federal job through a mild deception about his age, had been found out and fired. James Fitzgerald had won appointment as supervisor of the Treasury Department's Boston detail in charge of taxing alcoholic beverages. To qualify under civil service requirements, he had falsely sworn his age as sixty-four rather than seventy-two. On receiving news of Fitzgerald's dismissal, Joseph Kennedy went straight to the president to complain. John McCormack, Democratic congressman from Massachusetts and a family friend, also telephoned his objection. Roosevelt bucked the matter to the official under whose jurisdiction Fitzgerald fell, Henry Morgenthau.

Knowing the squeamishness of his fellow old Dutchess Country reformer about patronage matters, the president derived enormous pleasure from throwing such matters into Morgenthau's lap. After ordering an investigation, the secretary called Kennedy and McCormack to his office to discuss the case.

Armed with a treasury report, Morgenthau laid out the evidence for Fitzgerald's dismissal. The department had discovered that its alcohol tax supervisor had been a bootlegger during Prohibition. "He openly talks of having formerly been in the liquor business and has been referred to publicly as an ex-saloonkeeper and rum dispenser." Fitzgerald had evidently made a practice of trading distillery permits for promises that the distillery owners would employ his friends and relatives, including his own son. He refused to cooperate with treasury officials, was "curt, impolite, arrogant and hostile." Employees in Fitzgerald's office—"who are believed to be honest"—were afraid to speak openly to investigators from Washington. The supervisor had also neglected to scrutinize an operation counterfeiting liquor tax stamps—"probably enough to supply the whole of New England." Finally, Fitzgerald customarily leaked confidential messages from the Treasury Department to highly-placed friends in Washington. As a matter of fact, a recent letter commanding a personnel cut in Fitzgerald's office had found its way into the hands of Congressman McCormack himself within twenty-four hours.

McCormack rebutted this recitation by reminding Morgenthau that Fitzgerald had been a faithful Democrat for fifty years; he confessed that this was all he could say in favor of Mrs. Kennedy's uncle. The secretary explained that his hands were tied because the Civil Service Commission, not the treasury, had ordered Fitzgerald's dismissal. Kennedy leapt into the breach: if the civil service could be persuaded to withdraw its complaint, would Morgenthau rehire his wife's uncle? Morgenthau said he would have to dig further into Fitzgerald's record. At the end of the meeting Kennedy stormed out of the room. McCormack lingered to say that he owed it to Kennedy to put up a fight for Fitzgerald, but really didn't care whether the old man was put back or not.

Morgenthau related the entire story to the president. "You can't take that man back," Roosevelt said, "if for no other reason than that he had sworn falsely as to his age at the time of his application." The two men agreed, as a gesture to Kennedy, that Fitzgerald would be offered a ninety-day appointment in the Boston Customs House. This was enough to assuage Kennedy. "I can't help it if I married into an S.O.B. of a family," he apologized to Morgenthau. "Perhaps the old man won't live longer than ninety days and we won't have to worry about him anymore." The treasury secretary informed the president of Kennedy's response and was "astonished" by Roosevelt's comment: "No one can tell what an Irishman will do."

Against the backdrop of issues like securities reform, public works, and the utilities, the tale of Jim Fitzgerald again illustrated the Kennedy drawn between the ethic of Boston politics and his ideal of disinterested public service, between loyalty to the president who granted him office and Kennedy's own robust views on national affairs. He could support the First New Deal with little ambivalence because the first two years of the Roosevelt administration synthesized reform, relief, and recovery in a trinity of national goals. A Burton Wheeler who had long battled for securities and utilities reform; a Jim Farley, enchanted by the fountain of patronage in the relief program; a Bernard Baruch who wished to balance the budget and see economic confidence revived: all responded to the element in the trinity that satisfied their principal concerns.

Kennedy's primary public goal was national recovery; this priority sprang from his underlying dread of social upheaval and the unlimited confidence in confidence that was the hallmark of the nineteen-twenties businessman. Yet he was distinguished from most of his New Era associates in the belief that government also "must take care of people," as he phrased it to Lippmann; this priority harked back to Patrick Kennedy's politics of social welfare. Joseph Kennedy regarded their common views on benevolent government as an especial bond with Franklin Roosevelt. "From my acquaintance with the President, I say that his whole character, private and official, is based on a consuming desire to improve the lot of what he has called the underprivileged," he once told a British journalist. "Throughout his public life, he has campaigned for measures which, in his judgment, would make for the benefit of the majority. I believe that his every action can be understood if it is measured against this yardstick."

Kennedy linked relief with recovery by observing that the "security of human beings is the basis of business prosperity." On another occasion he made the point less elegantly by explaining that he became a New Dealer "after seeing how ugly and menacing hungry men become." Economic revival and, to a lesser extent, relief were ends for Kennedy to which reform was a limited means.

But the coming of the Second New Deal in 1935 revealed Franklin Roosevelt's abiding commitment to reform as end more than means, alienating many in the city machines and in the business community. The president recognized that the bosses would remain with him so long as he could bring them votes and jobs, but the large-scale desertion by business profoundly affected administration strategy. Roosevelt moved away from the conciliation urged by the Kennedys, Moleys, and Baruchs, to the outright confrontation prescribed by the Corcorans and Ickeses. Within a year, the president would denounce the economic royalists and say of Kennedy's old chief, "Go tell Charlie Schwab he'll never make another million!"

This continuing momentum would further challenge the division in Joseph Kennedy, pitting his political aspirations and allegiance to Franklin Roosevelt against his discomfort with many of the people and ideas rising to the surface of the New Deal.

Summer Solstice

"You know, when I took this job I told the Boss I didn't want to tie myself down or take on work that would be more than temporary," Joseph Kennedy said in mid-1935, "But you do get a kick out of it. You can't do the job in a minute or a week, and I don't know how long I shall be here. Anyway, there's something interesting in it every day."

It was the summer solstice in his political alliance with Franklin Roosevelt.

The White House call came in late afternoon, inviting Kennedy to join the president after dinner. It was the most prized summons in the capital. Kennedy was waved into the president's upstairs Oval Study, with its family portraits, political artifacts, and naval scenes. Then the hearty welcome from the president, Tom Corcoran, Henry Morgenthau, or other viziers invited that evening. A tray of refreshments was delivered, followed perhaps by a few hands of poker and political talk. Frequently Roosevelt would beckon Kennedy aside to chat about an upcoming bill, a patronage problem with Tammany Hall, a possible candidate for a top New Deal position.

"Don't trust him—he'd steal a red-hot stove!" was a characteristic Kennedy warning, or "He'd double-cross his own mother!" The reticence of his first visit to the White House was long faded. Kennedy prided himself on the bravado that permitted him to speak so straightforwardly to the president. "The bluntness and abrasiveness with which he often expressed his views could be startling," Bernard Baruch remembered. "The two argue constantly over acts and policies, and the President hears more objections than assents from his chairman of the SEC," Arthur Krock informed his readers. "But he consults Mr. Kennedy on everything, and when the argument is over, President and advisor relax like two schoolboys."

There were joyous and hair-raising rides through the Hyde Park countryside, with Roosevelt at the wheel of his special hand-controlled blue Ford; there were morning visits to the presidential bedroom and, on occasion, to the presidential bathroom. At Marwood the president splashed about in Kennedy's pool, enjoyed his fresh Boston lobster and the contents of his celebrated wine cellar, his first-run films and his entertaining company—these affairs Kennedy referred to as "late-night drinking and gab fests." Roosevelt sometimes stayed overnight; in the relaxed atmosphere, the host twice violated protocol by retiring for the evening before the president. "Father loved to match wits with Joe Kennedy," Franklin Roosevelt, Jr., recalled. "He used to say he enjoyed 'educating him.' " Kennedy reported what "the boys on Wall Street" were worrying about, and the president gave him messages to take back to his friends in finance.

Sometimes this dialogue was more direct. With the aid of Baruch, and perhaps of Moley, Kennedy arranged for prominent businessmen to come to Marwood and confer there in secret with the president. Away from the glare of publicity and the disapproval of New Dealers and Wall Street men, Roosevelt strove to effect some kind of concordance that would forestall an irreparable parting of the ways. This was not to happen, but Kennedy performed his function so smoothly that the meetings remained out of the public record.

Kennedy concentrated his considerable charm on the men and women in the Roosevelt circle. Missy Le Hand and Grace Tully were both fond of the jocular visitor to the White House; Kennedy and Missy penned notes back and forth signed "Love and Kisses." He invited everyone to Palm Beach; offered James Roosevelt advice on business in New York and Boston; aided Anna's new husband, John Boettiger, formerly of the *Chicago Tribune*, in finding jobs first with Will Hays in Hollywood and then as publisher of the Hearst paper in Seattle. Eleanor Roosevelt received orchids from Kennedy at Easter, the president a trunk packed with Scotch whiskey at Christmastime. The Roosevelts several times invited the Kennedys to stay the night at the White House. All of the Kennedy children met the president; ten-year-old Robert received some stamps from his fellow philatelist and an invitation to talk about their mutual hobby. Joseph Kennedy, Jr., and John Roosevelt, the president's youngest son, were close and rambunctious friends in the Class of 1938 at

Harvard. The senior Kennedy continually asked the president for small souvenirs of their relationship ("about three lines in longhand for my children") and bid for Roosevelt's attention—provoking occasional annoyance. The president complained to Henry Morgenthau of Kennedy's telephoned protestations that "he is hurt because I have not seen him."

Yet Franklin Roosevelt genuinely enjoyed Kennedy's companionship and, usually, his irreverent sense of humor. He drank in Burton Wheeler's story of the prank he played on Kennedy. The Montana senator had been asked by Kennedy to invite eight or nine Senate colleagues to come to Marwood for one of Kennedy's increasingly famous dinners for congressmen. At the last moment, Lynn Frazier of North Dakota was called away. Wheeler mischievously borrowed a lawyer from his subcommittee on American Indian affairs to attend Kennedy's soiree in the person of Senator Frazier. Kennedy was eager to win over his new acquaintance. "It was Senator Frazier this and Senator Frazier that," Wheeler recounted. At the end of the evening, Kennedy invited Wheeler and "Frazier" to remain at Marwood for the night. He served them breakfast the next morning and sent his guests on their way, confident he had made a new ally. Shortly thereafter, Wheeler revealed his charade. "To think a smart Irishman could be taken in by a hardheaded Swede," Kennedy said, grateful that few would know he had been outfoxed. But the next time Kennedy visited the White House the president plunged in the rapier:

"Say, Joe, I hear you met Senator Frazier."

Roosevelt could not resist a hoax of his own. Scheduled to ride in the Shriners parade in Washington, he called up one of the most conspicuous Catholics in the New Deal. "My God! I go to the Shriners parade?" Kennedy exclaimed. Roosevelt added that Jim Farley would be there. "Jim is coming? Is that a command?" It was. Mindful of the possible political injury to a Catholic seen in the clutches of the Shrine, Kennedy crouched behind the police guard to avoid being photographed while riding in the presidential automobile through a heavy night rain. He and Roosevelt spoke with Shrine officials while the president received his honorary fez at the end of the procession. Afterwards, Kennedy flew home to Hyannis Port.

A few weeks later a telegram arrived from a mysterious "M. T. Currier": "In pursuance of our delightful conversation on the night of the Shrine parade, may I express the hope that you will be here in Washington the week following Labor Day in order that we may induct you in due course and as painlessly as possible." The president had dispatched the wire from the Willard Hotel so that Kennedy could not trace it back to the White House. Later, Roosevelt related Kennedy's reaction, off-the-record, to newspapermen: "He told the wife and children and the whole Kennedy family went up through the roof and they remained up through the roof all of August. . . . About the twenty-fifth of August, I was talking to Joe on the telephone from the White House—he was still up on the Cape—and at the end of the conversation, I said, 'By the way, Joe, are you going to be down here the first week in September?'

"Joe said, 'You blankety blank blank blank!' Just like that—and to the President of the United States!"

It was said that Eleanor Roosevelt once told Kennedy she wanted him to "go right on telling Franklin what you think." But she and others in the New Deal began to worry about the conservative Wall Street operator who was seeing the president with such frequency. Roosevelt, confident of his expertise in perceiving the motivations of those around him and enlisting them for his own purposes, had no such apprehensions. He appreciated Kennedy's forthright ambition to bring distinction to his family as well as the sense of loyalty that the president felt he could depend on in a pinch. Yet, as serene as he appeared, Roosevelt was ever vigilant of Machiavelli's admonition about the minister who has any aspiration but the good of his prince. Prima donnas, as Kennedy had himself warned Raymond Moley two years earlier, did not remain for long in Franklin Roosevelt's inner council. The president, therefore, kept a wary eye on Joseph Kennedy's flight to prominence in Washington.

Perhaps no one in government received a better press during Franklin Roosevelt's first term than Joseph Kennedy. Impressed by Kennedy's administration of the Securities Commission, many members of the "one-party press" also celebrated his conservative influence at the White House. The journalistic hosannas multiplied because no one also courted the Washington press corps more prodigiously than Kennedy. He was "quick to recognize the value of newspapermen," Walter Trohan of the *Chicago Tribune* believed, "and to cultivate them across a wide spectrum of ideologies as sources of influence."

"Joe could peddle baloney like everyone else," remembered Frank Waldrop of the *Washington Times-Herald*, "but he was an immensely attractive fellow. He was one of the people you *had* to see in Washington." Other journalists concurred. Marquis Childs of the *St. Louis Post-Dispatch* saw in Kennedy an astute and purposeful man. Lawrence Spivak, editor of the *American Mercury* and later radio and television moderator of "Meet the Press," remembered Kennedy as one of the first in Washington to comprehend the political possibilities in broadcasting. Bascom Timmons, correspondent for a syndicate of Southern newspapers, recalled that Kennedy was known among the capital press as a "financial genius" and was popular for his wit and generosity.

Kennedy rarely attended Washington social functions but, as *Time* reported, he presided as "the urbane host at small dinners famed throughout the Capital for the excellence of *cave* and cuisine." He frequently invited journalists out to Marwood for evenings sometimes ornamented by Hollywood starlets; on leaving town for weekends, Kennedy turned the house over to reporters with an invitation to enjoy themselves and leave the bills to their host. Kennedy became fast friends with Frank Kent of the *Baltimore Sun* and investigative reporter Drew Pearson. He devoted attention to Walter Winchell and asked the staccato-speaking radio commentator for advice on public relations. Colonel Robert McCormick, the resolutely Republican and isolationist publisher of the *Chicago Tribune* and Groton schoolmate of the president, was a Kennedy neighbor in Florida. Walter Lippmann, two classes ahead of Kennedy at Harvard, thought so highly of his abilities that he recommended him for the university's Visiting Committee for Economics. Henry Luce found that Kennedy shared his toughminded commitment to free enterprise and the American destiny—as well as a canny instinct for the uses of power. Joseph Kennedy was accorded two cover stories in *Time,* the generous attention of *Life,* and a majestic feature article in *Fortune*.

His painful sensitivity to his press clippings was part of the folklore among capital newspapermen. After reading an early draft of the *Fortune* piece, an incensed Kennedy had Tom Corcoran, who served as his personal attorney in Washington, telephone the magazine to complain. "I am indeed very sorry that the whole subject of this article has come up," Kennedy wrote a *Fortune* editor, "I am convinced, after talking with your Mr. Wood, that it is the brainchild of a psychopathic case and as such, I am trying to forget." Kennedy strove almost as excessively to reward praise. "I want to let you know how deeply grateful I am for the editorial in Saturday's paper," he wrote Arthur Sulzberger of the *New York Times,* "I can hardly agree that I deserve such praise but it is heartwarming nonetheless." He assured Walter Lippmann that "your writings on the matters before Congress embrace by all means the fairest and most intelligent observations."

Eugene Meyer, publisher of the *Washington Post,* received a winning note from Kennedy after writing him that he had seen a photograph of the

Kennedy family in *Life*. Young Joe seemed to favor his father, Meyer had observed, Jack his mother; as for Mrs. Kennedy, she looked more like Kennedy's daughter than his wife.

"For a fellow that has been laying off chocolate ice cream and potatoes and wanted to keep his youthful figure, to be told again and again that his wife looks like his daughter, it is a hell of a disappointment!" Kennedy replied. He had read Meyer's letter aloud at the family luncheon table. "Joe, Jr., will probably never read the Washington Post again. Jack, on the other hand, thinks that any paper who has a publisher so discerning and with such fine judgment should be supported by the entire country." As for Rose, "she reminded me that you had been one of the most successful men in the country, both publicly and privately, and after all, if we weren't to follow a man of your judgment, who were we to follow?"

There was more to Kennedy's friendships with figures in journalism than simple calculation. Most newspapermen and publishers had seen public officials come and go and had long steeled themselves against idle flattery and favors. Joseph Kennedy generated a sense of comradeship with journalists that appeared somehow lacking in his relations with government officials. (In later years people observed this of John Kennedy as well.) Perhaps he felt less competitive toward reporters than toward other members of the New Deal. Many of his friendships in the press were among the most abiding he would ever have. When John O'Donnell of the *New York Daily News* fell mortally ill, Kennedy wrote O'Donnell's colleagues at the paper, offering to absorb his friend's medical expenses.

Kennedy's closest friend of all was Arthur Krock. They seemed oddly suited, at first glimpse—Kennedy who delighted in shattering convention, Krock the distant Grand Duke of the *New York Times*. Yet beneath these veneers they were both outsiders who had made their way in the capital. Although both used the rhetoric of principle and public service, neither fully accepted these ideals as overriding creeds. "I never had any idealism from the time I was a young reporter about anybody who touched the edges of politics or big business," Krock declared in his last years, "I expected, and still do, that politicians and big businessmen don't have any morals—that is, public morals." Ernest Lindley observed, "Both Kennedy and Krock had expensive tastes, conservative economic views and a love for banter, and they were therefore a perfect fit." After the friendship cooled, Krock recalled Kennedy's instruction to "look out the window Christmas morning and you'll see an automobile." In retrospect, the journalist considered this "a pretty coarse kind of bribe" and remembered replying, "I'll see nothing of the kind. I'll have it towed away if it's there."

But in the halcyon days, Krock was a frequent guest at the Kennedy homes and a Dutch uncle to the Kennedy sons. A constant source of political advice for Joseph Kennedy, he often favored his friend by floating trial balloons in his *Times* column.

Kennedy's friendships on Capitol Hill too were based more on personal chemistry than ideological affinity. They ranged from Burton Wheeler to Senators James F. Byrnes, a conservative New Dealer from South Carolina; Pat Harrison of Mississippi; Claude Pepper of Florida; George Norris, progressive Republican of Nebraska.

Many of Kennedy's allies in Congress and in the press included those most unreconciled to the New Deal. Rather than discourage this, the president employed Kennedy as a go-between. One example was William Randolph Hearst. Kennedy and the publisher remained in close touch, despite Hearst's impatience with Franklin Roosevelt. "Pop thought Joe was very smart," William Randolph Hearst, Jr., recalled. "They had movie interests and many friends in common. They had sort of a mutual admiration society." Relations between the publisher and the new president had begun cordially. Hearst wrote Kennedy that he was willing to go to "great lengths" to support Roosevelt because of the seriousness of the national crisis. He lunched with the president and wrote Roosevelt after his return to San Simeon that he had been "doing a little work since I got back telling the business people how fine you are. I guess at your next election we will have to make it unanimous."

He soon changed his mind. Hearst concluded that the New Deal was infiltrated by Communists and sent a man to Louisiana to discover whether Huey Long was serious about running for president in 1936. Kennedy kept working to keep Roosevelt and Hearst from loggerheads. He brought the publisher to the White House in October 1934. The meeting went poorly, however, and Hearst refused to return for fear of being "taken in" by the president.

Kennedy journeyed to California to listen to and agree with many of the publisher's complaints about Roosevelt's tax policies. After a perplexing session in May 1935 he received a soothing telegram from Missy Le Hand: PRESIDENT SUGGESTS YOU RETURN ON BATTLESHIP THROUGH PANAMA CANAL. HAPPY LANDING!

When the president came into possession of a confidential message from Hearst to his editors commanding that "Raw Deal" be substituted for all references to the New Deal, he restrained his impulse to issue an exposé and continued to encourage Kennedy's peace-making efforts. But the Hearst press continued to thunder against the New Deal.

The president who brought diverse men and women into the quadrille of government was entertained by the man who was at once the son of a ward leader, a Wall Street speculator, and a loyal New Dealer. "He liked Joe and especially liked the family image projected by his wife and nine children, yet he was a little bit afraid of him," James Roosevelt observed. The president offered Kennedy power, but he also caricatured him before Henry Morgenthau and Harold Ickes (although here he was indulging his listeners), played practical jokes that sometimes suggested censure as much as humor, reminded Kennedy in a hundred subtle yet unmistakable ways that he served at the pleasure of the president. With the visits to Marwood, the evening calls to the executive mansion, the graciousness to Kennedy's family and other good deeds, Roosevelt encouraged Kennedy—as he encouraged everyone—to overvalue his indispensability to the president. But Kennedy revised his view of Franklin Roosevelt from the manipulable figure he perceived in 1932 and 1917. He would say that it was while serving under Roosevelt at the Securities Commission that he learned "the uselessness of trying to change him."

Kennedy sometimes responded to his conflicting instincts of political ambition, strenuous beliefs on public issues, and allegiance to the president in self-damaging ways. Conservative friends like Frank Kent valued Kennedy's restraining effect on Roosevelt but in the instances where, in deference to the president, Kennedy pulled in his horns rather than criticize administration policy, these friends would rib him for subjugating matters of conscience to his eagerness to score points with Roosevelt. Few accusations more greatly wounded this man who so cherished his authenticity. As if to make up for his public obeisance to the president, Kennedy indulged in scathing attacks on Roosevelt in private. These jeremiads Kennedy knew would drift back to the White House.

Another explanation for his demonstrations of independence was the slight social tension that seemed to separate Kennedy from Roosevelt. Eleanor Roosevelt once observed the reverse snobbishness of the man who looked down on another man, like her husband, who had not pulled himself up by his own bootstraps. She was thinking of Al Smith, but the same malady may also have afflicted Joseph Kennedy. Like many others, Kennedy was hurt by the president's tendency to compartmentalize his companions into social and political friends. One of the few subjects that interrupted Jim Farley's good humor was his certainty of Franklin Roosevelt's condescension. Ed Flynn, who enjoyed the president's company as frequently as Kennedy did, inveighed acidly against Roosevelt's "Hasty Pudding Cabinet" aboard Vincent Astor's boat.

Occasionally, Kennedy's needling of the president lapsed into effrontery. Once when Roosevelt asked Kennedy for discretion regarding a lady friend too much in evidence, Kennedy reputedly replied, "Not until you get rid of Missy Le Hand!" Such hubris may have been Kennedy's conscious or unconscious device to preclude a vision of himself as an Irish Catholic courtier to a partrician Chief Executive.

"Neither had any illusions about the other," a newspaperman who was close to Joseph Kennedy in Washington observed. "Kennedy and Roosevelt found each other highly attractive men. Although each was, by nature, too suspicious to allow himself to genuinely like the other, they admired each other's performances. They were both masters at handling men." Franklin Roosevelt once confided to Kennedy, with a flourish, that "I can have Barney Baruch any time I let him put his feet under my dining room table." Kennedy had laughed, but did he wonder whether the president believed he could employ the same guile on him?

There were few hours for introspection in the tumultuous atmosphere of New Deal Washington. As Kennedy prepared to resign from the Securities and Exchange Commission, an election year loomed. At Franklin Roosevelt's insistence he kept up the pilgrimages to San Simeon and to the Shrine of the Little Flower in Royal Oak, Michigan.

The Priest of the Little Flower

Sunday afternoons at two o'clock. Strains of organ music issued from forty million radios, followed by an announcer's voice, deathly and sonorous. It was the weekly "discourse" of the Reverend Charles Coughlin. Audiences listened for the familiar, schoolmasterly opening, the brogue thickening portentiously, the indignant crescendo against the money changers, the Bolsheviks, the international bankers and, increasingly, Franklin Delano Roosevelt.

The priest of the Shrine of the Little Flower posed, with Huey Long, the most serious single threat to the president's reelection, or so many at the White House believed. Jim Farley commissioned a survey estimating how many votes a presidential ticket backed by Long and Coughlin could amass. The answer: six million, enough to throw the election to the Republicans. In March 1935 Hugh Johnson, the loudspoken former National Recovery Administrator, warned a New York audience, "You can laugh at Father Coughlin, you can snort at Huey Long, but this country was never under a greater threat."

The president took it philosophically. The American people, he wrote to a friend that same month, were "going through a bad case of Huey Long and Father Coughlin influenza—the whole country aching in every bone." Still Roosevelt was not daring enough to allow the disease to run its course. He charged Joseph Kennedy with the responsibility of keeping the good priest on the reservation.

Who was this man behind the microphone? Coughlin was born in 1891 to a Canadian seamstress and an American seaman who had suffered typhoid and found a sexton's job in Hamilton, Ontario. At a Basilian college of the University of Toronto the young man steeped himself in Social Catholicism. He accepted as his credo the encyclical of Pope Leo XIII, *Rerum Novarum,* on the changes wrought by the industrial revolution. The sanctity of private property, the immorality of usury, public regulation of working conditions, the natural harmony of labor and capital, the obligation of the state to provide social justice—many of these precepts were shared by American reform programs at the turn of the century. Some hoped that the document would bridge the chasm between urban Catholics and the reform movement.

The new priest found a sympathetic soul in Michael Gallagher, bishop of Detroit, who had been schooled in Social Catholicism in Vienna. He asked Coughlin to found a church in the Detroit suburb of Royal Oak, a stronghold of the Ku Klux Klan. Coughlin's welcome was a flaming cross. There were money problems too, for the few Catholic families in Royal Oak were hard pressed to sustain a parish church. "There I was, sleeping in the vestry, threatened with pneumonia, shivering with the cold, and unwilling to admit defeat," the priest recalled. "Something had to be done."

In 1926 Coughlin called on the manager of a Detroit radio station. The manager had heard of Coughlin's gift for lively sermons: what else could he do? The priest said he could play the organ and sing a little. "The Golden Hour of the Little Flower" began as a weekly showcase for Coughlin's talents as reader of children's stories, organist, sermonizer, and recitalist of Keats and Shelley. The program was adopted by CBS and beamed from coast to coast. When the depression came, Coughlin wet his feet in politics. "I knew damn well that the little people, the average man, was suffering. I also knew that no one had the courage to tell the truth about why this nation was in such mortal danger. I knew that if anyone was going to inform the American citizenry, it would have to be me."

He proposed the principles of Social Catholicism as the cure for the economic malaise, taking papal encyclicals as his touchstones. But the radio broadcasts were more dramatic than consistent; from week to week

Coughlin attacked financiers, supported economic nostrums, denounced Herbert Hoover as the arch-villain of mass misery. The size of his audience jumped as the allegations and solutions grew more imaginative. Letters containing hundreds of thousands of dollars descended upon Royal Oak; with the proceeds, Coughlin erected the Shrine of the Little Flower. Fearful of controversy, CBS canceled his contract, but the priest found no difficulty in forming his own national network.

In May 1931 the governor of New York received a letter from his wife's brother, G. Hall Roosevelt, controller of Detroit: "Father Coughlin is probably known to you by this time and is famous for being the director of fifty-two secretaries, which he has found necessary to handle his mail, which gets as high as 250,000 letters a day. He would like to tender his services. He would be difficult to handle and might be full of dynamite, but I think you had better be prepared to say yes or no."

Roosevelt said yes. In the spring of 1932 he and Coughlin joined in a cautious political embrace during a meeting in Albany. "We were supposed to be partners," the priest said later. "He said he would rely on me, that I would be an important advisor." Coughlin said he could not come out openly for a presidential candidate but that he would speak in favor of Roosevelt's "philosophy of government."

Joseph Kennedy befriended the priest and kept an eye on him for the Roosevelt campaign. The two men swiftly became fond of each other. If one was a speculator, the other a self-appointed gadfly of Wall Street, they paid little mind to this barrier. (Neither did the priest permit his outrage against international banking to keep him from secret speculation in silver and country weekends at the homes of Wall Street financiers.) But for the clerical collar and rhetoric, Coughlin was in fact the very picture of the man of the New Era. Athletic, an avid watcher of sports, he had the Main Street knack for making money and good fellowship. Both Kennedy and Coughlin liked publicity and jokes that were mildly naughty, disdained the Wall Street Old Guard, said things in anger that they later regretted, looked on life with some sense of the absurd. Both had been shaken by the depression and yearned for strong leadership and national planning. And, whether or not they ever spoke of it, both Joseph Kennedy and Father Coughlin believed they could each wield powerful influence, if not control, over Franklin Roosevelt.

After the 1932 election Coughlin arrived in New York for his audience with the president-elect. Earlier the priest had suggested, to Roosevelt's agreement, that the new president must appoint a greater number of Catholics as ambassadors in Latin America. He brought a list of qualified candidates to the home on Sixty-fifth Street. But, "Padre, terrible disappointment. I can't go through with that," Roosevelt replied; he had already permitted the new secretary of state, Cordell Hull, to make the Latin American appointments. "I'll tell you what I can do. You can have the Philippines if you want it." Coughlin immediately proposed Frank Murphy, mayor of Detroit and an early Roosevelt man who had been one of the priest's first altar boys. The next day the president-elect congratulated the new governor-general. "Frank, you are going to the Philippines."

Coughlin approved of most of the early New Deal—"It is either Roosevelt or ruin"—and his followers deluged the White House demanding his appointment as secretary of the treasury. Sixty-six congressmen signed a petition asking Roosevelt to make Coughlin an economic adviser. The priest directed his own stream of requests to Washington, so much so that by the end of 1933 the president told Jim Farley, "He should run for the Presidency himself. Who the hell does he think he is?" Coughlin began to have his own private doubts about Roosevelt. "Sometimes I am of the opinion that while I certainly rebuilt the confidence of the people in him, a confidence which had been greatly impaired, I sometimes wonder whether or not he favors my being with him," he wrote Frank Murphy in Manila in January 1934. Yet the voice on the radio declared, "I will never change my philosophy that the New Deal is Christ's Deal."

In April 1934 Roosevelt waved a red flag at Coughlin. Secretary Morgenthau revealed a list of prominent silver speculators to Congress. Near the top of the roster was the secretary-treasurer of the Radio League of the Little Flower, who had evidently invested some of Coughlin's earnings on the priest's behalf. Roosevelt could have saved Coughlin from embarrassment by removing his name from the list, but he did not.

Now the priest faced a dilemma. He was furious at the president yet afraid to gamble his popularity against Roosevelt's. Throughout 1934 Coughlin oscillated between supporting the president and opposing him. He offered a crazy quilt of proposals ranging from large-scale inflation to creation of a national bank to abolition of the Federal Reserve. Privately, the priest offered an oracular forecast to Frank Murphy: "The President within two years will have constructed a social order of a new type which will prevail. When I speak of this, I foresee that many of our so-called democratic functions must be discarded." A month later he wrote, "The entire fabric of democracy is moth-eaten. I am not intimating any inclination toward Naziism, but the possibility of viewing democracy too far to the right. It is an old story: if you go too far west, you go east."

By the end of 1934 Coughlin was poised to challenge Franklin Roosevelt. He formed his own political organization, the National Union for Social Justice, to lobby the Democratic and Republican parties for the Coughlin program. But in January 1935 he said he believed in Roosevelt "as much as ever." Two weeks later, abetted by William Randolph Hearst and other isolationists, Coughlin led the fight against the president's bill to bring the United States into the World Court. In March he informed his audience that Franklin Roosevelt had "out-Hoovered Hoover," protected plutocrats, and comforted Communists. Striking responsive nerves in Social Catholicism and Populism, drawing in elements of anti-Semitism, Coughlin seemed capable of fulfilling the old dream of alliance between Catholics and Populists. Those who knew Coughlin and Huey Long doubted the widespread rumors of a political partnership—each was too strong-willed to defer to the other—but others regarded the Kingfish and the radio priest as the forerunners of an American fascism.

The president slapped Coughlin with one hand while slapping him on the back with the other. Roosevelt believed he had a powerful restraint on the priest in the form of the Vatican's longstanding request for official recognition by the American government. If Coughlin kept up his criticism, the president told Henry Morgenthau, he would "send for the three cardinals and Apostolic delegate and show them the attacks that Father Coughlin has made on the sovereign of the United States—namely the President—and ask them how that jibes with their theory that the Church should have an ambassador in each country." At Roosevelt's request, Joseph Kennedy consulted Frank Murphy on strategies to keep peace with Royal Oak. ("By the way, I've yet to meet a girl in New York or Washington who doesn't know Frank Murphy," Kennedy appended a friendly letter. "Where in hell do you find the time to meet all these good-looking women?")

Since the inauguration, Coughlin had tried to work his will on the president through the Catholics at the White House. The priest's mother and Ray Moley's mother happened to be old friends. Coughlin traded jokes with Jim Farley and urged Missy Le Hand to talk politics; she prudently refused to stray from less perilous topics like novenae and the striking architecture of Coughlin's Shrine. Coughlin considered Frank Murphy his political protégé until he concluded that Murphy's ambitions were leading him to offer himself as a cat's paw for Franklin Roosevelt.

The priest's rapport with Kennedy increased. "Joe was fascinated by Coughlin's talent on the radio," James Roosevelt remembered. "He recognized it as demagoguery, but revelled in what the priest could accomplish. He was intrigued by Coughlin's use of power." Kennedy made periodic visits to Royal Oak and, on one occasion, brought his son Jack along to meet the celebrated radio priest. Kennedy and Coughlin often disagreed on politics—he would laughingly call the priest a "jackass"—but Coughlin perceived a genuineness in Kennedy that preserved their friendship long after the priest's links to others in Washington were severed. "We were just friends," Coughlin remembered later, "I had many friends who didn't support me. I never sought their support either, but they enjoyed conversation with me."

Taking a leaf perhaps from the president, Kennedy offered Coughlin enough of an impression of political agreement to lure the priest into speaking frankly. Coughlin informed Frank Murphy in 1935 that "the general criticism against Mr. Roosevelt is due to the fact that he has broken nearly every promise that he has made while he prefers to seek means and methods closely allied with socialism and communism to rectify our economic ills. Joseph Kennedy agrees with me in this analysis."

At the beginning of September 1935 Kennedy visited the president at Hyde Park. By then, Father Coughlin had boycotted the White House for several months. Roosevelt planned a final attempt to work his magic over the radio priest. The White House switchboard reached Coughlin at dinner with his parents in Michigan. Kennedy took the receiver and asked his friend where he had been keeping himself. "Home, I'm busy," was the curt reply. But the Boss wanted to speak with him, said Kennedy. "Where are you calling from, Joe?" Kennedy chuckled: "Up the river!"

Then the familiar voice came over the line: "Hiya Padre! Where have you been all the time? I'm lonesome. I've got a couple of days off down here. Come on down and see me." Coughlin declined with the explanation that he had "an important funeral" to attend the following morning. "You get ready and come down the next night then," Roosevelt replied.

Coughlin, relating the conversation many years after, explained his reluctance to see the president. His mentor Bishop Gallagher had received from the archbishop of Guadalajara a check allegedly made out by a Communist sympathizer in the Treasury Department to Mexican revolutionaries. The bishop had told Coughlin he must stay away from Roosevelt. After the president's telephone call, the priest asked Gallagher's permission for a visit to Hyde Park. Gallagher approved the trip on the condition that Coughlin confront Roosevelt with the mysterious check. The priest called Joseph Kennedy to say he would arrive on the early morning train in Albany.

The train pulled into Albany before dawn on September 10. Stepping onto the platform, Coughlin glimpsed a tall newspaper headline: HUEY LONG DEAD. A reporter rushed up from the darkness to record his reaction: "The most regrettable thing in modern history." Kennedy escorted the priest to his waiting Rolls-Royce and they motored down the Hudson, arriving at sunrise. The president was still asleep. Kennedy and Coughlin made breakfast for themselves and repaired to the study to wait for the president to awaken.

There was a rumbling at the top of the stairs. In the custom of the house, Coughlin ran up the staircase to assist Roosevelt, a newspaper under his arm. What did Coughlin have there? the president asked. Coughlin brandished the paper: "Your boyfriend is dead." After Roosevelt had his breakfast, he got down to business: "Cards on the table, Padre, cards on the table. Why are you cooling off to me?" Coughlin hemmed and hawed, uncomfortable with Kennedy present. Roosevelt invited Kennedy to "go out and look at the pigs."

"We've got some bad news from Mexico," Coughlin remembered telling the president. He produced the check. "Michael Gallagher's afraid that we're going soft on the Communists down there." Roosevelt, puzzled, examined the check and promised to look into the matter. Coughlin went on to say that the president's recognition of the Soviet Union was all right because no nation could go bankrupt without injuring the remainder of the world, but Roosevelt should pursue more inflationary fiscal policies and get rid of the Federal Reserve. The president replied to these entreaties as he typically did: "Don't be so innocent as to think that the President of the United States can also be the Congress of the United States. I'm only the President."

Roosevelt reminded Coughlin of the dire problems the nation faced and the catastrophe that would confront America should a Republican president be elected in 1936. If Coughlin went ahead to form a third party, it might result in a Republican victory. Was that what Coughlin wanted? The priest was noncommittal. After many hours of talk, the president invited Kennedy and Coughlin to stay for dinner, but they had already made plans to dine with a friend in the Berkshires. The priest related the long conversation with Roosevelt as he and Kennedy drove away. After listening sympathetically, Kennedy told Coughlin he was planning to resign from the Securities Commission in a few weeks; he still liked and respected the president but found few challenges left in the job.

"I went down to see Mr. Roosevelt and spent eight hours talking with him, during which time I did most of the talking," Coughlin reported to Frank Murphy. He was now convinced that reconciliation with the president was impossible. "I sincerely feel that Mr. Roosevelt is a socialist of the radical type . . . not for what he has done so much as what he has left undone and which he has no intention of doing as he told me." Coughlin predicted that Roosevelt would be reelected but that his second administration would have "a most stormy existence." He prophesied that the legislative and executive branches would revolt against the president, that the Republicans would be "even willing to help re-elect Roosevelt for the purpose of ruining him entirely together with the hopes of the Tugwells, the Frankfurters and the rest of the Jews who surround him. The plot is deeply laid. . . ."

At Hyde Park the president took pains to keep Father Coughlin's visit a secret. That evening, a reporter found presidential secretary Marvin McIntyre on his way into a Poughkeepsie restaurant. Was it true that the radio priest had seen the president? McIntyre denied the report. But the next day, after consulting with Roosevelt, he withdrew the denial. At the afternoon press conference, a newspaperman asked about the purpose of Coughlin's call. The president was cautious:

"He came yesterday to lunch. Joe Kennedy called up and said he was going to bring him through from Albany on his way to Massachusetts. He came down and we had a nice visit. He stayed for lunch and went on." Coughlin had told reporters that it was he who informed the president of the death of Huey Long—was that true? "No, what happened was that he was present when Missy came in and said so." Was the priest back on the reservation? "I don't know. It was a social visit." Hadn't they talked politics? "Just a social visit." Was Coughlin coming back for another talk? "Not that I know of." What was Joe Kennedy's mission? "I have no idea, except to act as chauffeur, I guess."

"I'm for Roosevelt" and "I'm for Kennedy"

A week later, at another press conference, Marvin McIntyre brought up the rumor of Kennedy's departure from government. "One or two of the boys have an inquiry and if you want to answer it, it ought to be not for morning paper release, but for immediate release. The news is that Joe Kennedy—"

"Yes, I think that can be announced," Roosevelt broke in. "The only thing is this—I have his letter and I have not written my letter. I do not want to kill the story for Joe. . . . I told you six weeks ago he was getting out this fall."

"Does he give any reason?"

"That is the trouble about making it. There are going to be two very nice letters." But when told that the story of Kennedy's resignation was already breaking in Washington, the president relented. "All right. Letters for the morning."

"Can you tell us why he is getting out now?"

"Because he has been hoping to get out for some time and he stayed a good deal longer than he expected to stay. He has to get back to his private work."

The "very nice letters" were issued on September 21, 1935. "To discontinue my official relations with you is not an easy task," Kennedy wrote to the president, "Rather it is one involving genuine regret assuaged only by the privilege of your friendship. As a chief, you have been unfailingly considerate and stimulating. . . . You know how deeply devoted I am to you personally and to the success of your Administration. Because of this devotion, after retiring from the post of Chairman of the Securities and Exchange Commission, I shall still deem myself a part of your Administration."

"Of course, I am very sorry to see you go," Roosevelt responded, "but you rightly reminded me that you accepted the Chairmanship of the Securities Commission with the distinct understanding that your private affairs would not permit you to stay beyond a year." He congratulated Kennedy for his successful implementation of the New Deal in finance. "Such a result never just happens. It comes to pass only through skill, resourcefulness, good sense, and devotion to the public interest." Kennedy was fully justified to continue regarding himself as a member of the New Deal. "In the future, as in the past, I shall freely turn to you for your support and counsel."

"I'm going to feel that I'm out of politics—if this is politics—for the rest of my natural life," Kennedy told newspapermen. One of his last acts as chairman of the Securities Commission was to write a batch of letters to publishers and journalists thanking them for their support: "I am now through with public life forever. . . ." Few believed it. Willard Kiplinger reported that Kennedy was in line for a cabinet position.

The president asked Kennedy to visit Europe as an unofficial emissary to report on economics and politics: "When I lie awake at nights, as I often do, I worry about the condition of Europe . . . more than anything else. I wish you would do a trouble-shooting job and find out for me just what the threat to peace amounts to." Kennedy sailed with presidential letters of introduction to the leaders of government and opposition in Great Britain, France, Italy, Switzerland, and the Netherlands. Before

Kennedy reached London, Bernard Baruch cabled his friend Winston Churchill: "Suggest your making appointment to see him as he is important and good relationship between you two might have far reaching results."

Churchill asked the Kennedys to luncheon at his home at Chartwell, Kent. During the meal, Mrs. Churchill asked Rose Kennedy whether she thought Eleanor Roosevelt was an exhibitionist, using her husband's high office to gain publicity. No, the president's wife was sincere, Mrs. Kennedy replied; gradually people would grow accustomed to her unconventional approach. Churchill carried the burden of the conversation; he suggested to his American guests that their two countries build a navy strong enough to protect the world from Nazism. This would be a difficult idea to sell in America, he warned Joseph Kennedy—prophetically. There were too many isolationists, "too many Irish haters of England, too many people that would prefer to remain outside England's sphere."

Churchill in 1935 looked askance at most of the domestic innovations of the New Deal, but Kennedy was surprised to find support for Franklin Roosevelt's policies among the chief men of British finance. "One thing we can be sure of," he wrote Jim Farley on Claridge's stationery, "and that is that if all the newspaper and business men of America had one tenth of the confidence in the President that they have here in England, he would be President for the rest of his life." The newspapermen of Fleet Street asked the American if he believed Roosevelt could be defeated in 1936. "There is no one to beat him, because no one has anything to offer. What could be the program of any opponent of Roosevelt?"

In mid-November Kennedy returned with a report on "the tensions and hypocrisies I had witnessed." He had found Europe "unsettled and confused" with an "Alice-in-Wonderland quality." Changing subjects during an evening meeting at the White House, Kennedy urged the president to keep trying to mend fences with William Randolph Hearst and Father Coughlin. Roosevelt was unreceptive. Referring to Hearst as "that bastard," he declared there was no man in the entire United States who was as vicious an influence. Kennedy dryly noted that there seemed little chance of concord. That same month, Father Coughlin announced to his radio audience that he and the president were now unalterably opposed. Was a bargain with the Vatican in Roosevelt's mind? He told Kennedy that he had "practically decided" to officially recognize the Catholic church.

At Farley's behest, the president tried once more for peace with the priest of the Little Flower. On January 8, 1936 Coughlin came to the

White House for the last time. Roosevelt tried to pin him down on his political plans, Coughlin to pin down Roosevelt on his plans if reelected. Neither succeeded. By the end of the meeting, the president was reduced to asking the priest how his Great Dane was feeling. "Fine," Coughlin replied. "How is Fala?"

A few weeks later, with the cunning of a ward boss, Father Coughlin tested his remaining political clout at the White House. He wired Kennedy that "the federal judgeship in Detroit is wide open and Washington is considering the appointment of a young man who doesn't know the date of Christmas. I have a man who is one of the eminent attorneys of Michigan and a Republican who is a real convert. Moreover, he is willing and desirous of wringing the necks of the Administration's enemies around Michigan." Coughlin offered to "give you his name and see if you can go to work." Kennedy sent the telegram on to James Roosevelt with the notation that "the President can decide whether it is worthwhile to make a gesture to Father Coughlin." There was no gesture.

Murphy received another missive from Royal Oak: "Frank, don't deceive yourself. Roosevelt is a liar and the truth is not in him."

Spending the winter in Palm Beach, Kennedy reported to the White House that local churches were filling up with Liberty Leaguers. The Roosevelt anthem for 1936, he joked, would not be "Happy Days Are Here Again," but "I'll Be Glad When You're Dead, You Rascal, You." The president sent Kennedy a list of businessmen, prepared by the Commerce Department, who were known to be favorable to the New Deal and whom Kennedy might approach for financial support in the coming campaign. Indicative of the chill between Franklin Roosevelt and business was the brevity of the list; it included only fifty names. Kennedy undertook short-term consulting work with RCA and Paramount Pictures but—in spite of the disclaimers—he was eager to return to public life. In the spring of 1936, James Roosevelt found Kennedy "unhappy and angry that no new job offer was forthcoming from Washington."

Kennedy asked Missy Le Hand to transmit a message to the president: "I'm fairly free now of any business activities, and so if he thinks I can be of any use to him, please let me know." On the editorial page of the *New York Times* Arthur Krock unsuccessfully proposed Kennedy as chairman of a new board overseeing public works.

Seeing no official position in his immediate future, Joseph Kennedy threw himself into the presidential campaign. He was the preeminent specimen of a rare breed—a big businessman in support of the New Deal. Kennedy drafted a book that would demonstrate to American businessmen that "they never had it so good." He sent a rough version to the president in June but received no response. Anxiously, he wrote Missy Le Hand, "Unless he feels some value in releasing it, it won't hurt my feelings at all if he just says, 'Let's use it in some other way.' " Roosevelt dispatched a reply: "I thought you got my message sent more than ten days ago—that I thought the manuscript splendid and that it will be of real service, not only from a campaign point of view, but also as a distinct step in sane education of the country."

Kennedy offered Arthur Krock five thousand dollars to rework his manuscript, reporting that the president was "anxious to have it done, and if it is done, I should like to have it done in bang-up shape." Krock consented but refused the fee.

I'm for Roosevelt was published by Reynal and Hitchcock in September 1936. Except for its mild objections to Franklin Roosevelt's 1936 tax proposals and certain of his fiscal policies, the book was a clarion defense of the New Deal. Kennedy reminded businessmen that even though some found the president's reforms distasteful, Roosevelt's programs had nevertheless saved the capitalist system. He advocated some type of permanent system of national planning to maintain the social and economic order. "Planned action is imperative or else capitalism and the American scheme of life will be in serious jeopardy." The question facing Americans was "whether we should intelligently regulate our social life as to assure the maintenance of a democracy or should smash our regulatory machine and thus pave the way for dictatorship. . . .

"My faith in Roosevelt and my belief in the ultimate triumph and broad benefit of his principles is much affected by my position as the father of a large family. Out of a chaotic condition which stunned everybody, out of a collapse which threatened the welfare of all of us, our nation has come to a relatively prosperous and harmonious era." Who would choose to return, he demanded, "to the terror of 1933 or step backward from the sound threshold of the future into the economic quicksand of the years before the New Deal?"

Some critics derided the protestation of "no political ambitions for myself or my children" with which Kennedy opened the volume, but most praised his arguments. A few reviewers worried about his seeming passion for federal supervision of American life. A critic for the *Saturday Review* asked, "Does he scoff at fears of excessive regimentation and bureaucracy because he is confident that the President can be trusted to avoid them or because he wants less individualism and more regimentation?" Did Kennedy know himself?

That autumn he contributed handsomely to the reelection campaigns of congressional friends. George Norris was given one thousand dollars. James Byrnes received a note from Kennedy—"I am convinced that South Carolina just couldn't get along without you"—and shortly thereafter, Edward Moore arrived at the senator's home in Spartanburg with a check for twenty-five hundred dollars. Byrnes declined on the grounds that his relations with Kennedy were not such that he should feel justified in accepting such a sum. But Kennedy never accepted excuses for failure, Moore said; the senator's refusal would hurt his position with Kennedy. As a compromise, Byrnes agreed to accept the check and reimburse Kennedy immediately.

The showcase businessman for Roosevelt promulgated his views in interviews, articles, and speeches. "If you shove your neck out, you're bound to get it slapped," he told a reporter. Some of his business friends had told him he had seen his last job with anyone in the financial world, but Kennedy was "tired of hearing rich and powerful men express their hatred for the President." He was "afraid some people are laying up bad trouble for themselves the way they are acting. . . . You can't tell the public to go to hell anymore. Fifty men have run America—and that's a high figure. The rest of America is demanding a share in the game and they'll get it."

"A Businessman's View of the New Deal," an article under Kennedy's byline in the *Review of Reviews*, was distributed by the Democratic National Committee. Another piece entitled "The Administration and Business" was published in the *New York Times Magazine*. "It is the partisanship of some and the essential selfishness of the economically powerful that explain the frequent use of the scare technique in the campaign against the President," Kennedy explained. "To be sure, the term economic royalist stings, but we all know that it is not directed to a whole class but to a few, the irresponsible wealthy who have no heed for the social obligations of money and power."

Kennedy's strategy was to separate the lions of Wall Street from small businessmen and executives in newer industries like motion pictures, radio, and computers, inclined to be more friendly to Roosevelt. His willingness to join the attacks on economic royalists and criticize the American power elite with the vigor of a Harold Ickes or Ferdinand Lundberg issued perhaps from Kennedy's failure to achieve complete acceptance by Wall Street. A call on J. P. Morgan one day in 1929 was rebuffed with the excuse that the great man was too busy to see him. James Roosevelt believed that this explained Kennedy's yearning for the treasury: "Joe realized that he would never be fully accepted by the members of the financial establishment and felt that this way he could circumvent them." Despite his attainments, Kennedy never ceased to identify more with the commoners than with the sultans of finance. "Six or seven times in my life, the pendulum swung my way," he once reminded a friend, "and for that, if it hadn't fallen favorably, life could be quite a bit different."

The president asked him to organize a series of dinners honoring Businessmen for Roosevelt. Only the candidate's insistence overcame Kennedy's reluctance to accept this thankless task. The invitations were not coveted. One man excused himself by explaining that his wife was afraid to be left alone in her Manhattan apartment; another declined with the observation that "Landon is in, anyhow"; a third wrote, "I'll vote for him. Ain't that enough?" The banquets were held on an October evening in major American cities. The president delivered an after-dinner address by telephone from Washington.

Kennedy proposed to take to the radio for Roosevelt. "The Boss thinks the idea for a broadcast is swell," replied the presidential press secretary, Stephen Early. He asked Kennedy to submit his speech for White House clearance and to follow a few suggestions laid down by the president: "If big business and big finance is different from the overwhelming majority of little businessmen and small bankers and think that they can stop government efforts to end long-standing abuses, they are playing a very dangerous game. The country is not going to revert to complete freedom for business where such freedom results in over-speculation, overproduction, tax avoidance through the corporate process, stock watering, price fixing."

Pressing Arthur Krock and a French journalist into service in the drafting, Kennedy delivered three radio speeches in October. He warned small businessmen to avoid being "jockeyed into a position of antagonism to the rest of the nation because a few stuffed shirts have lost their silk hats." Kennedy observed that when Franklin Roosevelt took office, "the most fundamental dogma of Americanism was that to become rich was not only a worthy aim in itself but the fulfillment of a beneficent duty toward the community. Since then, Mr. Roosevelt has repeatedly inferred that if a man had attained financial success, it did not necessarily follow that this man was either a better man or a more useful citizen."

Kennedy also locked horns with Father Coughlin. The priest was barnstorming for a Union party ticket headed by Congressman William Lemke of North Dakota. Coughlin now vilified the president as "Franklin

Double-Crossing Roosevelt." Stripping off his coat and Roman collar at a Union party convention, he denounced the "liar" and "great betrayer" in the White House, bringing the audience to its feet. Coughlin exempted Kennedy from criticism: his friend was "the shining star among the dim knights of the Administration." But in a Boston address at the end of the campaign, Kennedy assailed "the efforts made for low, practical purposes to confuse a Christian program of social justice with a Godless program of Communism." He reminded his listeners that in 1933 "we could have had a dictatorship in the twinkling of an eye—President Roosevelt's eye. . . . If there were any semblance of Communism or dictatorship or regimentation in this country, the words liar and betrayer would have been uttered only once."

Weary from campaigning, Kennedy returned to New York. He wrote wistfully to Senator Byrnes, "Well, boy—win, lose or draw—after Tuesday, one Joseph Patrick Kennedy retires from the political ring forever and a day."

Two days after the greatest presidential landslide in American history, Joseph and Rose Kennedy boarded a special train for Hyde Park with the papal secretary of state, Eugenio Cardinal Pacelli, who had been touring the United States for a month. The president had approved Kennedy's earlier request to receive the cardinal but had delayed the visit until after the election. There were murmurs among newspapermen that the chief subject of conversation would be Father Coughlin. The priest's presidential candidate, William Lemke, had fared poorly, but the weekly voice on the radio was prepared to continue its competition with Franklin Roosevelt.

Pacelli and the Kennedys were welcomed by the president and his mother at the Roosevelt doorstep. When president and cardinal returned from their talk, reporters asked Pacelli if the two men had discussed Father Coughlin. He gave no answer and the questioners were waved aside. Later that afternoon, the cardinal took tea with the Kennedys at their home in Bronxville. The exchange between Franklin Roosevelt and Cardinal Pacelli was never revealed. But years later Father Coughlin, in retirement, confided his view to a visitor at the Shrine of the Little Flower that a deal had been struck: if the Vatican ordained his removal from the radio, the president would sent an emissary to Rome. Two years after the meeting with Roosevelt Pacelli became Pope Pius XII. Coughlin indeed left the airwaves and the White House announced the appointment of a special presidential representative to the Vatican.

Joseph Kennedy pressed the White House after the 1936 election for a presidential note that the author of *I'm for Roosevelt* could pass on to his children. The president postponed the chore until Missy Le Hand prodded: "You *must* do this." When the letter arrived, it was framed and displayed at Hyannis Port. "Dear Joe," it began, "I'M FOR KENNEDY. . . ."

The Greatest Joke in the World

In a conversation during the interregnum between presidential administrations, James Roosevelt found that Kennedy still hankered to be secretary of the treasury, although he understood the president's reluctance to replace his old friend Henry Morgenthau. Franklin Roosevelt knew all about Kennedy's persistent ambition but shrank from the idea. "Joe would want to run the Treasury in his own way," he told Jim Farley, "contrary to my plans and views."

In February 1937 Kennedy was called to Washington. The president asked him to chair the new Maritime Commission. Congress had created the agency to rescue the American shipping industry from its perpetual doldrums. Roosevelt decided that his old counterpart at Fore River and miracle-worker of the Securities Commission was up to the task. But Kennedy was disappointed; he did not want to exhaust his political credit at the White House by accepting a job he did not want and worried that the problems of American shipping might tarnish his reputation for success.

"If it's all the same to you, let some other patriot take it on the chin for a while," Kennedy told the president, adding, "There's a lot of money to be made in the market. I'd like to skim off my share of the profits." His misgivings were overcome by the Roosevelt persuasiveness—and the implicit suggestion that if Kennedy completed the maritime job in good form, a greater reward would be in store. "To be very honest with you, I had great hesitancy in taking this job," he told James Byrnes. "I had received a couple of large assignments which were along the lines I like and they would have proved very profitable, but the President made his appeal on such a personal basis that there was nothing for me to do but go back into government service."

Kennedy wrote John Boettiger in Seattle, "I should love to tell you the story how I got into this mess and you and Anna would have plenty of laughs. I give up my business, give up my leisure to take up the most unworkable bill I ever read in my life, but you know that man's winning ways. It is pretty good when you can give up a perfectly good reputation and throw it into the ash can when you can be of service, but you know. If you are going through with a guy, you must go all the way through."

One of the most unworkable provisions of the Maritime Act was a congressional deadline of July 1 for Kennedy's commission to settle a storehouse of mail contracts and other outstanding claims. Working seven days a week, Kennedy met the deadline, a feat that impressed the president: "Congratulations. It was a grand job to get those contracts out of the way on time." Arthur Krock declared in the *Times* that Kennedy had performed another miracle. It was the anniversary of Kennedy's appointment to the Securities Commission. He scrawled a sentimental thank-you to his friend:

"It seems to me it would sound silly to call you up and say, 'Arthur, that was swell of you,' so I want to write it to you and tell you that three years ago this week you started me on my way with another article in the Times. I am practical enough to know that the help you have given me beginning with that article three years ago and all those in between and today's have been the real reason that the press of the country have given me all the breaks. So, Arthur, my father taught me, 'Be grateful and be loyal at whatever cost.' I am most appreciative and will never forget it."

"I may have lighted your Federal path, but I never started you on it," Krock rejoined. "Every inch of the way you won yourself and splendidly."

The maritime position propelled Joseph Kennedy into the bitter and often bloody warfare between management and labor, union and union for mastery of American shipping. Kennedy warned the president that strikes were costing American companies millions of dollars a year. Something had to be done—"or else the government is wasting money building ships." Although sympathetic to the condition of maritime workers—his own father had worked for a time on the Boston wharves—Kennedy was hired to restore efficiency to American shipping, a duty that brought him into conflict with the tenacious princes of the maritime unions.

In September 1937 crewmen aboard the U.S.S. *Algic* staged a sit-down strike in Montevideo to demonstrate solidarity with local longshoremen. Kennedy wanted to clap the ringleaders in irons and prosecute. The president understood Kennedy's wish to set an example but, sensitive to his relations with labor, he urged a more moderate solution. Arthur Krock was chatting with Kennedy at the Maritime Commission when the call came from the White House. He offered to leave the room but Kennedy beckoned him to remain, perhaps a trifle eager to show off for his friend.

"Yes, Mr. President," Krock heard Kennedy say. "Yes, sir, I know you're getting complaints. . . . Yes, Mr. President, but I'd do it again—we can't allow things like this and get the job done. . . . No sir, I don't go with that idea of a compromise. . . ." Kennedy dropped his formality: "Listen, boy, if we do that, we'll land in the shit house!" Krock heard an exuberant roar from the other end of the line. But when Kennedy asked the president what he would do if Kennedy were wrong, Roosevelt replied suavely, "I won't do anything. If you're wrong, you'll swing for it."

After the strikers were declared guilty, labor leaders like Joseph Curran of the National Maritime Union demanded Kennedy's resignation. *The Nation* considered the maritime chairman's performance "as neat an exhibition of pre-Fascist union-smashing as has ever been our lot to witness."

In the maritime industry as in the stock market, Kennedy was concerned about conditions that might contain the seeds of revolution. Noting the inhuman quarters and low wages offered to many seamen, Kennedy declared that "removal of grievances is the one sure road to elimination of Communistic influence on American ships." In his report to Congress in November 1937 he proposed compulsory arbitration of disputes between unions and management as well as training schools for American seamen. Secretary of Labor Frances Perkins, who represented a different constituency, testified against Kennedy's plan. The president refused to take sides and a relatively weak bill was enacted.

The experience of dealing with unions and attracting private investment to a sagging industry convinced Kennedy that government ownership was the only solution. Yet, if his conclusions were bleak, Kennedy settled old claims, enacted federal subsidies, and completed a study of American shipping that gained wide praise. The chairmanship of the Maritime Commission, Kennedy declared, was "the toughest job I ever handled in my life—without any reservations whatever."

His return to Washington brought Joseph Kennedy back into the heart of the New Deal. He had "grown tremendously in Roosevelt's esteem," *Business Week* reported, and "his voice will be potent on any question in respect to the handling of business, corporations and taxes." The *New Republic* called Kennedy the president's "protégé" and *Time*, more approvingly, Roosevelt's "most effective and trusted extra-Cabinet friend."

At the twenty-fifth reunion of the Harvard Class of 1912 there were many jokes at the expense of the New Dealer. In a musical revue, the curtain opened on a secretary struggling with a battery of telephones. "No,

On the facing page: Above, The Kennedys of East Boston (seated first and second from left), late 1880s.

Below, The Roosevelts of Hyde Park, 1896.

KENNEDY FAMILY COLLECTION

FRANKLIN D. ROOSEVELT LIBRARY

FRANKLIN D. ROOSEVELT LIB

Apprentice in politics: Franklin Roosevelt with Josephus Daniels at the Navy Department, 1918.

Apprentice in business: Joseph Kennedy with Charles Schwab at the Fore River shipyard, 1918.

KENNEDY FAMILY COLLECTION

FRANKLIN D. ROOSEVELT LIBRARY

Business statesman: Roosevelt poring over desk work at Hyde Park, 1924.

Rugged individualist: Kennedy in Hollywood with one of his leading players, the western actor Tom Mix, 1928.

KENNEDY FAMILY COLLECTION

The Roosevelt Party
Oregon - Californid
Line
September 23, 1932.
THE
ROOSEVELT
SPECIAL

Springtime of an alliance: Kennedy is standing directly below the candidate.

At a whistle stop, Joseph Kennedy (second from left) cheering as Franklin Roosevelt (lower right, partially obscured by hatted men) makes his way through a crowd absorbed by the sight of the candidate's lameness, 1932. Eleanor Roosevelt follows at right.

KENNEDY FAMILY COLLECTION

FRANKLIN D. ROOSEVELT LIBRAR

JOHN F. KENNEDY LIBRARY

Masters of the press (on the facing page). Above: Roosevelt at the White House. Below: Kennedy at the Securities and Exchange Commission.

A New Deal portrait: Members of the inner circle emerge from advising the president on public works, April 27, 1935. From left: Secretary of the Treasury Henry Morgenthau, Jr.; Joseph Kennedy; relief administrator Harry Hopkins; budget director Daniel Bell; Secretary of the Interior Harold Ickes; White House congressional liason Charles West; Undersecretary of Agriculture Rexford Tugwell; Admiral Christian Peoples, director of treasury procurement.

NATIONAL ARCHIVES

WIDE WORLD

William Randolph Hearst, 1936.

On the facing page, above: The priest of the Little Flower: Father Charles Coughlin delivering one of his Sunday radio "discourses," 1934.

Below: "The greatest joke in the world." In the presidential office, Franklin Roosevelt presiding over the oath-taking of his new ambassador to the Court of St. James's, February 18, 1938. Justice Stanley Reed is at center.

UNITED PRESS

UNITED PRESS

NATIONAL ARCHIVES

James Roosevelt with Joseph Kennedy aboard the U.S.S. Manhattan *before the envoy's voyage to Great Britain, February 23, 1938.*

Secretary of State Cordell Hull and the president discussing the European crisis at a cabinet meeting, September 1938.

FRANKLIN D. ROOSEVELT LIBRA

WIDE WORLD

The American ambassador conferring with two staff assistants, John F. Kennedy (left) and Joseph Kennedy, Jr., at the London embassy, 1938.

The path to Munich: Adolf Hitler and Neville Chamberlain at Godesberg, September 24, 1938.

UNITED PRESS

WIDE WORLD

Joseph Kennedy bidding farewell to King George and Queen Elizabeth on their departure

1939.

WIDE WORLD

UNITED PRESS

After a visit with Winston Churchill during Sumner Welles's "peace mission" to Europe, the president's emissary and Joseph Kennedy leaving the Admiralty, March 27, 1940.

"Nothing to say until I've seen the President": Kennedy on arrival at La Guardia Field, New York, October 27, 1940. Flanking the returning ambassador are Jean, Rose Kennedy, Kathleen, Patricia, and Eunice.

WIDE WOR

NATIONAL ARCHIVES

The president watching as Secretary of War Henry L. Stimson draws the first number in the "muster" of over a million American men for military service, Washington, October 29, 1940.

Amid the campaign hysteria against American intervention in Europe, a decisive third-term endorsement for Franklin Roosevelt, New York, October 29, 1940.

CBS

WIDE WORLD

NEW YORK TIMES

"We must always be wary of those who with sounding brass and tinkling cymbal preach the 'ism' of appeasement": The president delivering his State of the Union message to Congress, January 6, 1941.

Joseph Kennedy taking the witness stand to testify for five hours against Lend-Lease, House Committee on Foreign Affairs, January 21, 1941.

UNITED PRESS

The private citizen leaving the White House after a last confrontation with Franklin Roosevelt, October 26, 1944.

The nation's only four-term president riding in victory with the incoming vice-president, Harry Truman, through the streets of Washington, November 10, 1944.

UNITED PRESS

Springtime of a new alliance: John F. Kennedy and Franklin Roosevelt, Jr., greeting voters in West Virginia, April 1960. At center is Ward Wylie, state chairman of the Kennedy presidential

Mr. President, it can't be nine o'clock because Mr. Kennedy isn't here yet. . . . No, Mrs. Roosevelt, your clock must be fast." In walked "Kennedy," resplendent in top hat and cutaway. "Get me Franklin at the White House," he demanded, swinging his feet onto the desktop. "Frank, this is Joe. I'm here. It's nine o'clock and you can start the country." One classmate proposed that Kennedy enter his Harvard friends on the federal dole at ten thousand dollars a year. But not all the teasing was as lighthearted as this. When, on the final night of the reunion, Kennedy delivered a brief address in support of the New Deal, there were catcalls. Kennedy never attended another Harvard reunion.

The taunting in Cambridge must have been especially difficult to stomach because Kennedy was growing daily more disturbed by Franklin Roosevelt's economic policies. In 1937 the American economy suffered a decline that critics branded the "Roosevelt recession." Heeding the entreaties of Kennedy and Morgenthau, the president worked to balance the budget by trimming federal expenditures. But he also raised taxes. Kennedy complained that higher taxes would cripple the industrial expansion and investment required of the private sector to compensate for lowered government spending. He told the president that his solution treated symptoms but failed to produce cures. James Roosevelt found Kennedy fearful and pessimistic about the outcome. At the drop of an economic indicator, Kennedy would exclaim, "We're going to have another crash!" Kennedy lobbied and testified in Congress against the president's levy on undistributed corporate income.

He was willing to subjugate his personal beliefs to a sense of presidential loyalty, however, when asked to support the Boss's plan to expand the Supreme Court and circumvent the "nine old men" who threatened to continue to nullify the New Deal. In March 1937 James Roosevelt, now a secretary to the president, asked Kennedy to chair a national committee that would back the Court proposal. Despite his objections to Court-packing, Kennedy agreed—with the proviso that the Democratic National Committee repay the money it owed him; this he would in turn spend on a new committee. Kennedy wired Bernard Baruch to solicit his aid: "Before I ask you in the name of the Holy Father to help on a plan, are you for or against the Holy Father's suggestion on the Supreme Court, and if you are for his plan, would you care to go along and help me, care of the White House?" The committee—and the president's scheme—never got off the ground.

Few of his conservative friends begrudged Kennedy his support for Court-packing, but they questioned his public enthusiasm for an administration about which he was growing privately so doubtful. Kennedy told the New York Economic Club in December 1937 that he was "more of a New Dealer than ever." Franklin Roosevelt would be in the White House for three more years and it would get them nowhere to bellyache. "You say fear broke the market. I know something about the market. It very nearly kept me out of a job once as Chairman of the Securities Commission. I happened to be a member of a pool that was exposed by Ferdinand Pecora." It was time for cooperation between business and government—"not for Roosevelt, not for the New Deal, but for yourselves, because by doing something now, you can help the whole cause, and there never was a time when it was more important for you, for all of us to get behind now and stop bellyaching and try and do something for the cause."

"Joe wins the 1937 China Egg diamond belt prize with this one," snickered Frank Kent in a letter to Baruch after Kennedy's speech. He wrote in the *Baltimore Sun*, "No man ever held an important post in Washington who has had more praise and less abuse than Mr. Kennedy." The reason—"no one thought he was an enthusiast for the New Deal. On the contrary, the conviction was cherished that he heartily disapproved of the radical Brain Trust doctrines, that he strongly opposed the fiscal and tax policies pursued, and was so constituted that he bellyached loudly and effectively to the President against them."

Harold Ickes agreed with Kent's analysis—from the opposite end of the political spectrum. "Kennedy has probably a better press right now than any member of the Administration," he recorded in his diary that month. The interior secretary was worried that Kennedy—"a New Dealer merely out of personal loyalty to the President"—was pouring his conservative ideas into the sympathetic ear of James Roosevelt, who presumably relayed them to his father. "The result is that the liberals do not know whether they are coming or going and, more importantly still, they do not know what direction the President is likely to take in the near future. We all feel that unless the President makes a stand in the next two or three months, the whole New Deal fight will be lost. . . .

"It is of great importance that Kennedy, through Jimmy Roosevelt, does not have the almost exclusive ear of the President."

The prospect of higher office had remained on Kennedy's mind through the months at the Maritime Commission. "I felt that Joe deserved something better, something really special in the government and I told him so," Rose Kennedy remembered. After his broad hints about the treasury drew no reaction from the president, Kennedy riveted his sights on the Court of St. James's. Robert Worth Bingham, the Kentucky newspaper publisher who was the current ambassador, was mortally ill and soon to return. When Kennedy returned to Cape Cod on weekends, his wife asked, "What has the President said? Couldn't you tell him what you want?"

"Well, I can't just walk into the office of the President of the United States and say I want to be Ambassador to England."

But there were other channels. Discreetly, Kennedy mentioned his aspiration to friends in Congress, the press, and the White House who, he hoped, would transmit the message to Franklin Roosevelt. "Everybody seems to be for me but the White House," Kennedy said to a Senate friend in June 1937. "Poor old felt-minded Joe," Frank Kent wrote Baruch. "What a sucker he is going to look if he does not get this appointment."

The president knew that Kennedy was getting restless. "We've got to do something for old Joe, but I don't know what," he told his son. "Why don't you go see him and feel him out and see what you can come up with?" James called on Kennedy at Marwood and was taken aback by his friend's suggestion. "I really liked Joe," he remembered, "but he was a crusty old cuss and I couldn't picture him as an Ambassador—especially to England." Kennedy really didn't want London, did he? "Oh, yes I do. I've been thinking about it and I'm intrigued by the thought of being the first Irishman to be Ambassador from the United States to the Court of St. James's." James agreed that it would be "quite a precedent" and promised to report Kennedy's request to the president.

"Sure enough, when I passed it on to Father, he laughed so hard he almost toppled from his wheelchair." Roosevelt shook his head and said he was sorry—London was out too. Before James carried the bad news back to Kennedy, however, his father began to ponder the idea. There was an impressive array of circumstances in Kennedy's favor. He was wealthy enough to entertain at the London embassy in the requisite grand manner. He could be depended upon to transmit candid, perceptive reports on the British situation. The bargaining abilities he had displayed at the Securities and Maritime commissions would enable Kennedy to promote the Anglo-American trade agreement that was up for negotiation. There was also the novelty of an Irishman at the Court of St. James's; this appealed to Roosevelt's weakness for the droll gesture and his Revolutionary War–vintage indignation over the imperiousness of British officials toward their American counterparts. Once when the chancellor of the exchequer addressed a communication to the secretary of the treasury, he eschewed Henry Morgenthau's formal title. The president emboldened Morgenthau to address his reply simply to "Mr. John Simon."

Not far from Roosevelt's consideration was another factor. He knew that American assistance to Great Britain in the event of a European conflict was a distinct possibility. Having Kennedy in London making the arrangements would help to overcome the resistance of the anti-British, isolationist Catholic population of the Northeast. "Father never dreamed that Joe might put ideology above loyalty," James Roosevelt remembered. "He felt that if a policy disagreement ever arose between them, he would simply shift Kennedy to another job. He knew by then that this was the way Joe worked." When the president tried out the idea on some of the people at the White House, he discovered more amusement than disapproval.

Kennedy would be offered the London post—but he would have to earn it. In the autumn of 1937 James Roosevelt ushered Kennedy into the Oval Room. His father greeted the maritime chairman and asked, "Joe, would you mind taking your pants down?" Kennedy asked the president if he had heard correctly. He had indeed. Loosening his suspenders, Kennedy sheepishly complied.

"Someone who saw you in a bathing suit once told me something I now know to be true. Joe, just look at your legs. You are just about the most bowlegged man I have ever seen. Don't you know that the ambassador to the Court of St. James's has to go through an induction ceremony in which he wears knee breeches and silk stockings? Can you imagine how you'll look? When photos of our new ambassador appear all over the world, we'll be a laughing stock. You're just not right for the job, Joe."

"Mr. President, if I can get the permission of His Majesty's government to wear a cutaway coat and striped pants to the ceremony, would you agree to appoint me?"

"Well, Joe, you know how the British are about tradition. There's no way you are going to get permission and I must name an Ambassador soon."

"Will you give me two weeks?"

Roosevelt consented. Kennedy returned a few days later bearing his official letter of permission, evidently arranged through friends in the British embassy in Washington. Now the president worried that the Foreign Office might object to the appointment on the grounds of Kennedy's religion. He sent James back to Marwood, where Kennedy was dining with Arthur Krock. After the president's son departed, Kennedy returned to the table and fumed, "You know what Jimmy proposed? That instead of going to London, I become Secretary of Commerce! Well, I'm not going to! FDR promised me London and I told Jimmy to tell his father that's the job—and the only one—I'll accept."

Eager for an exclusive story, Krock asked Kennedy if he could release the news of Kennedy's appointment. Kennedy advised him to gain clearance from the White House. Ambassador Bingham had been transferred to a Baltimore hospital and the announcement of Kennedy's succession would have to be delicate. After a week, according to Krock, he received approval from James Roosevelt to publish his scoop. When Krock's exclusive appeared on the front page of the *New York Times* on December 9, the president was irate. At a press conference, he added another episode to the feud with Krock by accusing him of hastening the death of Ambassador Bingham. Privately, Roosevelt accused Krock of settling an old score with the publisher who had once passed him over for editor of his Louisville newspaper.

Surprisingly, people in government and the press seemed more interested in the end of Kennedy's immediate influence on domestic affairs than in his new influence over American foreign policy. Tom Corcoran, whose friendship with Kennedy was strained lately by ideological differences, told Ickes he had done everything he could to get Kennedy out of Washington. Why did Kennedy want London so badly? Ickes asked. "You don't understand the Irish," replied Corcoran. "London has always been a closed door to him. As Ambassador of the United States, Kennedy will have all doors open to him."

The *New York Times* soberly reported one rumor that Franklin Roosevelt was sending Kennedy abroad to ease his plans to establish a dictatorship in Washington. In Kennedy's absence, radicals like Harry Hopkins and Corcoran would be in complete charge. Conservatives regretted that Kennedy would no longer be present to exert a restraining influence on the president. When James Byrnes presented this argument to Kennedy, the new ambassador replied, "If the premise were correct that I could exert all the influence that I am supposed to have, then I would have no feeling but to stay here and do everything I can, but you are as good a judge of that as anyone and you know that no individual possesses that much influence.

"To continue where I am is certainly a waste of whatever talents I possess because, with the five-man commission and the outline that we have made for the future, it is silly for me to sit around there and waste my time." Kennedy continued, "I haven't any idea how well I will get along abroad, either from the point of view of doing much for the country or doing a job of which my friends will feel proud, but if I don't get the results that I feel are necessary, I would get out at once. I will stick along with this Administration as long as I can do any good or as long as I have the confidence of the leaders, regardless of the inconveniences that accrue to me. I have never had political ambitions and have none now. . . . I will stay and help in whatever job I can do the most good. If I can't help, I can always go back to my private affairs and be quite happy."

On the day the story of Kennedy's appointment broke, Franklin Roosevelt was in a dark mood. His quiet resentment of Joseph Kennedy's

"New Worlds to Conquer," December 11, 1937.

BERRYMAN, *Washington*

demands and his displays of independence rose to the surface. As Henry Morgenthau recorded in his diary, the president said "he considered Kennedy a very dangerous man and that he was going to send him to England as Ambassador with the distinct understanding that the appointment was only good for six months and that, furthermore, by giving him this appointment, any obligation that he had to Kennedy was paid for." Roosevelt repeated that "Kennedy is too dangerous to have around here." He told Morgenthau that "from three independent sources, he had gotten the story that Floyd Odlum [a utilities executive] had offered Kennedy one million dollars to represent the utilities in Washington and that Kennedy had even gone so far as to split this million with certain parties, that he faced Kennedy with this story and that he absolutely denied it."

Morgenthau interjected, "Well, Mr. President, England is a most important post and there have been so many people over there talking against the New Deal. Don't you think you are taking considerable risks by sending Kennedy, who has talked so freely and so critically against your Administration?"

"I have made arrangements to have Joe Kennedy watched hourly—and the first time he opens his mouth and criticizes me, I will fire him."

At a dinner at Hyde Park Roosevelt was more buoyant. The company included the president's mother, the president and Mrs. Roosevelt, and Dorothy Schiff, the president's friend and publisher of the *New York Post*. Someone at the table—Mrs. Schiff thought it was Eleanor—complained about the appointment of "that awful Joe Kennedy" to London. The president, who had once deflected objections with the defense that he was setting a thief to catch a thief, now threw back his head and laughed. Appointing an Irishman to the Court of St. James's was "a great joke, the greatest joke in the world."

None of the other diners laughed.

Six

STRUGGLE OVER FOREIGN POLICY

THE PUBLIC ANNOUNCEMENT evoked consternation, bemusement, delight. Career men at the State Department lamented the advent of an amateur in the eye of the European storm; it was a typical Roosevelt gesture, they said. Boston Yankees were slightly startled to learn that an Irishman—and especially this Irishman—would head the embassy that was considered the nation's most prestigious post abroad. The Boston Irish, with inherited memories of Cromwell and the early years in America, exulted as they had once celebrated the news about P. A. Collins.

Some Britons scoffed at the announcement—in private. London newspapers emphasized Kennedy's intimacy with the American president and hailed "the highest compliment Roosevelt could pay to Great Britain." Sir Ronald Lindsay, the perceptive British ambassador in Washington, cabled the Foreign Office that many Americans regretted Kennedy's departure "because they regard him as the sole surviving counsellor of moderation to President Roosevelt." His sources predicted grave results "now that Mr. Roosevelt is left without any such controlling influence."

Rose Kennedy wrote the president, "The children and I feel deeply honored, delighted and thrilled and we want you to know that we do appreciate the fact that you have made possible this great rejoicing." Roosevelt assured her that sending Kennedy's nomination to the Senate "gave me a feeling of real pleasure." He received a telegram from the ambassador-to-be: "I want to say right now that I don't know what kind of a diplomat I shall be, probably rotten, but I promise to get done for you those things you want done."

Kennedy was clearly to be an unorthodox envoy. Shortly after his appointment, he met with the president and Cordell Hull at the White House to become better acquainted with the secretary of state. Not long before was the public revelation that Hugo Black, Roosevelt's latest Supreme Court nominee, had belonged to the Ku Klux Klan. Arthur Krock had been astonished over Black's failure to disclose this fact to the president, Kennedy related. "When Krock said that, what did you say to Krock?" Roosevelt prompted. "I said to him, 'If Marlene Dietrich asked you to make love to her, would you tell her you weren't much good at making love?" The president roared at this, but the courtly Tennessean was silent.

On February 18, 1938, in the Oval Room, Justice Stanley Reed administered Kennedy's oath of office with the president and a band of photographers in attendance. Four days later the new envoy met Roosevelt after Sunday church at Hyde Park for a farewell talk. There was "the usual light and cheerful banter and gossip. . . ." Kennedy remembered, "with the President warning me before lunch to flit lightly over the issue of knee breeches in case his mother would question me on my plans to abolish them." Roosevelt's little joke continued to hound Kennedy. "You'll be a knockout in knee breeches!" he assured him after a discussion of European affairs in the president's study. Asked later if he would don the traditional garb to present his credentials to the king, the diplomat protested, "Not Mrs. Kennedy's little boy!" Wearing knickers, he explained to Whitehall, would "ruin me at home." Still later, an American reporter asked if, as rumored, Kennedy forwent knee breeches for reasons of bowleggedness. Kennedy offered to demonstrate the contrary to her in private.

Before Kennedy left Hyde Park, Roosevelt took out a photograph of himself and wrote, "To my old friend and new ambassador." The president shook hands and said goodbye—"with every wish in the world"—and Kennedy drove to New York to make his ship to England.

John Bull's introduction to Joseph Kennedy captured the imagination of newspaper readers in Britain and America. "You can't expect me to develop into a statesman overnight," he cautioned London journalists, his feet atop the ambassadorial desk. The tabloids raved about "America's nine-child envoy." Kennedy made the rounds of official London, seeing Lady Astor, Lord Halifax, the new foreign secretary, and Neville Chamberlain, the prime minister, who held guarded but fervent hopes that Kennedy would persuade his government to support an appeasement policy toward Germany. Reading the articles and dispatches back in Washington, Franklin Roosevelt was surprised by the warmth of Kennedy's welcome.

"It's a quarter past nine on Tuesday morning and I am sitting in a bathrobe at the Embassy and am supposed to dress in about an hour to get ready to be drawn to the Palace in a carriage with white horses to present my credentials to the King," Kennedy wrote Senator Byrnes with unconcealed excitement. Kennedy boasted to Arthur Krock after the ceremony that the king had been "much more nervous than I was." He offered Krock his first impressions of British officials. Chamberlain: "tough guy and going to run the Cabinet, hopes he can get away with his plan and if he doesn't, feels there will be plenty of trouble." Halifax: "looks and acts like a Cardinal or Abraham Lincoln (without a beard)." The king: "acts to me like a fellow that was doing all he could to keep people loving 'the King.' "

At the instance of Felix Frankfurter, who reminded him that an earlier Bostonian, John Adams, had done the same in London, Kennedy arranged for sons Joe and Jack to spend terms as staff assistants in the embassy. An immersion in international politics would be an invaluable aid to the career in public affairs the father anticipated especially for the eldest son.

"The children are enjoying it tremendously and we all went to a ball last night given by Lady Astor for the King and Queen," Kennedy wrote his sister Loretta in Winthrop, Massachusetts. "You would have had a lot of fun watching your little brother having the first dance with the Duchess of Kent and the second with Queen Elizabeth, who, by the way, is one of the best dancers I have ever danced with."

During a weekend at Windsor Castle, the American ambassador was asked by Lady Halifax for his impressions of President Roosevelt. "If you want him in one word," Kennedy replied, "it is gallantry. The man is almost paralyzed, yet he ignores it. . . . I have seen him when he is determined to win an argument rise to his full height and, bearing his weight solely upon his arms braced aganst the desk, make the point to bring him victory. This always brings a lump to my throat, although I consider myself pretty hard-boiled." Dressing with his wife before dinner with the king and queen, the ambassador extraordinary and plenipotentiary to the Court of St. James's consigned his experience of London to a single famous sentence: "Well, Rose, it's a hell of a long way from East Boston!"

Forebodings lurked beneath Kennedy's gaiety. He reminded American correspondents that he only "temporarily" enjoyed the president's confidence; their reporting would "make or break" him as a diplomat.

With characteristic pessimism, he added, "I hope all you boys will be down to see me off when I am recalled." Kennedy took time away to write a long letter to James Roosevelt: "Well, old boy, I may not last long over here, but it's going to be fast and furious while it's on. My love to Missy and tell her the minute I get any scandal, I'll start a social column for her, and tell the Boss that, leaving aside the Kennedy family, there are two things I am for—the U.S.A. and F.D.R., and you can put this last paragraph on the last letter I write when I leave here."

Influence from London

The nation-state, wrote Plato, is the soul magnified. In the modern world, the same distinction between idealism and power politics that cleft the American tradition of public service has divided the American way of diplomacy. One ethos of foreign affairs was suggested by Wilson, of abstract principle enacted in a world arena through acts of national sacrifice. The opposing ethic was represented in the more toughminded sensibilities of Washington and Monroe, a diplomacy of bold realism and international partnerships in power. Like the cleavage in American politics, the division between the two diplomacies has been indistinct and founded more in attitude than ideology. The same opposing visions of ends and means that separated Franklin Roosevelt and Joseph Kennedy in domestic affairs shaped each man's judgment of the issues crystallizing in Europe.

Kennedy reached London at a critical hour. Austria had been absorbed by Hitler's Germany in keeping with the Führer's blueprint for a new *Gross-Deutschland.* The next target was Czechoslovakia. For years Hitler had exhorted the rump state's minority of three million Sudeten Germans to demand greater autonomy from Prague. Fearful that Britain was unprepared to fight, hopeful that Germany's goals were isolated demands rather than insatiate expansionism, sneakingly optimistic that Washington could be induced to lend aid, Neville Chamberlain promoted appeasement.

Roosevelt kept his own counsel. Confined by neutrality legislation and militant American opinion against entanglements but suspecting that dictator nations must ultimately be faced down, he walked a diplomatic path that was tortuously ambiguous. International offenses by Germany evoked presidential protests and little more. To some in the inner circle, Roosevelt admitted that the European picture looked dark and that American involvement in some form was a distinct possibility. But to

Kennedy during their farewell talk at Hyde Park (as Kennedy remembered it), the president predicted the day when he would call the diplomatic corps to the White House to propose a world economic and political structure based on "fundamental rules" of international conduct. "Joe, I still have not lost heart. If Chamberlain succeeds in pacifying the dictators, the time may soon come when my plan can be put into effect." He added a warning: "Be careful about one thing, Joe. Don't forget that this country is determined to be neutral in event of any war. . . . We shall have to mark time until we see whether or not Chamberlain accomplishes anything." Roosevelt was intent on sustaining his delicate balance until the last possible moment.

Sending Kennedy to London was a risky, jarring note in this symphony of caution. The new ambassador had traveled to Europe on business, studied its economy in 1935, and settled international maritime disputes, but these episodes offered meager schooling in statecraft. The president knew that Kennedy would never be content as mere figurehead or messenger; he had been correct about the treasury—Kennedy would have run things in his own way. But he would operate no less independently at the embassy on Grosvenor Square.

Kennedy perceived the sharpening international differences in Europe more as economic imbalances than political disputes: "An unemployed man with a hungry family is the same fellow whether the swastika or some other flag floats over his head." His attitude toward diplomacy was essentially the same as his view of domestic affairs, but on a larger scale. In domestic policy, Kennedy's preeminent goal had been to prevent another market crash that would lead to national chaos and bankruptcy and threaten the security of his family. In foreign policy, his principal goal was to prevent another war that would lead to world chaos and bankruptcy and threaten the security of his family. As early as 1935 Kennedy told a friend, "I have four boys and I don't want them to be killed in a foreign war."

Although his views were more emotional and personal than those of most opponents of intervention, they thrust Joseph Kennedy into the mainstream of American isolationism. The new ambassador kept a finger in the air of national opinion by asking managers of the New England theaters he owned to circulate through the audiences, asking questions about public affairs; the managers reported almost unanimous opposition to an activist international policy. "The more I see of things here, the more convinced I am that we must exert all of our intelligence and effort toward keeping clear of any involvement," he wrote to the isolationist senator from Idaho, William Borah. "As long as I hold my present job, I shall never lose sight of this guiding principle." At the outset, therefore, Kennedy's purposes were opposite to those of his patron in the White House. Roosevelt was striving for freedom of action by keeping the reins of diplomacy in his hands. Kennedy was striving to influence the president, the Congress, and his countrymen to bar from American foreign policy the alternative of war.

Roosevelt and Hull initially assigned Kennedy a series of well-defined diplomatic tasks—to negotiate the British-American trade treaty, to settle a dispute over some Pacific islands, to relay messages in the difficult dialogue between Britain and Ireland. The president was delighted by Kennedy's democratic act of ending the custom of presenting American debutantes at court. "When do you expect to announce your candidacy for the presidential nomination?" wrote Senator Byrnes. "Whatever doubts we may have had about your intentions in the past have been removed by this political stunt of turning down requests for an opportunity to bow for the King."

Kennedy worked tirelessly to convince the British to sign a trade agreement with the United States. The prime minister was unenthusiastic, but the concept of free trade as the safeguard of world harmony was dear to both Kennedy and Secretary Hull. The American ambassador waxed eloquent one evening before a group of London bankers when the report arrived of a speech Roosevelt had delivered in Georgia. The president had implied that there was not a great deal of difference between feudal and fascist economies, an argument not designed to convince British financiers of America's kindly intentions. Piqued, Kennedy complained to Hull by telephone that Roosevelt had almost queered the treaty: "Who was responsible for that Gainesville speech? Whoever was ought to be horsewhipped!" The president would probably be "mad as hell" at him for "butting in from London," Kennedy added, but he felt it his duty to pass along the views of British finance. The State Department and Foreign Office finally signed an agreement, but it was negotiated essentially on British terms.

Kennedy found a warm friend in Chamberlain. He shared the prime minister's dread of war and communism, and saw appeasement as a step toward solving the economic problems that both men believed threatened the core of European security. He could "talk Chamberlain's language," as Kennedy told Hull. "He too was a businessman," Kennedy later wrote of the British leader. "He was hard, as befitted a man who had been teethed by six years of a vain effort to grow sisal in the Bahamas and who later had made a success of two struggling enterprises in Birmingham. But he was not narrow, and could see the advantages to business in fair and generous dealings." Both Kennedy and Chamberlain interpreted Hitler's eastward expansionism as a bid mainly for resources and markets. "I'm just like that with Chamberlain," the ambassador soon was able to say. "Why, Franklin himself isn't as confidential with me."

Kennedy bade the president support Chamberlain's policy: "The time is going to come, after Chamberlain has made the political offers necessary, for you to make a worldwide gesture and base it completely on an economic standard." He reported that the British were unwilling to fight and that they believed America would be "very foolish" to mix in Europe's affairs. "All they are interested in is to have the United States stay prosperous and build a strong Navy."

In April 1938 the Chamberlain government, in a pact with Italy, recognized Mussolini's domination of Ethiopia. Kennedy submitted a draft of a presidential statement supporting the agreement. Roosevelt read Kennedy's draft and observed that the police chief who dealt with gansters would remain heroic only so long as the gangsters failed to attack, but he issued a statement drawn almost verbatim from Kennedy's submission.

Complaining that the State Department leaked confidential reports and blocked action, Kennedy increasingly went over Secretary Hull's head to appeal directly to the president. He cabled a vehement protest on hearing that Roosevelt contemplated lifting the arms embargo against Spain. Revision would have aided the Spanish loyalists; it aroused a torrent of objections from American Catholics. There is no evidence that Kennedy's plaints carried especial weight in the president's decision not to revise, but the illusion of influence was enough to quicken the tempers of his adversaries. Harold Ickes thought he detected Kennedy's "malevolent" hand in Roosevelt's decision.

As the trees blossomed along the Thames, Kennedy worried that the Czech question would culminate in a shooting war. He resorted to another method of personal diplomacy that was bolder and more perilous. Hoping that better relations between America and Germany might help to prevent a European conflict, Kennedy began meeting quietly with the German ambassador to London, Herbert von Dirksen. According to von Dirksen's cables to Berlin, Kennedy said that President Roosevelt was poorly advised on Germany, partly because of the influence of Jewish leaders in journalism and government. Some of Kennedy's reported remarks amounted to acceptance of the German policy toward the Jews;

these could be only partially explained by von Dirksen's exaggerations and Kennedy's tactic of feigning agreement with those he hoped to convince. Other of Kennedy's comments may have convinced the German envoy that Chamberlain was eager for a German settlement, an impression which may have strengthened Hitler's intransigence. Although Kennedy promised von Dirksen that he would relate their conversations when he saw the president in June, he was evidently acting on no authority but his own.

The American ambassador cut a prominent figure in London, his popularity no doubt augmented by British hopes of American cooperation in international affairs. Kennedy visited Lord and Lady Astor at their country home at Cliveden. Claud Cockburn, publisher of the left-leaning British newsletter, *The Week*, gave the Astors' weekend company a name that caught on in the British and American press—the "Cliveden Set." According to legend, Cliveden was the site of secret intrigues to keep Britain out of war, a "second Foreign Office" where the talk turned horrifyingly pro-German. This was a misnomer, but Kennedy's occasional attendance was enough to irk critics at home. Kennedy wrote Drew Pearson after one item appeared in Pearson's column with Robert Allen, "I know you and Bob don't want to hurt me unless you have definite reasons, but your story on the Cliveden Set is complete bunk. There is not a single word of truth in it and it has done me great harm."

He did not relax his efforts to court the American press—if at a distance. Walter Lippmann, Arthur Sulzberger, and Henry and Clare Luce were entertained royally when they came through London. Kennedy skirted official procedure to arrange exclusive interviews with British officials for American reporters. He wrote Arthur Krock, "I certainly have the most interesting story that has come out of here for many years," and noted that "it would be a very helpful thing if agitation could be started to have me address the Senate and House Foreign Relations Committees." Walter Lippmann wrote Kennedy that he would be amused to hear that newspapermen were trying to find someone who visited the White House in the role of "another Joseph P. Kennedy."

Also keeping his name and deeds in the minds of influential Americans was an extraordinary series of letters. Emblazoned "Private and Confidential," Kennedy's missives were almost identical in content, although individually typed and usually appended with a handwritten postscript from the ambassador. William Randolph Hearst, Walter Lippmann, Arthur Krock, James Byrnes, Frank Kent, Drew Pearson, Jay Pierrepont Moffat of the State Department, and Bernard Baruch were among the many names in press and government that comprised the mailing list. The letters offered a running commentary on Kennedy's doings in London and his current thinking on international issues. A few of the recipients believed Kennedy's intention was to boom himself for president in 1940.

"The march of events in Austria made my first few days here more exciting than they might otherwise have been," began the first letter, sent March 21, 1938, "but I am still unable to see that the Central European developments affect our country or my job. . . . If and when a general European war breaks out, our people will review the situation and will decide that things are serious enough to face, but not before, as I see it. Therefore, I have been to no great pains thus far in reporting to the State Department the various bits of information which have come my way, because they don't mean anything as far as we are concerned."

March 28: "I wish our fellows at home would attend to the worries they have on their own doorsteps and keep Europe out of their minds until they have made some headway in their own country. . . . The German-Czech situation will solve itself without interference from France or Russia, it appears from here. As long as Great Britain will not give unconditional promises to back them up in a fight, the French will not do anything to stop the German domination of Czechoslovakia and the Czechs in power know that. The Russians are too disorganized and too far away. So where is your war?"

April 14: "The Anglo-Italian agreement, the terms of which you will doubtless know by the time you get this, is the high point in Mr. Chamberlain's foreign policy thus far. . . . The Italians apparently realize that the Germans are essentially competitors and not allies and that Mussolini and Hitler cannot live long under the same tent. . . . Whether it is averting or merely deferring war, I don't believe we or they can tell at this moment. All I can say is that no immediate war is in sight."

May 3: "The atmosphere here has changed decidedly since Germany took over Austria some seven weeks ago. That gave the British public a severe jolt and the British government a renewed sense of the importance of the time element. I get the feeling that the British military and diplomatic engine has now been put from second into high—it is jerking somewhat and some cylinders are definitely missing fire, but the speedometer begins to register an increase."

May 17: "Henlein's surprise visit was the chief topic of interest this week. . . . The Sudeten German leader left the impression that he and his lieutenants, if not their followers, have learned a good deal by watching the progress of events in Austria since the Anschluss. They have now decided that they would be much better off if they were in control of a practically autonomous portion of Czechoslovakia than they would be if they were swallowed up in the Greater Reich. . . . All usual indices on the economic side here continue to point downward."

May 31: "The momentary lull in Central Europe has not caused anyone here to think that the Czechoslovak business is settled. . . . The hard part lies ahead, of course, and the Foreign Office takes only what comfort it legitimately can from the fact that things had gone along thus far without greater friction. . . . We seem to be living through one crisis after another these days. . . . There is a certain fatalism in their attitude. . . ."

Downcast over Czechoslovakia, Kennedy began to ponder the outcome. As antidote for the upheaval suggested by the crash of 1929 and the recession of 1937, he had prescribed a system of national planning. Now Kennedy contemplated what course America should take if the European crisis resulted in the bleakest consequences. In the event of a totalitarian Europe, he concluded, the United States should make itself an armed fortress in which power would be even more centralized in Washington; some democratic ideals might have to be laid aside to ensure American survival in a hostile world.

In a gloomy frame of mind, Kennedy sailed for America in June. The State Department had granted him home leave to attend the Harvard commencement of his eldest son. Newspapers reported that the ambassador would receive an honorary degree at the ceremony, but when the Harvard committee considered the possibility, it ruled that an ambassadorship was insufficient evidence of distinction. Kennedy saved face by publicly "declining" the honor, but he was wounded by the rebuff.

Like a hummingbird in flight, Joseph Kennedy had darted about the British capital through the spring of 1938, winning over government officers and financiers; gathering support for his foreign policy views; gauging the possibility of a campaign for the White House. But, unwittingly or not, the hummingbird fluttered under a glass dome, and above the dome loomed the omniscient eyes of Franklin Roosevelt. For months the president had known of the gossip that Kennedy was indulging himself in the same denunciations of the president in London that he had in Washington. Kennedy's rivals cautioned Roosevelt that his ambassador was keeping the pot boiling for his own presidential candidacy in 1940; they hoped to stimulate the quarrel that would once and for all end Kennedy's influence at the White House. Conservative allies also hoped that Kennedy would break with the president and join other Roosevelt exiles such as Raymond Moley and Hugh Johnson in the opposition to the New Deal.

Fully conscious of the plots and counterplots, Roosevelt was all the less inclined to alienate Kennedy. Despite their annoyance to him, he had long ago learned to discount Kennedy's dinner-party railleries. The president occasionally expressed irritation over his ambassador's proximity to Chamberlain, but recognized that this access enabled him to submit reports that even the career men at State considered excellent. The members of Roosevelt's secretariat were confident that there would be no showdown between the president and his ambassador—until Arthur Krock bound up Kennedy's "Private and Confidential" messages and sent them to Franklin Roosevelt.

Kennedy for President

There was speculation in the capital all spring that Joseph Kennedy aspired to the White House. John O'Donnell and Doris Fleeson of the *New York Daily News,* both friends of the ambassador, interpreted Kennedy's appointment to London as evidence that he was "the Crown Prince of the Roosevelt regime—F.D.R.'s personal selection as his successor." Harlan Miller of the *Washington Post* acknowledged that Kennedy had "an excellent chance to be the first Catholic President" and added the intriguing assertion that "he has the nearest to a Rooseveltian personality among the viziers." A *Boston Post* editorial noted that Kennedy—"the left-wing New Dealers to the contrary"—was one of the ablest men in America. His only drawback? "He is too regular to be a politician. His expressed insight into human nature would probably cause a riot on the stump. But this country will either select a next President of the Kennedy type—or it will wish it had."

"Will Kennedy Run for President?" inquired a *Liberty* magazine piece in May 1938. The article might have been dismissed but for the prominence of its author, Ernest Lindley. "Professional political handicappers will give heavy odds against him at this stage. But a few connoisseurs of Presidential material are willing to make long-shot bets that the next Democratic nominee for President will be Joseph Patrick Kennedy." His assets: "brains, personality, driving power and the habit of success." Kennedy was also popular with businessmen. "In 1940, both the Democratic politicians and the country at large may demand a man who can make business and progressive reform pull together toward sound prosperity." Lindley continued, "European capitals have seen American diplomats who were picturesque in language or habits. Joe Kennedy isn't. He has an athlete's figure, a clean-cut head, sandy hair, clear straight-shooting eyes, a flashingly infectious smile and faultless taste in dress." The ambassador who attacked jobs "with the speed and untiring efficiency of a dynamo" was a presidential prospect "looming arrestingly large on the horizon." Later Lindley recalled, "I think Kennedy wanted to be President, but I never felt that was his greatest ambition. His ambition was always for his kids."

"Somebody is doing one of the best recorded publicity jobs for the Honorable Joseph P. Kennedy," observed Hugh Johnson, who would have known. Harold Ickes noted a Washington rumor that Kennedy and Arthur Krock had made an agreement to advance each other's ambitions. The columnist aspired to be managing editor of the *New York Times*. "Krock is doing all that he can to boost Kennedy and Kennedy is ready to support Krock financially for this New York Times job." Ickes thought there was "no doubt" that Kennedy was spending a great deal of money to further his own ambitions. "Neither is there any doubt that he is making a good deal of headway in conservative quarters." Support was lent to the rumor when *Times* publisher Arthur Sulzberger visited the London embassy in May and Kennedy requested him to grant the editor's post to Krock. Krock confirmed years later that Kennedy "actively promoted" his own presidential aspirations in 1938.

The *Ladies Home Journal* commissioned C. L. Sulzberger that spring to write an article on the new ambassador to Great Britain. As the journalist remembered, Kennedy "greeted me warmly and placed his staff at my disposal, requesting only that I show him my piece in advance so he might correct factual errors." In an interview, Kennedy "confessed" to Sulzberger, "I never thought about an ambassadorship and this offer came as a complete surprise." Kennedy had indeed heard the suggestions that he run for president but would not because he loved his family too much. "I've never given the Presidency a serious thought." Sulzberger was unconvinced by these protestations and suggested that the ambassador had accorded the White House something more than serious thought. When Kennedy saw the article, he demanded revision. Sulzberger refused. "The publisher of that magazine is a close friend of mine," Kennedy warned, "I'll see to it that your piece is never printed." The article was published, but Sulzberger found it so incredibly changed that "it almost seemed as if the Ambassador had written it himself."

Another who was unpersuaded by Kennedy's denials was the president. He learned that Kennedy had hired Krock's State Department correspondent, Harold Hinton, to join his London staff, undertaking some duties that were tantamount to those of a public relations agent. The ambassador supplemented Hinton's salary from his personal funds. Roosevelt doubted that any Catholic could win the presidency in 1940 and knew that Kennedy's chances were slight at best—a May public opinion poll ranked Kennedy at fifth place among potential Democratic nominees were Roosevelt not a candidate. Yet the president detected the mildest hint of a presidential bee in a New Dealer's bonnet: like Kennedy, Jim Farley was discovering a distinct coolness at the White House.

"There were many reasons that militated against my candidacy for that office, including my Catholic faith, but even these might be overcome," Kennedy later acknowledged. "But I knew that the time was not propitious. For many years, Mr. Roosevelt had been my chief; he still was. I wanted no such false issue to arise between us and endanger both an official relationship of some importance and a personal association which to me had been heavy with meaning."

On June 20 he sailed into New York Harbor aboard the *Queen Mary*. James Roosevelt rode out on a cutter with a group of newspapermen to welcome his friend home; he took Kennedy aside to warn him that reporters were curious about his rumored presidential ambitions. The ambassador had better have a statement ready. "I enlisted under President Roosevelt in 1932 to do whatever he wanted me to do," Kennedy told a press conference. "There are many problems at home and abroad and I happen to be busy at one abroad just now. If I had my eye on another job, it would be a complete breach of faith with President Roosevelt." Afterwards, James listened to Kennedy's dour appraisal of the months ahead. "He was worried that fascism might very well sweep the world and that we would have to prepare ourselves."

The next day, Kennedy talked with the president at Hyde Park. Roosevelt asked him to give Chamberlain a message that was studiedly vague: when the time came that Chamberlain had difficulty keeping the peace, the president would be glad to place the moral power of his office on the side of peace. Roosevelt repeated for reporters one of Kennedy's best comments: he had met the same kind of people in London that he used to meet in America, who wailed about how the world was coming to an end and that they would have to sell their Rolls-Royces. The only difference? In Britain, they did not blame it on their government—"which I think is a grand line, a brilliant line." Did Kennedy seem hopeful about Europe? Roosevelt gave no answer.

Meanwhile, Stephen Early telephoned the *Chicago Tribune*'s Walter

Trohan. The reporter was a bit surprised by the invitation to see the presidential press secretary, for his newspaper was one of the most outspoken opponents of the New Deal. "You're a good friend of Joe Kennedy's, aren't you?" Early asked. Trohan assented. "Would you write a critical story if we give you the facts?"

"I'd write a story against any New Dealer," replied Colonel McCormick's man, "and I haven't hesitated to aim higher, as you know."

Early laughed. "The Boss thought you would. Here it is. Joe wants to run for President and is dealing behind the Boss's back at the London Embassy. . . ." He unveiled the "Private and Confidential" letters. Trohan rushed off to write up his scoop.

KENNEDY'S 1940 AMBITIONS OPEN ROOSEVELT RIFT, trumpeted the *Tribune*'s page-one headline. "The chilling shadow of 1940 has fallen across the friendship of President Roosevelt and his two-fisted troubleshooter, Joseph Patrick Kennedy, United States Ambassador to Great Britain." Trohan had learned from "unimpeachable sources" that Kennedy and Roosevelt had met in a "frigid atmosphere" at Hyde Park. The reason? "Mr. Roosevelt has received positive evidence that Kennedy hopes to use the Court of St. James's as a stepping stone to the White House in 1940." Trohan cited the confidential letters, adding that "Kennedy has besought a prominent Washington correspondent to direct his Presidential boom from London." Kennedy's stirrings were "particularly irksome" to the White House because his name was being mentioned more frequently than any other for 1940. Presidential intimates "who once heralded Kennedy as the only representative of big business to see eye to eye with the Administration" were now calling him "the soul of selfishness" in language "crisp with oaths." Trohan included a quote from Early, disguised as a "high Administration official": "Joe Kennedy never did anything without thinking of Joe Kennedy."

The ironic aspect of Early's treachery was that the dagger had been provided by Arthur Krock. Krock had no inkling that the confidential letters were anything more significant than incisive reportage; he had forwarded them intending to boost Kennedy's stock at the White House. Kennedy's ruinous mistake—could it have been intentional?—was that he had omitted the president from his mailing list.

The ambassador took Saturday dinner at the White House a few days after the *Tribune* article appeared, but only afterwards did someone tell Kennedy who had actually leaked the story. "It was a true Irish anger that swept over me." He tried to get back to the president, but the president was unavailable. He caught up with Cordell Hull and offered his resignation. Hull refused it: his own treatment by Roosevelt was twenty times worse than Kennedy's. "An angry interview with Early brought a half-hearted denial and a further interview with the President, with whom it was not my habit to mince words, but he denied that he had anything to do with it," Kennedy remembered. "In this way, he assuaged my feelings . . . but deep within me, I knew that something had happened."

The president told Harold and Jane Ickes over lunch that he did not expect Kennedy to last more than a few years in London. Kennedy was the kind of man who liked to go from one job to another and then drop it just when the going got heavy. Although he cried "wolf," Roosevelt said, Kennedy was having "the time of his life" in London. Ickes mentioned seeing the newspaper story on Kennedy's declination of the Harvard degree. The president laughed mordantly: "Can you imagine Joe Kennedy declining a honorary degree from Harvard?"

Mrs. Ickes reminded Roosevelt that she and her husband had seen Kennedy on a London visit in May. How should the Duke and Duchess of Kent be addressed? she had asked. "When I am alone with them, I call them George and Marina," the ambassador replied, "but when in public, I address them as Your Highness." The president was delighted by this story: "Joe must like Marina pretty well because he was very insistent that she and the Duke of Kent be invited officially to the New York exposition."

Roosevelt related an astonishing exchange. Kennedy had remonstrated with him for criticizing fascism in his speeches. It was all right to attack Nazism—but not fascism. Why? Kennedy had said that he frankly thought we would have to "come to some form of fascism here." While Ickes and his wife digested this item, the president went on, "Joe Kennedy, if he were in power, would give us a fascist form of government. He would organize a small powerful committee under himself as chairman and this committee would run the country without much reference to Congress."

He later asked Ickes if he knew of the "cell" meeting at Cissy Patterson's house that was "backing Joe Kennedy for President." Mrs. Patterson, the conservative and sardonic publisher of the *Washington Times-Herald,* held one of the capital's best-known salons. The members of her circle seemed so isolationist to Roosevelt that he privately compared it to Cliveden and castigated the "Dover House set." Ickes said he had not heard of Mrs. Patterson's conspiracy, but he did not neglect the opportunity to remind the president that Arthur Krock was working hard to advance Kennedy's ambitions. Roosevelt dismissed "the idea that Joe Kennedy could be elected President" as "absurd."

The Path to Munich

Before returning to London, Kennedy acceded to John D. Rockefeller, Jr.'s request that he visit with one of the Rockefeller sons who was interested in public life. ("Nelson will, I know, be only too glad to meet any appointment day or night that will be convenient for you, and will count it a privilege to have the opportunity of a talk with you.")

He also undertook a chore he had promised the president. United States Steel was planning a wage cut that, Roosevelt feared, would deal a blow to the sluggish economy. To see if he could forestall the action, Kennedy contacted Thomas Lamont, Morgan banker for a number of major manufacturing interests. The ambassador suggested that if the company postponed the cuts for at least ninety days, U.S. Steel might receive more favorable consideration when it next applied for government contracts. Lamont refused: such a deal would be unfair and morally wrong. What was business to do with an administration that purveyed such ideas?

"Tom, you are a respectable man," Kennedy replied. "You can't understand these people. But you've got to. . . . I'm just telling you what you can expect if you hold off these wage cuts and follow my suggestion. But, forgetting the deal, my suggestion has greater value and some moral quality. Your statement will put the President in two holes. One, if business doesn't improve and you put on the wage cuts, there will be proof that the pump-priming has failed to work. Two, if you wait ninety days to see, he cannot again accuse business of failure to cooperate." After conferring with executives from U.S. Steel, Lamont again refused the arrangement, but management finally decided to forgo the wage cut without any quid pro quo from Washington.

A sensational magazine piece was published at the end of June. "Jimmy's Got It," by Alva Johnson, claimed that James Roosevelt had been involved in all manner of questionable business dealings, including helping Joseph Kennedy to make a killing in Scotch whiskey: "Jimmy has helped Kennedy to reach the two great positions he now holds—that of Ambassador to London and that of premier Scotch-whiskey salesman in America."

Kennedy brushed off the story while boarding the *Normandie*. "I'll admit I am the American Ambassador, but I'll deny I'm the premier Scotch salesman," he told reporters, adding, "I suffered by knowing

James Roosevelt. If the rest of the *Saturday Evening Post* article is no truer than the part about my connection with James Roosevelt, it's all a lie."

The exposure to Franklin Roosevelt's optimism had apparently improved his morale. "Kennedy has come back with the most roseate accounts of the change in American opinion in our favor and of the President's desire to do anything to help," Neville Chamberlain noted in his journal. When Kennedy saw Ambassador von Dirksen, he told the German that he had relayed the substance of their talks to Roosevelt. The president was thinking "calmly and moderately" about Europe, he reported, but if peace efforts failed, America would probably enter on the side of Great Britain.

Kennedy's roseate mood did not last. By August, Hitler was ready to plunge Europe into war by marching on Czechoslovakia. Kennedy struggled to keep the British on the road of appeasement. "He believes it his business in the first place to throw his whole weight into an effort to insure peace," an American correspondent reported from London. "Beyond that, he is anxious to get the dictators and the democracies together to work out ways and means to avert the economic disaster for which, in his belief, the world is now coasting straight and fast. . . . He says he is scared and I can believe that, for he frightened me."

In Washington the president carefully positioned himself between encouraging the British to resist German aggression and cautioning them that they must not depend on the United States. In London Joseph Kennedy worked on British officialdom to keep out of the war. Franklin Roosevelt evidently decided that he could do only one of two things—manage his London ambassador or cope with the hourly changes in Europe. During the fateful weeks of August and September 1938, the president worked to maintain the precarious balance in American diplomacy yet allowed Kennedy to work his own will under little more restraint than occasional reprimands from Secretary Hull.

In late August Kennedy asked the State Department for clearance on a speech; it included the observation, "Perhaps I am not well informed of the terrifically vital forces underlying all this unrest in the world, but for the life of me, I cannot see anything involved which would be remotely considered worth shedding blood for." When Roosevelt saw this, he parodied Kennedy's utterance as "I can't for the life of me understand why anyone would want to go to war to save the Czechs." He muttered to Henry Morgenthau, "The young man needs his wrists slapped rather hard." But the president merely asked Hull to cable Kennedy to omit the offending language.

The ambassador granted an exclusive interview to the Hearst press advising Americans "not to lose our heads." Again Roosevelt turned to Hull. "Frankly, I think that Joe Kennedy's attention should be called to this. . . . If all of our fifty-five or sixty Ambassadors and Ministers were to send exclusive stories to specially chosen newspapers in the United States, your Department might just as well close shop." He also applied soothing syrup, writing Kennedy in late August, "I know what difficult days you are going through and I can assure you that it is not *much* easier at this end!"

"Who would have thought that the English could take into camp a red-headed Irishman?" the president asked Morgenthau. But the only admonition he would give Kennedy came indirectly, through newspaper columnists known to be close to the White House. Joseph Alsop and Robert Kintner reported on the highest authority that Kennedy had become a prize exhibit at Cliveden, that he saw Chamberlain as a very great man, and loved every instant of his London life. "While Kennedy is loved in London, he is no longer popular at the White House. The President knows of his private talk, resents it and rebukes it when he can." After reading this piece, Arthur Krock confronted Alsop and demanded, "What do you mean by telling lies about Joe Kennedy?"

On September 12 Europe was jolted toward war. When Hitler demanded "justice" for the Sudetenland in the ominous speech at Nuremberg, London went into a frenzy. As Chamberlain met with cabinet members, the American ambassador circulated between his embassy, the Foreign Office, and Ten Downing Street. Central to the British debate over resistance or appeasement was a single question: What would America do? Earlier, Kennedy had warned Lord Halifax that the United States would probably maintain its neutrality. When Roosevelt discovered this, he suspected his ambassador was trying to force his hand "in his process of playing the Chamberlain game." Another reproof was sent by Hull: Kennedy should not injure the effect of careful Washington statements with his own diplomacy. The president had authorized Kennedy to tell Chamberlain that America would abide by Chamberlain's decision but, after Hitler's Nuremberg address, Roosevelt asked the British ambassador in Washington to the White House. Sir Ronald Lindsay afterward cabled home his impression that a compromise with Berlin would disappoint the president.

On the fifteenth, the Führer received the British prime minister at Berchtesgaden. Chamberlain agreed in principle to national self-determination and in fact to turn the Sudetenland over to Germany. The president called Ambassador Lindsay back to the White House for another ambiguous message. He said he understood the difficulties Britain faced and would be the first to cheer if negotiations succeeded, but he could not countenance a sell-out of Czechoslovakia. Still, neither could he publicly endorse resistance because that would only encourage the Czechs to fight and be crushed. He doubted that American troops could be sent overseas unless Britain were actually invaded, although he might be able to circumvent the neutrality laws if there were no war declaration.

Kennedy generally observed Hull's pleas for discretion until, on September 21, he executed a dramatic ploy of his own. He summoned Charles Lindbergh to London. The two men had been introduced at the home of the Astors in May and taken an instant liking to each other. "He is not the usual type of politician or diplomat," the aviator had observed. "His views on the European situation seem intelligent and interesting." Mrs. Lindbergh had found that her husband so enjoyed talking to the ambassador that she could barely pull him away. She too liked Kennedy and saw in him "an Irish terrier wagging his tail (a *very* nice Irish terrier)." After visiting German airfields and installations, Lindbergh had concluded that the *Luftwaffe* was the strongest in the world and would be well nigh unassailable in a war of the skies with the Western democracies. Now Kennedy asked him to submit these views in a letter that he would transmit to Washington and Whitehall. He also arranged a meeting between Lindbergh and an official of the British air ministry to warn of the grave consequences of an air war with Germany.

Neville Chamberlain required little cautioning, for the prospects looked darker than ever. Heady with the triumph of Berchtesgaden, Hitler reneged on his agreements and announced he would occupy the Sudetenland, setting an ultimatum with a deadline of October 1. Fighting Germany would be like "a man attacking a tiger before he has loaded his gun," Chamberlain told his cabinet. Once again he flew to see Hitler, this time at Godesberg. The meeting ended grimly. Rose Kennedy wrote in her diary that everyone in London was "unutterably shocked and depressed." Her husband wrote to Arthur Krock, "I'm feeling very blue myself today because I am starting to think about sending Rose and the children back to America and stay here *alone* for how long God only knows. Maybe never see them again. . . ."

Franklin Roosevelt tried to break the deadlock with a last, direct appeal to European leaders. ("It can't do any harm," he told Hull.) He asked the chiefs of state not to break off negotiations. "As long as negotiations continue, differences may be reconciled. Once they are broken off, reason is banished and force asserts itself." The leaders of Great Britain, France, and Czechoslovakia responded favorably, but Hitler refused. The president sent another message to the Führer suggesting a conference of the nations concerned with the Czech problem. Roosevelt would bid for a settlement, but he would not upset the American policy of balance; he vetoed the Czech president's request that the United States ask Britain and France to stand by Czechoslovakia. He also vetoed Kennedy's request that Chamberlain be allowed to broadcast a message directly to the American people. On the twenty-eighth, Charles Lindbergh arrived at the American embassy in London for gas masks. Kennedy bustled into the room: "You may not need them. There's some good news coming in."

Hitler had agreed to see Chamberlain for a third time. The president telegraphed a terse congratulation to the prime minister: GOOD MAN. Kennedy was joyful. "The President can feel that God was on his side and he was on God's side," he cabled Washington, adding, "It may be that England will thank Chamberlain, but certainly their second choice will be the President. . . ." As Chamberlain boarded the plane for Munich, the ambassador told Halifax that he was entirely sympathetic to everything the prime minister had done.

On the final day of September 1938, after an exhausting thirteen hours of bargaining with Hitler, Chamberlain returned with his Anglo-German agreement and his hopes for "peace in our time." Joseph Kennedy navigated through a mass of people—they were cheering, laughing, waving, running alongside automobiles—to the American embassy. He entered with a triumphant grin: "Well, boys, the war is off." Kennedy soon received a cable from the President for delivery to Chamberlain: "I fully share your hope and belief that there exists today the greatest opportunity in years for the establishment of a new order based on justice and on law."

"Instead of handing the cable to Chamberlain as is customary, I read it to him," Kennedy said in later years. But his recollection was subject to the revisionism of time. Still attempting to maintain his autonomy unhampered by embarrassing statements that might later be wielded against him, Franklin Roosevelt directed that even this carefully worded message be presented orally to the prime minister.

After Chamberlain's return, Joseph Kennedy encountered Jan Masaryk. "Isn't it wonderful?" the Czech minister to London remembered the American say. "Now I can get to Palm Beach after all!"

Brickbats Over the Atlantic

"I have just gone through the most exciting month of my life," the ambassador wrote to an American friend. "Between trying to keep up my contacts so we would know what really was going on before it actually happened so that we would not be caught unprepared and contemplating the possibility of the bombing of London with eight children as prospective victims, well, it is just a great page in my life's history."

Three weeks after Munich, Joseph Kennedy was invited to speak to the annual Trafalgar Day dinner of the Navy League in London. No American ambassador had ever before been asked to address the hallowed group. Kennedy carefully polished his address and cleared it with the State Department. "It has long been a theory of mine that it is unproductive for both the democratic and dictator countries to widen the division now existing between them by emphasizing their differences, which are now self-apparent," he told the audience. It was true that democracies and dictatorships had fundamental differences in outlook. "But there is simply no sense, common or otherwise, in letting these differences grow into unrelenting antagonisms. After all, we have to live together in the same world whether we like it or not."

The declaration sparked a firestorm. Chancelleries around the world perceived in Kennedy's words a sharp turnabout in American diplomacy. The proposal directly contradicted Franklin Roosevelt's view, delivered a year earlier in an electrifying address at Chicago, that a quarantine should be imposed upon the bandit nations. The American ambassador seemed to have resolved the ambiguity in international policy that the president had so painstakingly maintained. Telegrams flooded the White House, State Department, Foreign Office, and newspaper offices asking whether American policy had been changed. Heywood Broun, the columnist who was at Harvard with Kennedy, suggested dropping his classmate in Boston Harbor "so that his Americanism might be restored by resting a while among the alien tea." Others whispered that Kennedy favored the fascists and doted on dictators; political adversaries delivered every morsel to the Oval Room. Arthur Krock reminded his readers of "the difficulty faced these days by a government with an idealistic foreign policy that cannot be applied or very clearly explained," but this could not much soften the blow. The man who had once enjoyed some of the most flattering press coverage in America now endured the most critical. Later Kennedy wrote that he was "hardly prepared, despite years in public office, for the viciousness of this onslaught."

The president was more disturbed by the effect of Kennedy's speech than surprised by his ambassador's views. Roosevelt privately confessed to one friend after Munich that he was "not a bit upset over the final result" but, publicly, he continued to straddle the fence. The State Department had approved Kennedy's speech on the dubious grounds that he prefaced his remarks by saying that coexistence between democracies and dictatorships was his own theory. To undo the damage, the president delivered his own intentional display of belligerence: "There can be no peace if national policy adopts as a deliberate instrument the threat of war." Journalists wrote stories on the president's repudiation of his ambassador. Joseph Kennedy told friends he had been stabbed in the back.

"I am so god-damned mad I can't see. Of all the insidious lying I have ever read in my life I have read in these columns the last two weeks." Kennedy told James Byrnes that he had decided his ambassadorship would mark the end of his public career. "The only thing that could bring me into active political life again would be to hear that you were going to be a candidate for President and, with all the names I hear mentioned, why in the name of God you don't get busy is a mystery to me." Kennedy advised the South Carolinian to "start maneuvering around and if you go, I declare myself right here and now unquestionably and unqualifiedly for you and I don't give a damn who is against you." Franklin Roosevelt, already being mentioned for a third term, would have been interested to hear of Kennedy's 1940 endorsement.

Among the stacks of unfavorable mail and telegrams arriving at the London embassy was one heartening letter. John Boettiger, the president's son-in-law, told Kennedy he had been doing a grand job. "There are plenty of brickbats flying around, but that is an old-fashioned American custom that always comes as a reaction to anything unpleasant." Before Munich, people had been unanimous for preventing a war with Germany; now they behaved like the fellow who ran away after someone twice his size threatened to punch him in the nose—and later declared he should have hit the bully himself. "Out here in the wide open spaces, people are tremendously relieved. . . ."

"All I have been having poured into me for the last three months," Kennedy replied, "is how Roosevelt is off me, how the gang is batting my head off, and that I am persona non grata to the entire Roosevelt family." He realized that a lot of this was "hooey"—"but it is damned annoying three thousand miles away. . . . When I add up my contributions to this cause over the past five years—and I do not mean monetary ones—I get damned sick that anybody close to the Boss finds it necessary to do anything but say a good word. It has taught me one lesson: I am going to stay on the side lines for a while and mind my own business and let the boys worry about their problems."

Shortly thereafter was *Krystallnacht*, the attack against the Jews of Germany that threw into stark relief the distinction between democracies and dictatorships. An international committee on refugees was established in London, chaired by Washington attorney George Rublee. The American ambassador seemed at first to offer little encouragement; some in London explained that Kennedy feared overt assistance might jeopardize Chamberlain's cherished access to Hitler. Rublee complained to the president that his envoy was dragging his heels. "If there was a demagogue around here of the type of Huey Long to take up anti-Semitism," Roosevelt later remarked to Kennedy, "there could be more blood running in the streets of New York than in Berlin." He cabled Kennedy to ask Chamberlain to intervene personally with Hitler. The prime minister replied that he had given much thought to the matter; it was one of the issues that could now be raised with the Führer "in due course."

After *Krystallnacht* Kennedy toyed with a plan to transfer tens of thousands of German refugees to Africa and the Americas: "If political and personal considerations could be gotten out of the way, if the plight of the Jews would not only countenance to be subordinated, particularly in American Jewish circles, to the destiny of Palestine, progress could be made with rapidity provided that funds could be supplied." *Life* predicted that if the "Kennedy Plan" succeeded, "it will add new luster to a reputation that may well carry Joseph Patrick Kennedy into the White House." Some New Dealers attributed Kennedy's newfound concern to an attempt to recover politically from the Trafalgar Day speech. When Roosevelt and Hull were asked about the Kennedy Plan, they told reporters they knew nothing about it.

Kennedy departed for the United States in December 1938. When he arrived, Boake Carter reported, there would be a tremendous confrontation between Franklin Roosevelt and his maverick ambassador. In prose as purple as Hugh Johnson's and Father Coughlin's, the columnist wrote, "The White House has on its hands a fighting Irishman with blazing eyes and a determination to strip the bandages of deceit, innuendo and misrepresentation bound around the eyes of American citizens." Kennedy told another journalist that he supposed he might be fired: "I am going home to face the President and tell him what I think—and what I think won't please him." The president discounted the rumors that he would recall or rebuke his envoy: Kennedy was merely coming home for a holiday. But in a talk with Morgenthau, Jim Farley noted that Roosevelt was "terribly peeved with Joe. . . . When Joe comes back, that will probably be the beginning of the end."

Newspapermen greeted Kennedy at the port of New York in mid-December. What did he think of Hitler? "Come and see me the day I resign." Did he consider himself part of the Cliveden set? "I don't know what it is." Did he still consider Munich the wisest solution? "With me, it is not a question of the Munich agreement. I am pro-peace. I pray, hope, and work for peace." But the situation was changing daily for the worse, Kennedy reported. There were only two alternatives—chaos or war. "And if there is any way of doing better than either of those, then it is worth trying."

For two hours at the White House, Kennedy and Roosevelt discussed the European outlook (the Munich pact was failing, the ambassador said); the plight of the Jews (Kennedy believed it all depended on the financial support of the American Jewish community); and America's role when and if warfare began. For the first time, Kennedy detected "a trace of impatience" in the president's attitude toward Chamberlain's policy of watch-and-wait. Some saber-rattling might now be in order, Roosevelt said. His main objectives of the moment? Rearm and repeal the Neutrality Act.

The ambassador agreed: this was the best way of keeping the United States out. Kennedy promised to see Thomas Lamont about consolidating banking and manufacturing sentiment behind rearmament. He complained of White House maltreatment while in London—the failure to consult Kennedy on important matters, Roosevelt's private contacts with people in Britain through letters and personal emissaries. "I told him again that I was willing to step out anytime that he wanted me to, but he insisted that I must stay and he discounted as of little importance to our relationship the crop of rumors that I pointed out to him were being fed to the press by persons close to him . . ." Kennedy recorded. "He dismissed the whole business with assurances of confidence in my objectives and my work."

Kennedy left the president an apocalyptic memorandum. Its title: "What would be the effect on the United States of the decline or collapse of the British Empire?" Kennedy's answer: danger, unless America initiated a grand new world design. He outlined three alternatives for American diplomacy. First was the Wilson doctrine of making the world safe for democracy by working to overthrow totalitarian regimes. Second was the Fortress America idea of occupying all vital positions within a thousand miles from American shores. Kennedy's recommendation? Divide the globe into four or five independent spheres of influence—systems composed of the Americas, France and Britain, Germany, Russia, and Japan and China. These systems would support themselves politically and economically; resources required from outside a particular region would be obtained through barter and free trade. Under his scheme, Kennedy argued, the world would "settle down to a long peace and security in which the forces for freedom everywhere would once more have an opportunity to develop." Kennedy's stride toward a new departure in international policy found only a faint hearing at a White House and State Department already miffed at his efforts to exceed his chartered responsibilities. There is no record that either the president or Secretary Hull studied Kennedy's proposal with any degree of seriousness.

While Mrs. Kennedy and eight of the children skiied at St. Moritz, the ambassador spent Christmas at Palm Beach with Jack. Kennedy sat at poolside, telephoning friends across the country to assay American opinion. He concluded that Americans stood foursquare behind isolation. A Boston journalist who visited the Kennedy home in January 1939 found "a virtual publicity bureau." Walter Winchell and Boake Carter were houseguests, enjoying long conversations with the ambassador in the Kennedy pool and solarium. Kennedy spoke to Colonel McCormick of the *Chicago Tribune.* Father Coughlin, no longer disseminating his views over radio but now through his weekly *Social Justice*, badgered his friend to fly out to Royal Oak. (When Kennedy mentioned this to Thomas Lamont, the Morgan banker replied, "God help Father Coughlin or God help you—perhaps both of you—if you get together!") Tom Corcoran regarded Kennedy as a possible obstacle to his hopes of engineering a third term for Franklin Roosevelt. He warned Henry Morgenthau that Arthur Krock was "running a campaign to put Joe Kennedy over for President, that if any prominent Catholic gets in the way, he's to be rubbed out. . . . If anybody with financial training gets in the way, he's to be rubbed out."

By January 1939 the president was nearly convinced of the bankruptcy of appeasement. He asked Congress for a quantum leap in defense appropriations. Ever conscious of the imposing national sentiment against warlike maneuvers, Roosevelt proposed the mightiest array of strength in American history as a deterrent to war. To support his recommendation he summoned Kennedy and William Bullitt, ambassador to Paris, from their Florida holidays to testify secretly before the Senate and House Military Affairs committees. Both Kennedy and Bullitt presented a dim outlook and backed rearmament to maintain America as a peaceful island amid the deepening world storm.

Later Kennedy caustically remembered Franklin Roosevelt's private declaration around this time that "he would be a bitter isolationist, help with arms and money, and later, depending on the state of affairs, get into the fight." This recollection may have been altered by hindsight, but by now Kennedy and Roosevelt knew they were working at cross-purposes. Although they agreed on military strength, the president was considering intervention as a possibility, real if remote. Kennedy was more than ever resolved to prevent American involvement.

The ambassador returned to Palm Beach and stayed there well into February until Roosevelt telephoned Kennedy to suggest that he consider returning to his post. Kennedy's attitude on leaving for London was recorded in a column by Boake Carter, written after talking with the ambassador at length. The previous autumn, Carter wrote, Kennedy had "bucked the State Department and Mr. Roosevelt, who is of course the State Department." Kennedy had complained to the president about his duplicity in diplomacy—"in language that Mr. Roosevelt does not care to hear." The president had "sold out his Ambassador lock, stock and barrel." When he spoke with Roosevelt in December, he had intended to tell the president to "quit making a sucker out of me," but friends had warned, "He'll twist whatever you say and make himself appear with the credit and you with the discredit." Kennedy would not resign. Instead he would prevent the appointment of a Roosevelt "marionette." "He feels that he can serve America, not Mr. Roosevelt, better by sticking than in any other job."

Carter's report probably mirrored Kennedy's spoken explanation of his attitudes, but the ambassador himself knew that considerations more complex than digging in his heels were keeping him in London. As in the highpoint of the New Deal, Joseph Kennedy was again torn between loyalty to the president and disagreement with his policies. Like Father Coughlin five years earlier, he knew his influence was waning, but was reluctant to pit his power against the White House. He felt abused yet appreciated Roosevelt's kindnesses. He may well have wanted to keep an interventionist out of the London embassy, yet (as Roosevelt accurately concluded) Kennedy always tried to leave a job at the peak of his performance. Still, the indifference paid the Kennedy Plan and his proposal for a grand world design indicated that Kennedy's old influence was diminished beyond repair.

"You know how I feel about things and people," he told Roosevelt almost plaintively before leaving for Britain. "I have never made a public statement criticizing you. As to what I say privately, you know perfectly well that I will never say anything that I have not said to you face to face. But you know the way I feel about you and I won't be any good to you unless we are on good terms."

"Don't worry," the president replied, "I know how you feel—and as for those cracks at you, some people just like to make trouble."

Kennedy decided to remain in London, trying to convince himself of Roosevelt's sincerity in pursuing peace, searching for every opening to shape American diplomacy, hoping against hope that the president would resume seeking his counsel.

In the event this did not come about, Kennedy discreetly prepared the way for resignation. He asked Arthur Krock to inquire quietly whether Princeton was willing to offer an honorary degree to the ambassador. On Kennedy's authority, Krock advised the university that the envoy was considering resignation in June 1939 and could return then to accept the degree, if offered. (It never was.) "Do you hear anything about Kennedy wanting to quit?" Drew Pearson asked his partner. "I hear Joe has his eye on a Morgan partnership and also that he has spent so much dough—$250,000 a year—that he wants to get back into harness and make some money." Pearson had heard "he wants to get out but Roosevelt wants him to stay because he'd rather have Joe in England than here on his neck."

Pearson was correct. The same friction between policy and power was working on Franklin Roosevelt. The statesman realized that if he opted for intervention, Joseph Kennedy would pose a barricade to the conduct of American foreign policy. The political manipulator realized that dismissing Kennedy might unleash a Frankenstein demon who would denounce Roosevelt's policies from a platform of the president's own making. Roosevelt's strategy: keep Kennedy in London and simply circumvent the embassy on important transactions. "By 1939, Father knew that Kennedy had to go," James Roosevelt recalled. "But he did not want to make the change. He wanted it to evolve on its own."

"The End of Everything"

"People here are a good deal more optimistic than when I left, but there is still plenty of trouble on the horizon," wrote Joseph Kennedy on returning to Great Britain. The troubled horizon moved the ambassador to narrow his vision from world strategies to the immediate exigencies of the United States. In another attempt to influence Franklin Roosevelt, Kennedy mailed to the White House an even more ardent proposition than his December message.

Kennedy agreed with the president that America must build an almighty arsenal—particularly a two-front navy—but he feared that even this equipment could not be depended upon to guarantee the survival of the United States. In the event of a two-front attack in which Latin America fell under totalitarian control, the ambassador foresaw only a fifty percent chance that the United States might avert defeat.

Americans faced an even greater danger from within. Building a great military, Kennedy reasoned, would require public sacrifices that would be difficult for a popularly elected government to defend. The needy, resentful, defeated populations might join their conquerors to destroy the final stronghold of democracy. The heavy taxation and regimentation required for defense would "inevitably mean the destruction of the American form of Government as at present conceived, in the very effort to defend the country from alien authoritarian forms of control"—effects that "would soon penetrate into every American home."

Kennedy believed the United States would be compelled to duplicate many of the features of the fascist system. To diminish the economic slack resulting from decreased exports, the American economy would have to be ruled by Washington. "To fight totalitarianism, we would have to adopt totalitarian methods." Did Kennedy himself endorse totalitarianism in the event of such an emergency? His memorandum was inconclusive. It noted the costs of isolation but promoted isolationism. It enumerated the dangers of fascism but seemed to imply that an American fascism might be necessary, if unpalatable, to ensure American survival. Still, Kennedy's thesis approached this conclusion so tentatively that it seemed designed not to fuel the president's suspicions about Kennedy's confidence in democracy during crisis.

Kennedy's argument threw more light on the different assumptions on which the president and his ambassador were working. Through all Roosevelt's maneuverings—the waffling, temporizing, feigned agreement with militant isolationists alongside avowals that he too had seen and hated war—the preservation and advancement of democratic ideals was his ultimate goal, although this objective was sometimes obscured by the short-term manipulations toward that end. Joseph Kennedy—although he lauded Chamberlain's flight to Munich as a noble act and labored to gain public acceptance for coexistence—saw the crisis from the standpoint of a toughminded diplomat. He was most vitally concerned with the preservation of the United States as a sovereign entity, whether or not strictly founded on democratic principles. The optimist in the White House looked beyond Kennedy's doubts about American self-preservation—Raymond Moley considered Roosevelt "the fairy prince who did not know how to shudder"—to rest his faith on the strength inherent in democratic ideals. The pessimist in London rejoined that ideals meant little to the average citizen in an emergency. The paths of Roosevelt and Kennedy diverged further in the spring of 1939 but, as Frank Kent wrote, "each needs or wants what the other can give." Joseph Kennedy's memorandum on America in a totalitarian world met the same silence that greeted his November proposal on refugees and his grand design of December.

March 1939 marked the end of independent Czechoslovakia. Neville Chamberlain said his hopes had been "wantonly shattered." At the end of the month, appeasement ended when Great Britain guaranteed the independence of Poland. In this guarantee Kennedy saw the tinder for war. "Roosevelt's urging of Chamberlain had a lot to do with the guarantee of Poland," he later told Herbert Hoover. (Hoover doubted Kennedy's explanation, noting that only a week elapsed between Germany's ultimatum on Poland and the British guarantee.) The ambassador worried that the United States would enter because of the liquidation of British investments and the resulting strain on the American economy. He still viewed Hitler's ambitions in an economic context. "I'm just as convinced that he doesn't want to fight as anybody else is, but I'm not convinced as to how he can save his own situation for his own people," Kennedy told Hull in April. The Führer's dilemma was that "he has no money and he can't change all those people who are engaging in wartime activities into peacetime activities without having a terrific problem."

Kennedy's abiding support for policies akin to appeasement contradicted public opinion in both the United States and Great Britain that was shifting toward firmness against the dictatorships. The gossip mill in Washington ground on into the summer. The Felix Frankfurters regaled Harold and Jane Ickes with stories of their visit to the London embassy. Frankfurter, whom the president would soon appoint to the Supreme Court, had once been friendly with Kennedy in Boston and had accompanied him on the final day of the Roosevelt campaign in 1932, but the old Anglophile's loyalties diminished with Kennedy's continued shouldering of appeasement. "At the first meeting, Joe was all that he ought to be—redundant with expressions of admiration for and devotion to the President." Frankfurter said, adding that he suspected Kennedy hoped he would report these expressions to Roosevelt.

Marian Frankfurter mentioned that at another dinner, Kennedy discomfited the punctilious Chamberlain by explosively and frequently referring to him as "Neville." "Chamberlain's adam's apple would work up and down convulsively three or four times and then he would emit a forced 'Joe.' "

Her husband reminded Ickes—as if he needed to be reminded—that

Kennedy was "perfectly certain that he will be the compromise candidate for President on the Democratic ticket next year." Frankfurter also mentioned that when Arthur Krock's name once came up in Kennedy's presence, Kennedy blurted out that he was "supporting that fellow."

At the White House Ickes told the president of the "perfectly insulting manner" in which the ambassador spoke of Roosevelt in front of the embassy servants. He evoked a presidential laugh by reporting the riposte, current in London, that Chamberlain had decided to expand his cabinet to provide a place for Joe Kennedy. After a cabinet meeting, the interior secretary flourished a copy of *The Week*, which a friend had mailed from London. It reported that the American ambassador had been assuring London friends that "the democratic policy of the United States is a Jewish production" and that "Roosevelt will fall in 1940." (Ickes need not have bothered, for J. Edgar Hoover with his usual generosity had furnished a copy to the White House, as he did other items about Kennedy in London.)

The president gave the newsletter back to Ickes and declared, "It is true."

In the spirit of his conversations with Herbert von Dirksen, Kennedy continued to search for a basis of conciliation with Germany. In May 1939 James Mooney, head of General Motors in Germany, invited him to dine in Paris with "a personal friend of Hitler and the topside influence in the Krupps," as the ambassador cabled the State Department. "The dinner will be private and nobody will know I am there and I am returning early Sunday morning. Do you see any objection to my going and have you any suggestions?" Sumner Welles feared the meeting would indeed become known and asked Kennedy not to go.

Kennedy continued to place primary blame for his circumvention not on the president but the State Department. "My experience in business and politics has been that one really gets the best results when one works for somebody or with somebody in whom one has great confidence." State was too impersonal, he complained to Senator Byrnes. "A fellow might just as well be working for a wooden Indian."

A monument of Kennedy's circumvention was the American visit of the king and queen in June. He had been the first to suggest the idea to their highnesses the previous autumn. "I only know three Americans—you, Fred Astaire, and J. P. Morgan—and I would like to know more," the queen told Kennedy. But the American ambassador was barred not only from accompanying the royal couple but even from aiding in the arrangements. "I suppose if the President wanted me to be aware of any discussion he was having, he would notify me," Kennedy peevishly told

Hull, adding, "I suppose nothing can be done about this and that I can continue being a dummy and carry on the best I can." When Al Smith asked Kennedy to arrange a visit to his Empire State Building for "a really royal welcome," Kennedy had to reply that the plans were "entirely in the hands of the British ambassador in Washington and the President." Roosevelt tried to placate Kennedy by noting that it was easier to iron out details in Washington; but there might have been a more compelling reason for Kennedy's exclusion. As Thomas Corcoran recalled, "The announcement of the royal visit infuriated the Irish at the White House. It signalled an impending alliance and we interpreted it to mean that America would soon be at war." Allowing Kennedy to take part in the event seemed a risk-laden proposition.

The president jollied Kennedy along while increasingly objecting to his independence. Kennedy professed allegiance while denouncing Roosevelt in the drawing rooms of London. Each understood the public and private feelings of the other; each kept up the veneer of friendship and cooperation. In late July the ambassador wrote Roosevelt to complain that his abilities were being wasted in London. He felt like a "glorified errand boy," Kennedy wrote, doing petty chores "which seem to have no close connection with the real job at hand." He pledged, however, that "regardless of any personal inconvenience, as long as I am of any assistance to you, I shall remain for whatever time you like." Kennedy invoked his father's credo of gratitude and loyalty. "Remember that whatever you want, I always stay put."

Franklin Roosevelt replied with a letter direct enough to let Kennedy know he was not being fooled, yet ambiguous enough not to precipitate a rupture. With the letter, Roosevelt enclosed one of the more damaging articles on Kennedy's alleged disloyalty. "I tried to correct the impression by telling several people the other day that I have complete confidence in you, that you have never mentioned leaving London, that you are doing a good job there, and that in these critical days, I count on your carrying on. It is true that some people are getting things printed like the enclosed, which you have doubtless seen, but things like this have small distribution and are so frankly hostile and silly that they do you no harm."

A few days earlier, Arthur Krock had reported Kennedy's readiness to resign because of his ebbing confidence in the president's policies and his worry that the attacks on Kennedy were inflicting harm on Roosevelt. "I suppose you know of the latest 'Krock' in the Times about you," the president's letter continued, "and I think you begin to agree with me that this particular gentleman, with his distorted ideas of how to be helpful, has done you more harm in the past few years than all of your enemies put together." Krock had "never in his whole life said a really decent thing about any human being without qualifying it by some nasty dig at the end of the praise. He is, after all, only a social parasite whose surface support can be won by entertainment and flattery, but who in his heart is a cynic who has never felt warm affection for anybody—man or woman."

Harold Ickes listened to Roosevelt recite the gist of his letter with obvious delight: "Of course, the purpose of the President was to hit Krock over Kennedy's shoulders, knowing full well that Kennedy would lose no time in getting this letter, or the substance of it, back to Krock."

By summer's end and the signing of a nonaggression pact by Hitler and Stalin there was little hope for a peaceful solution in Europe. "The real smart thing for the United States to do," Kennedy wrote home, "is to keep themselves financially rich so that they will be able to sit at the table when this mess is over, for a mess it is going to be. . . ." On Chamberlain's behalf Kennedy urged Washington to pressure Poland into backing down: "In the event President Roosevelt has in mind any action for the preservation of peace . . . the object of his efforts should be Beck in Poland, and to be effective, it must be done quickly." Roosevelt refused; he asked Kennedy to "put some iron up Chamberlain's backside." This did no good if the British had no iron with which to fight, Kennedy replied.

The president issued a last-minute peace appeal to the king of Italy, Victor Emmanuel. Late on the night of August 24 Kennedy telephoned Sumner Welles, as Roosevelt listened in, to renew his plea for action on Poland. Welles tactfully said that Washington would do something, but not quite as Kennedy suggested. "I don't care how it is done as long as something is done and done quickly," the ambassador replied. What did Kennedy think of the message to Victor Emmanuel? "Lousy. The idea of anybody addressing anything to the King of Italy who has been a nonentity for years doesn't make sense."

The next morning another presidential message went out, this time to Hitler and President Moszicki of Poland, asking for direct negotiations. Kennedy cabled Washington a summary of a report from Sir Neville Henderson, the British envoy to Berlin who had just spoken with Hitler: the Führer was determined to achieve only limited ambitions. Once these were realized, Hitler would "make a deal with England that would guarantee the British Empire forever." Then he would "go back to peaceful pursuits and become an artist, which is what he wanted to be." The president was much amused by Kennedy's cable.

On the final day of August Europe was on the brink. To a letter to Eleanor Roosevelt on a routine matter, Kennedy added, "This morning we are praying that, miraculously, war may be avoided, when only a month ago everyone thought things were definitely on the upgrade. . . . What worries me more than anything else is the effect it is sooner or later going to have on the social, political and economic life of the United States, regardless of what we do."

Mrs. Roosevelt calmed Kennedy's fears with a response that was characteristic of her: "I feel with you that when one sees civilization disappearing before one's eyes on a whole continent, one cannot help but worry about one's own country. However, we must live from day to day and do the best we can. We cannot plan the future; that is for youth to do."

September 1, 1939, before daybreak. The president's bedside telephone rang. It was William Bullitt in Paris. German battalions had thrust into Poland. "Well, Bill, it's come at last. God help us all." Cordell Hull was awakened by a call from the president. He dressed quickly, his mind racing with nightmarish images of human suffering and destruction. Pacing the carpet at the State Department, the secretary waited for his staff to arrive. They strained to hear the scratchy, demanding cries of Adolf Hitler, broadcast from the Reichstag. "We are ending our death watch over Europe," said Adolf Berle.

Joseph Kennedy was on the telephone from London. News of the invasion was sketchy, he said, but Great Britain would declare war by day's end. "It's all over. The party is on." Was there any chance to avert the conflict? "Oh, unquestionably none." Yet for two days the prime minister and his cabinet held back.

On the third of September Neville Chamberlain summoned the American ambassador to Ten Downing Street. Tears in his eyes, Joseph Kennedy read the words he would hear in Parliament later that day: ". . . Everything that I have believed in during my public life has crashed in ruins." Kennedy made his way back to the embassy. A triple-priority cable went to Hull.

The president's telephone rang again. Roosevelt could barely recognize the choked voice from across the Atlantic. Kennedy unreeled his impressions of Chamberlain's Parliament talk, and predicted that a new Dark Age would descend upon Europe. Whoever won the war would inherit a legacy of only chaos and upheaval. Franklin Roosevelt tried to comfort his old ally, but the voice was inconsolable. Over and over Kennedy cried, "It's the end of the world . . . the end of everything. . . ."

Seven

TURNING OF THE LEAVES

THE DARKNESS over Europe plunged Joseph Kennedy into melancholy. A decade earlier, the Wall Street speculator had sought out Franklin Roosevelt as the man who could save the country. Now the ambassador beseeched the president. "It seems to me that this situation may crystallize to a point where the President can be the savior of the world," Kennedy wrote Washington a week after the invasion of Poland. "The British government as such certainly cannot accept any agreement with Hitler, but there may be a point when the President himself may work out plans for world peace. Now this opportunity may never arise, but as a fairly practical fellow all my life, I believe that it is entirely conceivable that the President can get himself in a spot where he can save the world. . . ."

"I want to tell you something and don't pass it on to a living soul," Roosevelt confided to Jim Farley. Kennedy had sent "the silliest message to me I have ever received. It urged me to do this, that and the other thing in a frantic sort of way." To Henry Morgenthau the president complained that his ambassador was nothing but a pain in the neck. "Joe has been an appeaser and will always be an appeaser. . . . If Germany and Italy made a good peace offer tomorrow, Joe would start working on the King and his friend the Queen and from there on down to get everybody to accept it."

This was somewhat unfair, because Roosevelt himself had not entirely ruled out the possibility of a negotiated settlement. But he directed Secretary Hull to send one of his curtest reprimands to London: "This Government, so long as present European conditions continue, sees no opportunity nor occasion for any peace move to be introduced by the

President of the United States. The people of the United States would not support any move for peace initiated by this Government that would consolidate or make possible a survival of a regime of force and aggression."

"My days as a diplomat ended Sunday morning at eleven o'clock," Kennedy lamented. "Now I'm just running a business, an officer of a company. I'm back where I was ten years ago." The American ambassador worked late into the night behind blackout curtains in a lonely embassy, his wife and children sent home to safety. "None of the family have the slightest regret at having been here at this time or being separated probably for God knows how long," Kennedy wrote Arthur Krock. "I don't want Rose to get lonesome, so call her up occasionally and tell her the American news because, while she will be all right with all the children, after a while, she is bound to get a bit depressed. . . . The results of modern warfare on women and children will be so catastrophic that something must be done."

Kennedy was adamantly opposed to the concept now ascendant in the Foreign Office: total war fought to unconditional surrender. The American envoy warned British officialdom that a long conflict would bankrupt their country, open Europe to radicalism, and endanger the American economy. An astute British diplomat noted that the ambassador's views were "based on some fundamental and emotional attitude of mind than on reason." The widespread if polite refusal of Kennedy's arguments led him to warn Franklin Roosevelt that the European war would be "concluded with British eyes constantly on the United States." If Britain triumphed in drawing America into its predicament, "the burden will be placed more completely on our shoulders by one hundred percent than it was in 1917." Kennedy's admonition: "We should be on guard to protect our interests."

This guardedness brought Kennedy into direct conflict with Neville Chamberlain and the king. Now desperate for assistance, George VI was distressed by the ambassador's warnings that Great Britain must not depend for rescue on the United States. The king laid out his thinking in a letter to Kennedy:

"As I see it, the U.S.A., France and the British Empire are the three really free peoples in the world, and two of these great democracies are now fighting against all that we three countries hate and detest, Hitler and his Nazi regime and all that it stands for. . . . But what of the future? The British Empire's mind is made up. I leave it at that."

Diplomatic Tug-of-War

After a month of Blitzkrieg, Poland fell. The warfare ceased in an eerie silence. The Nazi armies, ranged along the Maginot Line, informed France of orders from Berlin not to attack unless fired upon. Encountering studied indifference at Whitehall, Joseph Kennedy exploited the unreal quiet of the "phony war" to persuade Franklin Roosevelt of the futility of American involvement.

He had talked to military experts, Kennedy reported, and could not find a single one who gave Britain more than "a Chinaman's chance" in an alliance with France against Germany, Russia, and their potential allies. The president must beware "the facility with which the Anglo-Saxon can play power politics while talking in terms of philanthropy." Why was Great Britain really fighting? "For her possessions and place in the sun just as she has in the past." And the British would continue to fight, although "confused about what they want and what they'll get if they win." Roosevelt must drive home the point that America wanted no part of the mess. "Democracy as we conceive it in the United States will not exist in France and England after the war."

The president asked Congress to revise the Neutrality Act; assisting Britain with weapons and matériel would preempt the need for America troops. Still, Kennedy warned Hull that the British might take advantage of this development. "If Germany does not break and throw Hitler out . . . they will spend every hour trying to get us in." Roosevelt sidestepped Kennedy's warnings: "I am inclined to think the British public has more humility than before and is slowly but surely getting rid of the muddle-through attitude of the past."

The president also initiated an unprecedented correspondence between the leader of a neutral power and the subordinate official of a nation at war. The new First Lord of the Admiralty, Winston Churchill, had been Franklin Roosevelt's British counterpart at the same time Joseph Kennedy's shipyard manufactured armaments for Britain and America. Now the chagrined American envoy was delivering sealed communications between Roosevelt and Churchill with little knowledge of their contents. Churchill courteously asked Kennedy to the Admiralty to hear the first message, but the ambassador remained on guard. "Maybe I do him an injustice," he confided to his diary, "but I just don't trust him."

Kennedy continued his independent efforts for peace. He met again with the German ambassador to discuss unbroken trade between the United States and Germany. Von Dirksen concluded that Kennedy was angling for an invitation to Berlin, perhaps to attempt the first step toward a negotiated settlement, but he would not entertain the idea unless Kennedy first obtained official sanction from Washington. Kennedy's continuing contacts with the German embassy erupted in more unfavorable publicity. *The Week* reported on those in London who believed "the war must not be conducted in such a manner as to lead to a total breakdown of the German regime and the emergence of some kind of 'radical' government in Germany. These circles are certainly in direct touch with certain German military circles—and the intermediary is the American Embassy in London (after all, nobody can suspect Mr. Kennedy of being unduly prejudiced against Fascist regimes and it is through Mr. Kennedy that the German government hopes to maintain 'contacts')."

"There is a lot of truth to that," observed Franklin Roosevelt on being shown the article by the faithful Ickes.

Despite criticism from the press and the noteworthy lack of interest at the White House, Kennedy asked the president to reconsider a peace settlement. "Some of my English friends believe that only one man can save the world, not only in peace but in planning for the future, and that man is yourself." Kennedy told Roosevelt he was "a combination of the Holy Ghost and Jack Dempsey." There was "a very definite undercurrent for peace" among the British people that would force the government to define its war aims. When it did, "it will be apparent to the world and particularly to the English and French that they are fighting for something they probably can never attain."

His counsel largely ignored in both Washington and London, Kennedy found himself on the losing side of the diplomatic tug-of-war. When the monarchs of Holland and Belgium asked warring nations to lay down arms, Kennedy scheduled an appointment with Neville Chamberlain. The old proponents of appeasement had drawn light years apart. The prime minister refused the ambassador's plea to pull back; he thought the war had not brought sufficient suffering to the German people; when it had, they would throw off the shackles of the Nazi regime. By spring 1940, Chamberlain prophesied, the Germans would buckle under a British blockade, their hopes for victory dashed. He merely asked Kennedy to thank the president for his effort in revising American neutrality legislation.

Chamberlain needed no propaganda effort in the United States, Kennedy bitterly replied, because the latest poll found that ninety-five percent of Americans favored the Allies. Chamberlain must be thinking of only one motive—bringing the United States into Britain's war. The prime minister denied the charge with a defense he knew Kennedy would understand: this was an economic war and Britain needed equipment and resources, not men. But the once-intimate relations between Kennedy and Chamberlain would never again be the same.

The ambassador began to indulge in the same private criticism of the British government that he used to direct at Franklin Roosevelt and his policies and subordinates in Washington. Reports circulated throughout London of Kennedy's assurances that Britain would lose the war, that President Roosevelt was finished, that democracy was over in Europe as it might be in America if it entered the war. Conscious that the American president was circumventing his envoy, the men of the Foreign Office concluded that Roosevelt had lost confidence in Kennedy. Once friendly to the ambassador who was a valued conduit to the White House, Whitehall now regarded him as an obstacle to American cooperation and a threat to British morale.

The minute books at the Foreign Office filled with confidential accounts of the deeds and sayings of the American envoy. As one diplomat noted, it was gossip—"but gossip which very probably has more than a grain of truth in it." Occasionally cruel, occasionally exaggerated, the reports scrawled across bound foolscap reflected growing antagonism. A few wits referred to the senational reports as "Kennediana." They were not to be made public for thirty-five years.

On the day Great Britain declared war, Sir John Balfour recorded that Kennedy had "informed some acquaintances of his during the summer that if we fought the Germans, we would be beaten." He ventured that Kennedy "wishes us well but, being himself a hustler, is inclined to depreciate our less ostentatious British merits."

"Quite likely," replied the chief of the Foreign Office, Sir Alexander Cadogan.

A report on an American embassy dinner: "Mr. Kennedy had (after a somewhat competitive exchange of toasts) expressed the opinion that we should be badly thrashed in the present war." The ambassador appeared "rather to relish expressing this opinion"—evidently because of his delight in "seeing the lion's tail twisted (and perhaps in twisting the lion's tail!)." The reporter went on to warn that the harm in Kennedy's talk was "very considerable and I fear that, whatever steps we take, it will continue, though perhaps less indiscriminately than hitherto. The only way to stop it is to convince Mr. Kennedy that he is wrong."

The dialogue fastened on the question of whether Whitehall should attempt to put a muzzle on the American ambassador. "Mr. Kennedy is entitled to his opinion and to express it when and where he likes and I am afraid I can't think of any action which would be likely to make him refrain from talking as he does," read one entry. "The trouble is that he is no doubt regarded by some people—probably including some of his own colleagues—as being particularly 'in the know' owing to his close contacts with members of the Government whereas, of course, being primarily interested in the financial side of things, he cannot, poor man, see the imponderabilia which, in a war like this, will be decisive."

Cadogan disagreed: Kennedy was not free to express himself at will. The envoy occupied "a privileged position by virtue of his being accredited here, and he enjoys access to people in the highest authority."

Victor Perowne of the American desk recommended notifying the British ambassador in Washington, Lord Lothian, who had succeeded Lindsay. Lothian should "be aware of the situation in case it should at any time become suddenly necessary to ask him to speak to Mr. Roosevelt."

Sir Berkeley Gage acknowledged that "a complaint might make him shut up, but in that case we shall neither know what he is thinking nor what he is telling the U.S. Government. 'Putting the wind up' President Roosevelt may also conceivably have advantages as we know that he, at least, has no illusions about the threat to America should we be beaten."

In October 1939 Lord Lothian received several samples of Kennedy's conversation with the warning that "Kennedy has been adopting a most defeatist attitude in his talk with a number of private individuals. The general line which he takes in these conversations as reported to us is that Great Britain is certain to be defeated in the war, particularly on account of her financial weakness." The British envoy was not requested to complain to the White House, but Lothian was advised that it might later "become necessary to ask you to drop a hint in the proper quarter. . . ."

The reports continued to flow into Whitehall. Charles Peake of the Foreign Office had discussed Kennedy with William Hillman, an American correspondent and friend of the ambassador. According to Hillman, Kennedy was "a professing Catholic who loathed Hitler and Hitlerism almost, though perhaps not quite, as much as he loathed Bolshevism, but he was also a self-made man who had known poverty and who did not want to know it again." Hillman observed that bankruptcy and defeat had become obsessions for Kennedy. "He was not amenable to reason, his argument being that Hitler and the Nazis could not have lasted forever and that there was bound to be a change in regime in Germany one day if we had only let it alone."

"I wish that I could resist the feeling that Mr. Kennedy is thinking all the time about (1) his own financial position, and (2) his political future," wrote Balfour.

"Kennedy's real ambition is the White House," observed a British intelligence officer, "and he has a great chance of achieving it."

Perowne suggested that the ambassador's certainty of a British defeat "*may* have its good side in jogging the Americans out of their eighty-two percent (Gallup poll) wishful thinking that the French and we are going to win."

Winston Churchill was less sanguine. At an affair in London, hearing accounts of Kennedy's predictions of defeat, he replied, "Supposing, as I do not for one moment suppose, that Mr. Kennedy were correct in his tragic utterance, then I for one would willingly lay down my life in combat rather than, in fear of defeat, surrender to the menaces of these most sinister men." Kennedy continued to nurture his suspicions of Churchill's secret correspondence with the president. He told Franklin Roosevelt that he distrusted Churchill's influence on certain groups in America.

"Estimated Effects of Britain's Entry into the War upon the American Economy" was the title of another dismal prediction Kennedy mailed to Washington in late November. After a sharp decline in American trade, he ventured, Great Britain might decide to favor its own colonies and dominions in international commerce and drive America out of the marketplace. Latin America too might turn away from products made in the United States in favor of lower-priced goods. Attend to the business of educating Americans on world economics, Kennedy implored the president; he was more convinced than ever that some form of regimentation must be imposed to meet the demands of impending emergency. American citizens would have to be schooled to accept greater government control over capital and labor, extending beyond even the relationship between government and business of the conciliatory First New Deal.

"The job now is terribly boring and with all the family back in America, I am depressed beyond words," Kennedy told Arthur Krock. He was hoping to return home for Christmas, "since all the important work is lined up here now and it is a matter of routine and anybody in the Embassy could handle it from now on."

What of his future? "I suppose, if Roosevelt is not a candidate, I will properly retire to private life, regardless of whether another Democrat is elected." Kennedy's business interests were "really shot to pieces" as the result of war. "I will have finished almost six years—and important years of my life—in government service. But of course I am prepared if any emergency arrives to stay here as long as I am needed. . . ."

Granted home leave, the ambassador dined with the king and queen before departing. George looked drawn, Kennedy noticed, and the king's tendency to stutter was more pronounced than usual. While picking at an entree of hare, Kennedy reiterated his view: America should assist Great Britain—but not with American men. "That is what I thought you would say," replied the queen with a laugh.

Elizabeth mentioned how dismayed she had been to hear Charles Lindbergh say that Britain was fighting only for the preservation of the Crown. The ambassador was hardly free to concur as he had been saying the same thing to friends in London; he defended Lindbergh as an honest man. The king wondered if President Roosevelt would agree to run for a third term in 1940. "All of England hopes so."

Kennedy provided no answer. "There was only one thing I really wanted to do," he wrote later, "and that was to have at least two weeks in Palm Beach. Then I would not have to be on guard. I could read detective stories and sleep and swim and sleep again."

Reprise: Kennedy for President

The newspapermen who assembled around the arriving ambassador at New York heard a familiar refrain. "I'm all through. This is my last public job. I'm going to spend the next five years watching my family grow up." When would the five years begin? "I'll be dead and buried five years from now," Kennedy answered lugubriously. Asked if he planned to participate in the upcoming presidential campaign, the ambassador replied, "I haven't any idea." After the press conference, however, a newspaper friend and fellow Irishman took Kennedy aside to ask how he stood on the third term. He received a startling reply:

"I can't go against the guy. He's done more for me than my own kind. If he wants it, I'll be with him."

On the White House steps two days later Kennedy made his decision public. "The problems that are going to affect the people of the United States—political, social and economic—are already so great and becoming greater by the war that they should be handled by a man it won't take two years to educate. . . . We know from what we have seen and heard that President Roosevelt's policy is to keep us out of war—and war at this time would bring to this country chaos beyond anybody's dream. This, in my opinion, overshadows any possible objection to a third term."

Friends who had sat through Kennedy's excoriations of Franklin Roosevelt and his warlike intentions were mystified. Even Arthur Krock wrote that the ambassador was "almost the last man in the Administration from whom anti–New Dealers and New Dealers alike expected such a statement." Perhaps Kennedy hoped his declaration would be a self-fulfilling prophecy. If he was grateful for the president's kindnesses in the past, Kennedy's mind dwelled on future jobs; if the president had so far opposed European intervention, Kennedy hoped that he would continue his opposition. Kennedy's early backing was invaluable to Roosevelt for it bolstered the idea of the president's indispensability that men like Tom Corcoran were advancing. They had no idea that the endorsement would later crumble.

Kennedy had taken the night train from New York. Weary and unshaven, he was whisked up in the White House elevator to see the president. Roosevelt sat magisterially in bed, pouring coffee from a thermos bottle, looking "terribly tired but cordial," Kennedy thought. The ambassador offered his latest observations of the London scene. "Bearish," said Roosevelt. Bearish they were, Kennedy replied, but that was how he saw it. As the president listened with interest, Kennedy made a proposal: let America keep international trade channels open by taking over some of Britain's shipping.

Kennedy also bore a message from Churchill. The First Lord of the Admiralty was eager to mine Norwegian waters and disrupt German ore shipments; he wanted the president's consent. With his finger, Kennedy traced imaginary Norwegian routes on Roosevelt's bedroom highboy. The request was approved; later Kennedy transmitted to London the code message he had worked out with Churchill: MY WIFE CANNOT EXPRESS AN OPINION.

Kennedy had saved the best for last. He told Roosevelt about his third-term endorsement in front of the mansion. "No, Joe, I can't do it," the president said, "but we'll talk about that later." He was half an hour late for a press conference and must dress in a hurry.

Downstairs, Kennedy looked on as Roosevelt cited his British shipping proposals with praise and evaded reporters' questions about the third term. The president sat that afternoon behind his desk: "Did you see me finish off another Republican presidential candidate this morning? I never mentioned his name, but that relief question in Ohio finishes Bricker off completely."

"What about this third term?" Kennedy asked, sounding him out. "You'll have to run."

"Joe, I can't. I'm tired. I can't take it. What I need is a year's rest. You do too. You may think you're resting at times, but the subconscious idea of war and its problems—bombings and all that—is going on in your brain all the time. I just won't go for a third term unless we are in war." Roosevelt remembered his audience and caught himself: "Even then, I'll never send an army over. We'll help them, but with supplies."

"What about Hull?"

The president laughed. "I'll tell you a story, Joe. The other day, it seemed to me absolutely clear that the Russians were going to attack Finland. I was at Warm Springs and Cordell called me and said he had information—he always talks about his 'information'—that Russia was about to march and that we ought to prepare a statement offering to mediate. . . . Well, Cordell didn't get the statement out until six o'clock that night. . . . By that time, the Russians were on their way to bomb the Finns."

"Well, if Hull won't do, whom have you got?"

"Lots of them. We've got a better group of young men than England has." There was Paul McNutt of Indiana: "a go-getter if he has a definite assignment, but he's only good if he has a definite assignment." Harry Hopkins: "He's gained sixteen pounds and he hasn't got cancer, despite what the Mayos said." There was Frank Murphy, now attorney general.

"Is Frank doing a good job?"

"He's doing a swell job. There's Bob Jackson. He's a fine fellow and very able. There's yourself—and Bill Douglas. England hasn't got a group as able as that." (From this soliloquy Kennedy divined that Roosevelt "did not want the job but that he wanted his own man.")

The discussion moved on to the cabinet, British finances, Winston Churchill. Why the secret correspondence with Churchill? Kennedy asked.

"I have always disliked him since the time I went to England in 1918. He acted like a stinker at a dinner I attended, lording it all over us. . . . I'm giving him attention now because there is a strong possibility that he will become the prime minister and I want to get my hand in now."

The afternoon had slipped away. Missy Le Hand came into the room with a sheaf of papers to be signed. "I want to see you again, Joe," said Roosevelt. "Meanwhile, get the rest you came back for—and give my best to Rose." The curtain dropped, and a momentarily dazzled Kennedy left the White House.

A large audience gathered several days later at the East Boston church where the red-haired lad who was always devising schemes to earn money had served as altar boy. "As you love America, don't let anything that comes out of any country make you believe you can make a situation one whit better by getting into the war," Joseph Kennedy told them. They must not be carried away by a "sporting spirit" or a reluctance to see "an unfair or immoral thing done." A British journalist noted acerbically that there were enough Americans giving bad advice without the ambassador "who knows all our anxieties, all our ordeals" joining their number. But Sir Alexander Cadogan scrawled his relief into the Whitehall minute books: "I should not have been surprised by worse."

The ambassador entered the Lahey Clinic for a physical examination. He had lost fifteen pounds since the Polish invasion and the stomach disorders dating back to Fore River days were acting up again. A few years earlier, Kennedy feared he had stomach cancer. Now he withdrew to Palm Beach for weeks of rest and conversation with guests including Krock; Bill Douglas, newly named to the Supreme Court; Sumner Welles; and Lord Lothian, the new British envoy to Washington. Kennedy wished to recuperate through February but felt guilty about taking two months away from his post during wartime; he asked the Lahey Clinic to affirm the seriousness of his illness in a letter to the president. The ambassador wrote Roosevelt himself that if the European crisis erupted anew, "regardless of what the results might be to me in disregarding doctor's orders, I would take a plane and get over there."

Kennedy's holiday was interrupted not by new fighting overseas but by the political winds that were beginning to blow. Franklin Roosevelt's nonstrategy for 1940 was to keep the presidential waters unnavigable by encouraging as many candidates as cared to enter the race. The Sphinx urged Harry Hopkins to run, told Secretary Hull he hoped he would be his successor, reminded Alben Barkley, senator from Kentucky, that "some of the folks here at the White House" wanted him. The president encouraged and foiled the ambitions of such disparate possibilities as Secretary of Agriculture Henry Wallace, Harold Ickes, and the rather vacuous Governor McNutt.

Roosevelt's most serious rival was Jim Farley and Farley rested many of his hopes on a major victory in the Massachusetts primary. The Bay State seemed tailor-made for the postmaster general, heavily weighted toward the Irish and Catholics as well as the old system of machine politics in Boston. Casting a sidelong glance at Farley's movements in Massachusetts, Franklin Roosevelt told Joseph Kennedy that it was unfair of Farley to intrude on Kennedy's own bailiwick. Kennedy deserved the votes of the Massachusetts delegation. He ought to run in the primary himself.

Knowing of the rivalry between Farley and Kennedy, the president found in Massachusetts further ammunition for his divide-and-conquer strategy. If Kennedy should run as a favorite son in the Bay State and perhaps in other northeastern primaries, he might keep Farley from victory and make a third-term draft at the convention easier that summer. Kennedy's presidential prospect, dormant since the failure of the appeasement policy with which he was so closely identified, now rose from the ashes as the ambassador considered the idea in Palm Beach.

KENNEDY MAY BE CANDIDATE, proclaimed a *Boston Post* extra on February 12, 1940. "Strong Move to Have Him Run for President—Ambassador Refuses Definite Answer—Friends Lining Up Delegates in Massachusetts and Other Eastern States / Intensely Loyal to Roosevelt—Has Urged Him to Run Again—Close Friend of Farley / Heads for The Capital Tonight to Confer with President and Other Party Leaders." The source of the exclusive story was probably Kennedy, attempting to test the political waters. "While he has maintained complete silence in his residence at Palm Beach, Florida, concerning the affair, it was learned last night that powerful pressure has been placed upon him to offer his candidacy." The article went on to note that the ambassador's "loyalty to the President has been unswerving" and that "he would not be in public life today unless he considered it a patriotic duty"—both statements that sounded peculiarly as if they originated with Kennedy. The *Post* reported that "if some strength is shown in delegations from this state and others, he may give his permission to place his name in nomination."

The result was a brief act in the comic opera of the factious Massachusetts Democracy. The head of Farley's slate, state Democratic chairman William Burke, known throughout the commonwealth as "Onions," attempted to overcome the reservations of Democrats waiting for Roosevelt by pledging that his delegation would back the president, if he should run. But Burke predicated his pledge on the unlikely prospect that Farley would himself step aside for Roosevelt.

Democratic mandarins, including Senator David Walsh, Attorney General Paul Dever, and former Governor Joseph Ely, were suspicious. They declined to join Burke's slate, holding out for a candidate more likely to defer to the president, a man like Joseph Kennedy. Party regulars girded for "one of the biggest fights the Bay State Democracy has ever staged." Petitions were filed for Kennedy's nomination by one of the ambassador's cousins. Newspapermen who studied the proposed slate found another clue to the mysterious origins of the Kennedy boom. A prospective Kennedy delegate was one John Roosevelt of Boston. The haste of Kennedy's candidacy found the candidate's own father-in-law on the opposing side, for Honey Fitz had signed on with the Farley men weeks earlier.

In the end Joseph Kennedy resisted temptation. After a conference with the president, he announced that he would not run: "I cannot forget that I now occupy a most important government post which at this particular time involves matters so precious to the American people that no private consideration should permit my energies or interests to be diverted. To my numerous friends who have been anxious for me to submit my name for the consideration of the American electorate, I am deeply grateful. However, the paramount consideration of public duty compels me to decline to permit my name to be presented."

Now Onions Burke heaped praise on the ambassador. "There is no man in Massachusetts more popular than Joe Kennedy. Neither has President Roosevelt any greater friend than Joseph Kennedy. He is a builder, not a destructionist. . . ."

The nondestructionist may have exacted a price for his withdrawal. Two days later, Joseph Kennedy, Jr., announced his candidacy for the Farley slate from Brookline. Chairman Burke magnanimously overcame a chorus of objections that the young Kennedy had not resided in Brookline for over a decade; he immediately installed the ambassador's son on the official delegation.

His presidential candidacy safely reinterred, Kennedy dropped by the State Department before flying back to London. He called on William Bullitt, on holiday leave from Paris, who was giving an interview to Kennedy's friends Joseph Patterson and Doris Fleeson of the *New York Daily News*. As Harold Ickes related Bullitt's account of the incident, "Joe cheerfully entered into the conversation and before long, he was saying that Germany would win, that everything in France and England would go to hell, and that his one interest was in saving his money for his children." Kennedy denounced the president with fervor; the journalists, embarrassed, left the room. Bullitt told Kennedy he was disloyal and had no right to speak that way in front of members of the press. "Joe said he would say what he god-damned pleased before whom he god-damned pleased." Bullitt said Kennedy was "abysmally ignorant on foreign affairs" and had no grounds on which to utter such opinions. As long as he was a member of the administration, he should be loyal—or at least keep his mouth shut.

Bullitt and Kennedy had been intense rivals as long as they had been in Paris and London. ("I talk to Bullitt occasionally," Kennedy once wrote his wife. "He is more rattlebrained than ever. His judgment is pathetic and I am afraid of his influence on F.D.R. because they think alike on many things.") The president delighted in pitting both ambassadors against each other; he told each that he had been outdone by the other on a particular chore. Bullitt actually was having some of the same doubts about the president as Kennedy that spring, but after their contretemps he told Ickes that he doubted he would ever speak to Kennedy again.

"I Do Not Enjoy Being a Dummy"

By March 1940 the cordiality that had welcomed Joseph Kennedy to London was almost spent. "It soon became evident that a coolness had developed towards me in those circles, official and otherwise, whose main use for America was to embroil her in the war," he wrote of his return. A Foreign Office man reported that the American ambassador had come back "not because he wants to or because the President or State Department have the slightest degree of confidence in him, but in order to get him out of the way." Lord Beaverbrook, the Fleet Street publisher whose fondness for Kennedy was dwindling, wrote a friend that "a man who takes hydrochloric acid after every meal is apt to be pessimistic."

Kennedy agonized over a way out, complaining that the official duties left to him could be handled by a "fifty-dollar-a-month clerk." "I should hate to wind up six years of government service by getting out of a job and subjecting myself to criticism, because from what I gather, the American public believes Ambassadors are supposed to perform some satisfactory service, even in times like this, and to walk out would convince them that I was letting American interests down," he mused aloud to Arthur Krock. On the other hand, he was wasting his time and damaging his health. "Of course, if the President really needed me and offered me some kind of a job that I could fill, that would solve it, but I don't think he has that kind of a job available."

Shortly after the ambassador's return, Sumner Welles arrived in London. The undersecretary of state, friendlier to Kennedy than most of the others in his department, was sent on a European peace mission by Franklin Roosevelt. Kennedy's spirits might have been lifted by the president's official openness to a negotiated settlement, but he saw the Welles mission as merely another instance of personal humiliation by the White House—more evidence to Whitehall that Roosevelt had no faith in his ambassador. When a foreign service colleague murmured to Kennedy that the Welles trip seemed little more than a stage play, he replied with a nod. "It's like Roosevelt. . . . He does those things. . . ."

Bearing old proposals on disarmament and international trade, Welles traversed the continent, gauging the chances to end the "phony war." In London Kennedy joined the Welles party for a dinner held by Prime Minister Chamberlain at Ten Downing Street. He took the occasion to needle Winston Churchill in front of the visiting Americans: "If you can show me one Englishman that's tougher than you are, Winston, I'll eat my hat." Kennedy went on to announce that before leaving America he had given a warning to Secretary Hull: even if Kennedy's ocean liner was blown up, Washington should not consider the action a provocation to declare war. "I thought this would give me some protection against Churchill's placing a bomb on the ship!" Through the laughter, Churchill muttered, "I am certain that the United States will come in later anyway."

Kennedy stubbornly refused to believe that Washington was no longer listening to him. He urged the president to propose legislation preventing British purchases in gold because the purchases might injure the American economy. Secretary Morgenthau saw the encroachment on his domain; he persuaded Roosevelt to remind Kennedy that gold purchases were a matter for the treasury to decide—not the embassy in London.

On April 9, 1940 the Nazis entered Denmark and Norway. The Danes surrendered. Along the Norwegian coast the British navy was turned back. Kennedy cited the episode to the president as still another instance of Great Britain's lack of preparedness. This time he was not alone. Roosevelt was overcome by a fit of gloom so encompassing that Morgenthau worried the president was growing defeatist as well. Yet Roosevelt wired Kennedy, "These are sad days for all of us who remember always that when real world forces come into conflict, the final result is never as dark as we mortals guess it in very difficult days."

A month after Norway and Denmark the German army moved into the Low Countries and France. Chamberlain passed the reins of government to Winston Churchill. Kennedy telephoned congratulations to the new prime minister; he jocosely informed Churchill that it was he who was responsible for his promotion to Ten Downing Street. Why? When the First Lord of the Admiralty had conceived the ill-fated mining of Norwegian waters, Kennedy had been the one to cable Franklin Roosevelt's concurrence to London—"hence Norway, hence Prime Minister." There is no record that Churchill was at all amused. The two men barely concealed their antagonism. Churchill saw Kennedy as an impediment to Anglo-American cooperation and Kennedy considered Churchill a self-righteous imperialist striving to disguise a war for empire in the garb of a moral crusade. Kennedy never permitted the president to forget the new prime minister's designs on America. When Churchill finally succeeded in drawing the United States into war, Kennedy predicted, "he'll reach for that brandy, charge his glass, lift his hand on high and say, 'I have discharged my duty. Victory is ours! This is my crowning achievement! God save the King!' "

The Dutch surrendered to Hitler in mid-May. Churchill prepared to send a letter to Franklin Roosevelt. After seeing Churchill, Kennedy warned the president that the prime minister's forthcoming message would plead for American assistance. "I asked him what the United States could do to help that would not leave the United States holding the bag for a war in which the Allies expected to be beaten. . . . He said it was his intention to ask for the loan of thirty or forty of our own destroyers and also whatever airplanes we could spare right now."

At the end of the month the British armies retreated to Dunkerque. Kennedy grasped the hour to implore the president once again to make peace. "I think the possibility of the French considering a peace move is not beyond the realm of reason and I suspect that the Germans would be willing to make peace with both the French and British now—of course, on their own terms, but on terms that would be a great deal better than they would be if the war continues." His request spurned by Washington, it seemed there was little Kennedy could do now to prevent his country from further steps toward intervention. But then came an exceptional opportunity.

Tyler Kent was an American embassy clerk, one of two hundred employees under Kennedy's jurisdiction. Before coming to London in 1939 the Virginian had worked in the embassy in Moscow. There he concluded that Franklin Roosevelt's foreign policy was "contrary to the interests of the United States." Kent believed that the president was deliberately keeping the American people from being adequately informed on American diplomacy. One of Kent's responsibilities in London was manning the embassy code room, where he had access to messages from American missions in Europe as well as many of Winston Churchill's communications to the White House. Kent was also involved with a number of pro-German organizations.

On May 20 Scotland Yard officials stormed his London flat to discover hundreds of confidential documents copied at the American embassy. Kent was taken to confront the ambassador, who was summoned from dinner with Clare Boothe Luce. How on earth he could violate the trust with his own country? Kennedy asked. Couldn't Kent comprehend the effects on his own parents back in the United States? Kent told the ambassador to forget about him. Kennedy was informed that his employee may have forwarded secret embassy communications to Berlin: "I telephoned the President in Washington, saying our most secret code was no good anymore."

Whether the code had actually been broken by Germany was uncertain, but Joseph Kennedy was confronted with a dilemma. As an American citizen, Kent would routinely have been returned home for trial under American law. It was in the ambassador's authority, however, to waive Kent's diplomatic immunity to allow the British to try him. The problem offered Kennedy precisely the opportunity to influence American policy for which he had been striving for two years. If he did not waive immunity, Kent's trial would be publicized in every newspaper in America. The evidence of Anglo-American cooperation, perhaps even including the secret correspondence between Roosevelt and Churchill, would be splashed before every citizen, launching a public furor against Franklin Roosevelt's private machinations in Europe. The congressional investigations and journalistic denunciations that would have conceivably resulted might have eliminated any chance of a third term for the president and made it nearly impossible for him to move public opinion so swiftly toward aid to the Allies. A British trial, on the other hand, would be conducted under a cloak of wartime secrecy.

Kennedy authorized a British trial. He was unwilling to influence American policy at the cost of an act that seemed illegitimate and disloyal. "If we had been at war," he said later, "I wouldn't have favored turning Kent over to Scotland Yard or have sanctioned his imprisonment in England. I would have recommended that he be brought back to the United States and been shot." Kent's hearing and sentencing to prison were only briefly noted in the American press.

In mid-June Paris fell. Kennedy had reported two days earlier Winston Churchill's assurance that "he expects the United States will be in right after the election, that when the people in the United States see the towns and cities of England, after which so many American cities and towns have been named, bombed and destroyed, they will line up and want war." The Reynaud government was prepared to make a separate peace with Adolf Hitler unless America came in with substantial aid. Churchill appealed to Roosevelt to strengthen French resistance. The president replied with a reassuring message.

Churchill tried to persuade Premier Reynaud that Roosevelt's statement of reassurance was the equivalent of a war declaration and urged the President to publish his message in order to strengthen its effect. Kennedy immediately wired Roosevelt to warn against publication; since the British prime minister saw in it "an absolute commitment of the United States that if France fights on, the United States will be in the war." The president did not make his message public. As Herbert Hoover later recorded Kennedy's recollection of his role, "He delivered the message to Churchill but told him that he did not stand for it and had put in a telephone call to Roosevelt which he was expecting any minute. The call came through while he was with Churchill and he persuaded Roosevelt to withdraw it in Churchill's presence. Said Churchill hated him from then on."

In July Neville Chamberlain, mortally ill with cancer, recorded in his diary, "Saw Joe Kennedy, who says everyone in the U.S.A. thinks we shall be beaten before the end of the month." Even the president observed at the fall of Paris that chances for an Allied victory were no more than one in three. A poll found that less than a third of Americans predicted that the Allies would triumph.

Franklin Roosevelt's next moves depended on a cool evaluation of genuine British strength, independent of his ambassador's gloom and the disappointment of recent setbacks. To do the job he dispatched a personal emissary, Colonel William Donovan, a Republican and Columbia Law School friend who was widely known as "Wild Bill." It was a bipartisan choice in a bipartisan hour. Roosevelt had just appointed Henry L. Stimson, Hoover's secretary of state, to the War Department and Colonel Frank Knox, publisher of the *Chicago Daily News* and 1936 G.O.P. vice-presidential nominee, to the navy. Accompanying Donovan to London was a distinguished foreign correspondent for Knox's newspaper, Edgar Mowrer.

"I will render any service I can to Colonel Donovan, whom I know and like," Kennedy promised Secretary Hull—although he noted that his staff was perfectly able to provide any information the president needed and that sending Donovan was "the height of nonsense and a blow to good organization." He was less restrained on the subject of Mowrer. "We don't need a newspaperman to make this investigation for the government and it is most embarrassing to me. I think he should be called off the complete assignment." Apprised of Kennedy's complaints, Roosevelt observed that "somebody's nose seems to be out of joint." Donovan and Mowrer inspected installations, saw the king and queen, interviewed enlisted men and diplomats, officers and industrial workers. They reported to the president that Great Britain stood an excellent chance of withstanding a German invasion.

"I hope that at Washington they have got the Ambassador's number!" Sir John Balfour rejoiced into the minute books at Whitehall.

*

The party of Jefferson, Jackson, Wilson, and Roosevelt descended on Chicago that summer. In London Winston Churchill asked the American ambassador whether he believed Franklin Roosevelt would agree to campaign for a third term. "Probably he would if it were necessary to keep things right in the United States," Kennedy replied. As Kennedy remembered, Churchill declared, "Of course, we want him to run, but we must take care that the United States does not know that. If we stirred up some action here in July, which seems more than likely, Roosevelt might then be more inclined to run." The ambassador was startled to hear a similar comment from Lord Halifax a few days thereafter. "It led me to wonder what, if anything, had been said by Roosevelt privately to Churchill, or whether it was merely their own wishful thinking," he wrote later.

Eight years before, Joseph Kennedy had entered Chicago with the triumphant Roosevelt. Now he remained in London, almost a prisoner of his own embassy. As the gavel sounded in the Chicago Stadium, the president's nomination for a third term seemed all but certain. Roosevelt's only remaining active rival was Jim Farley. The president's agents in Chicago, James Byrnes and Harry Hopkins, considered a unanimous vote for Roosevelt crucial to the strategy of a third-term draft. They applied excruciating pressure to the last few delegates pledged to Farley, clustered mainly in the delegation from Massachusetts.

The confusion of March, when Chairman Burke had promised that his slate would switch from Farley to the president if he ran, now erupted into a shouting match. Should they honor their promises or back Roosevelt? The men from the White House reminded delegate Joseph Kennedy, Jr., of the honors their candidate had showered upon Kennedy's father. The young Kennedy made no secret of his ultimate intention to become president of the United States; he was warned of the effect ingratitude might have on the political careers of both father and son. Senator Byrnes even telephoned London to ask the senior Kennedy to put his son in line. "No," Kennedy replied firmly to the man to whom he had offered his own support in 1938, "I wouldn't think of telling him what to do." Young Joe consulted with Arthur Krock, Walter Trohan, and others of his father's friends; they counseled him to keep his pledge to Farley. When the roll call reached the Bay State, he was one of a covey of dissenters to deny Franklin Roosevelt his unanimous anointment. When Farley later cabled thanks to the ambassador, Kennedy responded, "As you can imagine, I had heard about the struggle to get him to change his vote and was delighted he took the stand he did."

After the nominations of Franklin Roosevelt and Henry Wallace, Jim Farley resigned as chairman of the Democratic party. The president offered the job to Senator Byrnes, but Byrnes worried that party responsibilities would interfere with his Senate work. He suggested Kennedy. In London the ambassador heard that his name was being considered by the White House. Arthur Krock had suggested for months that the party chairmanship could be just the route out of the embassy that Kennedy had so long been seeking.

Roosevelt did not offer the job. On August first he telephoned Kennedy in London. The Democratic National Committee wanted him to leave the embassy to run the fall campaign, the president reported, but the State Department wanted him to remain. "They were very anxious to have you and you know how happy I would be to have you in charge, but the general impression is that you would do the cause of England a good deal of harm if you left there at this time." (This was said not long after a sardonic British diplomat pondered whether Whitehall should be so bold to ask for a friendlier envoy "should we be so 'unlucky' to be deprived of Mr. Kennedy.") "I didn't want you to hear that you had been named and that your name had been turned down by me," said Roosevelt.

"Well, that's all very good," Kennedy replied, "but nevertheless, I am not at all satisfied with what I am doing and I will take a look at it in another month and then see what my plans are." He added, "I am damn sorry for your sake that you had to be a candidate, but I am glad for the country." Kennedy later admitted to Eddie Moore that he had been "damned fresh on the phone" and wrote Clare Luce of the "amazing" conversation: "The President telling me that the State Department wants to do something different from what he wishes is something new in my life."

On American best-seller lists that month was *Why England Slept* by John F. Kennedy. "When I was in the States with Jack and heard some professors talking about Munich, I realized they knew nothing about it," the father told a journalist friend. "I said to Jack, 'You get down to it and tell them all about it.' " The book was based on the younger Kennedy's senior thesis at Harvard and strengthened by interviews arranged through the London embassy with British journalists and officials. Jack did not share his father's confidence in the Great Man theory of history. Appeasement was the result less of misguided leadership, he argued, than an array of "underlying factors" including unwarranted confidence in the League of Nations, self-indulgent partisanship, pacifism, and the narrow visions of capital and labor. So determinist was Kennedy's argument in an early draft that the ambassador wrote to remind him with some insight that a politician must not only represent the wishes of his constituency—"he is also supposed to look after the national welfare, and to attempt to educate the people." Arthur Krock aided his friend's son in finding a literary agent and publisher and in reworking the manuscript. Krock was asked to write a foreword to the book, but Jack was overruled by the ambassador, who asked Henry Luce for the reason that Luce's name was better known. Joseph Kennedy mailed copies of the book to Churchill, the king and queen, and others in Britain and America. The British royalties were donated by the author to help rebuild the bombed city of Plymouth, the American proceeds used to purchase an automobile.

By August 1940 fully half of Great Britain's destroyers had been sunk. A group of American government officials, lawyers, and businessmen devised a plan to trade fifty World War One–vintage battleships for ninety-nine year leases of military bases on British soil. This would meet the need that Churchill had described to Kennedy in May. Henry Luce spent an evening at the White House to lobby the president on a destroyer deal. Roosevelt, who required little persuasion, used the occasion for some lobbying of his own: "Harry, I can't come out in favor of such a deal unless I can count on the support of the entire *Time-Life* organization for my foreign policy."

Kennedy was worried that the ships would fall into German hands if Britain surrendered, but wired Washington: "No matter what criticism may be leveled at the giving of a few destroyers, the President can very properly say: At least I have conducted the affairs of this country in such a manner that it has been possible to obtain these important bases for ninety-nine years with no real loss of anything worthwhile to America." Among the American vessels may have been a destroyer or two contracted for by the assistant secretary of the navy in a telephone call to the assistant manager of the Fore River shipyard during the First World War.

The ambassador was kept out of the destroyer bargaining by the president, who chose to conduct negotiations through the British embassy in Washington. Kennedy suspected that Roosevelt was trying to prevent him from learning of confidential conversations and promises to British leaders. He was embarrassed to learn from Whitehall, not Washington, of a presidential mission led by Admiral Robert Ghormley in late August. "As far as I can see, I am not doing a damn thing here that amounts to anything," he complained to Roosevelt. "For twenty-five years, I have been fairly active in any enterprise I took up. To be honest with you, I do not enjoy being a dummy." Kennedy sent a blunter message to Hull: "I am very unhappy about the whole position and of course there is always the alternative of resigning."

Roosevelt was vexed that, in a perilous hour, his envoy seemed primarily concerned with the importance of the work he was given, but both he and Hull mollified Kennedy with calls and letters. "There is no thought of embarrassing you and only a practical necessity for personal conversations makes it easier to handle details here," the president wrote. "Don't forget that you are not only not a dummy, but are essential to all of us both in the Government and the Nation." Hull wanted the ambassador to know that "the President and I appreciate the magnificent way in which you and your staff are carrying on your work. . . ." Though grateful for these gestures, Kennedy was not easily placated. "I am not fooling myself and I haven't the slightest doubt that they would turn around tomorrow and throw me in the ash can," he told his wife. The reason Roosevelt was being so attentive was "because he was afraid I would walk out and he wanted to soft-soap me." To Lord Halifax Kennedy complained that "if it were not that I did not want to walk out under the threat of bombing, I would resign rather than put up with such nonsense."

The Battle of Britain enveloped London in September. Night after night of the Blitz, Germany tried to force surrender by decimating the city and devastating British morale. "Confucius say man who gets to be American Ambassador should make up mind first whether he looks best in pine or mahogany," Clare Luce wired Kennedy. The ambassador kept a running tally of the number of air raids he survived. He complained to Welles that "no one in the State Department had any idea of what we were going through and seemed to care less." Kennedy later recalled that when the president telephoned in mid-September "and said perfunctorily that he hoped we were all right, I wasn't very cordial."

Later in the month, Britain was compelled to retreat at Dakar. Kennedy to Washington: "I cannot impress upon you strongly enough my complete lack of confidence in the entire conduct of this war. I was delighted to see that the President said he was not going to enter the war because to enter this war, imagining for a minute that the English have anything to offer in the line of leadership or productive capacity in industry that could be of the slightest value to us, would be a complete misapprehension. It breaks my heart to draw these conclusions about a people that I sincerely hoped might be victorious. . . ."

European policy was the main issue of the American presidential campaign; the tide was moving with Wendell Willkie. Accepting his third nomination, Franklin Roosevelt had declared that the foreign crisis would prevent him from leaving Washington; only in reply to "deliberate falsification of fact" would he turn his attention from Europe to the hustings.

In July the world had concentrated on every bulletin from the front lines, but by October, a successful invasion of Britain seemed less probable. The threat to the world appeared somehow less menacing than the dire picture painted by the president.

"Who really thinks that the president is sincerely trying to keep us out of war?" Willkie demanded of a New York audience. The Republican nominee insisted that Franklin Roosevelt reveal any "international understandings to put America into the war that we citizens do not know about." Events seemed to be falling into place for Willkie—the lull in Europe, an isolationist backlash, then a repudiation of Roosevelt by union leader John L. Lewis. Members of the Willkie entourage cast about for the final blow that would ensure the presidency for their candidate. Their view turned to London.

The previous spring, Joseph Kennedy had told Clare Boothe Luce and scores of others that he was "absolutely certain Roosevelt is going to push us into the war." Yet by autumn the ambassador seemed to be wavering between an array of conflicting emotions: his allegiance to the president, his frustration in London, his resentment that his warnings against war were going unheeded, his lingering hope that Franklin Roosevelt was sincere in promising not to send American boys into Europe. Arthur Krock found his friend "quite confused and at loose ends because of his distress at the turn policies had taken."

"It is my personal judgment you should return to this country immediately and tell what you think about everything totally," Henry Luce had wired Kennedy in July, "regardless of ordinary antiquated rules." But Kennedy was reluctant to leave London without official sanction for fear of being accused of fleeing the Blitz. The rumored designs of Luce to bag Kennedy for the Republicans were known at the White House when Roosevelt instructed Hull to deny the ambassador home leave. Then Kennedy informed Hull, Halifax, Welles, and other officials of the scathing article he had sent to Edward Moore in New York. "An indictment of President Roosevelt's administration for having talked a lot and done very little," he called it; the piece would appear coast to coast on November first if "by any accident" Kennedy was not permitted to leave London.

Political conspiracy was also being hatched at a less likely locale—the Supreme Court. Felix Frankfurter, all through October, had watched millions of American Catholics slipping away from the Roosevelt camp. How could the Catholic vote be recaptured? he asked Frank Murphy, recently appointed to the bench. Murphy's answer: an address by Joe Kennedy. Justices Frankfurter, Murphy, and Douglas went to the White

House to discuss with the president and Harry Hopkins how Kennedy could be persuaded to speak out for Roosevelt. All agreed that the president must himself do the chore.

Kennedy was "a troublemaker," Roosevelt complained in the hearing of the State Department's Breckinridge Long, "entirely out of hand and out of sympathy." The president approved his ambassador's return only on Sumner Welles's assurance that Kennedy would be delivered to the White House "before anyone else got at him to talk." Roosevelt insisted to newspapermen that Kennedy was not returning to resign. But the ambassador wired Welles, "I am pretty sick and sore at a lot of things. . . ."

October 7, 1940.

Before leaving the British capital, Kennedy saw Neville Chamberlain for the last time. The enfeebled man whispered, "I can tell you, though I haven't told my wife. I want to die." Kennedy said he still could not see what war would accomplish. "We are supposed to be fighting for liberty and the result will be to turn the last of the democracies into socialist, Communist or totalitarian states." From Chamberlain Kennedy received nine pages written in a quavering hand assuring him that if only their views had been adopted, the world would have been saved.

On October 22, 1940 the American ambassador bade farewell to his staff and posed for photographers on the steps of the embassy. A diplomatic correspondent and friend watched Kennedy walk down Grosvenor

Square, his steps growing shorter and shorter. "There he was, turning the corner, and he looked just an ordinary man," the journalist wrote in his diary. "This was Kennedy, whose labors in the United States, whether he be in complete accord with Roosevelt or not, may change our political pages decades hence. . . ."

As Joseph Kennedy flew toward America, Franklin Roosevelt left the White House for the first speech of his campaign. "For a President especially, it is a duty to think in national terms," he told a Philadelphia audience. "He must think not only of this year but for future years when someone else will be President. . . . He must think not only of keeping us out of war today, but also of keeping us out of war in generations to come."

Fateful Return

In Kennedy's hand as he stepped onto the gangplank at New York was a British air raid siren. A grim reminder of the nights spent under the Blitz, it would summon the Kennedy children to meals at Hyannis Port. Ranged before him was a troop of foreign service officers, policemen, and other officials that was as much barricade as reception committee. They were led by Robert Stewart, British Empire man at the State Department, and Max Truitt, a former colleague at the Maritime Commission. Any idea that Kennedy would beat a hasty departure to the Luce home in Manhattan ended immediately. He was handed two messages—a handwritten presidential invitation to the White House and a telegram from James Byrnes underscoring Roosevelt's note.

The telephone rang in the Oval Room while the president was lunching with Speaker Rayburn and Lyndon Johnson. The young congressman watched, awestruck, as his mentor lifted the receiver. "Ah, Joe, it is so good to hear your voice." Roosevelt asked Kennedy to "come to the White House tonight for a little family dinner. I'm dying to talk to you." With that, the president made a theatrical gesture suggesting he was about to cut somebody's throat.

Clutching a bulging briefcase and homburg, the ambassador strode into a lion's den of reporters. "What's this?" he asked. "Do I have to go through this before I can see my family?" Kennedy's wife and daughters burst in and embraced him. (The automobile bearing Master Edward Kennedy was caught in airport traffic.) Flashbulbs exploded. The envoy was battered with questions. "Nothing to say until I've seen the President," Kennedy declared with the smile of a Cheshire cat. Would he issue a statement? "After I've seen the President I'll make a statement." Did he intend to resign? "No statement." What were his plans? "I'm going to the White House—and I'll talk a lot after I'm finished with that."

With a motorcycle escort, Joseph and Rose Kennedy were piped aboard an airplane bound for Washington. In Manhattan, the Luces wondered whether the ambassador would ever arrive.

The journey to the White House had been carefully orchestrated. "Be sure and butter Joe up when you see him," the president reminded Grace Tully. Roosevelt knew that Kennedy would be more open to persuasion now, after days flying home and months of sleepless nights in London, than after having a chance to rest and think. He also made a point of inviting Mrs. Kennedy, who thought the president had "more charm than any man I ever met."

During the flight to Washington, Rose reminded her husband of a political truth instinctive to both of them: "The President sent you, a Roman Catholic, as Ambassador to London, which probably no other President would have done. . . . You would write yourself down as an ingrate in the view of many people if you resign now." Flamboyant ingratitude might also injure the political aspirations of their sons. Kennedy admitted later to Arthur Krock that his wife's argument permitted Roosevelt to disarm him.

Against this appeal to political loyalty, however, weighed another consideration. With the power to reveal the many months of collaboration between the British and Americans, Joseph Kennedy could wield decisive influence to keep the United States out of war. Awaiting the ambassador on his arrival in America was a letter from General Robert E. Wood, chairman of the America First Committee. Wood entreated Kennedy to disclose everything he knew of secret commitments the president might have made to Great Britain. "To my mind, the whole future of our country is at stake, and the present is one of those times in history when the truth must be told." If Roosevelt had made any kind of unofficial alliance with Great Britain, "the truth ought to be told by you and it ought to be told before the election. Certainly as far as the Middle West is concerned, if my suspicions are correct and the facts known, the President will be defeated. . . . I believe you owe to your country and to your fellow citizens the duty of telling those facts, regardless of partisanship or any personal friendships."

At the White House the Kennedys were joined by Senator Byrnes and his wife ("proving that Roosevelt didn't want to have it out with me alone," the ambassador later noted). In the company of the South Carolinian who he knew was close to the president, Kennedy softpedaled his differences with Roosevelt. "I've got a great idea, Joe," Byrnes said. "Why don't you make a radio speech on the lines of what you have said here tonight and urge the President's re-election?" The Democratic National Committee had reserved time for Tuesday night. Shaking his head, Kennedy said it was not in his heart until he had gotten a few things off his chest.

They joined the president and Missy Le Hand in the upstairs Oval Study where Kennedy and Roosevelt had talked and joked in the early days of the New Deal. But tonight there was a tense undercurrent. As the guests entered the room, the president was seated at his desk, Rose Kennedy recorded, "shaking a cocktail shaker and reaching over for a few lumps of ice with his powerful hands." Over a Roosevelt Sunday dinner of scrambled eggs and sausages, the ambassador reported on conditions under the Blitz and his visit with the dying Chamberlain. Byrnes again raised the question of a Kennedy speech for Roosevelt; the president chimed in that such an address was "essential to the success of the campaign." Kennedy gave no direct reply. Undaunted, Roosevelt wooed Mrs. Kennedy with a succession of stories about her father. "The President worked very hard on Rose, whom I suspect he had come down because of her great influence on me," Kennedy later wrote.

The ambassador was keen to withdraw from the group for his showdown with Franklin Roosevelt, but before long it became obvious that the president had no intention of leaving the room. "Since it doesn't seem possible for me to see the President alone, I guess I'll just have to say what I am going to say in front of everybody," Kennedy burst out. As her husband spoke, Mrs. Kennedy observed that Roosevelt looked "rather pale, rather ashen, and I always noticed the nervous habit he had of nervously snapping his eyes."

"In the first place," the ambassador began, "I am damn sore at the way I have been treated. I feel that it is entirely unreasonable and I don't think I rated it. Mr. President, as you know, I have never said anything privately in my life that I didn't say to you personally, and I have never said anything in a public interview that ever caused you the slightest embarrassment." Whenever the president or a member of the Roosevelt family got into a jam, whom did they turn to but Kennedy? Despite all the public doubts, he had come out for the third term a year ago. Over and over again he had pledged his loyalty to the president. For all this, presidential messengers like Sumner Welles, Donovan, and Ghormley had paraded through London to transact business over his head, while Kennedy was kept on the shelf. Even when issues as critical as the destroyer deal were being negotiated, nobody had bothered to inform the ambassador. "All these things were conducive to harming my influence in England if I had not gone to the British government and said, 'If you don't let me know all about this, your country is going to find me most unfriendly toward the whole situation.' So I smashed my way through—with no thanks to the American government." He would not go back to London.

Rose Kennedy tactfully suggested that perhaps it was hard to get the right perspective on a situation three thousand miles away. But the president offered no rebuttal to Kennedy's stream of consciousness. He said that, as far as he was concerned, Kennedy was being charitable. The officious men at the State Department should not be permitted to treat old, dear friends and valued public servants like Joe Kennedy with such callousness. Roosevelt had not been aware of their cavalier attitude ("which isn't true," Kennedy said later). Only the pressures of the European crisis had forced the president to brook such outrageous behavior. After the election there would be "a real housecleaning" to ensure that the most important members of the administration like Joe Kennedy would never again be abused. As the president improved upon his ambassador's complaints, Byrnes thought Kennedy was "even beginning to feel a touch of sympathy for the State Department boys."

The next portion of the dialogue remained a mystery. John Kennedy said later that Franklin Roosevelt gave his father the impression that evening that he had the president's blessing for the 1944 Democratic nomination. It would have been characteristic of Roosevelt, who "offered" the 1940 nomination—or so the "nominees" believed—to a sufficient number of ambitious men to fragment the field and bring on the draft at Chicago. Now Roosevelt probably dangled the bait ambiguously enough before Kennedy to whet his political appetite. Others later insisted that the president confronted Kennedy with transcripts of his indiscreet London conversations, acquired through British intelligence. Not only would this have been untypically heavyhanded for Roosevelt, but, as Kennedy noted, his cocktail criticism was hardly a surprise at the White House. James Roosevelt believed his father warned Kennedy that abandoning him now would mark him as a Judas Iscariot for the rest of his life: Kennedy's boys were fine boys—and the president wanted to help them in politics—but Kennedy would ruin their careers if he deserted Roosevelt now.

All sources were agreed on the conclusion of the conversation. The president asked Kennedy to deliver the speech endorsing his reelection.

"All right, I will," Kennedy replied. "But I will pay for it myself, show it to nobody in advance, and say what I wish." No sooner did he speak than Missy Le Hand telephoned the Democratic National Committee to ask that the Tuesday radio time be turned over to Kennedy.

During dinner, a White House aide had prematurely informed newspapermen that Kennedy would accompany the president by train to New York, where Roosevelt would speak at Madison Square Garden. It was Sunday night and the tired reporters assumed from the announcement that Kennedy had decided to support the president. All but a few departed. But the old Hollywood man would not relieve the suspense he had so masterfully created. Leaving the executive mansion, Kennedy told a skeleton crew that he had turned down Roosevelt's invitation. He would fly immediately to New York and hold a press conference at the Waldorf-Astoria at eleven o'clock Monday morning. The reporters came alive with talk of Kennedy's stormy departure from the White House. (They were unaware of one piece of evidence that would have belied this conclusion: Mrs. Kennedy had accepted the president's invitation to stay overnight at the mansion.)

The next morning Kennedy canceled his press conference. Edward Moore told reporters instead that "Ambassador Kennedy will speak over the nationwide Columbia network on Tuesday at nine p.m." Willkie supporters rejoiced at the news. Analysts at the Foreign Office in London also concluded that Kennedy was endorsing the Republican. A *Washington Star* reporter was less certain, writing that Kennedy's plans remained "as much of a mystery as ever. It all depended on what the President told him Sunday night." Suspicions intensified that evening when the president spoke to twenty-two thousand cheering Democrats at Madison Square Garden. Prominent on the platform was one infidel, Jim Farley. But where was Kennedy?

Election day was now one week away.

"Good evening, my fellow Americans," Kennedy began on Tuesday evening. "On Sunday, I returned from war-torn Europe to the peaceful shores of our beloved country renewed in my conviction that this country must and will stay out of war." Kennedy stated his feeling that both presidential candidates shared this conviction. Then he offered the assurance that millions were waiting to hear: "Unfortunately, during this political campaign, there has arisen the charge that the President of the United States is trying to involve this country in the world war. Such a charge is *false*." In an age of lightning events, "the man of experience is our man of the hour." Kennedy confessed that he disagreed sharply with the president's positions on some issues, but how many employees ever agreed entirely with the policies of their employers? Now national teamwork was vital—and only the most inescapable differences could be allowed to interfere. From London he had watched the collapse of Denmark, Norway, Belgium, Holland, "proud and honorable France." It was "later than you think"—no time to train a new and inexperienced president.

"In my years of service for the government, both at home and abroad, I have sought to have honest judgment as my goal. From the other side, I sent reports to the President and the Secretary of State which were my best judgment about the forces that were moving, the developments that were likely and the course best suited to protect America.

"After all, I have a great stake in this country. My wife and I have given nine hostages to fortune. Our children and your children are more important than anything else in the world. The kind of America that they and their children will inherit is of grave concern to us all.

"In the light of these considerations, I believe that Franklin D. Roosevelt should be re-elected President of the United States."

Like a Broadway director on opening night, Kennedy awaited his reviews. They were resounding. Telegrams poured into the White House and Democratic National Committee. "Get Kennedy on the radio every day and night for the rest of the campaign," wired an Ohio precinct captain. A North Carolinian reported that Kennedy's speech had converted him to the Roosevelt cause. The *New York Times* and other newspapers published the complete text. "As a vote-getting speech, it was probably the most effective of the campaign," thought *Life*. Wendell Willkie woefully agreed. Ernest Lindley considered it the best case for Roosevelt to come from the conservative side. Henry Morgenthau told Kennedy his speech was "perfectly swell." Jerome Frank, Kennedy's successor at the Securities Commission: "One of the finest things I have ever heard." The most heartwarming praise came from a master of radio. "I have just listened to a great speech," wired Franklin Roosevelt. "Thank you."

The Democratic National Committee took out newspaper advertisements: "This one simple, sincere statement by Ambassador Joe Kennedy smashed into smithereens Wendell Willkie's brutal charge that President Roosevelt is planning to send our boys to England. . . . For months on end, Joe Kennedy remained at his post in London, braving the fire and bombs and death to perform his duty to the American people and the land he loves. . . . And then Joe Kennedy boarded an airplane and flew home—to tell the American people the truth. . . ."

Some were unconvinced. A disappointed General Wood thought Kennedy had been something less than forthcoming and chided him with the hope that "after the election it may be possible to speak a little more frankly and freely." Kennedy's air attaché in London, Colonel Raymond Lee, regarded the speech as proof that "Kennedy has no depth of political philosophy" and "is exactly the opportunist that everyone now thinks he is." Wendell Willkie, on the stump in Baltimore, fulminated against the notion of American diplomats "back here making cheap political speeches like any hirelings trying to hold their jobs." (He left to the imaginations of his audience whether he would have objected to a cheap political speech for Willkie.) The Republican nominee croaked a challenge into the microphones: "Mr. Third Term Candidate, is your pledge about peace and the acceptance of the Democratic platform in 1940 more or less sacred than the pledge you made about sound money in 1932? Are you kidding Joe Kennedy the way you kidded Carter Glass?"

Henry and Clare Boothe Luce were astonished by Kennedy's address. For some reason he had failed to warn them of his change of heart and offered little more than a halfhearted apology to the publisher a few months later. But Mrs. Luce continued to wonder what had happened that evening at the White House to make Kennedy change his mind. Sixteen years later she asked him.

Kennedy explained that he had had no choice but to fly straight to Washington because "you just don't refuse a Presidential invitation." He said that the president had assured him that there was no real difference between Roosevelt and Willkie on the war issue. Willkie's image as a man who would keep out of the fighting was merely "a ploy that worked too well." Then Kennedy flashed the disarming grin that Clare Luce considered the clue to his most compelling reason:

"I simply made a deal with Roosevelt. We agreed that if I endorsed him for President in 1940, then he would support my son Joe for governor of Massachusetts in 1942."

On Halloween eve the president came to Boston for one of the culminating rallies of the campaign. From South Station, he motored with Honey Fitz and Joseph Kennedy, Jr., to join the ambassador at Boston Garden. There he delivered a speech so convincingly isolationist that Wendell Willkie would cry, "That hypocritical son of a bitch! This is going to beat me!" All eyes were on the East Bostonian sitting at the president's elbow. Roosevelt welcomed "back to the shores of America that Boston boy, beloved by all of Boston and a lot of other places, my Ambassador to the Court of St. James's, Joe Kennedy." The reference to "my Ambassador," though technically correct, would be seized as proof of Roosevelt's dictatorial ambitions in the last days of the campaign.

But the audience that evening responded demonstratively to a more significant declaration. When the applause died away, the maestro worked up to his peroration: "I have said this before, but I shall say it again and again and again: *Your boys are not going to be sent into any foreign wars!*" Joseph Kennedy joined in the ovation.

"The fight is close and vicious," he cabled a British friend. Six nights later, the president emerged from the Big House at Hyde Park for the traditional torchlight victory procession. Once more, Joseph Kennedy had played an important role, and once more he anticipated an important post in the new administration. Perhaps a cabinet position or perhaps, according to rumor, Kennedy would chair the new commission on national defense. But this time there would be no reward.

The Greatest Cause in the World

Franklin Roosevelt returned to Washington two days after the counting of the ballots. Encouraged by a local newspaper, the capital city cast away its cloak of nonchalance. Washingtonians burst through police lines at Union Station as the president shook hands with congressmen and cabinet members. Thousands followed the black limousine through the streets while a marching band performed. They spilled onto the lawn of the White House, where the Roosevelts and the Henry Wallaces acknowledged the ovation from the north portico. Later that morning, Joseph Kennedy arrived to offer his congratulations and his resignation.

He had called at the State Department the previous day. Breckinridge Long, assistant secretary of state, listened as Kennedy spun his vision of a crumbling British Empire and a Europe dominated by Hitler. "He thinks that we ought to take some steps to implement a realistic policy and make some approach to Germany and to Japan which would result in an economic collaboration," Long recorded. "He does not see how or what." But of one thing the ambassador was convinced. "He thinks that we will have to assume a Fascist form of government here or something similar to it if we are to survive in a world of concentrated and centralized power."

Kennedy revealed that he had twice received invitations from Hitler for a conference; these he had refused. "Hitler must have got the impression Kennedy had views which Hitler might use as an approach to us," Long surmised. "As a matter of fact, Kennedy thinks we ought to lay the basis for some cooperation. He does not go to the extent of appeasing . . .

but he is positive in the thought something should be done—some uncharted way found." Kennedy told Long that he was flying to the West Coast to generate opposition to intervention in Europe. He would see prominent publishers and longtime friends such as Hearst, McCormick, and Patterson. But first he would talk to the president.

Entering the Oval Room Kennedy saw "a very tired but very happy-looking man." "Well, you've got it. I certainly don't begrudge you the next four years," he told Roosevelt. "I think I should hand in my resignation at once," Kennedy went on, "I've told you how I feel being Ambassador without anything to do. . . . To sit there doing nothing and have whatever has to be done handled through the British Embassy—I'd rather come home." The president did not try to dissuade Kennedy; he could not blame him after suffering so at the hands of the State Department. He asked Kennedy to keep his departure a secret until his successor was chosen. They discussed Anthony Biddle for the post. Kennedy put in a closing shot: if Germany continued to devastate British ports, America would not only be powerless to help but defenseless if the Axis turned to the Western Hemisphere. The nation must stay out of war. Roosevelt said he agreed with both conclusions. Kennedy departed to deny he was resigning and Roosevelt went off to lunch with Henry Morgenthau—but not before a frank exchange. "You will either go down as the greatest President in history," declared Kennedy, "or the greatest horse's ass."

"There is a third alternative," Roosevelt remonstrated. "I may go down as the President of an unimportant country at the end of my term."

The editor of the *Boston Globe* wanted a Sunday piece on the local luminary who had been such a pivotal figure in the final week of the presidential campaign. He gave the assignment to one of his ablest reporters, Louis Lyons. On Saturday, November 9 Lyons arrived at the ambassador's suite at the Ritz-Carlton Hotel. Two journalists from the *St. Louis Post-Dispatch* were also waiting there to do a background interview with the returned envoy. A secretary presented the three men to Kennedy, who was dining casually on apple pie and cheese, his suspenders drooped by his sides.

They heard ninety minutes of the rapid-fire opinions that had made Kennedy so popular with the Washington and London press. But this afternoon he spoke even more freewheelingly than usual. "It was almost as though he were making a campaign speech," Lyons remembered, "but not for Roosevelt. . . ." His editors were equally startled; to keep the story from sensationalism, they asked Lyons to bury Kennedy's most explosive comments in the text of a feature article.

The next morning Neville Chamberlain died in London. The *Globe*'s city editor telephoned Kennedy for comment; he also mentioned that the ambassador had given quite an interview to Louis Lyons. "Why?" Kennedy asked nervously. "What did he say?" The editor read out some quotes from the article. There was silence, and then: "He wrote all that?"

Kennedy's interview made headlines across the United States and throughout Great Britain. The remarks were not new for Kennedy, but British censorship and journalistic discretion had kept them out of almost every channel but the gossip circles and the minute books at Whitehall. "Democracy is all finished in England," Kennedy was quoted as saying. "It may be here. Because it comes to a question of feeding people. It's all an economic question. I told the President last Sunday, 'Don't send me fifty admirals and generals. Send me a dozen real economists.' It's the loss of our foreign trade that's going to change our form of government. . . .

"What's there to be gay about? If we get into war . . . a bureaucracy would take over right off. Everything we hold dear would be gone. They tell me that after 1918, we got it all back again, but this is different. There's a different pattern in the world."

Kennedy had shot off salvos on a range of subjects. The queen had "more brains than the Cabinet." Eleanor Roosevelt was another wonderful woman, but "she bothered us more on our jobs in Washington to take care of the poor little nobodies who hadn't any influence than all the rest of the people down there altogether." The leitmotif however was Kennedy's apprehensions over the coming storm. He had supported Franklin Roosevelt, he said, because the president was "the only man who can control the groups who have got to be brought along in what's ahead of us. . . . I mean the have-nots. They haven't any stake of ownership. They've got to take it whatever faces us." Kennedy was "willing to spend all I've got to keep us out of the war. There's no sense in our getting in. We'd just be holding the bag."

His opinions found their way into print through a misunderstanding. Kennedy believed that at least some of his remarks would remain off the record, Lyons that the entire exchange was intended for publication—except for the comments that Kennedy had specifically branded as confidential. Kennedy repudiated the article, holding that his published statements provided a different impression from what he had intended and also that Lyons had reported the interview without benefit of notes. He demanded a retraction. The *Globe* stood by its reporter. Kennedy retaliated by withdrawing thousands of dollars in liquor advertising from the newspaper.

But the damage could not be withdrawn. Many of Kennedy's London friends were bitter. William Allen White's Committee to Defend America by Aiding the Allies petitioned the president to repudiate Kennedy as "an enemy of the democratic way of life." Arthur Krock faithfully wrote Kennedy that "if there is anything I can do to dispel the ill effect of that unfortunate interview, I stand ready, as usual, to do it." Krock persuaded White to apologize to Kennedy and told the ambassador that the Kansas editor was actually less unfriendly than he appeared. "These people who like me privately and give me hell publicly don't warm my heart much," Kennedy replied.

His rivals savored the faux pas. Ickes and Frankfurter both made sure that the president had read Kennedy's interview. Frankfurter went so far as to send a copy to the White House, adding that "what is printed watered down some of the things Joe said. They were so raw the Globe did not want to print them." He might have spared himself the effort. Roosevelt could hardly have missed the furor. He asked Archibald MacLeish, librarian of Congress, to confirm the authenticity of Kennedy's published remarks.

Thoughtful commentators, although critical, debated Kennedy's hypothesis on a level more serious than the yammering of an enemy of democracy. Professor Harold Laski, the British socialist who taught both of the ambassador's eldest sons at the London School of Economics, assumed that Kennedy's fears for democracy stemmed from the belief that "the growth of state power—inevitable in wartime—is an irresponsible growth, which develops a vested interest of its own alien from public well-being." Laski reminded Americans that "with a nation, as with an individual, it profits nothing to retain its whole world if it thereby loses its own soul." Walter Lippmann, less admiring of Kennedy than during the First New Deal, observed wryly that if one decided that "democracy is finished because it is making these extraordinary sacrifices to save itself from destruction, he is of course entitled to his opinion, and even in England, where democracy is supposed to be finished, his opinion will be published."

Other Americans lacked this scholarly detachment. "I hope you put Joe Kennedy in a bag and pull the string tight," read one of the angry letters to the White House. As after the Trafalgar Day address two years before, many asked whether Kennedy's opinions represented administration policy. Franklin Roosevelt tried to muffle the reverberations from

Kennedy's interview with another militant declaration. At the Tomb of the Unknown Soldier, he reminded an Armistice Day audience that the United States must defend democracy and all that it stood for.

Three days after the interview was published Kennedy arrived in California. Harry Warner, Samuel Goldwyn, Louis B. Mayer, and other motion picture magnates welcomed their old colleague back to Hollywood with a grand luncheon at Warner Brothers. After dessert, the guest of honor rose to deliver an impromptu talk that staggered his listeners. The remarks were off the record, but they spread quickly around the film colony. Douglas Fairbanks, Jr., sent a confidential report to the president. The actor apologized for his "hurried and probably too passionate letter" but he and many of his friends had been disturbed by the ambassador's comments. Kennedy had declared that "the Lindbergh appeasement groups were not so far off the mark when they suggest that this country can reconcile itself to whomever wins the war and adjust our trade and lives accordingly. . . . He apparently threw the fear of God into many of our producers and executives by telling them that the Jews were on the spot and they should stop making anti-Nazi pictures or using the film medium to promote or show sympathy to the cause of the democracies versus the dictators." Fairbanks felt Kennedy had been "violently influenced by strong Catholic appeasement groups and is in favor of a negotiated peace."

The actor told Roosevelt that he did not like to "tattle" but had observed that "many people are beginning to feel that because he is still accredited to you as Ambassador . . . he is voicing new Administration thoughts. On the other hand, there are many of us who do not, can not and will not believe that that is so." British intelligence in New York reported a "very strong feeling of fear that there is a great deal in what Mr. Kennedy said." Still, not all in Hollywood were frightened. Darryl Zanuck of Twentieth Century-Fox told friends that Kennedy wanted to "scare the Jews out of the film business so that he can get back into it." It took no more than two weeks for sensational reports of Kennedy's talk to emerge in the newspapers. "Ambassador Joseph P. Kennedy has been denying newspaper stories lately," Drew Pearson wrote, "but in Hollywood recently, he had the movie moguls almost pop-eyed. . . ."

Kennedy flew north to Wyntoon, William Randolph Hearst's wilderness retreat outside San Francisco. There was talk that he might help the publisher by taking over the helm of the troubled Hearst empire. At a cocktail party, the ambassador encountered Anna and John Boettiger. According to Hearst's longtime companion Marion Davies, Boettiger con-

SOME ARMISTICE DAY OBSERVATIONS

It will be interesting to know how Future Historians will rate Neville Chamberlain.

President Roosevelt speaks of Democracy in his Armistice day address.

Ambassador Kennedy gives an important interview.

November 12, 1940.

McCUTCHEON, *Chicago Tribune*

fronted Kennedy: What right had he to oppose the president's principles? "Now wait a minute," Kennedy replied, "I have not in any way said I'm not in accord with what your father-in-law says. Let's not argue now." Miss Davies suggested that they all have a drink. But the two men squared off as the ladies withdrew. Later Boettiger sent a warning to the president: "After our talk with Joe in California, both Anna and I were considerably worried about what we thought were Fascist leanings."

After returning to New York Kennedy called on Herbert Hoover. Despite their places on opposite sides of the political fence in 1932, Kennedy and the former president were growing closer as Kennedy's relations with Franklin Roosevelt grew more difficult. Hoover recorded Kennedy's observation that "there was no long-view statesmanship left in England. That Churchill had a precarious position, largely because of his short view, and that he was an entirely bellicose character." Kennedy confided that "the British had received an offer of peace in September, through Sweden. That the offer provided for the full maintenance of the British Empire, their fleet and everything else. It provided also for the Germans making the entire continental settlement without interference from the British. Churchill had refused it." Had the president been consulted? Hoover asked. Kennedy seemed unclear, but he did say he had told the British that "they had better take it." Why had they refused the German proposal? "Nothing but Churchill's bullheadness."

Kennedy went on to report that the confidence of the British was based "solely on their obsession that Roosevelt would bring the United States into the war, or at least that the war psychosis of the United States would develop to this end." He said he had told the president, "Whatever aid you extend to Britain you must regard as a bet on a losing horse." Hoover listened to Kennedy's fear that "if we went into the war, we would have a National Socialist state—he could see no return to democratic forms." The former president disagreed; he believed "we could plan a self-contained economy here, which would enable us to live, perhaps on a lower standard of living, but under which we could maintain democratic forms."

The sitting president told members of his cabinet that he believed the *Globe* interview was authentic. Kennedy had said substantially the same thing in Hollywood and had apparently also been seeing the nation's newspaper publishers to gain support for his views. "There is not any doubt that a powerful group is being formed that will make a public fight for some policy of appeasement," Harold Ickes concluded after cabinet. "Kennedy will be up to his neck in this and it will be well financed."

Franklin Roosevelt decided that it was time for the confrontation he had postponed for over two years.

The president and first lady had come to Hyde Park for a quiet weekend with the president's mother before Thanksgiving. Roosevelt brought with him a well-guarded secret—he would unveil Lend-Lease by year's end. The blazing colors of autumn were extinguished now and a bitter wind shook the elms along the Hudson. The Roosevelts spoke of Joseph Kennedy's Boston interview and his travels on the West Coast. "We'd better have him down here and see what he has to say," the president concluded.

Eleanor Roosevelt met the morning train at Rhinecliff and brought the ambassador straight to the president. The two men disappeared into the president's tiny study at the front of the house. Kennedy's vision of a vanquished Britain and an America adjusting to an authoritarian world was no more provocative than his conversations with Breckinridge Long, Louis Lyons, the Hollywood executives, William Randolph Hearst, Herbert Hoover, and the president himself only a month earlier. But now the election had passed and Franklin Roosevelt was freer to indulge the frustrations he had pent up for months.

Not ten minutes elapsed before Mrs. Roosevelt was called back to the Big House. The president asked Kennedy to step out of the room. His wife had rarely seen him so angry. His face was drained, his voice almost tremulously restrained:

"I never want to see that son of a bitch again as long as I live. Take his resignation and get him out of here!"

But Kennedy had been invited for the weekend, she reminded him, "and we've got guests for lunch and the train doesn't leave until two."

"Then you drive him around Hyde Park, give him a sandwich, and put him on that train!"

Mrs. Roosevelt could not understand her husband's wrath, she told friends, until she lunched with the ambassador at her cottage at Val-Kill. It was then that she listened to Kennedy's gloomy description of an omnipotent German air force. She took him back to the Rhinecliff station for the afternoon train. Twenty years later, she would look back on the president's angry episode with Joseph Kennedy as "the most dreadful four hours of my life."

Yet not even this showdown opened the breach for which Kennedy's critics had so long hoped. Franklin Roosevelt rarely allowed himself the pleasure of willing an errant ally entirely off the reservation, especially one who could so skillfully throw a hammer into his diplomatic machinery in the coming months. And despite the travails in London, the hostility around the White House, and his words with the president at Hyde Park, Kennedy still hoped for a new government appointment.

On the first of December Kennedy delivered his resignation letter. He was sorry to bother the president, he said, but hated people to think the ambassador was sunning himself in Florida while London was being bombed. Roosevelt asked Kennedy to continue his diplomatic functions until his successor was sworn in. "That's O.K. as long as I'm out," Kennedy replied. He read the formal statement he had prepared and once again warned the president against Churchill.

"I know. He is one of the few men in public life who was rude to me." Perhaps to evoke some sympathy, the president reminded Kennedy of his problems. Fitting labor into the defense program, naval contractors into the naval program—people didn't realize all the burdens that the president had to shoulder.

"For God's sake," Kennedy replied, "don't let anything happen to you and then have to take Wallace. You're responsible for him and he has no experience."

Outside the West Wing, the retired ambassador told reporters, "Today the President was good enough to express regret over my decision." He quieted speculation that his departure had been precipitated by the *Globe* interview, noting that he had told Roosevelt on November 6 that he was planning to resign. "My plan is, after a short holiday, to devote my efforts to what seems to me to be the greatest cause in the world today—and means, if successful, the preservation of the American form of democracy. That cause is to help the President keep the United States out of war."

Alarm flared again that Kennedy's words reflected Roosevelt's policy. "When the President's own Ambassador to London, Mr. Kennedy, contributes to the general defeatism and announces that he is 'helping the President,' " wrote columnist Dorothy Thompson, "the public becomes weary, confused and even more apathetic." Alsop and Kintner predicted that Kennedy was about to "peddle appeasement all across the United States," (Kennedy heatedly reminded Kintner that he was responsible for many of the two columnists' most fruitful sources.) Harold Ickes wrote in his journal that Kennedy was "an outstanding example of what the President can do in the way of an appointment when he is at his worst. Despite the fact that Kennedy was nothing but a stock market gambler, with no political background and no social outlook, the President brought him here to make him chairman of the SEC. There he did everything he could for the stock market gamblers. Kennedy made a stiff fight to become Secretary of the Treasury and Morgenthau blocked him there. Against a less stubborn man than Morgenthau, or one less close to the President, he might have won. As a consolation prize, the President sent him to the Court of St. James's. . . . Now he is back here undertaking to sabotage the President's foreign policy."

At a cabinet meeting, Roosevelt discussed a covert campaign by a group of American businessmen and financiers to arrange a negotiated settlement between Great Britain and Germany. The movement was evidently led by a speculator named Bernard E. Smith, known on Wall Street in the days after the crash as "Sell 'Em Ben." Smith had traveled to Vichy at the beginning of December to sound out leaders of the collaborationist Pétain government. Attorney General Robert Jackson suggested to the president that they solve the problem immediately by revoking the financier's passport. A few days later, on December 4, the *Chicago Daily News* broke the story and suggested that the man behind Smith's mission was Joseph Kennedy. Telephoned in Palm Beach, Kennedy told the newspaper that Smith was merely an acquaintance whom, as best he could recall, he had not seen for over two years. Had Kennedy anything to do with the financier's meetings with collaborationist leaders in Vichy? "I think my first statement answers all questions."

Later, Carroll Binder, the foreign editor of the *Daily News*, confided to a British diplomat that Joseph Kennedy had been doing "everything in his power" to bring about a peace settlement. As Whitehall was informed, Kennedy had allegedly sent Ben Smith "to see Pétain and Hitler and to try to find some formula for the reconstruction of Europe to which they would both set their names." After achieving such a formula, Kennedy was to join two prominent, unnamed Britons to "start an agitation in England in favor of a negotiated peace." According to Binder, Franklin Roosevelt then discovered Kennedy's plan. Through the American ambassador in Vichy, Admiral William Leahy, the president persuaded Marshal Pétain to refuse an audience with Smith.

Roosevelt cited Kennedy and Smith to his cabinet as prominent examples of the problem of "our appeasers." It was reported elsewhere that the administration was investigating Kennedy's private activities and his tax returns. The president planned the most unmistakable stroke of all for the end of the month. He told the cabinet that he was drafting a major address that would signalize the future course of American foreign policy.

Harold Ickes, among many, was delighted. "It would put us right on the firing line and very clearly against the appeasement campaign that Joe Kennedy and others are supposed to be planning."

Officially, Kennedy was still ambassador, awaiting the naming of his successor. He was as divided as ever between maintaining his ties to Franklin Roosevelt and breaking away to promote his independent views. General Wood offered him a splendid platform, the chairmanship of America First. But Kennedy turned him down: "My own hunch is, at least for the time being while I am Ambassador in name, I won't join any committees, and after I get out I think I will have to decide just how I think I can work best." Wood replied with a reproof: "You are the one man who can speak with authority. I believe that if you made some speeches or wrote some articles explaining why it would be disastrous for this country to get into the war, it would turn the tide. I believe it is your duty to do so."

On December 17 the president revealed at a press conference his plan to provide billions of dollars in war supplies to Great Britain. Two days later, Joseph Kennedy criticized Lend-Lease in a letter to Congressman Louis Ludlow, author of the amendment requiring a national referendum to declare war that was defeated in the House by only a single vote. "While our own defenses are weak, we are limited as to what we can do for Britain, even though we want to," Ludlow read on the House floor from Kennedy's statement. "Therefore, our first obligation is to speed up defense with all our might." But even this equivocal letter Kennedy quickly denied was a criticism of the president. The congressional isolationists though otherwise. "Thank God for Joseph P. Kennedy," declaimed Ludlow.

Franklin Roosevelt delivered his long-awaited address to the nation two days before the end of 1940. "Never before since Jamestown and Plymouth Rock has our American civilization been in such danger as now," he began. The president warned that highly placed Americans—"unwittingly, in most cases"—were furthering the cause of foreign agents. "The experience of the past two years has proven beyond doubt that no nation can appease the Nazis." He cautioned against these "American appeasers" who cried that "the Axis powers are going to win anyway, that all this bloodshed in the world can be saved, that the United States might just as well throw its influence into the scale of a dictated peace, and get the best out of it that we can. They call it a 'negotiated peace.'

"Nonsense! Is it a negotiated peace if a gang of outlaws surrounds your community and on threat of extermination makes you pay tribute to save your own skins? . . . We must be the great arsenal of democracy. For us, this is an emergency as serious as war itself."

Joseph Kennedy received a letter from John Boettiger: "Anna and I have been wondering concerning your thoughts on hearing FDR's address of last evening. We do hope you will stay on his side!" But when the House of Representatives scheduled hearings on the president's Lend-Lease bill, Kennedy volunteered to be the opening witness for the opposition.

Eight

WINTER OF DISCONTENT

LEGISLATORS AND DIPLOMATS, justices and journalists, cabinet secretaries, photographers, family and friends gathered in the well of the House. It was six days into 1941. There was a signal, an announcement, and then waves of applause engulfed the chamber as the president made his way to the rostrum. Coming on the heels of the call for an "arsenal of democracy," Franklin Roosevelt's State of the Union address might have been expected to be deliberately uncaptivating. The president himself had observed years before that public psychology could not long be tuned to the highest note on the scale. But Roosevelt presented his audience a summons to a nation grounded on an economic Bill of Rights and a world founded on the Four Freedoms.

As in the fireside chat a week earlier, the president injected a warning into this highminded appeal that was scarcely veiled. "In times like this, it is immature—and incidentally, untrue—for anybody to brag that an unprepared America, singlehanded, and with one hand tied behind its back, can hold off the entire world." From a dictator's peace, no realistic American could expect "international generosity, or return of true independence, or world disarmament, or freedom of expression, or freedom of religion—or even good business. . . . We must always be wary of those who with sounding brass and tinkling cymbal preach the 'ism' of appeasement."

ROOSEVELT BRANDS FOES OF HIS FOREIGN POLICY, proclaimed an article in *Life*, whose editors believed they knew whom the president meant. Illustrating the piece was a veritable rogues' gallery of suggested appeasers, including General Hugh Johnson, Lawrence Dennis, philosopher of fascism, the Lindberghs, Ben Smith, and Joseph Kennedy, identified as "defeatist about Britain, in favor of a quick peace."

Several days later Kennedy left Palm Beach for Washington. At the airport he found that a fellow passenger was Franklin Roosevelt, Jr., on leave from the navy. Chatting with his father's old companion during the flight, young Roosevelt was struck by Kennedy's despair: "He was convinced that Hitler would ride right over Europe and that we should pressure England into negotiating the best peace it could." Kennedy criticized the people around the president, the names pouring out in a torrent—Harry Hopkins, Sumner Welles, Bill Donovan. . . . The president's son deflected Kennedy's challenges with "I'm only a naval officer" and "That's between you and my father." Kennedy's monologue grew so zealous, however, that another passenger tapped him on the shoulder to ask if he would kindly lower his voice. Kennedy asked Franklin if he knew who the man was. Franklin did not know, but thought the man's accent sounded English. "I thought so," Kennedy blustered. "I hate all of those goddamned Englishmen from Churchill on down."

In Washington Kennedy announced that he would speak on radio to resolve the controversy over his views on international affairs. One correspondent predicted he would break with the president and " 'tell all' in a peace-at-any-price broadcast." Behind the scenes, however, Kennedy tried to come back into Franklin Roosevelt's government. Arthur Krock discreetly suggested to the British embassy in Washington that the retired ambassador might be the perfect choice to help Britain ease its nagging troubles with neutral Ireland. A Kennedy visit to President Eamon de Valera might move the government of Eire to open its ports to British warships. Interested British officials broached the idea to Secretary Hull.

On January 16, two days before Kennedy's broadcast, he met with the president for ninety minutes at the White House. Roosevelt's vow never to see this man again had dissolved in the face of Kennedy's potent threats to mobilize American opinion against Lend-Lease. Kennedy complained, as he had during the home leaves from London, about the injuries inflicted upon him in the newspapers by Roosevelt's "hatchetmen." The president dryly remarked that he had himself suffered worse. And as in days of old, Roosevelt tried to keep Kennedy on the reservation with the suggestion of another government job. As Kennedy recorded, the president said "he would like to have a long talk with me about the Irish situation which, according to Welles, I was the only one who could help in straightening it out." Kennedy said it was too bad that all the important jobs had to go to Republicans like Stimson, Knox, and James Forrestal, men who had done nothing to aid Roosevelt's reelection. The president "astounded" him by declaring that there were "no good administrators" among the Democrats.

Then, talk of Lend-Lease. Kennedy told Roosevelt (in Kennedy's recollection) that he "didn't think it was fair to wind up seven years of service in his Administration with a bad record and I had gone in for everything he wanted, and this time I had to do something for the Kennedy family." The president could probably force the bill through Congress, Kennedy said, but the request for such vast power left a bad taste in the mouths of many people. Roosevelt confessed that he was asking for a great deal, but hoping for much less: "I could stand on my head under this bill, but I don't propose to do it."

"That's one of the difficulties the country worries about. They are not sure you want to keep out of war."

"I've said it a hundred-and-fifty times at least," the president exclaimed. "For the last seven years, I have been going to get them into every war that has taken place in Europe—and I haven't done it yet." Ken-

January 18, 1941.

BERRYMAN, *Washington Star*

nedy wrote later, "I don't know whether it was due to my suspicions, but it didn't sound as convincing as it did before when he said the same thing."

Kennedy decided to remain with Franklin Roosevelt, at least for the time being. "One of the most discouraging things that I have experienced the few months before I came home, and the time I have been home, is the very evident desire of those around the President to split us up," he wrote John Boettiger. "Of course, that would be a loss only for me, but nobody ever mentions that I have done any service for him ever; just let anybody get any angle at all they can twist and they are running around like a lot of mosquitoes. . . ."

On the afternoon of his visit with the president, Kennedy avoided an old friend who had become one of Roosevelt's worst adversaries. Burton Wheeler, now a grand marshal of the isolationists, had infuriated the president not long before by denouncing the foreign policy that would "plow under every fourth American boy." Roosevelt told the press that Wheeler's remark was "the most dastardly, unpatriotic thing that has been said in public life in my generation." (Kennedy reminded a White House aide that the president had broken one of his own political commandments—by mentioning Wheeler's comment, Roosevelt had ensured that the senator's message would be heard not by five thousand but five million.) Kennedy had invited Wheeler to come to his hotel suite to talk after his White House meeting. But when the senator knocked, there was no answer. He asked a chambermaid to let him in with a passkey. Kennedy bashfully emerged from behind the door.

To Be and Not to Be

"Shortly after I came home from London, I spoke over the radio for the re-election of President Roosevelt," Joseph Kennedy said into the microphones of the NBC Red network. "I declared then that my sincere judgment was that we ought to stay out of war. I urged that we give England all possible aid. I feel the same way about it today. . . ."

Kennedy's speech had been billed as his answer to the appeasement charges that were led by Franklin Roosevelt. "Many Americans, including myself, have been subjected to deliberate smear campaigns—merely because we differed from an articulate minority." His voice rising, Kennedy noted that "a favorite device of an aggressive minority is to call any American questioning the likelihood of a British victory an apostle of gloom—a defeatist." But if he had reported to Washington anything but the truth as he saw it, Kennedy argued, he would have betrayed both his trust and his country.

"Another label used as a smear against certain citizens who favor keeping America out of the war is the word appeaser. . . . If by that word, now possessed of hateful implications, it is charged that I advocate a deal with the dictators contrary to the British desires, or that I advocate placing any trust or confidence in their promises, the charge is *false* and *malicious*. . . . But if I am called an appeaser because I oppose the entrance of this country into the present war, I cheerfully plead guilty."

Now listeners across America anticipated the denunciation of Lend-Lease that had been widely advertised. There was no denunciation; instead, Kennedy tried to throw a catwalk between isolation and intervention. He backed aid to Britain—but only as a play for time, allowing the United States to rearm and withdraw into a well-guarded fortress in the Western Hemisphere. What about granting Roosevelt the momentous powers implied in the Lend-Lease bill? Kennedy confessed that he was "a great believer in centralized responsibility and therefore believe in conferring all powers necessary to carry out that emergency." But he questioned whether the national danger was dire enough for Congress to surrender such authority. Kennedy hoped that "after the hearings have been completed, there will be revealed less drastic ways of meeting the problem of adequate authority for the President." But he suggested none. Still, whatever happened, "all of us must rally behind the President so that he may carry on with a nation which has debated in the democratic manner. . . ."

In a great debate as impassioned as any in this century, Kennedy's caution was ridiculed as an effort to dodge the issue. Dorothy Thompson wrote that the envoy had out-Hamleted Hamlet—Kennedy's position was "to be *and* not to be." A fellow Boston Latin alumnus wired Kennedy that he had delivered a fine statement of the problem but had reached the wrong answer: "Regret to advise you that according to our strict Latin School standards, you are marked zero on this test." The *New York Herald-Tribune* praised Kennedy's talk as "a welcome voice for unity" and others advanced his position as a harmonizing middle ground between the most extreme camps. General Wood, somewhat surprisingly, told Kennedy his speech was "splendid" and "struck just the right note. I am sure it is going to be of great help in keeping this country out of the war." America First reprinted and circulated excerpts from the broadcast, but an internal memorandum at committee headquarters recorded the widespread comment that Kennedy had "straddled too much."

On the morning after Franklin Roosevelt was sworn into office for the third time, Kennedy took his place before the House Committee on Foreign Affairs. Through five hours of questioning, he managed to elude members such as Hamilton Fish of New York, the president's own congressman and political enemy, who probed for an unambiguous criticism of Lend-Lease. Kennedy continually referred his interlocutors to the text of his ambiguous radio broadcast. Did aid to Britain really require such an extreme grant of power as the bill provided the president? "In order to get things done, you have got to have power in one hand—and to that extent, I am one hundred percent for granting it," Kennedy replied, but even during emergencies, the president should consult Congress. Kennedy's proposal was a liaison committee between the Hill and the White House. "You would still have Congress functioning and at the same time, have a body that is not unwieldy."

But wasn't Kennedy worried by the prospect of Congress abdicating its constitutional authority? "I imagine they will have to surrender some prerogatives in this emergency, and it is a question of how great. . . ." What was the line of demarcation? "That seems to be the question you gentlemen have to decide." Didn't Kennedy have an opinion of his own? "I want to give the President it. I think he should have it. I think he is the best-fitted man to exercise it because I think he knows more about the situation than anybody else." Asked if he thought this solution might produce an American dictatorship, Kennedy cryptically replied, "I would not want to answer that question." Did he have faith in Franklin Roosevelt's integrity and patriotism? "Completely."

Drawn between his old confidence in centralized national authority and his doubts of the president's intentions, his ambitions to reenter the administration and to take his case to the people, Kennedy irked both his supporters and detractors by failing to stand squarely behind or against Lend-Lease. "Knowing that Britain couldn't survive without the Lend-Lease, I made no public statement against the bill despite my own objection to it," he wrote later in an explanation that shed scant light on his reasons for opposition. Kennedy's testimony differed little from the views of later supporting witnesses such as Wendell Willkie and William Allen White, but while Willkie and White acknowledged that Lend-Lease was more likely a step toward intervention than away, Kennedy represented the bill as a preventive against American involvement. This permitted him to preserve the notion that he could oppose intervention and support Franklin Roosevelt's policies. Kennedy's position skirted the conclusion that had already been reached by most public thinkers—that Lend-Lease embodied a commitment in itself from which there could be no shrinking back.

Columnist Raymond Clapper found Kennedy "almost as good a witness for the Administration as for the opposition" and suspected he had "earned another good reward from the Administration." Father Coughlin's *Social Justice* decided that any idea that Kennedy and Roosevelt had parted was fatuous. "Behind their sham-battling is a solid unanimity. Mr. Kennedy wants all aid for Britain short of war, which is tantamount to having his cake and eating it too." Congressman John

BERRYMAN, *Washington Star*

"The historic debate of Joe Kennedy vs. Joe Kennedy," January 21, 1941.

O'Connor, a staunch isolationist from New York and brother of the president's old law partner, complained, "If Roosevelt cannot win the so-called leaders over completely by calling them over to the White House and smiling at them, he at least does a ninety percent job on them so that they meet themselves coming back because of the fear of offending the throne."

Leaders on both sides of the war issue seized Kennedy's position as support for their views. Senator Byrnes assured reporters that Kennedy had presented a strong case for the president's policy. Hamilton Fish was equally certain that Kennedy had "hit the nail on the head" and said he agreed with the witness "one hundred percent." The presentation somewhat improved Kennedy's standing with his British friends but many resented that he did not do still more. Returning from his mission to London Wendell Willkie confided to Joseph Alsop that "the British people hate Joe Kennedy." He reported his jest with the queen that he hoped she would be more successful in influencing him than she had apparently been with the recent American ambassador.

When Harry Hopkins departed for London on presidential assignment in early January, he had paid a courtesy call on the former ambassador in New York, assuring Kennedy that Roosevelt was "not sold on the British at all." "Maybe my warnings to him to look after himself in dealing with Churchill were making an impression," Kennedy mused afterwards. But journalists attributed Kennedy's ambiguous stance on Lend-Lease to other White House persuasion that was less friendly. The *Christian Century* reported a whispering campaign about damaging documents on Kennedy that had been "secreted in confidential files of the White House." John O'Donnell and Doris Fleeson speculated that Harry Hopkins sought ammunition in London "for use against Kennedy if the Ambassador really opens up on the Administration's war policy." They reported that the president's top assistant was "checking up with Churchill and other English leaders on just what Kennedy might have said in confidence and off the record about the folks back home here—observations that might come in handy if Kennedy shoots the works."

These stories contained more than a kernel of truth. Harold Ickes, through a third party, received a message from Jan Masaryk in London that "just before Czechoslovakia fell, Joe Kennedy had sold Czech securities short and had made a profit of twenty thousand pounds." The interior secretary had been informed that "if Harry Hopkins should talk to Masaryk, he would get this story and that he might even be able to verify the fact through Kennedy's London brokers." Ickes wasted no time in transmitting this item to the president through Grace Tully.

The day before Kennedy's meeting with Roosevelt in mid-January, Ickes asked the president over lunch whether he had received the message from Miss Tully. "Yes," Roosevelt responded, holding up a sealed envelope, "and this letter is going by clipper to Harry Hopkins asking him to investigate." Ickes crowed into his journal, "Of course, if this can be nailed to Kennedy, we need have no fears of what he may do along the appeasement line over here, because a story of this kind, if it is sustained by the facts, would utterly ruin him in public estimation." But nothing was ever publicly "nailed" to Kennedy.

Alsop and Kintner revived the rumor of the campaign for a negotiated peace led by Kennedy and Ben Smith. A few months later, J. Edgar Hoover forwarded an FBI report to the White House. According to a source "for whom we cannot vouch," Kennedy and Smith "sometime in the past had a meeting with Goering in Vichy" and thereafter "donated a considerable amount of money to the German cause." Hoover's information doubtless did few wonders for Kennedy's standing at the White House.

During the spring of 1941 Joseph Kennedy finally reached the conclusion that opposing intervention and supporting Franklin Roosevelt were irreconcilable. He now realized that the president's promises to stay out of war had no meaning, he told Herbert Hoover. To the president's son-in-law, Kennedy wrote, "Now, if my statements and my position mean that, outside of the ever loyal Boettigers, I am to be a social outcast by the Administration, well so be it. I will be sorry, but if that's the way it is, it's just too bad. I will, at least, have the satisfaction of having fulfilled all my obligations."

In a commencement speech at Oglethorpe University in May Kennedy cast off the conditions and careful phrasing that had modified his statements on Lend-Lease and world war. "Let us not be deluded by a claim that self-interest should make us the guardians of the peace of the rest of the world." A British victory would be "helpful from the viewpoint of our foreign markets—but it is nonsense to say that an Axis victory spells ruin for us." The "crusaders' argument for war" was the "silliest of all." Increases in government spending, taxes, and federal regulation would have the effect of limiting production and consumption in the private sector forever. Then the United States would lie vulnerable to an even more perilous transformation. "When the war machine has run down and the economic shock is being felt by every man, woman and child, new and sweet-sounding slogans will fill the air. Shortcuts to utopia will be advocated on all sides." Franklin Roosevelt went unnamed, but Kennedy left little doubt about his target. "The people who must suffer and give up their lives are entitled to know all the facts before their judgment can be won to the interventionist cause. It is a mockery of liberty to withhold from a democratic people the essential facts upon which this, the most awful decision of our times, must be based."

This declaration of independence collapsed a few days later when the president announced a state of national emergency. Kennedy dutifully told another commencement audience at Notre Dame that Roosevelt's proclamation was "a most historic and most solemn pronouncement" that demanded the "unlimited loyalty" of all Americans.

Joseph Kennedy, Jr., a Harvard Law School student now, echoed his father's views on international affairs. With Langdon Marvin, Jr., the president's godson, and Quentin Roosevelt, grandson of the earlier president, the younger Kennedy formed the Harvard Committee Against Military Intervention. He invited his father as one of the first speakers. Joe enlisted in the Naval Aviation Cadet program and in June was sworn into the naval reserve as a seaman, second class. Also entering the navy in the same Boston ceremony was his friend John Roosevelt, who was to be a supply officer.

That month Great Britain made its alliance with the Soviet Union. Herbert Hoover asked Kennedy to sign a petition holding that the new partnership revealed finally that the European war was merely another incident in the Old World struggles for power. Was there any difference between a Nazi dictatorship and a Communist dictatorship? the document inquired. The United States should continue to serve as the arsenal of Britain and China, but the president must "abstain from further warlike and provocative deeds." Despite Hoover's notation that Alf Landon, Robert Hutchins of the University of Chicago, and others had already agreed to endorse the petition, Kennedy said he preferred to go it alone: "I can then take any position on any subject without consultation with anyone."

"It is a strange experience to watch the reaction of the public nowadays," Kennedy wrote in another letter to the former president in July, "I'm sure that they are lulled a bit into acquiescence in our foreign policy by the reports from Europe that indicate that Russia is holding her own. I think the minute the Germans are successful in that territory, public opinion will become surprisingly less interested in getting into any phase of the war."

This complacency penetrated Kennedy's private life. After a quiet summer on Cape Cod, he admitted to Arthur Krock in October that "the longer I stay away from Washington, the easier I find it to stay away. . . . Strangely enough, I find myself very comfortable in my mind at not being employed at this particular hour."

After Thanksgiving Kennedy departed for Palm Beach. There, on the afternoon of December 7, 1941, he received the news from Pearl Harbor.

In the Leper Colony

For all his resistance to intervention, Kennedy had never questioned that America should fight if attacked. Now he was eager to throw himself into the war effort. He shot off a telegram to the president: "In this great crisis, all Americans are with you. Name the battle front. I'm yours to command." He received only a form letter from Stephen Early.

In January 1942 John McCormack telephoned Kennedy after a White House meeting to report the president's surprise that Kennedy had failed to volunteer after Pearl Harbor. McCormack said he had corrected Roosevelt; the president had promised to look up Kennedy's message. But a month later Kennedy again learned of Roosevelt's annoyance at his supposed reluctance to serve—this time from Senator Alben Barkley. Kennedy called the White House to find that the president was unavailable. He was assured that the president would return his call. The president did not.

"I've found out one thing from an editorial in yesterday's newspaper," Kennedy wrote John Boettiger, "and that is that some former member of the intimate circle of President Franklin D. Roosevelt at some time or another has taken a stand that the President doesn't like. . . . I offered my services, of course, the Sunday the Japanese struck and I have never heard anything from it. However, it is one of those things you can't do anything about and I've called them as I saw them and I'd be perfectly willing to do anything that would be of any real value."

After two months of silence, Kennedy wrote a letter to the president, taking care to attach a copy of his December 7 telegram and Early's reply. He sent the envelope to Grace Tully with a request that it be delivered directly to the president. "I don't want to appear in the role of a man looking for a job for the sake of getting an appointment," Kennedy wrote, "but Joe and Jack are in the service and I feel that my experience in these critical times might be worth something in some position. I just want to say that if you want me, I'm yours to command at any time."

Roosevelt this time sent back a friendly response. Thousands of telegrams had been handled after Pearl Harbor without his ever seeing them, he explained. "I was, of course, sure that you wanted to do everything possible to help and I have had the suggestion from the Maritime Commission that you, knowing its earlier work and having had experience with the Fore River people, could be of real service in stepping up the great increase in our shipbuilding. . . . I know, for example, that you do not want to be merely a member of one of the many commissions—that you do want actual, practical and effective responsibility in turning out ships."

So many times had he been foiled by the president, Kennedy told a friend, he would not accept another job unless it was specifically defined. Kennedy called the new emergency shipping coordinator, Admiral

Emory Land, who had served under him on the Maritime Commission. He asked what kind of position the president had in mind, what results he would expect, what authority he was prepared to grant. Land called back the following day with three offers. Kennedy could launch a new shipbuilding corporation, aid management in existing yards that were flagging, or chair a labor board if one should be established.

Disappointed, Kennedy wrote Roosevelt that a new shipyard "might have been practical ten months or a year ago, but it certainly isn't today and I don't want to get into private enterprise and have a relationship with the government." Strengthen shipyard management? "It certainly wouldn't take me to do that." And a labor board was not even in the offing. Kennedy proposed instead that ship construction be separated from the remainder of the shipping program and that a full-time coordinator be appointed. He said nothing to suggest that he would not be interested in such a post. "I think you know that if I am given a job cleanly and concisely, I will work hard to get you the results you want, but running around without a definite program and authority—I'd just be a hindrance to the program."

It did not take long for the burden of Kennedy's letter to make the rounds of the White House and cabinet. Bill Bullitt told Ickes of how "Kennedy had insolently written to the President outlining the conditions under which he would take the job." Roosevelt indeed resented Kennedy's unwillingness to serve in any war capacity for which his services were requested. He returned to the gamesmanship of yore, keeping Kennedy in mind only for positions he knew were beneath those Kennedy would probably accept. 'What do I do about this?" the president asked Land about Kennedy's letter. "My personal slant is that you offer him a specific, definite job: (a) to run a shipyard, (b) to head a small hurry-up inspecting organization under Vickery to iron out kinks and speed up production in all yards doing Maritime Commission work."

The only position Land could think of was a job improving organization at two shipyards in Portland, Maine. This would reduce a general to the rank of first lieutenant. Kennedy dismissed the idea out of hand in a letter to James Byrnes: "There is not much point in adding confusion to chaos in my personal case and unless I can really do the President and the effort some good, it is silly to be just taking a job. Perhaps as the thing progresses, now that the ice is broken as far as the White House is concerned, something may turn up."

On April 16, 1942 Kennedy saw the president for the first time since his testimony on Lend-Lease over a year earlier. He told reporters afterwards that he had informed Roosevelt that "if there is any job he thought I could do, I would like to do it." But no further offers arose. A major reason was the antipathy of New Dealers springing from Kennedy's days in Washington and hardened by his activities in London and in America before Pearl Harbor. Harold Ickes's reaction when Bullitt mentioned the president's offer of the shipping position was not uncommon. The news, wrote Ickes, "made me gasp. I know, or think I do, that Kennedy is still an appeaser. Even if there is any doubt on this score, it cannot be denied that, as Bill reminded us, Kennedy continues to speak of the President in the most unfitting language. One of his choice expressions is 'that son of a bitch.' But he uses other expressions that I do not even feel like putting down in a private memorandum.

"I know that the President hates Kennedy. Bill's explanation of how it came about that the President made this offer is that it was the result of the importunings of Jimmy Roosevelt." Hoping to generate objections to Kennedy's return to Washington, the interior secretary spread the news to Frank Walker. He happily recorded Walker's remark that Kennedy had never done "anything in the government service that proved he was such a man as such people as Arthur Krock insists that he is. . . . Frank spoke of him as a stock market manipulator and he seemed to have as low an opinion of him as I have."

The uproar in the capital over a Kennedy appointment occasioned the president to consider Kennedy only for jobs that were informal or relatively in the background. Roosevelt had to contend, too, with the array of interest groups and elements in the press who exploded at the mere mention of Kennedy's name. "All-Outers Fear Pressure Will Put Kennedy In Job," headlined the progressive New York tabloid *PM*. The Coordinating Committee for Democratic Action saw Kennedy as "the choice of former isolationists, appeasers and pro-Vichy propagandists" whose appointment would wreak "almost incalculable effects both on the war effort and public morale, especially in the light of Kennedy's own antagonism to democratic ideals." Arthur Krock was told by a reader that offering Kennedy a public post higher than the level of day worker would be an insult to Britain and a comfort to Hitler. Krock replied by accusing the reader of slander. A FATAL MISTAKE TO APPOINT THIS APOSTLE OF APPEASEMENT TO ANY SHIPPING POSITION, Kennedy's old National Maritime Union foes wired the White House.

By 1942 Franklin Roosevelt seemed to play down his relationship with Joseph Kennedy in a manner once reserved for such controversial men as Father Coughlin, now constrained to cease publication of *Social Justice* in order to escape indictment for sedition. When reporters prodded the president on the purpose of Kennedy's April visit to the White House, Roosevelt reported "a very pleasant talk—that was all." Was there any possibility of Kennedy's return to the administration? "No, no."

There were occasional newspaper flurries. House Republican leader Joseph Martin, a not-unfriendly acquaintance from Massachusetts, proposed Kennedy as head of the president's shipping program, with "full and complete power to supervise the whole show." Arthur Krock continued to beat his drum. The *Washington Times-Herald* speculated on Kennedy's nomination as second man to Joseph Eastman, war transport administrator. But, as a Boston columnist close to Kennedy accurately reported, "It's the bureaucrats, the Perkinses, Frankfurters, Hopkinses and other on and off the record advisers who want no part of him, and mostly because he never wanted any part of them and was unpolitic enough to say so."

"When I saw Mr. Roosevelt, I was of the opinion that he intended to use me in the shipping situation," Kennedy reported in a letter to his friend Lord Beaverbrook, "but the radicals and certain elements in the New Deal hollered so loud that I was not even considered. Naturally, I am very unhappy that I have not had a chance to do anything, but I've made every effort that I could and unless things get a little worse, I'm not likely to be called. . . ."

In the spring of 1942 Senator Gerald Nye, the isolationist Republican made famous by investigating World War One "merchants of death" during the nineteen-thirties, received some information which, he thought, might be used to embarrass Franklin Roosevelt on Capitol Hill. The subject was James Roosevelt's association with Joseph Kennedy on British liquor franchises, made public by the *Saturday Evening Post* four years earlier. But according to Nye's impeachable informant, it was young Roosevelt rather than Kennedy who had procured the contracts prior to Repeal. Spurred on by resentful American liquor interests, several congressmen had allegedly confronted the president, threatening an investigation unless Roosevelt's son gave up his franchises. James was supposed to have transferred the contracts to Kennedy to avoid harming his father. In order to calm the British liquor companies who had granted the franchises, "it was considered a good idea to have the latter go to Great Britain in the capacity of Ambassador." J. Edgar Hoover informed the White House of the planned exposé before the senator dropped his idea, fearing damage to national unity.

That fall Senator Henry Cabot Lodge stood for reelection in Massachusetts. To oppose Lodge, the president had persuaded a New Deal congressman from Clinton, Joseph Casey. It was too bad that some anti-Roosevelt man could not be persuaded to oppose Casey in the primary, Joseph Kennedy remarked to a friend. He might have run himself but for having changed his legal address to Florida a year earlier—and the knowledge that the chances for victory against the popular Lodge were dismal. Kennedy's cousin, Joseph Kane, reminded him lightheartedly that his father-in-law was "not doing anything at the moment." John F. Fitzgerald was now seventy-nine years old. Honey Fitz liked the idea; he had lost narrowly to Lodge's grandfather in a Senate race in 1916 and was eager to settle old scores. Scrappy as ever, he entered the race, denouncing Casey as Franklin Roosevelt's "rubber stamp." Kennedy was the mastermind of the campaign, convincing William Randolph Hearst to turn his Boston paper over "lock, stock and barrel" for Fitzgerald, soliciting speech drafts and borrowing ideas from Jim Farley. (Bearing his own grudge against he president, Farley was intent on defeating John Bennett, the White House candidate for governor of New York.)

"We've had more fun than a barrel of monkeys," Kennedy wrote his friend Frank Waldrop before the September primary, "I don't know what the results will be, considering that our candidate was eighty years old, had against him all the government employees, including the W.P.A., all the Congressmen, state organization, everybody who wanted a contract or commission, James Michael Curley, Mayor Tobin and his group, and most of the Representatives, I think John F. will make a great showing." Kennedy's father-in-law had "attacked the Administration unmercifully and caused more talk and discussion in the state than has been here for a long time."

Kennedy described "one of the things about which we had the most fun. For weeks, Casey had been telling how as a World War veteran, he understood the rigors of war and the lonesomeness of the boys at the front and he told it off by accusing Lodge of being a faker in that he had never seen action. Well, John F. looked up his record and found that he entered the service on October 10, 1918, and spent the four weeks until Armistice Day as a student at Boston University, and he was mustered out on the twenty-third of November, two weeks after the Armistice."

Kennedy was yet too chary to throw his full resouces behind a spoiler's effort. Shown a series of advertisements that might have won the nomination for Fitzgerald, he asked his cousin how much they would cost. About two- or three-hundred thousand dollars, Kane replied. Did Honey have any chance of beating Lodge? "Not a chance in the world."

Kennedy kept his checkbook closed. Shortly before the primary, John McCormack called Kennedy to ask him to speak for Casey. Twenty minutes after Kennedy refused, the president telephoned with the same request. After an anxious pause, Kennedy told Roosevelt that it would be improper for him to speak against his wife's father. "I quite agree," the president replied. "I've been in politics." Fitzgerald lost by almost thirty thousand votes, but Kennedy's hand remained in the fall campaign; he reputedly provided money to Senator Lodge to help defeat Franklin Roosevelt's chosen candidate. For Kennedy the election was more than a grudge match against the president. If Casey had won the seat, Massachusetts would have been represented in the Senate by two Irishmen, Casey and David Walsh, limiting the opportunities for other Irishmen such as Joseph Kennedy, Jr., to move into the top ranks.

The election of 1942 saw the frustration of New Deal congressional candidates across the country. Kennedy sensed a growing "lack of unity in the belief that the conduct of the war and the conduct of our internal affairs are being properly managed." He reported to Beaverbrook that "the public just don't think Roosevelt and Churchill should run the war." Kennedy found "a great many large-sized groups of people who are with Roosevelt one hundred percent to win the war but are definitely against him on his domestic policies." The result was "a very bitter anti–New Deal feeling in the country" that was "more against the New Deal than against Roosevelt personally." Kennedy perceived that "dissatisfaction is rife and lack of confidence in the leaders and in Congress is definitely high and there is a great undercurrent of dissatisfaction with the appointment of so many Jews in high places in Washington." The Irish Catholics of the Northeast, such as Farley, Curley, Walsh, and Kennedy, once so pro-Roosevelt and later so isolationist, seemed less in evidence in Washington after Pearl Harbor. Many of the ancient social and economic collisions with Jews, Italians, and other rival groups were reviving on the home front.

A month after the midterm elections, Joseph Kennedy saw the president. He reminded Roosevelt that he had "failed to appoint an Irish Catholic or a Catholic to an important war position since 1940," a course that was "not conducive to strengthening the Democratic party or to unity on the home front." The president corrected him—nineteen of his most recent twenty appointments in Massachusetts had been awarded to Catholics. Kennedy was not impressed; both men knew that it required little generosity to grant patronage to Catholics in the Bay State, where the Democratic voting bloc was constituted mainly of the Irish and Italians.

Roosevelt related his visit with Kennedy at his weekly meeting with the leadership of Congress a few days later, an assembly including Vice-President Wallace, Senator Lister Hill, and Congressman McCormack. Probably for McCormack's benefit he noted how much he had always liked Joe Kennedy but that he had especially liked Mrs. Kennedy. McCormack agreed that Mrs. Kennedy was "very fine" and declared, not for the first time, what "a fine thing it would be if Joe Kennedy could be appointed to something." Roosevelt replied that, unfortunately, Kennedy had the habit of telling everything he knew to Arthur Krock and Frank Kent. There were many executive officials who leaked stories, Wallace said in his defense. McCormack reminded the president that bringing Kennedy back was particularly important because of the persistent problem of the Catholics of the Northeast. Senator Hill suggested Kennedy be tapped to solve the problems of small business.

"What would you think of the rather wild idea of putting Joe Kennedy in charge of the Smaller War Plants Corporation?" Roosevelt asked James Byrnes. "He *might* do a good job with it and he *might* do us no harm." The president also raised the possibility with Donald Nelson of the War Production Board, adding, "Maybe a new face and a new approach would succeed." Byrnes, who had hopscotched from Senate to Supreme Court to the White House as economic stabilization director and acquired a reputation as a kind of "assistant President" (a term that Roosevelt predictably did not care for), thought the idea splendid. In January 1943 the president gave him the green light. "In regard to this Joe Kennedy matter, if you and Nelson and the rest think it would be a good idea, will you go ahead with it? I think it requires no signature by me and if you put it through, let Joe Kennedy know that it was my idea—and nobody's else."

Byrnes called his friend with the good news, only to find that John McCormack had tipped him off on the impending appointment two weeks earlier. Kennedy said he had investigated the possibility and concluded that, with no more authority than a corporation head, there was little he could do in the position. Byrnes reported back to Roosevelt, "He said that if he felt that it was possible for him to be of any service that he would take the job, but he is convinced that he could not accomplish anything and he could not accept it." Intending the message to be swiftly transmitted to Kennedy, the president lamented to Arthur Krock, "How hard-headed Joe is about this. Can't he see that it won't work out the ideal way he wants it to?"

Kennedy reported his side of the refusal in a letter to Frank Kent: "I told him to stick it because I feel that, in the first place, if I were of any use at all from an executive point of view, I was entitled to something I could really get my teeth into and if it was merely an excuse for putting me under cover, I resented that equally, so that didn't work out very well and I am still in the leper colony."

Roosevelt's openness to Kennedy's return was all the more impressive in light of the persistent cabal intent on preventing any government position for the old nemesis. Dr. George Sperti of the War Production Board was searching for an accomplished businessman to head the new Office of Production, Research and Development, which was tackling wartime shortages in rubber and chemicals. He settled on the former ambassador: "I discussed the possibility with Mr. Kennedy, who was receptive, then discussed the matter with several people in Washington who, to my surprise, assured me that he would not be acceptable to the President." Among them was Maury Maverick, the former Texas congressman who was Sperti's superior. Kennedy wrote a friend, "I am so damn well fed up with everything and so disgusted at sitting on my fanny at Cape Cod and Palm Beach when I really believe I can do something in this war effort. . . ."

In March 1943 the president received a note from the White House secretariat: "Joe Kennedy is in town and wants to see you before he returns to Florida. Says it has nothing to do with his getting job or politics, but is personal matter." Kennedy outlined for Roosevelt the possibility of importing maté from Brazil as a wartime substitute for coffee. At the president's behest Kennedy later submitted a written report. After reading it, Roosevelt replied that it was "mighty interesting that the Coca-Cola people have been trying out caffeine from maté. Being scientists, they are probably not interested in the allegation by maté users that the caffeine from maté is 'different'—that it does not keep you awake at night, and it is a better restorative the morning after." The president's letter, although friendly and well-intentioned, seemed a slightly painful parody of the weightier matters the two men used to discuss. It closed jocularly with: "Yours for more and better maté drinks!"

In calmer moments Kennedy would explain that he objected more to the president's people and policies than to Roosevelt himself. "You can differ with a man and depart from him without hating him." Yet as the months of exile wore on, Kennedy found it increasingly difficult to maintain his detachment. From Florida he telephoned a newspaper friend to report that he could see American ships being sunk by the Germans offshore. Told that censors would prevent such information from being published, Kennedy carped, "You know that's ridiculous. The Germans know they sank those boats. That's just Roosevelt trying to keep the country from knowing how badly he's screwed everything up."

In May 1943 an anti–New Deal congressman struck at the president on the House floor with an attack on one of Roosevelt's assistants, David Niles. Burton Wheeler told Felix Frankfurter that the attack had been inspired by Kennedy. Frankfurter assumed, as he wrote in his journal, that Kennedy "was not only venting his gorge against the New Deal, but more particularly his personal resentment against Harry Hopkins and me, whom he, in his foolish and ignorant way, blames for his exclusion from participation in the conduct of the war. I don't suppose it ever enters the head of a Joe Kennedy that one who was so hostile to the war effort as he was all over the lot, and so outspoken in his foulmouthed hostility to the President himself, barred his own way to a responsible share in the conduct of the war."

Kennedy's feelings took the shape of indignation that he had been exploited by the president in the course of Roosevelt's secret efforts to bring the United States to war. He began to sift his diplomatic papers to write with James Landis a memoir of the London years. It would "set the record straight" on his relations with the president, Kennedy told friends, and expose the "Roosevelt follies" in diplomacy. He told Herbert Hoover that the book would "put an entirely different color on the process of how America got into the war and would prove the betrayal of the American people by Franklin D. Roosevelt." But the necessities of wartime unity and, later, his sons' political careers kept Joseph Kennedy's diplomatic memoir out of print, where it remained.

Beginning with the conversation at Hyde Park before Kennedy's departure in February 1938, the manuscript documented the three-year dialogue between president and ambassador on American strategy in the world. Kennedy's ending, American intervention, skillfully contradicted the long narrative of assurances by Franklin Roosevelt that he was committed to peace. Other presidential associates would publish memoirs recording the other side of the president's ambiguous diplomacy. It was little wonder that in the decades after Pearl Harbor, historians and political scientists could draw on a wealth of evidence for vivid portraits of Franklin Roosevelt as both Wilsonian internationalist and American appeaser.

Kennedy's self-imposed quietude only intensified his frustrations: "I am withstanding all efforts to get me to make speeches or to write articles because I don't want to do anything that won't help us all win the war and get out of this mess, and they expect criticism from me, so I am suffering in silence." Kennedy considered writing an article against the policy of unconditional surrender for the *Reader's Digest* but decided against the idea. He told Arthur Krock at great length of his certainty that Pearl Harbor could have been prevented. He revealed to another friend that, while Kennedy was in London in 1940, Franklin Roosevelt had promised Churchill that "we would be at war with Japan before Christmas" and that "he couldn't promise anything about Germany at that time since the American public was not ready for that as yet." But when asked if he intended to speak out, Kennedy said that he did not and would not. A social columnist found the former ambassador at a table in a New York restaurant, "telling all and sundry how the war should be fought."

In September 1943 Joseph Kennedy volunteered for the only wartime government service he would perform. He offered to act as a special service contact for the Federal Bureau of Investigation. Kennedy had long admired the FBI and had entertained J. Edgar Hoover and his assistant, Clyde Tolson, in Palm Beach. A Boston agent reported to Hoover after seeing Kennedy that the former ambassador had "indicated that if he were ever in a position to make any official recommendations, there would be one Federal investigative unit and that would be headed by J. Edgar Hoover. He considers the Naval and Army Intelligence Services 'amateurs' in comparison to the Bureau and regrets that they have often meddled in investigations coming within the jurisdiction of the Bureau."

Asked what services he could provide, Kennedy had noted that he was still engaged in the liquor business and owned several movie theaters. "He stated that he maintains very close connections, financial and otherwise, with the moving picture industry in California and presently fears that the Communists and their fellow travelers have succeeded in obtaining for themselves the key positions in the moving picture industry." Hoover was informed that Kennedy was "a devout Catholic and is well versed on Communism and what it might possibly mean in the United States." He also enjoyed "innumerable contacts in the international diplomatic set and he is willing to use his entry into these circles for any advantage the Bureau might desire in this field." Kennedy was seldom called upon. His only significant contribution was to assist the Bureau on one case in the shipbuilding industry.

By the end of 1943 Kennedy was convinced that the Democratic party's days in power were numbered. In a letter to Max Beaverbrook he noted a national trend toward conservatism: "I think that the swing will only be for possibly one term, but it's definitely on at the minute. . . . People are getting fed up with promises and conversation and, for my part, I believe that the winning of the war is not only the movement of manpower and winning battles, but on seeing that every part of the home front moves forward in the general scheme of things. The President says he is concerned with winning the war. He definitely is. It is just a question of what the definition of the term 'winning the war' is. . . .

"It is my well-considered opinion that, short of a miracle, the New Deal is finished."

Final Reunion

Joseph Kennedy was weathering his long season of discontent with some serenity. He invested in a racetrack, backed a Broadway play, started the fliers in real estate and oil that within a decade would make him one of the wealthiest men in the world. By 1944, however, his hopes were settling on the next generation. "My world may pass. It can't go on forever. . . ." he told a journalist in May. "The generation that follows me may have to stand for everything I stood against—and I realize that this includes even my own sons."

The cynosure of Kennedy's aspirations now was his oldest son, who was serving alongside Colonel Elliott Roosevelt in Europe. Any dreams of the governorship of Massachusetts had been set aside when the former ambassador pinned navy cadet's wings on Joe, Jr., in a Florida ceremony. The elder Kennedy had begun to deliver a talk to the new officers but as he looked on his son, tears welling in his eyes, he had to sit down.

In March 1944 Joe was named to receive a navy commendation for valor through repeated air missions. James Byrnes suggested to the president that he might want to present the award in a special White House ceremony. Roosevelt customarily presented only the Congressional Medal of Honor, but told Byrnes he would be glad to pin the award on Kennedy's son. But by the time Byrnes called the former ambassador, a navy board had reduced the rank of commendation. A disappointed Kennedy told Byrnes that it would be better for his son if the president made no exception.

It was another presidential election year. Kennedy had hoped for months that the Democrats would nominate William O. Douglas. His admiration for the civil libertarian Supreme Court justice puzzled many; Kennedy himself joked that Douglas was one of those in public life whom he loved the most and with whom he disagreed the most. The old chemistry of personal allegiance was at work. Kennedy had taken the young Yale lawyer under his wing at the Securities Commission and brought Douglas along to White House meetings: "Bill, you have to get to know the Boss." In September 1937, after a talk with Roosevelt, Kennedy telephoned Douglas to expect an important call; it was the president, offering the chairmanship of the commission. Little more than a year thereafter, Douglas went to the high court. The political conspirators of 1940, Justices Murphy and Frankfurter, now traded rumors on the presidential prospects of their colleague. "Well, no Democrat will be elected in 1944, but Bill will be named, I believe," said Murphy. "I am only sorry that in order to gain what he believes to be the Catholic vote, the financial end of his campaign is being managed by Joe Kennedy. . . ."

By late spring, however, war was still raging. Joseph Kennedy and almost everyone else believed that Franklin Roosevelt would stand for a fourth term. But Kennedy was certain that the president would be defeated. "Roosevelt undoubtedly is very, very strong as Commander-in-Chief with most of the labor forces and with most of the people who despise him but who hesitate to change a Commander-in-Chief while we are in the terrific spot that we are now in," he informed Beaverbrook. The problem was that the president would probably insist on the renomination of Henry Wallace. "That will weaken the ticket because, whether Roosevelt likes it or not, there's still an undercurrent of feeling that his health is not of the best and while he will keep that reasonably well concealed, they can't help but expect that there's a bare chance that if he were elected, he might find it necessary to resign to take some international job for health reasons, and the Vice President would become President—and certainly there are countless Democrats who could never accept Wallace as President."

Kennedy predicted that the election outcome would depend on the timing of the Allied invasion of Europe. If the assault were delayed until after November, the president would "suffer terrifically" from accusations that he was "playing politics with the boys' lives." If the war were over by November, "Roosevelt wouldn't have as much chance of being elected as I have." Compounding the president's problems, he wrote, were public worries about incompetence in Washington as well as the strength of the Republican nominee-apparent, Thomas E. Dewey of New York. "He's making a very good governor and his main strength is that he's making good appointments." Kennedy's prophecy: "I'm still reserving to myself the right to change after the next three months' developments, but I think the trend is definitely Republican and Dewey will be elected."

Kennedy was awaiting his son's return from the European theater. "Although he's had a large number of casualties in his squadron, I'm still hoping and praying we'll see him around the first of July." But at the beginning of August Joe volunteered for the perilous assignment of flying explosives over the Belgian coast. Elliott Roosevelt was part of the air escort; the president's son was momentarily blinded by the flash as Kennedy's plane exploded in mid-air.

A navy priest arrived at the Kennedy home. The patriarch assembled his children on the sunporch. "I want you all to be particularly good to your mother." Kennedy climbed the stairs and locked his bedroom door.

There was a consoling note from the president. James Forrestal, secretary of the navy and a friend, ordered the naming of a battleship for the war hero; the vessel was christened by the former ambassador and his family at the Fore River yard. Joseph Kennedy drifted into an isolation of his own making, listening for hours to Beethoven as he gazed out the window at the sea. A month later came word that his daughter Kathleen's new husband had been killed in battle. The president had chuckled on hearing of her marriage to the marquess of Hartington; he had known the groom's family for years and they were devout Anglicans. Now Roosevelt asked Kennedy to "please tell Kathleen I am thinking of her in her crushing sorrow."

In a letter to a Washington friend Kennedy wondered "what I would have thought if I had had any part in causing the war to be fought. I am sure, with the kind of imagination I have, that my religious convictions would have had a hard time saving me from myself."

Franklin Roosevelt seemed equally battle-weary. "Yes, I *am* tired," the president joked. "So would you be if you had spent the last five years pushing Winston uphill in a wheelbarrow." But friends and family worried over the toll exacted by the war years. Roosevelt's color was grayer than it had been and the characteristic tremor in his hands was growing more severe. The president had also lost weight—actually on doctor's orders, but Republican newspapers published photographs emphasizing the hollow eyes and slack jaw to quicken the rumor mill against the "sick man in the White House." He no longer had the patience for the political skirmishes in which he once took pleasure. "He just doesn't give a damn," observed a presidential assistant.

The president announced that "as a good soldier" he would accept a fourth nomination. Contrary to Joseph Kennedy's prediction, he did not expend the energy required to maneuver Henry Wallace back onto the ticket. In 1940 Roosevelt had threatened to refuse renomination rather than be overruled on his choice of running mate. Now, after a late-night session at the White House with Democratic officials, he signed a letter stating he would be "very glad" to run with either William O. Douglas or

Harry S. Truman. After the ratification of Roosevelt and Truman at Chicago, the president returned to the daily demands of the war.

Was it an instance of déjà vu? In the final weeks of the presidential campaign, stories abounded that Joseph Kennedy would execute some dramatic attempt to deny the president reelection. A Boston news bureau reported that the former ambassador had purchased radio time for an eleventh-hour endorsement of the Republican candidate—"unless he changes his mind." Kennedy was summoned to the White House. Grace Tully telephoned to say that the president would like to hear Kennedy's views on the postwar economy. On October 26, 1944, a day short of four years after his return from London, Joseph Kennedy saw Franklin Roosevelt for the last time.

It was sunny and crisp in Washington. Government workers and military men took their lunches outdoors, under trees shaded in scarlets and oranges. The White House did not appear notably more fortresslike than in the days of the New Deal—the president had vetoed plans to defend the old mansion with troops and light tanks—but the black iron gates had been reinforced with armor and artillery was hidden on the roof.

In the Oval Room Kennedy was unprepared for the gaunt figure who came into view. The president briskly opened the conversation. What did Kennedy think of Henry Kaiser's plan for postwar employment? Roosevelt had immediately struck a sore spot. During the war years Kaiser had gained the admiration of press and public as "the President's favorite businessman," offering advice on all manner of government projects—a place that had once been held by Joseph Kennedy.

Kennedy thought the plan was "so much ——," using an epithet that was unrecorded for history. With the candor of a decade earlier, he warned the president that he should not adopt the idea without further study. "You will get in trouble if you do." Roosevelt asked him to summarize his thoughts in a memorandum.

Now it was Kennedy's turn. Encouraging the president's courtship in a fashion become almost ritualized, he acknowledged that he had "great affection" for Roosevelt. The president had given him several opportunities for important public service. But Kennedy could not abide "the crowd around you." He reeled off the names of Harry Hopkins, David Niles, Sam Rosenman. "They will write you down in history, if you don't get rid of them, as incompetent—and they will open the way for the Communist line." If Roosevelt lost the election, these men would be to blame. "They have surrounded you with Jews and Communists."

Kennedy observed that the current odds on the president's victory were three to one. These were ridiculously high, but the odds were "very valuable in terms of public psychology." Many who would otherwise oppose the president were intimidated by the overwhelming odds. It would be worth a million dollars to the Republicans if they could succeed in knocking them down. "If they go as low as seven to five, you will be beaten—and two to one will give you trouble." Kennedy warned that the Italians, the Poles, and many of the Irish Catholics were defecting to Dewey.

Roosevelt mentioned rather abruptly that he was planning to come to Boston in a week for a campaign speech. But Kennedy remained ostentatiously silent. Oddly, the president refrained from employing the incentives he would have used in earlier days to change Kennedy's mind. He let the matter drop.

The appointment by now was running overtime, but Kennedy threw out two observations before leaving. First, financing of the war was on such "rotten ground" that the American people and the next administration would be grieved. Second, what about Henry Morgenthau's intrusion into the problem of postwar Germany? (A month earlier, the treasury secretary had proposed to Roosevelt and Churchill at Quebec that the conquered nation be transformed into an unthreatening pastoral state.) This was "sheer madness," Kennedy complained, "the meddling of a proved incompetent."

The president confessed that the Morgenthau Plan had caused him a lot of worry. Then why had he permitted Mortenthau to appear at Quebec? Kennedy demanded. Now Roosevelt was silent.

The conversation ended in standoff, they discussed what Kennedy should say to the press. Kennedy told reporters outside the West Wing that he had not discussed politics with the president. He denied the reports of a radio broadcast for Dewey. He declined to predict the winner of the election.

The president arrived late for luncheon with his daughter Anna and Harold Ickes. A table had been set on the south lawn of the White House, overlooking the military shantytown that stood near the Washington Monument. Had he "gotten anywhere with Joe?" Anna asked. Roosevelt made a wry face and reported that he had not. Talking with Kennedy had left "a bad taste" in his mouth. What was more, the only reason he had invited Kennedy to the White House was that Kennedy had sent a message that he wanted to talk. "After the meeting, Kennedy gave it out to the newspapers that the President had sent for him without indicating that he himself had set the thing in motion."

Ickes grumpily observed that the administration had already done too much for the Irish Catholics. He reminded the president for the thousandth time of Kennedy's "almost unprintable" criticism in London.

Kennedy went to lunch with Arthur Krock. "The President looks sick," he declared. He had been shocked by Roosevelt's appearance. The president should never have run for reelection in his condition. "That crowd can put anything over on him. He hasn't the mental energy to resist." This time his mind was made up. He would not support the final election bid of his old ally.

"He is not the Roosevelt I knew."

Three days later Kennedy drove from Hyannis Port to Boston. It was a placid Sunday afternoon. Harry Truman, campaigning in Massachusetts, had invited the former ambassador over to the Ritz-Carlton Hotel to talk. The two men had been acquainted in Washington; Truman was a dinner guest at Marwood. Wearing a tam o'shanter, Kennedy strode into the candidate's suite. As Truman remembered, it did not take long for the guest to begin "throwing rocks at Roosevelt." The diatribe against the president and his policies ended with a challenge: "Harry, what are you doing campaigning for that crippled son of a bitch that killed my son Joe?"

"If you say another word about Roosevelt, I'm going to throw you out that window," Truman replied.

Robert Hannegan, the new Democratic national chairman, took the senator aside and whispered, "Come out here. I'm going to get ten thousand dollars out of the old son of a bitch for the Democratic party." Somehow Kennedy was persuaded to contribute half that amount to the Democratic campaign, although friends believed he donated a similar sum to Thomas Dewey.

After Kennedy departed, Truman evidently had misgivings over dismissing Kennedy out of hand. He turned to a member of his entourage and said, "I'd like to know what that fellow thinks of me." The aide was Edward Gallagher, once a Boston secretary for James Roosevelt and an old friend of the ambassador. Gallagher caught up with Kennedy as he was claiming his convertible in the hotel parking lot. He related Truman's message. Kennedy replied, "You go back and tell him that he's my friend and you're my friend—and I want him to know it."

The following Saturday night Franklin Roosevelt addressed almost fifty thousand Bostonians at Fenway Park. Kennedy was absent, but in the stadium that evening was the resonance of the pledge four years before to keep the sons of Boston mothers out of foreign wars. "We got into this war because we were attacked," the president declared now. "Under the same circumstances, I would choose to do the same thing—

again and again and again." Two nights later came the torchlight victory rite at Hyde Park.

That winter Joseph Kennedy confided to Drew Pearson that he was interested in joining Frankin Roosevelt's fourth administration. In March 1945 there was talk that Kennedy might succeed Jesse Jones as head of federal lending agencies. "From all reports, Joe is an active and eager candidate," Harold Ickes observed. He wished the president would "forget all about Joe Kennedy. . . ."

Pearson mentioned Kennedy's interest to Henry Wallace and found the new commerce secretary encouraging. "I gather that Wallace would like to talk to you when you come north," the columnist wrote Kennedy in Palm Beach. "Naturally, I didn't try to pin him down on anything definite, but I tried to tell him about your enthusiasm for doing something to help win the war and reminded him of the swell jobs you had done previously in the Administration, which I know something about first hand." Pearson promised to "keep on plugging the idea in whatever way I can." Kennedy thanked him and said he would be coming to Washington in mid-April. They could explore the possibilities then.

But by the time Joseph Kennedy arrived in Washington, Franklin Roosevelt was dead.

Asked by a capital newspaper for a statement, Kennedy declared, "As a member of President Roosevelt's official family for many years, I know that he felt that justice had been violated seriously by this war, and he dedicated his life that the grave injuries to states and inhabitants should be rectified." There was a hint of the admiration that, even during the war years, Kennedy could never fully conceal. "A greater love hath no man than he who gives his life for his country."

Still, a letter to his daughter Kathleen in Great Britain revealed more bitterness than sentiment. There was "real sorrow" for two or three days, Kennedy reported, "but there is also no doubt that it was a great thing for the country." The president had stirred up such hatred that "no matter whether he proposed anything good or bad, half the country would be against it."

The wound of their parting remained, but the exigencies of policies and the healing of time softened Kennedy's memories of his old partner. He did not care for many of the people who were around the president, Kennedy told a friend years later, but Franklin Roosevelt was a good man. "Despite all of our fights and all the reconciliations later, I would never have done anything to hurt him."

Epilogue

THE DENOUEMENT

NOT LONG AFTER Harry Truman's succession, Joseph Kennedy expressed sympathy for the plight of the new chief executive. It would be Truman's task, he wrote privately, "to carry out the policies of a man who is dead who, even if he were alive, couldn't carry them out himself." Of the new president, Kennedy wrote Kathleen, "I know him very well," adding that one of Truman's chief assets was "his advocating Americanism as the Mid West knows it and not as the elements in New York want it."

In July 1945 Robert Hannegan wrote Truman in Berlin to suggest Kennedy as head of the Reconstruction Finance Corporation. "I know he is very much interested in being considered for this appointment and I recommend him to you." Kennedy was not appointed. Another possibility was nomination to the Export-Import Bank. But *Time* reported that James Byrnes, now secretary of state, had vetoed the appointment out of respect for the memory of Franklin Roosevelt. Byrnes assured an indignant Kennedy that the report was inaccurate. "Personally, I wouldn't have taken the job if it had been offered to me," Kennedy replied, "but as I told Arthur Krock, I was horribly hurt if such a thing had happened."

Kennedy confided to Kathleen his thoughts on entering the Truman administration: "I'm seriously considering . . . whether I might not say to him that I'd like to help in any way I can; but if he's going to give me a job, I'd rather have him give it to Jack and maybe make him minister to some country or Assistant Secretary of State or Assistant Secretary of the Navy." The senior Kennedy would return to government sporadically during the next decade—on a Massachusetts commission to study state commerce, as a member of both Hoover commissions, on an intelligence oversight committee under Eisenhower—but he recognized that his major role in public life had ended.

Many of the conservative impulses Kennedy had suppressed during the New Deal began to reexpress themselves. He criticized the growth of state socialism—"some vast, nebulous institution which will somehow or other assume all the burdens of life and support the individual who lacks the ambition or energy to support himself." He became friends with Westbrook Pegler and wrote the truculent Hearst columnist, "We are just going into an era in which we will need you to fight for what's left of America before they push it all down the drain. It is much closer than most people think." Perhaps the most prominent symbol of Kennedy's nostalgia for the days before the New Deal was his public veneration of Herbert Hoover. In a tribute to the former president on his seventy-fifth birthday, Kennedy observed that the American people had "finally realized" that in Hoover "they had one of the great fighting forces for the kind of America we all want to live in."

Still, Kennedy's fundamental commitment remained the advancement of his family. Conscious of the albatross represented by the old controversies that lingered about him, Kennedy told a friend after the Second World War that there would be no speeches for him—his sons were going into politics. He who had once basked in the spotlight now turned down public invitations by the score, including one that was poignant—a request to deliver the principal speech at a dinner celebrating the twenty-fifth anniversary of Franklin Roosevelt's Securities and Exchange Commission.

A New Generation

The sons of both men competed in the politics of the postwar era. But while the Roosevelts seized the mantle of their father's principles and achievements, the Kennedys—with the understanding compliance of the patriarch—strove to demonstrate their independence. Later, Arthur Schlesinger, Jr., saw the paradox in the Roosevelt sons having lived beneath their promise and capacity, "while the sons of Joseph Kennedy, endowed somewhere with a capacity for self-discipline, had risen beyond their father and, no doubt, because of him."

"Two Young Roosevelts Race for the White House," began an article in *Look*. "Both Have FDR's Political Charm / Both May Become Governors in 1950." After illness compelled him to resign from the White House secretariat in 1938, James Roosevelt settled in California. In the years after the war he occasionally visited his father's old ally in Palm Beach. Not once did Kennedy mention the name of Franklin Roosevelt, James remembered. "He seemed pained about how the end came, although grateful for the years of friendship with me."

In 1950 the late president's oldest son won the Democratic nomination to oppose Governor Earl Warren. He asked Kennedy for financial help, but Kennedy's contribution was smaller than the candidate had hoped. "He bluntly told me that it was a waste of time and that he had long made it a practice not to delude people by letting them think they might win because of the pseudo-enthusiasm of some of their friends." Several years later, Kennedy was more generous when James requested a gift to the Eleanor Roosevelt Cancer Foundation. At first, Kennedy refused. "Why should I contribute to something in honor of your mother? I don't think she likes me and I don't think she likes my son." Roosevelt replied, "Some of your money was made because of my father and, to a lesser extent, because of my mother. You owe it to them." Kennedy stipulated that his donation remain anonymous.

Franklin Roosevelt, Jr., was elected to Congress from New York City in 1949. He remembered later that he was perhaps John Kennedy's closest friend in the House, recalling his fellow Harvard man and congressman as something of a loner. He toured the Middle East and Asia with John and Robert Kennedy in 1951 and spoke for the senatorial candidate in Massachusetts the following year. In 1954, largely at the hands of Tammany leader Carmine De Sapio, Roosevelt was defeated in the Democratic nomination battle for governor of New York; he left Congress to manage an import automobile business and his Dutchess County farm. "You know, Franklin," Joseph Kennedy told him during the presidential campaign of 1960, "if it hadn't been for that guinea, now we would all be working for you."

Instead, James, Franklin, and Elliott Roosevelt joined ranks behind John Kennedy. (John Roosevelt, a New York investment banker, was a Nixon supporter, and Anna assumed no active role in the campaign.) The three sons encountered the vehement opposition of their mother. Eleanor Roosevelt was troubled by the failure of the Massachusetts senator to assume a firm stance against McCarthyism. But in a moment of particular frustration, John Kennedy offered a different explanation: "She hated my father and she can't stand it that his children turned out so much better than hers." At the 1956 Democratic Convention, he had vainly attempted to win her support for vice-president. "It was like eighteen people in a telephone booth and she was giving it just half attention, not really listening to what I said, but giving her views on McCarthy," Kennedy remembered. "My point was that because I had never been particularly vigorous about McCarthy that it would really make me out to be a complete political whore for me to be really champing and jumping."

Mrs. Roosevelt remained unreconciled. In December 1958 she told a television audience that she would "hesitate to place the difficult questions that the next President will have to make with someone who understands what courage is and admires it, but has not quite the independence to have it." She noted rumors that Joseph Kennedy was spending "oodles of money all over the country" and "probably has paid representatives in every state by now." Kennedy objected, starting a long exchange of letters than ended only when both agreed to forget the matter. He appeared on Mrs. Roosevelt's television program in January 1960, but the coolness persisted.

That spring she told friends she knew the sins of the father should not be visited upon the son, but she must confess her strong feelings about Joe Kennedy. Gore Vidal, a congressional candidate in Dutchess County that year, came to lunch with Mrs. Roosevelt at Hyde Park. Also present was Eleanor's uncle, David Gray, who had served as Franklin Roosevelt's wartime minister to Ireland. "When Joe Kennedy came back from London," she recalled, "during the war—"

"Damned coward, Joe Kennedy," her uncle sputtered (as Vidal recorded the conversation). "Terrified they were going to drop a bomb on him."

"Anyway, he came back to Boston and gave that *unfortunate* interview in which he was, well, somewhat critical of us. You see, it's a very funny thing, but whatever people say about us, we almost almost hear—"

"Unpleasant fellow, that Joe. Thought he knew everything. Damned coward."

"Well, my Franklin said, 'We'd better have him down here. . . .' " She related the explosive meeting at Hyde Park after the 1940 election when the president said he never wanted to see Kennedy again. The uncle continued to interject such observations as "Wanted us to make a deal with Hitler" and "Damned coward." Mrs. Roosevelt concluded, "I wonder if the true story of Joe Kennedy will ever be known. . . ."

The elder man accepted, if a trifle ruefully, that the public success of his sons would depend largely on their ability to embrace beliefs that were anathema to their father. "Just stand for everything your old man's against," Kennedy puckishly advised, "and you might even become President." John Kennedy once said that his father would have supported him just as enthusiastically were he running as the nominee of the Communist party.

The father labored behind the scenes in 1960, alternately working his old charm and remonstrance over politicians like Charles Buckley of New

York, O'Connell of Albany, Daley of Chicago—men who spoke a political language little removed from that of Patrick Kennedy of East Boston.

With varying degrees of success, Kennedy also tried to enlist behind his son journalists who had once admired the father's conservative influence on Franklin Roosevelt. "Harry, you know goddamned well that no son of mine could ever be a goddamned liberal," he assured Henry Luce after dinner on the evening of John Kennedy's acceptance speech. Roy Howard was invited to Hyannis Port. Walter Lippmann received a birthday congratulation: "To hell with this being 'dean of columnists and political writers.' Keep telling the American people the real facts of life!"

Kennedy wrote Walter Trohan of the *Chicago Tribune*, "I know that nobody on the *Tribune* is going to toss his hat in the air for us, but I can tell you that as far as Walter Trohan is concerned, if I have any influence at the White House, he will always be persona grata because he was my friend at all times." When Trohan expressed worry about the younger Kennedy's fiscal proposals, the former ambassador calmed him. "Walter, you and I remember that after the closing of the banks in '33, the bankers were begging Roosevelt to take them over and it was Roosevelt who told them to hold their horses and continue as a private enterprise. . . . Don't be too tough on us the next two weeks, because you know and I know the country would be a damn sight better off with Kennedy than it would be with Nixon."

The most moving predicament was Arthur Krock's. "I wanted to see Jack Kennedy President," the old warhorse admitted in his final years, "I loved him all his life and still do." But Krock concluded that the country would be better served by Richard Nixon as president. After the Democratic Convention, Kennedy invited Krock for dinner and assured his old friend that he knew "how everybody in the Kennedy family feels about you and, as far as I am concerned, will always feel the same. . . . We're all for you always." But Krock's columns that autumn reflected his misgivings over the progressive stands taken by Kennedy's son. In mid-October there was an angry telephone call from the father. Kennedy admonished Krock to "quit the dull line" he had been following and write "the kind of stuff you alone are capable of." He assured the columnist that the excessive Democratic platform had been imposed on the nominee against his will.

The seemingly imperturbable Krock was shaken. "I have thought of nothing else than the counsel you gave me on the telephone yesterday," he wrote Kennedy. "Our personal relations, my deep admiration of your qualities and Jack's as persons and as public leaders and my affection for all the Kennedys account for the effect this conversation has had on me. To follow your advice would give me great pleasure and relief. But even though I have never considered that my newspaper function does or should include suggesting how readers should vote, I am unable to follow it. . . ." After outlining his reservations about the candidate's positions, Krock wrote, "These I hope you will comprehend, if not accept, with the sympathetic fellow-feeling of one who in 1940 was able to support the President who had honored him only after getting a pledge of action (which incidentally Roosevelt did not keep)."

"I don't know what counsel I gave you on the telephone, but it certainly wasn't that you are to use your newspaper to tell readers to vote for Kennedy," came the reply. "I am surprised that you would think that I had so little regard for your integrity that I would make such a suggestion." What he had actually wanted, Kennedy wrote, was to have Krock "stop writing those fuzzy columns that you have been writing and try to see such favorable sides of Jack as you are able to see in your other personal friends. *THAT I ASKED AND NO MORE.*" Kennedy said he was not "a damned bit" worried. "If we win, it will be great. If we don't, it will be great also. The winner will be carrying a burden on his shoulders, the likes of which he may wish he had never seen. At any rate, I am not going to lose any sleep over it and if you do, you are very foolish."

Krock lamented to Jim Farley after the election that "this young man, for whom and whose family I have done so much, attributes to my influence everything he doesn't like in the paper." Later Krock concluded that Joseph Kennedy "probably never liked me at all, but found me useful and thought he might be able to make use of me."

The Uneasy Alliance

A dinner companion asked Joseph Kennedy, near the end of his life, what had been his main aspiration. "I wanted power," he was said to have replied. "I thought money would give me power and so I made money, only to discover that it was politics—not money—that really gave a man power. So I went into politics." His old partner too was known to friend and foe as a vigorous pursuer of power. Franklin Roosevelt was "a man in whom the possession of power had not diminished his joy of life," wrote a biographer, "but rather augmented it."

Kennedy and Roosevelt were *hommes engagés*. To classify them simply as men of power overlooks the most illuminating contrasts between them—between the motives for which each man sought influence, the methods and mores with which he acquired and exercised it, the purposes toward which he used it. Different arenas demand different brands of leadership. How did this distinction between Kennedy and Roosevelt shape their performances as businessmen and political men, as allies and adversaries?

For Joseph Kennedy, power represented a sense of public recognition, acceptance, security, perhaps even invincibility. The social discrimination of Victorian Boston and his father's demands spurred Kennedy on to win a place in the American ascendancy; he acquired a fortune in business and honors and office in politics. "I was born here. My children were born here," he said in an oft-quoted plaint, "What the hell do I have to do to become an American?" The eagerness for approval manifested itself in multifarious ways: the anticipation at "meeting people like the Saltonstalls," J. P. Morgan, the king and queen; the prized association with the Great Man (Roosevelt, Chamberlain, the pope) preserved through letters and souvenirs; the striving for offices like the treasury and London for reasons of prestige as much as policy; the inordinate tinkering with press coverage and honorary degrees; the intricate strategies to "let it be known" that he had been "drafted" against his will for every public appointment. Kennedy never enunciated his reasons for seeking office more forthrightly than in 1937: the eagerness of men to enter public life, he told a newspaper audience, was "due almost entirely to that psychological element of honor and prestige."

Underlying this element was a more compelling instinct—the abiding specter in Kennedy's consciousness of personal and family ruination, ruination brought on by a mistaken move of Kennedy's own, a national revolution, a world war. Perhaps no one will ever know the source of these apprehensions—Kennedy gloomily remembered the chaos of the First War and was once thrown to the ground by an anarchist's bomb blast in front of the House of Morgan—but the apprehensions were aroused again and again. The depression moved this self-styled "tough guy" to imagine surrendering half his fortune in order to preserve the other half under law and order. The outbreak of a second European war moved him to seek a quick peace with Hitler. Never fully secure in his social and financial position, no matter how many millions or how prestigious the office, Kennedy sought stability where he could find it, whether in New Deal reform to preserve; in peace at a heavy price; in strong, centralized national governance; or, later, in political reaction.

Power held a very different meaning for Franklin Roosevelt. The squire of Hyde Park had been granted what the Irishman from East Boston coveted—an old fortune, a legacy of leisure and security. One side of Roosevelt studied family history, went boating with Vincent Astor on the *Nourmahal,* observed the proprieties, humored his mother. But another side, the activist Roosevelt, rebelled against the quiet life on the Hudson. He would not waste his considerable talents; he wished to enter the arena, as Theodore Roosevelt had. Heir to self-assurance and optimism, Roosevelt took highly speculative fliers as businessman and transformed the American order as president. His instinct for power was less emotional than Kennedy's; it was the fulfillment of self rather than the preservation of self. A defeated Roosevelt would have no doubt accepted his fate with more equanimity than a defeated Kennedy. Roosevelt was happiest not with stasis but with change, a happy amalgam of aristocrat and activist.

Still, it is difficult to imagine Roosevelt in high spirits for long in a subordinate position, however active. Had the boy been overwhelmed by the demanding mother and father; had he felt something of an outsider at Groton and Harvard; or did he simply desire to replicate in public life the seigniorial standing he enjoyed at Hyde Park? It was no accident that only once in his life, as Josephus Daniels's deputy at the navy, was he compelled to defer to a superior, and that this relationship was frayed by impatience and mistrust. Roosevelt's will to dominate betrayed itself in the constant tests of loyalty to the president, the elaborate schemes to discipline the "prima donnas" of the New Deal like Baruch and Kennedy, the razor-edged teasing, and the tendency—through all the charm and informality—to condescend. At no time, Henry Morgenthau observed, was Franklin Roosevelt anything but a ruler.

As formidable personalities and as political operators, Kennedy and Roosevelt bore striking resemblances. Both were irrepressibly egotistical, loved the theatrical, the unorthodox, the outrageous. Skilled actors, they both hid cunning and an element of cynicism behind ingenuous masks. Neither was an intellectual; they regarded ideas not as goals but as guides. Both men were indifferent planners, brilliant improvisers, and artists in attracting, managing, and mobilizing people of talent; both worked amiably with people whom at times they disdained (including each other). Although each could be irresistibly beguiling, they each operated with one hand under the table. Nor was either man known for prodigal friendship. Kennedy was ultimately committed only to family and a few close associates whom he considered family. Roosevelt's wife could never grow accustomed to his "real lack of attachment to people."

The differences impressed people who knew Kennedy and Roosevelt more than the similarities. Where Kennedy was proud of his candor, Roosevelt loved to circumnavigate a thorny question and then assume an air of pious innocence. Where Kennedy was intense, explosive, single-minded in the manner of the hedgehog, Roosevelt was urbane, collected, and operated on a variety of levels in the manner of the fox. Kennedy was generally pessimistic about human nature; Roosevelt believed one could appeal to both good and evil impulses in people. Kennedy's was a focused intelligence, as in many who are uncomfortable with doubt; he tended to fit political issues into the narrow frameworks of economics and personalities. Roosevelt enjoyed a confident, wide-ranging sensibility; he was not rattled but invigorated by the simultaneous advice of monetary quacks and Wall Street bankers, pacifists and militarists, regulators and trust-busters, subsidizers and collectivists. Henry L. Stimson compared the president's thought processes to "chasing a vagrant beam of sunshine around a vacant room."

Kennedy and Roosevelt differed conspicuously in their views of the ethics of political transactions. To Kennedy, personal allegiances and bargaining were paramount; few other public officials could have promised their presidential endorsement to Franklin Roosevelt in 1936, James Byrnes in 1940, and William O. Douglas in 1944 without some sense of inconsistency. In the tradition of the Boston wards, Kennedy's political morality upheld the values of conduct that made bargaining work. "When I was a youngster, my father taught me two principles: gratitude and loyalty," he wrote Roosevelt in 1939. "About the first, he told me that I should never let any act of kindness go by without in some way returning it. . . . Of the second principle, he said, no matter how you fail in ability, you can make it up by being unfailingly loyal to your friends. I have tried to live up to those principles and to you personally, I owe a debt on both counts."

Roosevelt was concerned with the ethics more of ends than means, although he realized that ends could be corrupted by means. Were the two men's places reversed, it is improbable that the president would have suppressed his reservations over policy as loyally as Kennedy. Reformers like Theodore Roosevelt and Woodrow Wilson made an art of betraying the city bosses who had engineered their elections; Franklin Roosevelt, so his wife testified, "discards people when they no longer fulfill a purpose of his." Neither Kennedy nor Roosevelt, however, lacked the capacity to manipulate and misrepresent, to be toughminded and oneminded, to risk making enemies in quest and exercise of power—and this made them worthy confreres as well as opponents. Both believed that in an imperfect world the legitimacy of means rested not on the means themselves, but on their relation to an ultimate purpose.

"Am I planning the illustration of my family," John Adams brooded into his diary in 1802, "or the welfare of my country?" Not a brooder by nature, Joseph Kennedy declined to distinguish between the two. Identifying public with private purpose, he sought a society that would ensure the right of his and every family to advance themselves in security and safety. "Having accumulated a substantial competence, not without hard work, my every instinct makes me a conservative," he said in 1936. "By that, I mean that I want to see the things I have worked for conserved for myself and my children." In *I'm for Roosevelt,* he declared that "the future happiness of America" meant to him "the future happiness of my family." Election eve 1940: "Our children and your children are more important than anything else in the world."

Committed above all to an efficiently functioning system that protected the rights of liberty, life, and the pursuit of happiness, Kennedy was a thoroughgoing Lockean. Government's mission for him was the idea of negative liberty, under which the responsibility of government is limited to defending individual rights from chaos and oppression—not the positive notion of liberty, which ordains the expansion of personal rights and the enactment of broader values such as justice and equality.

Kennedy adopted certain lineaments of the visionary tradition of public service—self-sacrifice (the continual reminders of the personal gain he forwent to serve the president); the office seeking the man (Kennedy's delight in being "drafted" for office); disinterested rhetoric—but these instincts sprang chiefly from the desire to emulate the public-spirited families of the ascendancy. Beneath the rhetoric, Kennedy operated under the assumption that the public interest was best served not by the commitment of citizens to an overriding vision of the common good, but by the engagement of contending interests in business and politics.

James MacGregor Burns draws a distinction between the transactional leader and the transforming leader. The transactional leader bargains with other leaders and followers in the economic and political arenas, exchanging money, votes, or other forms of influence for the self-interest of each. The transforming leader makes bargains too, satisfying the existing needs of leaders and followers, but enlists that bargaining in a higher common purpose.

Joseph Kennedy was supremely a transactional leader. On Wall Street and in Washington he was renowned for his wizardry in ascertaining and appealing to the motives of other businessmen and politicians. Kennedy the financier masterfully arranged mergers, traded stocks, assembled market pools with an eye more to the mutual betterment of himself and his colleagues than to strengthening a company or an industry. Kennedy the public official turned in magnificent performances at the Securities and Maritime commissions by persuading financiers and shippers to accept regulation because it would serve their own interests. But once he had resolved the contending demands at each agency, Kennedy considered his task complete. A transforming leader would have stayed on to use the "bully pulpit," through cajolery, persuasion, legislation, to goad the denizens of the regulated industries to a higher level of values such as economic justice or equal opportunity.

"I've seen the President's job from the inside and I think I know what it requires," Kennedy once said. "The biggest part of the President's job is stepping into fights between the Secretary of State and the Secretary of Defense, between the Secretary of the Treasury and the Federal Reserve System, or between the Secretary of the Army and the Secretary of Navy, and putting his fist down and deciding what is going to be done. . . ."

What kind of president would Joseph Kennedy have made? He would have delighted press and public with his plain speaking and winning ways, his unaffectedness and his attractive family. He would have handled congressmen, cabinet officials, and party leaders with skill and been energized by the brokerage and arbitration that comprise the daily rituals of politics. Kennedy would have sought an orderly administration, of business principles applied to government. He would have relied heavily —probably too heavily—on the advice of businessmen, economists, and financiers, and would have tended to overlook issues that were not easily explained by personal relations or economics. The wellsprings of new public policy would reside less at the White House than on Capitol Hill; the nation would experience a spell of congressional government. Joseph Kennedy would have presided amicably—if not especially creatively—over a period that demanded no articulation of national purpose beyond vague notions of prosperity and peace.

But a more tumultuous age, like the years in which Franklin Roosevelt led, would have been an ordeal for Kennedy. In no time more than in emergency does a nation require a leader who can evoke faith. While Kennedy's financial judgment and confidence in *Realpolitik* yielded conclusions that America was headed for upheaval in 1932, Britain for debacle in 1940, Roosevelt understood that ideas are weapons with an enduring strength of their own. The president's talent in conveying that faith to a troubled citizenry was a potent source of his leadership, not least over

Kennedy. In 1938 Roosevelt confided to Harold Ickes his view that Kennedy as president would have instituted a centralized, dictatorial, even a fascist form of government. This was hyperbole, but it touched on a critical contradiction in Kennedy that especially emerged in his ambivalent congressional testimony on granting the president bold authority under Lend-Lease. On the one hand, Kennedy believed in robust competition and its corollary of decentralized decision-making; on the other, he feared the instability of the Hobbesean state of nature. As a follower, Kennedy yearned for powerful leadership to order the chaos; as a leader, he would have lacked the political faith that comes from emotional self-confidence to exercise such authority himself.

Like John Adams, who studied politics and war so that his descendants could study philosophy and the arts, Kennedy strove to provide the secure foothold from which future generations of Kennedys could concern themselves with higher needs. He never gained for himself the sense of stability that might have instilled a broader vision of public purpose. As John Kennedy prepared to assume the presidency, Lord Beaverbrook wrote to the father, "Looking back on your own career, I am convinced that had you not had to strive so hard in your early years for money . . . you would have had a term or two in the White House yourself." Yet in the spirit of a member of Napoleon's court, Kennedy might have said, "Sir, you are only a descendant. I am an ancestor."

A descendant, Franklin Roosevelt retained a Yankee attachment to individualism, but he believed ultimately that the clash of enlightened self-interest must be checked by leaders with a strong vision of the commonweal. The belief in *noblesse oblige* stood at the core of his social position, his admiration for cousin Theodore, the teachings of Endicott Peabody. Linking his power-striving with larger purposes, whether doing battle with Tammany or defending Western civilization, Roosevelt was always a leader in search of a cause, his constituency not a family but a nation. It is intriguing to note that while Kennedy identified the national welfare with his family's welfare, Roosevelt cherished his self-image as the father of a great national family. Kennedy had extravagant empathy with those he knew personally and could comprehend; Roosevelt seemed at times less responsive to those closest to him than to his national following. He never seemed to understand his wife's difficulties with his mother or move to alleviate them; his children remembered with a trace of resentment the way they had to schedule appointments to see their father.

The New Deal embodied Roosevelt's vision of government as something greater than Kennedy's agent of stability. Its role was not only to provide immediate relief and recovery but to implement justice, equality, liberty, and other higher principles through collective action (though these end values would always be in conflict). This overarching national purpose was implicit in domestic policy; the coming of war compelled the president to codify it in declarations such as the Four Freedoms and the economic Bill of Rights. Yet Roosevelt also knew—as he felt Wilson and William Jennings Bryan and other "dear, good people" did not know—that the effective leader had to be an effective operator. "You will never know any more about it, I hope," he told one New Dealer after the man's Senate confirmation, "but today, I traded you for a couple of murderers." The president could horsetrade with the best of transactional leaders like Father Coughlin, Jesse Jones, and Kennedy, but his admiration was reserved for men and women like Hopkins, Wallace, Ickes, Perkins, and Morgenthau, who saw politics as the handmaiden of public purpose.

The presidency represented for Joseph Kennedy mainly the duty to mediate the claims of public officials. To Franklin Roosevelt it was a platform for transforming leadership: "All our great Presidents were leaders of thought at times when certain historic ideas in the nation had to be clarified. . . . That is what the office is—a superb opportunity for reapplying, applying in new conditions, the simple rules of human behavior to which we always go back."

Rexford Tugwell considered Joseph Kennedy "one of the people Roosevelt knew how to use without allowing them more scope than was appropriate to his intentions." Kennedy provided the president with lavish advice and entertaining companionship, financial help, and a pipeline to Wall Street and the Vatican. He delivered public hortatives at election time, performed administrative services both official and unofficial, granted favors to the Roosevelt children (for Kennedy, the highest act of friendship), transacted presidential business with the difficult—Hearst, Coughlin, Chamberlain, financiers, and city bosses—and as chieftain of the New Deal, served as a persuasive symbol to the Irish of the Northeast and to many elements of business and finance. Was there no more to the two men's partnership than this?

For Kennedy, Franklin Roosevelt had a central and profoundly emotional meaning. "He's done more for me than my own kind," he had said in 1939. Kennedy craved the sunlight of the president's approval, his attention, his proximity. Whose acceptance could be more treasured than that of the president of the United States? (It was not coincidental that when the friendship failed, Kennedy turned to Herbert Hoover.) Roosevelt knew precisely how to appeal to his man; after a new presidential appointment, a handwritten note for Kennedy to display in his home accompanied "the pen which gives you another job to do for the U.S.A." He also knew that presidential kindnesses would be better appreciated if not taken for granted. Kennedy would get the Securities Commission but not before an agonizing wait; he would get London but would have to plead for the nomination. Roosevelt complained of the unending requests for invitations, gimcracks, and presidential audiences ("the trouble with Kennedy is that you always have to hold his hand"), but knew that Kennedy would come when called.

The president enjoyed even a stronger hold: he served as a personal leader for Kennedy, to guide and simplify the seemingly unexplainable. "When I became President in 1932, it looked as if any extremist group could gain a tremendous following from among the underprivileged and unemployed," he reminded Kennedy more than once. "Who knows? The United States might have had a dictator if the New Deal hadn't come along with a sensible program." By defining them in terms of a broad social movement, Roosevelt satisfied Kennedy's needs for personal and national stability. Kennedy provided no finer leadership than as chairman of the Securities and Maritime commissions. Roosevelt was there to enlist the stream of transactions in a general purpose.

The First New Deal sought relief, recovery, and reform in no scrutable order of priority; the president's hand was not betrayed. But the continuing reform of the Second New Deal in 1935 threw Roosevelt's notion of positive liberty into conflict with Kennedy's limited "conception of what is wisdom in government," as he phrased it in opposing utilities regulation. Kennedy believed that the tax and fiscal policies of the Second New Deal would hinder corporate investment, diminish his children's inheritance, perhaps usher in another crash. He was torn between root values and goals he had never sorted out for himself—his loyalty to Roosevelt and eagerness for further honors and his increasing worry about the president's policies. Earlier, Roosevelt had calmed Kennedy's uncertainties in order to enlist his services; now he aggravated them to keep Kennedy out of the clutches of the opposition, reminding Kennedy of the dangers of political ingratitude, dangling promises of future appointment, assuring Kennedy that they were both really working toward the same public objectives. Dismayed by his dependence on the president, Kennedy made half-hearted efforts to strike out on his own: he appealed to a constituency more conservative than Roosevelt's and dreamed of seeking the presidency. But as Kennedy admitted, "I can say no to that fellow on the telephone, but face to face, he gets me." Hence he remained with the president and tarnished the image of forthright public servant he prized. Friends complained that Kennedy lacked the courage of his convictions. His political influence diminished.

Roosevelt employed similar wiles to keep Kennedy in line in London. As in the First New Deal, the president's priorities were indecipherable because they were still evolving. He temporized for months, professed hatred of war, encouraged Chamberlain, issued eleventh-hour peace appeals, declined to arouse Congress or constituents or Kennedy until the final possible moment. Once Roosevelt forged unmistakably toward intervention, Kennedy was forced to choose again—between political loyalty and his militant opposition to a war that might take his sons.

The classic definition of Economic Man is the pursuer of private goals in the economic marketplace. Political Man pursues private goals in the political marketplace and rationalizes them in terms of the public interest. The actual distinction is less bald than this, of course, but it helps to explain Kennedy and Roosevelt in the context of the business and political cultures in which they operated.

Kennedy mastered a business environment that rewarded individual ambition over public purpose. The battle of the Argentine ships in 1917 was an instructive contest between transforming and transactional leader. Roosevelt of the navy first appealed to Kennedy's sense of purpose: failure to deliver the vessels would injure American foreign policy. But delivering ships without payment might have cost Kennedy his job. The resource that brought Roosevelt victory was not his superior moral purpose but his superior brute power; he could dispatch the navy tugboats to take the ships from the harbor. The entrenchment of the pragmatic ethic in business was struck home once more to Roosevelt when his pleas for business voluntarism fell on deaf ears at the American Construction Council. This time he could command no navy battalions to enforce his ideals.

Twenty-three years later saw another great European war but a wholly different battleground for Kennedy and Roosevelt. Political loyalty, the possibility of future presidential appointments, his worries over Roosevelt's attitude toward war—these conflicting considerations swirled through Kennedy's mind as the *Atlantic Clipper* approached New York in October 1940. How did the president defuse Kennedy's election-eve "bombshell" and instigate the speech accounted one of the most effective of the campaign? He exploited the disorder in Kennedy's soul. If the accounts of that Sunday evening can be credited, Roosevelt appealed to

Kennedy's weakness for presidential hand-holding with a "family dinner" at the White House; reminded his envoy how much he appreciated his loyalty and friendship; heard out Kennedy's complaints about his treatment in London—and enlarged on them; hinted at upcoming job prospects; offered his help in getting Kennedy's sons started in politics; reminded Kennedy of the importance of loyalty in politics and the public service they had performed together; assured him that it was really Willkie who was the warmonger—the president was just as committed to peace as Kennedy himself was.

Politics commands consistent purpose. Had Kennedy resolutely ordered his goals beneath the supreme aim of staying out of war, he might have resisted Roosevelt's blandishments and assumed an influential role as leader of the opposition. Instead, he allowed the president again to immobilize him, preserving the fiction that he could serve Roosevelt faithfully, advance his own career, and oppose intervention at the same time. People who had admired Kennedy's outspokenness dismissed him. Franklin Roosevelt succeeded in guiding American opinion from isolation to intervention, strengthening his own authority in the process, because he articulated a persuasive conception of American purpose. Joseph Kennedy's lack of an overriding sense of public purpose prevailed, in the end, at the expense of his political power.

This was the lesson that Kennedy took away from the uneasy alliance with Franklin Roosevelt. His son came to write a book on political men whose careers where thrown into collision with their beliefs; as candidate and president, he strove to enter in the American mind a rousing vision of national purpose. Had the father no influence over the denouement?

In April 1960 citizens of a West Virginia hamlet lined the streets to watch Joseph Kennedy's son arrive with Franklin Roosevelt, Jr. It was the springtime of a new alliance. "That young Kennedy reminds me of Roosevelt," an old man said. "None of us will ever forget what he did for West Virginia people in the Depression." In the symbolism of the Roosevelts giving way to the Kennedys, Arthur Schlesinger, Jr., perceived an historic contrast, a dynastic change like the Plantagenets giving way to the Yorks. The young Roosevelt introduced the young Kennedy with enthusiasm that rang through hill and valley. Holding two fingers aloft, scout-fashion, he declared:

"My father and Jack Kennedy's father were just like this!"

Acknowledgments

Bibliographical Note

General Sources

Chapter Notes

Index

ACKNOWLEDGMENTS

THIS VOLUME is the outgrowth of a senior thesis written while I was an undergraduate at Williams College. In the course of its composition I have acquired obligations to a great many people.

The book has gained from the guidance of experts who took time from demanding lives to provide critical readings: Joseph P. Lash, historian of the Roosevelts and the Big Three, who offered encouragement at an early juncture; Joan Simpson Burns, who brought to bear her skills as poet, author, and editor; Jeannette Hopkins, whose expertise in the social sciences aided me in considering theory; and Doris Kearns, biographer of Lyndon Johnson and, soon, the Kennedy family, who provided many valuable suggestions and discussed matters of historiography. Theron Raines offered indispensable counsel. Professors Kurt Tauber and Richard Krouse of Williams College also gave most generously of their time and attention.

As noted in the General Sources, I have benefited from the views of numerous participants in the period covered by this work; they helped to bring these years to life for an author who did not live through them. Of these, Franklin Roosevelt, Jr., and Ernest Cuneo provided especial assistance in arranging interviews and in navigating the waters of the New Deal.

I am indebted to Senator Edward Kennedy and to Stephen Smith, who threw open a portion of the Joseph Kennedy papers as well as the ambassador's unpublished diplomatic memoir. Tyler Abell, John R. Boettiger, Henry Luce III, Mrs. Drew Pearson, and Frank C. Waldrop also kindly made private papers available.

For other archival material, I am grateful to the knowledgeable and helpful staffs of the presidential libraries, particularly Dan H. Fenn, Jr., and E. William Johnson of the John F. Kennedy Library, Boston; William R. Emerson and Raymond K. Teichman of the Franklin D. Roosevelt Library, Hyde Park; and archivists at the Herbert Hoover, Harry S. Truman, and Lyndon B. Johnson libraries.

John C. Broderick and the Manuscript Division of the Library of Congress aided in gaining access to a number of its collections. Equally cooperative were the staffs of the House of Lords Record Office, London; the Public Record Office, Kew Gardens, Surrey; the National Archives; the Columbia Oral History Project; the Boston Athenaeum; and the Williams College Library.

The Federal Bureau of Investigation and the Securities and Exchange Commission made government records available under the terms of the Freedom of Information Act, which, despite its shortcomings, opens an important new lode for American scholars.

The Sentinels of the Republic, Boston, provided assistance which aided my research. Barbara Boltz typed several drafts of the manuscript with skill and good humor.

I am very happy to express gratitude to an exemplary publisher, George P. Brockway, chairman of W. W. Norton & Company, for his unfailing encouragement and attention.

Finally, I would like to record a debt, above all, to James MacGregor Burns, who presided over the evolution of this book, and whose scholarship and friendship have been its principal inspiration.

BIBLIOGRAPHICAL NOTE

STUDENTS OF Joseph Kennedy and Franklin Roosevelt are benefited by an abundance of literature on the two men, their families, and their era. Rather than survey the field of published sources, I suggest here only those secondary sources that were of the greatest influence on this study.

James MacGregor Burns's two-volume biography is a classic of history and political science. *Roosevelt: The Lion and the Fox* (New York: Harcourt, Brace and Company, 1956) examines its subject in terms of his political development through 1940. *Roosevelt: The Soldier of Freedom* (New York: Harcourt Brace Jovanovich, 1970) is the history of the war years, studying the president from an international perspective. Also indispensable are three works that are unfinished as of this writing. Frank Freidel's *Franklin D. Roosevelt* (Four volumes, Boston: Little, Brown and Company, 1952, 1954, 1956, and 1973) is scrupulous and rife with detail, the standard reference on Roosevelt's life. Kenneth S. Davis sets Roosevelt in his historical and social context in *FDR: The Beckoning of Destiny, 1882–1928* (New York: G. P. Putnam's Sons, 1972) with the eye of both historian and novelist. Arthur M. Schlesinger, Jr.'s majestic *The Age of Roosevelt* (Three volumes, Boston: Houghton Mifflin Company, 1957, 1959, and 1960) captures the times and those who shaped them with the author's characteristic grace and interpretive skills.

Richard J. Whalen's *The Founding Father: The Story of Joseph P. Kennedy* (New York: The New American Library, 1964) is a vivid portrait and groundbreaking biography. David E. Koskoff's *Joseph P. Kennedy: A Life and Times* (Englewood Cliffs, N.J.: Prentice-Hall, 1974) is a thorough treatment and a wide-ranging sourcebook on its subject and his family. Joseph Kennedy's years in London are the subject of doctoral dissertations by Roger C. W. Bjerk (Washington State University, 1971) and Jane K. Vieth (Ohio State University, 1975). A full biography must wait until Joseph Kennedy's papers have been completely opened to historians.

GENERAL SOURCES

Interviews

Marquis Childs, October 19, 1977
Benjamin V. Cohen, March 5, 1977
Thomas G. Corcoran, March 5, 1977
Ernest Cuneo, November 3, 1976
Eva Hinton, December 14, 1977
Ernest K. Lindley, December 14, 1977
Clare Boothe Luce, April 5, 1978
Anne Landis McLaughlin, March 3, 1978
Franklin D. Roosevelt, Jr., December 5, 1977
James Roosevelt, May 17, 1978
John A. Roosevelt, December 1, 1977
James Rowe, Jr., March 4, 1978
Gen. Martin F. Scanlon, March 5, 1977
Dorothy Schiff, January 11, 1978
Lawrence Spivak, October 20, 1977
Bascom N. Timmons, November 9, 1977
Walter Trohan, July 13, 1978
Grace G. Tully, March 4, 1978
Frank C. Waldrop, October 21, 1977

Manuscript Collections

Joseph and Stewart Alsop papers, Library of Congress, courtesy of Joseph Alsop.
America First collection, Hoover Institution on War, Revolution, and Peace, Stanford University.
Newton D. Baker papers, Library of Congress.
Bernard M. Baruch papers, Princeton University.
Lord Beaverbrook (William Maxwell Aitken) papers, House of Lords Record Office, London.
Adolf A. Berle, Jr., papers, Franklin D. Roosevelt Library, Hyde Park, New York.
John Boettiger papers, Franklin D. Roosevelt Library.
William E. Borah papers, Library of Congress.
James F. Byrnes papers, Clemson University.
Raymond Clapper papers, Library of Congress.
Father Charles E. Coughlin collection, Northwestern University.
Thomas E. Dewey papers, University of Rochester.
James A. Farley papers, Library of Congress.
Federal Bureau of Investigation files, Washington, D.C.
Foreign Office archives, Public Record Office, Kew Gardens, Surrey.
Jerome N. Frank papers, Yale University.
Felix Frankfurter diary and papers, Library of Congress.
Anna Roosevelt Halsted papers, Franklin D. Roosevelt Library.
Harvard Business School archives, Harvard University.
Herbert Hoover papers, Herbert Hoover Library, West Branch, Iowa.

Louis Howe papers, Franklin D. Roosevelt Library.
Cordell Hull papers, Library of Congress.
Harold L. Ickes diary and papers, Library of Congress.
Frederick P. Kappel papers, Columbia University.
Joseph P. Kennedy papers, John F. Kennedy Library, Boston, Massachusetts, courtesy of Senator Edward Kennedy and Stephen Smith.
Joseph P. Kennedy diplomatic memoir. This refers to the uncompleted and unpublished manuscript drafted by James M. Landis under Kennedy's supervision. Drawing on diaries and ambassadorial papers, the memoir was intended to represent Kennedy's account of the London years. Fragments of an earlier draft are housed in the Landis papers. References to the Kennedy diplomatic memoir below refer to the version in the Joseph P. Kennedy papers, cited by chapter.
Frank Kent papers, Maryland Historical Society, Baltimore.
Arthur Krock papers, Princeton University.
Thomas W. Lamont papers, Harvard Business School.
James M. Landis papers, Library of Congress.
Walter Lippmann papers, Yale University.
Breckinridge Long diary, Library of Congress.
Henry R. Luce papers, New York, courtesy of Henry Luce III.
Eugene Meyer papers, Library of Congress.
Jay Pierrepont Moffat diary, Harvard University.
Raymond Moley papers, Hoover Institution on War, Revolution and Peace.
Henry Morgenthau, Jr., diary and papers, Franklin D. Roosevelt Library.
Charles B. Parsons papers, Yale University.
Drew Pearson papers, Lyndon B. Johnson Library, Austin, Texas, courtesy of Tyler Abell and Mrs. Drew Pearson.
Westbrook Pegler papers, Herbert Hoover Library.
Amos Pinchot papers, Library of Congress.
Eleanor Roosevelt papers, Franklin D. Roosevelt Library.
Franklin D. Roosevelt papers, Franklin D. Roosevelt Library.
James Roosevelt diary and papers, Franklin D. Roosevelt Library.
Securities and Exchange Commission chairman's files, Washington, D.C.
State Department archives, National Archives.
Henry L. Stimson diary, Yale University.
Time archives, New York, courtesy of Henry Luce III.
Walter Trohan papers, Herbert Hoover Library.
Harry S. Truman papers, Harry S. Truman Library, Independence, Missouri.
Frank C. Waldrop papers, Washington, D.C., courtesy of Mr. Waldrop, Washington, D.C.
Henry A. Wallace diary, University of Iowa.
William Allen White papers, Library of Congress.
Robert E. Wood papers, Herbert Hoover Library.

Basic Book List

Authors whose works are cited in more than one chapter are referred to in Chapter Notes only by last name; the full citations appear in the Basic Book List. Authors for whom more than one work is cited are referred to by last name and superior numeral as indicated below.

• • •

Blair, Joan and Clay, Jr. *The Search for J.F.K.* New York: G. P. Putnam's Sons, 1976.
Blum, John Morton. *From the Morgenthau Diaries*, 3 vols. Boston: Houghton Mifflin Company, 1959–1967.

Burns, James MacGregor. *John Kennedy: A Political Profile.* New York: Harcourt, Brace and World, 1960: Burns[1].

———. *Roosevelt: The Lion and the Fox.* New York: Harcourt, Brace and Company, 1956: Burns[2].

———. *Roosevelt: The Soldier of Freedom.* New York: Harcourt Brace Jovanovich, 1970: Burns[3].

Davis, Kenneth S. *F.D.R.: The Beckoning of Destiny, 1882–1928.* New York: G. P. Putnam's Sons, 1972.

de Bedts, Ralph F. *The New Deal's SEC: The Formative Years.* New York: Columbia University Press, 1964.

Dinneen, Joseph F. *The Kennedy Family.* Boston: Little, Brown and Company, 1959.

Divine, Robert A. *Foreign Policy and U.S. Presidential Elections, 1940–1948.* New York: New Viewpoints, 1974.

Documents on German Foreign Policy, 1918–1945, Series D. Washington, D.C.: State Department series, cited as *German Documents.*

Farley, James A. *Jim Farley's Story: The Roosevelt Years.* New York: The McGraw-Hill Book Company, 1948.

Freidel, Frank. *Franklin D. Roosevelt.* Boston: Little, Brown and Company. Vol. I, *The Apprenticeship* (1952): Freidel[1]. Vol. II, *The Ordeal* (1954): Freidel[2]. Vol. III, *The Triumph* (1956): Freidel[3]. Vol. IV, *Launching the New Deal* (1973): Freidel[4].

Goldman, Eric F. *Rendezvous with Destiny.* New York: Alfred A. Knopf, 1952.

Gunther, John. *Roosevelt in Retrospect.* New York: Harper and Brothers, 1950.

Hess, Stephen. *America's Political Dynasties: From Adams to Kennedy.* Garden City, N.Y.: Doubleday and Company, 1966.

Hull, Cordell. *The Memoirs of Cordell Hull,* 2 vols. New York: The Macmillan Company, 1948.

Kennedy, Joseph P. *I'm for Roosevelt.* New York: Reynal and Hitchcock, 1936.

Kennedy, Rose Fitzgerald. *Times to Remember.* Garden City, N.Y.: Doubleday and Company, 1974.

Kleeman, Rita Halle. *Gracious Lady: The Life of Sara Delano Roosevelt.* New York: Appleton-Century, 1935.

Koskoff, David E. *Joseph P. Kennedy: A Life and Times.* Englewood Cliffs, N.J.: Prentice-Hall, 1974.

Krock, Arthur. *Memoirs: Sixty Years on the Firing Line.* New York: Funk and Wagnalls, 1968.

Langer, William L., and Gleason, S. Everett. *The World Crisis and American Foreign Policy,* 2 vols. New York: Harper and Brothers, 1952–1953.

Lash, Joseph P. *Eleanor: The Years Alone.* New York: W. W. Norton & Company, 1973.

McCarthy, Joe. *The Remarkable Kennedys.* New York: The Dial Press, 1960.

Manchester, William. *Portrait of a President.* Boston: Little, Brown and Company, 1962.

Moley, Raymond. *After Seven Years.* New York: Harper and Brothers, 1939: Moley[1].

———. *The First New Deal.* New York: Harcourt, Brace and World, 1966: Moley[2].

Rollins, Alfred B., Jr. *Roosevelt and Howe.* New York: Alfred A. Knopf, 1962.

Schlesinger, Arthur M., Jr. *The Age of Roosevelt.* Boston: Houghton Mifflin Company. Vol. I, *The Crisis of the Old Order* (1957): Schlesinger[1]. Vol. II, *The Coming of the New Deal* (1959): Schlesinger[2]. Vol. III, *The Politics of Upheaval* (1960): Schlesinger[3].

———. *Robert Kennedy and His Times.* Boston: Houghton Mifflin Company, 1978: Schlesinger[4].

Stevenson, William. *A Man Called Intrepid: The Secret War.* New York: Harcourt Brace Jovanovich, 1976.

Stiles, Lela. *The Man Behind Roosevelt: The Story of Louis McHenry Howe.* Cleveland: The World Publishing Company, 1954.

Sulzberger, C. L. *A Long Row of Candles.* New York: The Macmillan Company, 1969: Sulzberger[1].

———. *The Last of the Giants.* New York: The Macmillan Company, 1970: Sulzberger[2].

Talese, Gay. *The Kingdom and the Power.* New York: The World Publishing Company, 1969.

Tully, Grace G. *F.D.R., My Boss.* New York: Charles Scribner's Sons, 1949.

Whalen, Richard J. *The Founding Father: The Story of Joseph P. Kennedy.* New York: The New American Library, 1964.

CHAPTER NOTES

The following abbreviations are used in chapter notes:

DM Joseph P. Kennedy unpublished diplomatic memoir.
EMK Edward M. Kennedy, ed. *The Fruitful Bough* (privately published, 1965).
FDRL Franklin D. Roosevelt Library, Hyde Park, New York.
FO Foreign Office archives.
FRUS *Foreign Relations of the United States*. Washington, D. C.: State Department series, cited by year.
JFKL John F. Kennedy Library, Boston, Massachusetts.
KP Joseph P. Kennedy papers. John F. Kennedy Library.
NA National Archives, Washington, D.C.
NYT The *New York Times*.
OHP Oral History Project, Columbia University.
PC Press Conferences. Franklin D. Roosevelt Library, cited by date.
PL Elliott Roosevelt, ed. *F.D.R.: His Personal Letters*, 4 vols. New York: Duell, Sloan and Pearce, 1947–1950.
PPA Samuel I. Rosenman, ed. *The Public Papers and Addresses of Franklin D. Roosevelt*, 13 vols. New York: Random House, Macmillan, and Harper and Brothers, 1938–1950, cited by year.
PRO Public Record Office, Kew Gardens, Surrey.
RP Franklin D. Roosevelt papers. Franklin D. Roosevelt Library.
SD State Department archives.

Prologue / OCTOBER 1940

Description of *Atlantic Clipper*'s arrival is based on a Paramount newsreel, October 29, 1940, NA, as well as accounts dated October 28, 1940, in *NYT* and *Boston Post*. Dr. Gallup's comment on closeness of election is cited in Divine, pp. 64–68. "Sudden anti-war psychology": Turner Catledge in *NYT*, October 27, 1940. Willkie doubts about Roosevelt promise to keep out of war: Burns[2], p. 443. Lord Beaverbrook reported Kennedy's boast of controlling American Catholic votes in a letter to William Stephenson, quoted in Stevenson, p. 149. Kennedy on resisting "to the bitter end" and endorsing the Republican nominee on radio: Clare Boothe Luce interview. Randolph Churchill related Henry Luce's purchase of broadcast time and Roosevelt's discovery of the scheme to C. L. Sulzberger, noted in Sulzberger[2], p. 629. In a letter to Arthur Schlesinger, Jr., Luce called Churchill's account "an odd mixture of true and untrue" (July 6, 1965, Luce papers), but Mrs. Luce confirmed the story in its essentials for this author. Kennedy to Hull on anti-Roosevelt article: memorandum by T. Graham Hutton, October 18, 1940, FO 371, PRO. Roosevelt to Kennedy at Lisbon: October 17, 1940, KP. Kennedy to newspapermen at Lisbon: *NYT*, October 24, 1940, p. 5. Kennedy recounted his 1917 conflict with Roosevelt to James Wright, *Boston Sunday Globe*, September 25, 1932, editorial section, p. 3, and Ernest K. Lindley, *Liberty*, May 21, 1938, p. 15.

One / CONTEST OF TRADITIONS

Quotes from Founding period writers: Gordon S. Wood, *The Creation of the American Republic, 1776–1787* (Univ. of North Carolina, 1969), pp. 418–419. Adam Smith on personal interest is, of course, his definition of the "invisible hand" in Book IV of *The Wealth of Nations*. James Madison's assessment of state legislatures: *The Federalist*, No. 62. George Washington on public and private interests: Richard B. Morris, *Seven Who Shaped Our Destiny* (Harper and Row, 1973), p. 57. Clinton Rossiter's *The Political Thought of the American Revolution* (Harcourt, Brace, 1953) also sheds light on this aspect of the debate. Plunkitt on politics is from William Riordon, *Plunkitt of Tammany Hall* (Knopf, 1948), a classic declaration of the machine creed. Additional sources on the contest after the Civil War include Merle Curti, *The Growth of American Thought* (Harper and Row, 1964), Goldman, Richard Hofstadter's *The Age of Reform* (Knopf, 1955) and *The American Political Tradition* (Knopf, 1948), Matthew Josephson's *The Politicos* (Harcourt, Brace, 1938) and *The Robber Barons* (Harcourt, Brace, 1934), and Clinton Rossiter, *Conservatism in America* (Knopf, 1955).

The Roosevelts of Hyde Park Philip Hone on James J. Roosevelt: Allen Churchill, *The Roosevelts* (Harper and Row, 1965), pp. 107–108. Friend on Theodore Roosevelt, Sr.: Hess, p. 178. Journalist on Theodore Roosevelt in Albany: Churchill, p. 167. Isaac Roosevelt to James is from family letters quoted in Davis, pp. 25–26. Eleanor Roosevelt noted the river families' attitude toward politics: *New York Times Magazine*, December 15, 1946, p. 15. James Roosevelt's address to the St. James's Guild is a forty-eight page document entitled "Work" among family papers at FDRL. I am indebted to Dr. Nona S. Ferdon for calling it to my attention. Mrs. Theodore Roosevelt, Sr., to daughter: Churchill, p. 149. Sara Roosevelt's diary entry is recorded in Kleeman, p. 132. Davis, pp. 9–44, Freidel[1], pp. 3–19, Hall Roosevelt, *Odyssey of an American Family* (Harper, 1939) and Karl Schriftgiesser, *The Amazing Roosevelt Family* (Funk and Wagnalls, 1942) also provide material on the Roosevelt ancestors.

The Kennedys of East Boston Patrick Kennedy as "mayor" is recorded in a letter from an East Bostonian, James Fish, to Westbrook Pegler, March 30, 1954, Pegler papers. Robert Kennedy on his family's emigration: Lord Longford, *Kennedy* (Weidenfeld and Nicholson, 1976), p. 8. The Dublin immigrant quoted on upward mobility in America was Charles O'Conor, quoted in Goldman, p. 9. Patrick Kennedy on the Irish as "levellers" was quoted by Joseph Kennedy, *Boston Sunday Globe*, September 25, 1932, editorial section, p. 3. Martin Lomasney on the three interests of the masses: John Henry Cutler, *"Honey Fitz"* (Bobbs-Merrill, 1962), p. 50. Catholic writers' opinions on Anglo-Saxon philosophers: Oscar Handlin, *Boston's Immigrants* (Harvard, 1941), pp. 142–143. James Michael Curley gibes the Board of Strategy in his autobiography, *I'd Do It Again* (Prentice-Hall, 1957), p. 44. John Paul Bocock on the conquest of the cities: Hofstadter, *The Age of Reform*, p. 177n. John F. Fitzgerald on good government groups: *Boston Telegram*, undated clipping, 1911. Curley records his own reaction to the "Goo-goos" in his memoir, p. 72.

My examination of the Irish method of politics is guided by Edward M. Levine, *The Irish and Irish Politics* (Notre Dame, 1965), Lawrence J. McCaffrey, *The Irish Diaspora in America* (Indiana, 1976), George M. Potter, *To the Golden Door* (Little, Brown, 1960) and William V. Shannon, *The American Irish* (Macmillan, 1965). Fruitful sources on the Kennedy antecedents include Burns[1], Rose Kennedy, and pieces in the *Boston Sunday Globe*, December 12, 1937, editorial section, p. 12, and the *Boston Sunday Post*, December 26, 1937, p. A-2.

Two / APPRENTICES IN BUSINESS AND POLITICS

A perceptive study of the Cleveland coalition as it particularly affected Massachusetts is Geoffrey Blodgett, *The Gentle Reformers: Massachusetts Democrats in the Cleveland Era* (Harvard, 1966). For Benjamin Butler's wide-ranging life, see Richard S. West, Jr., *Lincoln's Scapegoat General* (Houghton Mifflin, 1965). Patrick Kennedy's devotion to P. A. Collins is noted in the *Boston Sunday Post*, December 26, 1937, p. A-2. Sara Roosevelt's diary notation: Kleeman, pp. 144–145.

Patrician in the Arena Roosevelt claimed recollection of the Cleveland torchlight parade in his address on election night 1940, text in *NYT*, November 5, 1940, p. 1. Sara Roosevelt's reminiscences of her son's unhappiness at Campobello, his attitude toward friends, as well as her ambition for Franklin are from "My Boy Franklin," *Good Housekeeping*, January 1933, pp. 20–22. Roosevelt's essay: Freidel[1], p. 6. Endicott Peabody on Grotonians in public life: Frank D. Ashburn, *Peabody of Groton* (Coward-McCann, 1944), pp. 112–113. Roosevelt to Peabody: Freidel[1], p. 37. References consulted for Theodore Roosevelt's political career include William H. Harbaugh, *Power and Responsibility: The Life and Times of Theodore Roosevelt* (Farrar, Straus and Cudahy, 1961) and Henry F. Pringle, *Theodore Roosevelt* (Harcourt, Brace, 1931). Roosevelt on Harvard Political Club: *PL*, I, p. 509. Eleanor Roosevelt on Franklin's first exposure to Lower East Side is quoted in Bernard Asbell, *The F.D.R. Memoirs* (Doubleday, 1973), pp. 214–225. Roosevelt's discontent as lawyer: Robert D. Graff, Robert E. Ginna, and Roger Butterfield, *FDR* (Harper and Row, 1962), pp. 46–47. Roosevelt to Poughkeepsie Democrats: Freidel[1], p. 91.

Newspaperman on Roosevelt's aid to insurgents is from *Buffalo Enquirer*, quoted in Ernest K. Lindley, *Franklin D. Roosevelt* (Bobbs-Merrill, 1931), p. 85. Syracuse bishop on reviving Know-Nothingism: Freidel[1], p. 107. Roosevelt on democratic conception of government in Albany: Friedel[1], p. 117. Exchanges between Roosevelt and his Tammany colleagues in the legislature are recorded also in Friedel[1], p. 131. Roosevelt's acceptance of the assistant secretaryship of the navy: Josephus Daniels, *The Wilson Era: Years of Peace, 1910–1917* (North Carolina, 1944), p. 124. Roosevelt's telegram to Bethlehem: *NYT*, January 7, 1917, VII, p. 3.

Rise of a Businessman Election-night report of Patrick Kennedy's "repeaters": Burns[1], p. 34. Kennedy's worship of his father: James A. Fayne oral history, JFKL. Mary Kennedy as dynastic antecedent: *Boston Sunday Post*, December 26, 1937, p. A-2. Patrick Kennedy's credo of gratitude and loyalty was quoted in a letter from Joseph Kennedy to Arthur Krock, July 1, 1937, Krock papers. Kennedy's "progenitor's sense": Thomas Corcoran interview. Charles Eliot on Boston Latin: *Two Hundred and Seventh-Fifth Anniversary of the Boston Latin School* (privately published, 1910), p. 15. Baseball coach on young Kennedy's braggadocio: Koskoff, p. 16. Kennedy on Boston Latin: Address to Boston Latin School Tercentenary Dinner, copy of draft in Frankfurter papers. Harvard economics teacher to Kennedy: essay by Thomas J. Walsh in EMK, p. 41. The Porcellian classmate who was unacquainted with Kennedy was Kingsland Macy, quoted by Frank C. Waldrop in interview. Dinner with Professor Copeland: essay by Thomas J. Campbell in EMK, p. 18. John F. Fitzgerald to Boston banker: Burns[1], p. 32. Kennedy on Boston discrimination: McCarthy, p. 22. Kennedy's resentment at being turned down for bank loan: Frank C. Waldrop interview.

Kennedy's description of position as bank examiner: *American Magazine,* May 1928, p. 146. Kennedy's secretary on his kindnesses as bank president: Ethel C. Turner, quoted in Koskoff, p. 18. Roosevelt's absolution of shipbuilders from war duty: Freidel[1], p. 318. Kennedy on original relations with Roosevelt: *Boston Sunday Globe,* September 25, 1932, editorial section, p. 3. Roosevelt to Schwab: February 11, 1915, RP. An additional source on Kennedy's wartime encounters with Roosevelt is a Helen Essary column, July 4, 1934, in the Clapper papers. This account notes only a single battleship in dispute and identifies its destination as Brazil. The weight of the evidence, however, remains with two battleships destined for Argentina. Archivists at JFKL, FDRL, NA, and SD were unable to document the transaction. Kennedy on Roosevelt as trader: *Liberty,* May 21, 1938, p. 15.

The Businessman and the Politician Roosevelt relative on Franklin's rebuff by Porcellian: Gunther, p. 176. Kennedy's description of winning Columbia Trust presidency as "surprise": *American Magazine,* May 1928.

Three / MEN OF THE NEW ERA

Woodrow Wilson to Roosevelt on lifting nation above material things: *PL,* III, p. 219. Roosevelt on materialism and caution: Schlesinger[1], p. 366. Roosevelt drops reform from political vocabulary: Freidel[2], p. 94. Charles N. Fay on human nature is from his *Business in Politics: Suggestions for Leaders in American Business* (privately published, 1926), p. 96. The Harding administration member, Ben W. Hooper, is quoted in James W. Prothro, *The Dollar Decade* (Louisiana State, 1954), a compendium of much of the business doxology of the New Era. *Nation's Business* editorial is from the issue of July 1926, p. 14. George Perkins on competition: Schlesinger[1], p. 21. Herbert Hoover's definition of American Individualism is from his book of the same title (Doubleday, 1922). Roosevelt's appreciation of the book is cited in Schlesinger[1], p. 372. Goldman and Schlesinger[1] offer evocative discussions of the debate within the bounds of the nineteen-twenties business community.

Business Statesman The testimonial at Delmonico's was reported in *NYT,* January 8, 1921. Roosevelt's letter to old friend: Roosevelt to Matthew Hale, November 6, 1920, RP Roosevelt's orthodox opinions on business: Freidel[2], p. 93. Roosevelt on Fidelity business in Boston: Roosevelt to Van Lear Black, October 22, 1923, RP. Principal sources on Louis Howe include Stiles, a memoir by his secretary, and Rollins, which provides a particularly full account of Howe's role in Roosevelt's business career. Howe on "cunning little pardon case": Rollins, p. 194. Request for bond order from navy acquaintance: Roosevelt to A. C. Dinkey, June 21, 1922, RP. Impatience with Emmet and Marvin: Roosevelt to Van Lear Black, September 24, 1924, RP. Need to devote four or five years to recovery: Roosevelt to Grenville T. Emmet, September 24, 1924, RP. Description of United European Investors to Harvard classmate: Roosevelt to John Tucker, September 26, 1922, RP. Howe on internecine dispute: Howe to Roosevelt, July 29, 1922, RP. Optimism on dirigibles: Roosevelt to Grenville T. Emmet, July 26, 1921, RP. The story on the Sanitary Postage Service appeared in the *New York World,* March 13, 1926, perhaps through the intercession of editor Herbert Swope.

Morgenthau's anticipation of working with Roosevelt: Morgenthau to Roosevelt, February 13, 1927, RP. A copy of the Camco prospectus is included in RP. The critic of automatic vending was John T. Flynn in his election-year broadside *Country Squire in the White House* (Doubleday-Doran, 1940), pp. 31–32. Roosevelt's notation on hope springing eternal appears on a Montacal Oil Company press release, August 16, 1928, RP. Joseph Kennedy distinguished speculation from gambling in the *Saturday Evening Post,* January 18, 1936. Roosevelt's reprimand on business practices: Fred D. Andree to Roosevelt, July 20, 1923, RP. Roosevelt's reply: July 31, 1923. "A fit candidate for a receiver": Roosevelt to Wendell P. Blagdon, December 11, 1919, RP. A copy of the American Construction Council prospectus is in RP. Roosevelt on construction seasonality: Freidel[2], p. 147. Roosevelt's reply to editorial: *Manufacturer's Record,* June 21, 1923, p. 63. Roosevelt on national preference for reaction and material things: speech of July 22, 1925, copy in RP. Howe on Warm Springs fundraising: Howe to Roosevelt, April 1, 1927, RP. Al Smith's appeal to run for governor: Davis, pp. 843–853 and Friedel[2], pp. 243–253. Progressive hopes pinned on Roosevelt: *The Outlook,* November 21, 1928, p. 1195. "Our own great hero": *NYT,* December 5, 1928. Alva Johnson offers a synopsis of Roosevelt's business adventures in an election-eve piece, "Mr. Roosevelt as a Businessman," *Saturday Evening Post,* October 31, 1936. John Roosevelt shared with the present author his conclusions after his own study of his father's business career.

Rugged Individualist Kennedy's version of the Yellow Cab battle: *American Magazine,* May 1928, p. 148. "Easy to make money in this market": Whalen, p. 66. Sources for Kennedy's rendezvous with Burton Wheeler include *New York Post,* January 11, 1961, p. 37, Wheeler's essay in EMK, p. 61, Wheeler's autobiography, *Yankee from the West* (Doubleday, 1962), pp. 252–253, and Whalen, pp. 68–69. Kennedy on Hollywood "pants-pressers": Whalen, p. 75. Marcus Loew on a banker in Hollywood: quoted by Joseph Kennedy in *Saturday Evening Post,* January 18, 1936. Kennedy's exchange with Hollywood reporter: Joseph P. Kennedy, *The Story of the Films* (A. W. Shaw, 1927), p. 28. Material relating to Kennedy's lecture series at Harvard is in the archives of the Harvard Business School. Congressman William Sirovich on RKO insiders: *Congressional Record,* May 12, 1933, p. 3353. Will Hays claimed in his *Memoirs* (Doubleday, 1956) that Kennedy later influenced Franklin Roosevelt to limit an investigation of the film industry proposed by Sirovich (p. 460). Sirovich colleague's attack on motion picture interests: Congressman Adolph Sabath in *Congressional Record,* May 12, 1933, p. 3348. Joseph Kennedy's acknowledgment that the nineteen-twenties corporation was run for management appears in an article written for the *Saturday Evening Post,* January 16, 1937, p. 11. Thomas Corcoran was the friend to whom Kennedy quoted Bacon. Corcoran told the author that he later tried to locate the reference, without success.

Luce on Kennedy's emotions: Robert T. Elson, *Time, Inc.: The Intimate History of a Publishing Enterprise* (vol. 2, Atheneum, 1973), p. 471. Robert Kennedy on his father's motivation: essay in EMK, p. 222. Patrick Kennedy's worries about his son: Whalen, p. 72. Kennedy's certainty of dying young was expressed in his interview with C. L. Sulzberger, quoted in Sulzberger[1], p. 21. Kennedy to William Randolph Hearst on children's trust fund: essay by Eunice Kennedy Shriver in EMK, p. 218. "I used to eat guys like you for breakfast": Burton Hersh, *The Education of Edward Kennedy* (Morrow, 1972), p. 27. Kennedy on overrating of big businessmen: Manchester, p. 174. "All values disappearing": Joseph Kennedy, p. 3. Kennedy as legendary figure: *Fortune,* September 1937, p. 138. Kennedy's prophecy of Roosevelt as President: Whalen, p. 113. Henry T. Johnson, a Kennedy friend, reports that Kennedy predicted Roosevelt's election as early as the summer of 1928: essay in EMK, p. 27.

Citizens in a Business Civilization Kennedy's self-made rules: Eunice Shriver in EMK, p. 218.

Four / SPRINGTIME OF AN ALLIANCE

Rose Kennedy on her husband's fear of national explosion: Rose Kennedy, p. 194. Kennedy's search for "a leader who would lead": *NYT,* August 12, 1934, VI, p. 3. Sources on Kennedy's 1930 visit with Roosevelt in Albany are Whalen, p. 113, and Rose Kennedy, pp. 193–194. Other accounts of the reunion identify the intermediary as Frank Walker and others, and date it as early as 1928. The greatest substantiation exists for the Albany meeting of 1930. "I was really worried": McCarthy, p. 58. Kennedy on Roosevelt as man to save the country: Rose Kennedy, p. 195.

Nomination at Chicago Will Rogers on Roosevelt's reelection as governor: *NYT,* November 6, 1930. Farley on Roosevelt's nomination for president: *NYT*, November 7, 1930. Roosevelt's response: Farley[2], p. 6. Howe's assessment of Jesse Jones: Rollins, p. 336. Kennedy's introduction to Louis Howe: Stiles, p. 148. Like most campaign contributions of that era, the exact amount of Joseph Kennedy's gift to the Roosevelt pre-convention campaign remains in doubt. An official report by campaign treasurer Frank Walker to the U.S. Senate, November 1932, records donations by Kennedy of $5,000 on June 20 and by Edward Moore of $2,500 on July 2, the day after Roosevelt's acceptance at Chicago, copy of report in Roosevelt papers. Kennedy told Raymond Moley, however, that he contributed $20,000 to Roosevelt before the convention (Moley[2], p. 380). The standard biography of William Randolph Hearst is W. A. Swanberg, *Citizen Hearst* (Scribner, 1959). William Randolph Hearst, Jr. informed this author that his father left virtually no papers. Kennedy's May 1932 lunch with Roosevelt at Warm Springs: Ernest K. Lindley interview and *NYT*, May 7, 1932, p. 8. Kennedy to keep in touch with Hearst: Moley[2], p. 380. For the atmosphere of the Chicago convention, I have relied principally on the vivid accounts in Burns[2], pp. 134–138, Freidel[3], pp. 291–311, and Schlesinger[1], pp. 295–314.

Kennedy's role in battle over two-thirds rule: essay by Burton Wheeler in EMK, p. 63. For Kennedy's pivotal role in Hearst's endorsement of Roosevelt, see Farley[2], pp. 19–24, Krock, p. 45, Ralph G. Martin and Ed Plaut, *Front Runner, Dark Horse* (Doubleday, 1960), p. 117, Schlesinger[1], p. 305, Swanberg[1], pp. 437–438, Roy Howard to Newton D. Baker, July 12, 1932, Baker papers, Arthur Krock oral history, OHP. Schlesinger[1], pp. 307–310, provides a thorough account of Hearst's message to Garner and the result. Kennedy on bringing Hearst around for Roosevelt: Martin and Plaut, p. 117. Kennedy on Hearst check: Rose Kennedy, p. 198. Kennedy on reading Moley's draft of Roosevelt's acceptance: Moley[2], p. 380.

The Man of Mystery Kennedy's meeting with Roosevelt before cruise departure: *NYT*, July 12, 1932, p. 1. Kennedy's conversation with Roy Howard: Roy Howard to Newton D. Baker, July 12, 1932, Baker papers. Kennedy's comings and goings on Roosevelt cruise: John Roosevelt interview and *NYT*, July 13, 1932, p. 1. Edward Moore on greatness of Joseph Kennedy: Eddie Dowling oral history, OHP. Kennedy's refusal of executive committee post: *PL*, III, p. 294. Kennedy's version of campaign contributions: McCarthy, p. 59. Kennedy's counsel to Swope: Alfred Allan Lewis, *Man of the World* (Bobbs-Merrill, 1978), p. 198. Kennedy's claim of early discussion of securities reform with Roosevelt: *NYT*, July 4, 1934, p. 29. Roosevelt's speech at Columbus: *PPA*, 1928–1932, pp. 669–683. Kennedy's assimilation into Roosevelt circle: Moley[2], p. 380. Kennedy as "Little Bernard Baruch": Bascom Timmons interview. Arthur Schlesinger on "triangle of advice": Schlesinger[1], pp. 415–428. Kennedy's hand in Pittsburgh speech: James Roosevelt interview. James Wright, "Joe Kennedy Sits in Inner Circle of Roosevelt Campaign Train," *Boston Sunday Globe*, September 25, 1932, editorial section, p. 3, is the most complete contemporary account of Kennedy's part in the fall campaign.

Kennedy as host at Chicago World Series: Harold Brayman to the author, November 29, 1977. Giannini congratulations on Kennedy's performance in campaign: Marquis James and Bessie Rowland James, *Biography of a Bank: The Story of the Bank of America* (Harper, 1954), pp. 359–361. Kennedy to Warner at Los Angeles: essay by Jack Warner in EMK, p. 66. James Roosevelt on Kennedy aboard train: essay by James Roosevelt in EMK, p. 68. Ernest K. Lindley described Kennedy's role in the 1932 campaign to the author in an interview. Kennedy on his own campaign function: *Boston Sunday Globe*, September 25, 1932, editorial section, p. 3. Kennedy as "man of mystery": *Boston Globe*, November 3, 1932.

The Ways of Providence Kennedy's congratulations to Raymond Moley: telegram, November 18, 1932, Moley papers. Kennedy's desire to be secretary of the treasury: Rose Kennedy, p. 197. Possible appointment as treasurer of the United States: Freidel[4], p. 138. Moley on Kennedy's disappointment: Moley[2], p. 381. Kennedy to Wheeler on demanding repayment of campaign loan: Whalen, p. 131. Moley's New York luncheon with Kennedy: Moley[2], pp. 380–381. Spring 1933 correspondence between Kennedy and Roosevelt: Kennedy to Roosevelt, March 14; Roosevelt to Kennedy, March 29; Roosevelt to Kennedy, May 11; Kennedy to Roosevelt, May 17, all in RP. Swope to Kennedy: letter of March 30, 1933, reprinted in E. J. Kahn, *The World of Swope* (Simon and Schuster, 1965), pp. 378–379. Roosevelt's greeting to Kennedy: Whalen, p. 131. Kennedy's recollection of his bashfulness: Manchester, p. 28. Kennedy to Joseph, Jr.: quoted in Schlesinger[4], p. 8. Kennedy rumored for N.R.A. position: *NYT*, March 10, 1957, p. 22. Suggestion of Kennedy for South American commission: Roosevelt to William Phillips, July 31, 1933, SD file 711, NA. Moley's suggestion of Kennedy for London delegation and Warburg's objections: James P. Warburg oral history, OHP. Kennedy's visit to Moley's hotel room: Moley[2], p. 442.

Libbey-Owens-Ford pool: *Hearings on Stock Exchange Practices,* Committee on Banking and Currency, U.S. Senate, 73rd Congress (Government Printing Office, 1934), pp. 6221–6239. Kennedy on "revival of the national conscience": *Washington Post,* July 7, 1934, p. 1. Dowling's meeting with Roosevelt on telegram to Henry Ford: Eddie Dowling oral history, OHP. The most thorough recitation of James Roosevelt's rumored role in helping Joseph Kennedy win British liquor franchises is Alva Johnston, "Jimmy's Got It," *Saturday Evening Post,* July 2, 1938, p. 60. This author was told by sources close to the Roosevelt family that James had agreed to accept one-fourth of Kennedy's liquor enterprise, the other three-fourths to go to Kennedy and a trust fund for the Kennedy children. An authoritative source also told the author that the president's son asked a prominent Washington attorney to prepare a suit against Kennedy for breach of agreement but demurred on being told the case would not stand up in court. In an interview, James Roosevelt told the author that he had not anticipated that Kennedy would include him in the proposition. Kennedy to Frankfurter: Schlesinger[4], p. 9. Kennedy's restlessness over Christmas 1933 and James Roosevelt's response: James Roosevelt interview. Moley to Kennedy: January 16, 1934, Moley papers.

"Set a Thief to Catch a Thief" Description of the Pecora investigation is based on accounts in Schlesinger[2], pp. 434–445, and by Donald A. Ritchie in Arthur M. Schlesinger, Jr., and Roger Bruns, *Congress Investigates: A Documented History,* 1792–1974 (Chelsea House, 1974, vol. 4), pp. 2555–2578. Kennedy's comment on the probe: Joseph Kennedy, p. 93. Loudest applause for Roosevelt's criticism of banking and business: *NYT*, March 5, 1933, p. 1. Roosevelt proposes statutes on securities trading: *PPA*, 1933, pp. 93–94. Roosevelt signs Securities Act of 1933: *PPA*, 1933, p. 214. Rayburn on lobby against securities exchange bill: *Congressional Record,* LXXVII, Part VII, pp. 7694–7700. Standard references on the inception and implementation of the Securities and Exchange Commission are de Bedts and Michael E. Parrish, *Securities Regulation and the New Deal* (Yale, 1970). Moley's list of proposed members for the new Securities Commission is in the Moley papers. Moley on "ethics of politics": Moley[2], p. 519. Roosevelt tells Moley he has virtually decided on Kennedy: Moley[1], p. 287. Farley's worry over Kennedy nomination and dislike of Kennedy: Walter Trohan interview. Walker's unsuccessful persuasion of Kennedy: Eddie Dowling oral history, OHP. Moley's argument with Roy Howard: Moley[1], pp. 287–288. Howard advises Kennedy to decline: *Fortune,* September 1937, p. 56. *Washington News* editorial: edition of June 30, 1934.

Evening meeting of Roosevelt, Kennedy, Moley and Baruch: Moley[1], p. 288, Moley[2], pp. 519–520, and unpublished essay by Bernard Baruch on Joseph Kennedy, Baruch papers. Roosevelt to newspapermen on late night: PC, June 29, 1934. The *Boston Post* article on Kennedy's "draft" appeared on July 1, 1934, p. 12. Harold Ickes on Kennedy appointment: Ickes diary, June 30, 1934. Roosevelt to Swope: August 2, 1934, RP. Roosevelt's jocular "Set a thief to catch a thief" was reported to the author in interviews with numerous members of the New Deal and Roosevelt family. Kiplinger Newsletter on Kennedy appointment: July 14, 1934. Flynn in *The New Republic:* July 18, 1934, pp. 264–265. Wheeler's reassurance of colleagues: essay by Burton Wheeler in EMK, pp. 63–64. Moley exchange with Corcoran: Moley[1], p. 289. Sources for the initial meeting of the SEC and its aftermath include James Landis oral history, OHP, Moley[1], p. 289, Moley[2], p. 520, *NYT*, July 3, 1934, p. 1, *New York Herald-Tribune*, July 4, 1934, p. 3, *Fortune*, September 1937, pp. 56–57, and interviews with Benjamin V. Cohen and Thomas G. Corcoran. I have also had the benefit of seeing portions of Donald A. Ritchie's biography of James Landis (Harvard, 1980) in manuscript form. The fullest sources on Arthur Krock include his autobiography, cited as Krock, as well as the brief sketches provided in Gay Talese's study of the *New York Times*, cited as Talese; both volumes are in Basic Book List. Krock letter demanding special privileges from the White House: Ickes diary, April 29, 1939.

Roosevelt, Baruch, Swope ask Krock for piece on Kennedy: Manchester, p. 70, and Arthur Krock oral history, JFKL. "J. P. Kennedy Has Excelled": *NYT*, July 4, 1934, p. 14. Letter from broker: Stella P. Colman to Krock, Krock papers, July 7, 1934. Kennedy's response: Joseph Kennedy to Krock, July 16, 1934, Krock papers. Krock's challenge: July 17, 1934, Krock papers.

New Dealer in Finance Text of Kennedy's maiden address at SEC is in *NYT*, July 26, 1934, p. 1. Roosevelt to Berle: August 13, 1934, RP. Kennedy to Berle: August 1, 1934, Berle papers. Lippmann to Kennedy: July 26, 1934, Lippmann papers. Kennedy on end of stock manipulation: *NYT*, July 4, 1934, p. 29. Landis on Kennedy acumen: James Landis oral history, OHP. Journalist on Kennedy method: Theodore Knappen in *Magazine of Wall Street*, July 21, 1934, p. 330. Wiretapping rumors are from confidential conversations with Washington sources. Kennedy boldness toward anti–New Deal business elements: de Bedts, p. 98. Kennedy on new registration rules: *NYT*, January 13, 1935, p. 1. Kennedy on breaking of investment logjam: *NYT*, March 8, 1935, p. 1. *Wall Street Journal* survey: April 17, 1935, p. 1. *Washington Post* on Kennedy's performance: September 21, 1935, p. 2. Flynn retracts objections: *The New Republic*, October 9, 1935, p. 244. Lippmann's comment: quoted in Walter Lippmann, *Interpretations: 1933–1935* (Macmillan, 1936), p. 272. *New York Times* on frequency of Kennedy visits to White House: May 26, 1935.

Five / MEN OF THE NEW DEAL

Description of the evening at Marwood is from a private memorandum by Arthur Krock, July 1, 1935, Krock papers (excerpt in Krock, pp. 169–171); and interviews with Thomas G. Corcoran and Grace G. Tully. Kennedy's life of "Roosevelt frugality": Harold Brayman to author, November 30, 1977. Roosevelt on Krock's support of majority of New Deal: Krock, p. 150.

Kennedy and the New Deal Kennedy sends Colony Restaurant ledger to Roosevelt: September 29, 1934, RP. For Roosevelt's plight in early 1935, see Burns[2], pp. 209–215, Schlesinger[3], pp. 1–11. H. G. Wells on American discontent is from *The New America, The New World* (Macmillan, 1935). A copy of Roosevelt's undelivered speech on the gold clause is in RP. The text of Kennedy's memo and Roosevelt's reply are in Tully, pp. 157–161. October 1934 meetings on public works are recorded in the Ickes diary, October 11 and 24, 1934. Morgenthau's suggestion of Kennedy for public works and Roosevelt's response: Morgenthau diary, April 13 and 22, 1935. Kennedy to Lippmann on requirement for further deficits: May 23, 1935, Lippmann papers. Kennedy withdraws resignation: *Time*, July 22, 1935. Raymond Clapper on Roosevelt and utilities: *Review of Reviews*, August 1935. For discussion of the utilities battle, see de Bedts, pp. 113–143. Kennedy to Wheeler opposing death sentence: *NYT*, July 10, 1935. Source for the flap over James Fitzgerald is the Morgenthau diary, June 18, 19, 24 and 26, and July 1, 1935. Kennedy on Roosevelt and underprivileged: *Strand* (London), August 1938. Kennedy equation of individual security with business prosperity: *Review of Reviews*, September 1936. Kennedy a New Dealer after seeing hungry men: *Boston Sunday Post,* August 16, 1936, p. 14. Roosevelt on Schwab: *NYT*, July 17, 1935, VI, p. 7.

Summer Solstice Kennedy on government position: Dinneen, p. 49. Baruch on Kennedy bluntness: unpublished essay on Kennedy, Baruch papers. Arthur Krock on growing closeness of Roosevelt and Kennedy: *NYT*, April 28, 1935. Kennedy described the evenings with the president at Marwood during a December 1, 1960 conversation with Dorothy Schiff touching on his relationship with Franklin Roosevelt. Mrs. Schiff read portions of her memorandum on this conversation to the author. "Father loved to match wits": Franklin Roosevelt, Jr., interview. Secret meetings between Roosevelt and businessmen arranged by Kennedy: interviews with James, John, and Franklin Roosevelt, Jr. Roosevelt to Morgenthau on Kennedy sensitivity: Schlesinger[2], p. 542. Wheeler's joke on Kennedy: Whalen, p. 157; and Wheeler essay in EMK, p. 63. Roosevelt related the story of Kennedy at the Shriners' parade to reporters at a press conference, November 6, 1935. The telegram from "M. T. Currier" survives in RP, July 25, 1935. Eleanor Roosevelt asks Kennedy to speak mind: *Washington Times-Herald*, September 18, 1937. Walter Trohan on Kennedy and Washington press: interview. Frank Waldrop, Marquis Childs, Lawrence Spivak, Bascom Timmons on Kennedy in Washington: interviews. *Time* on Kennedy dinners: July 22, 1935. Kennedy the absent weekend host to newspapermen: Ickes diary, December 18, 1937. Kennedy friendship with Drew Pearson and Walter Winchell: Ernest Cuneo interview. Lippmann's recommendation for Harvard visiting committee: Lippmann to Kennedy, June 30, 1937, Lippmann papers. Kennedy to Russell Davenport on *Fortune* piece: May 28, 1937, *Time* archives. Kennedy to Wheeler on criticism: Whalen, p. 356. Kennedy to Sulzberger: September 23, 1935, SEC chairman's files.

Kennedy to Lippmann: May 23, 1935, Lippmann papers. Kennedy to Meyer: December 21, 1937, Meyer papers. Kennedy offers to absorb O'Donnell expenses: Edward T. Lewis to author, November 3, 1977. Krock on his own lack of idealism, Blair and Blair, pp. 6–7. Ernest K. Lindley on Krock and Kennedy: interview. Krock on Kennedy's offer of automobile: Blair and Blair, p. 43. William Randolph Hearst, Jr., on his father and Kennedy: letter to author, September 12, 1977. Hearst to Kennedy on willingness to support Roosevelt: Freidel[4], p. 63. Hearst to Roosevelt after luncheon: undated, 1933, RP. Missy Le Hand to Kennedy after San Simeon visit: telegram, May 15, 1935, RP. Hearst order on "Raw Deal" is described in Burns[2], p. 241. James Roosevelt on his father's attitude toward Kennedy: interview. Kennedy to Stimson on uselessness of trying to change Roosevelt: Stimson diary, pp. 1046–1047. Eleanor Roosevelt on reverse snobbishness is from her second volume of memoirs, *This I Remember* (Harper, 1949), pp. 49–50. "Neither had any illusions": Frank C. Waldrop interview. Kennedy quotes Roosevelt on mastering Baruch: Schiff interview.

The Priest of the Little Flower Description of Coughlin broadcast is based on a recording in the Father Coughlin collection. Hugh Johnson on threat of Long and Coughlin: Schlesinger[3], p. 246. Roosevelt on Long and Coughlin influenza: Roosevelt to Breckinridge Long, March 9, 1935, RP. Principal references on Father Coughlin are Sheldon Marcus, *Father Coughlin* (Little, Brown, 1973) and Charles J. Tull, *Father Coughlin and the New Deal* (Syracuse, 1965). G. Hall Roosevelt to Roosevelt: May 5, 1931, RP. "We were supposed to be partners": transcript of Sheldon Marcus interview with Coughlin, April 11 and 12, 1970, Father Coughlin collection. Murphy appointment to Philippines: Marcus interview transcript. Roosevelt to Farley on Coughlin: Marcus, p. 64. Coughlin to Murphy: January 5, 1934, Murphy papers. Coughlin predicts new social order to Murphy: July 26, 1934, Murphy papers. Roosevelt to Morgenthau on strategy if Coughlin attacks persist: Morgenthau diary, May 23, 1935. Kennedy to Murphy: May 18, 1937, Murphy papers. James Roosevelt on Kennedy's interest in Coughlin: interview. Kennedy on Coughlin as "jackass" and Coughlin description of their friendship: interview with Coughlin published in *Focus/Midwest,* February 1963, p. 9. Coughlin to Murphy on Kennedy's agreement with criticism of Roosevelt: September 5, 1935, Murphy papers.

Sources for the September 1935 meeting of Coughlin, Roosevelt and Kennedy are Marcus interview transcript and interview with Coughlin published in *American Heritage*, October 1972, pp. 103–104. Coughlin's report to Murphy on meeting: November 13, 1935, Murphy papers. Roosevelt sidesteps questions about meeting: PC, September 11, 1935. My discussion of the relationship between Roosevelt, Kennedy, and Coughlin has benefited from the guidance of Martin S. Hayden, who covered Father Coughlin for the *Detroit News*.

"I'm for Roosevelt" and "I'm for Kennedy." Roosevelt confirms Kennedy's resignation: PC, September 20, 1935. Exchange of letters and Kennedy "out of politics": *NYT*, September 21, 1935. Kennedy "through with public life forever": Kennedy to Eleanor Patterson, September 23, 1935, SEC chairman's files. Kiplinger Newsletter report: February 8, 1936. Roosevelt on Kennedy mission: DM, Chapter 1. Baruch to Churchill, telegram September 25, 1935, Baruch papers. The Chartwell luncheon is recorded in a memorandum by Rose Kennedy quoted in Schlesinger[4], p. 10. Kennedy to Farley, October 9, 1935, Farley papers. Kennedy on unlikelihood of Roosevelt defeat: *NYT*, October 12, 1935, p. 15. Roosevelt on Hearst: Ickes diary, November 1935. Roosevelt on recognizing Vatican: Robert I. Gannon, *The Cardinal Spellman Story* (Doubleday, 1962), p. 118. Final meeting of Roosevelt and Coughlin: Marcus, p. 106. Coughlin to Kennedy and Kennedy's notation: January 29, 1936, RP. Coughlin to Murphy, March 13, 1936, Murphy papers. Kennedy on Liberty Leaguers in Palm Beach: Kennedy to Missy Le Hand, February 25, 1936, RP. Roosevelt sends list of businessmen: *PL*, III, p. 547. James Roosevelt finds Kennedy unhappy and angry: interview. Kennedy to Missy Le Hand, June 15, 1936, RP. Krock proposes Kennedy for public works: *NYT*, April 29, 1936, p. 20.

"Never had it so good": Kennedy to Morgenthau in Morgenthau diary, April 28, 1936. Kennedy to Missy Le Hand, June, 15, 1936, and Roosevelt reply, June 17, 1936, RP. Kennedy to Krock on campaign book, June 24, 1936, Krock papers. Review of *I'm for Roosevelt* in *Saturday Review of Literature*, September 5, 1936, p. 12. Kennedy contribution to Senator Norris: Alfred Lief, *Democracy's Norris* (Stackpole, 1939), p. 489. Byrnes returns Kennedy contribution: memorandum and canceled check in Byrnes papers. "If you shove your neck out": *NYT*, July 26, 1936, III, p. 1. "A Businessman's View of the New Deal": *Review of Reviews*, September 1936. "The Administration and Business": *New York Times Magazine*, September 6, 1936, p. 1. James Roosevelt on Kennedy treasury ambitions is from interview. "Pendulum swung my way": Edward M. Gallagher oral history, JFKL. Kennedy difficulties in recruiting businessmen for Roosevelt: Arthur Krock in *NYT*, December 17, 1936, p. 26. "I'll vote for him": notation by Frederick P. Kappel on Kennedy invitation to New York dinner, October 15, 1936, Kappel papers. Early to Kennedy on radio broadcast: undated, 1936, copy in Krock papers. Kennedy radio speech: *NYT*, October 22, 1936, p. 13. Other speeches were reported in *NYT*, October 6, p. 14, and November 1, p. 49.

Coughlin criticism of Roosevelt and exemption of Kennedy: *Detroit News*, July 17, 1936; and *Boston Post*, August 16, 1936, p. 14. Kennedy's defense of Roosevelt: *NYT*, October 25, 1936, p. 33. Kennedy to Byrnes, October 30, 1936, Byrnes papers. Cardinal Pacelli's visit to Hyde Park: *NYT*, November 6, 1936, p. 1. Coughlin related the alleged agreement between Roosevelt and Pacelli to Clare Boothe Luce: Luce interview. Roosevelt to Kennedy, October 10, 1936, RP.

The Greatest Joke in the World Kennedy's persistent desire to be secretary of the treasury: James Roosevelt interview. Roosevelt to Farley on Kennedy at treasury: Farley, p. 115. Kennedy to Roosevelt on reasons for refusing maritime post: *American Magazine*, November 1937. Kennedy to Byrnes on maritime appointment, March 15, 1937, Byrnes papers. Kennedy to John Boettiger on maritime appointment, March 22, 1937, Boettiger papers. Roosevelt congratulations on meeting deadline: Roosevelt to Kennedy, July 10, 1937, RP. Kennedy to Arthur Krock, July 1, 1937, Krock papers. Krock reply, July 1, 1937, Krock papers. "Else the government is wasting money": Kennedy to Roosevelt, June 19, 1937, RP. Krock's version of Kennedy's telephone conversation with Roosevelt: Krock, pp.

332–333. (The precise obscenity Kennedy employed was confirmed for posterity by Koskoff, p. 508.) Roosevelt's reply: McCarthy, p. 21. *The Nation* on Kennedy performance in *Algic* incident, February 26, 1938, p. 234. Kennedy on removing grievances: Joseph F. Thorning, *Builders of the Social Order* (Catholic Literary Guild, 1941), p. 74. "Toughest job": *Time*, November 22, 1937, p. 20. *Business Week* on Kennedy's rise: December 5, 1936, p. 32. *The New Republic*, August 11, 1937, p. 7. *Time*, March 22, 1937, p. 64.

References for Harvard skit on Kennedy are Whalen, pp. 196–197 and an unpublished essay on Joseph Kennedy by Oscar W. Haussermann, November 13, 1964, copy in Krock papers. For an insightful discussion on Kennedy's attitudes toward taxes and New Deal economics, see Koskoff, pp. 110–113. James Roosevelt told the author of Kennedy's misgivings about the New Deal and fears of another stock market crash. Kennedy's testimony against the undistributed income tax on corporations is noted in the Morgenthau diary: Blum I, p. 441. James Roosevelt request of Kennedy to chair national committee on court reorganization: James Roosevelt diary, March 3, 1937, James Roosevelt papers, and James Roosevelt interview. Kennedy to Baruch on joining national committee: March 4, 1937, Baruch papers. Kennedy to New York Economic Club: *NYT*, December 8, 1937, p. 1. Kent to Baruch on "1937 China Egg diamond belt prize": December 8, 1937, Baruch papers. Kent in *Baltimore Sun*, "On Bellyaching": undated clipping in Baruch papers. Harold Ickes on Kennedy danger to New Deal: Ickes diary, December 8, 1937. Rose Kennedy on asking Roosevelt for appointment to London: Rose Kennedy, pp. 211–212.

"Everybody seems to be for me" and "Poor old felt-minded Joe": Frank Kent to Bernard Baruch, June 14, 1937, Baruch papers. For the account of Roosevelt's offer of London to Kennedy, I have relied on interviews with James and Franklin Roosevelt, Jr., and James Roosevelt, *My Parents: A Differing View* (Playboy Press, 1976), pp. 208–210. Kennedy on James Roosevelt's offer of Commerce: Krock, p. 333. Sources for Krock's publication of Kennedy story and Roosevelt's reaction are a private memorandum by Krock, December 9, 1937, Krock in *NYT*, December 9, 1937, p. 1, and Talese, pp. 188–189. *New York Times* reports impending Roosevelt dictatorship rumors: December 12, 1937, IV, p. 3. Kennedy to Byrnes: December 23, 1937, Byrnes papers. Roosevelt to Morgenthau on Kennedy appointment: Morgenthau diary, December 8, 1937. The dinner at Hyde Park was described to the author by Dorothy Schiff.

Six / STRUGGLE OVER FOREIGN POLICY

London newspaper on Roosevelt compliment: *London Daily Telegraph*, quoted in Whalen, p. 202. Lindsay on Kennedy's departure: Sir Ronald Lindsay to Foreign Office: March 8, 1938, FO 371, PRO. Rose Kennedy to Roosevelt, undated, 1938, and Roosevelt reply, January 27, 1938, RP. Kennedy's meeting with Roosevelt and Hull after appointment: McCarthy, pp. 68–69. Roosevelt on knee breeches: Tully, p. 157. Kennedy recounts farewell talk in DM, Chapter 1. Kennedy not to wear knee breeches at court: Whalen, p. 212. Kennedy to reporter on bowleggedness: McCarthy, p. 72. Kennedy to London reporters on overnight statesmanship: *Time*, March 14, 1938. Roosevelt surprised by Kennedy's warm welcome: James Roosevelt interview. Kennedy to Byrnes: March 8, 1938. Byrnes papers. Kennedy to Krock: same date, Krock papers. Kennedy to Loretta Kennedy Connelly: June 24, 1938, KP. Kennedy on Roosevelt: DM, Chapter 5. "A hell of a long way": Whalen, p. 205. Kennedy's pessimistic greeting to American correspondents in London: Whalen, p. 215. Kennedy to James Roosevelt: March 3, 1938, copy in Hull papers.

Influence from London My discussion of Roosevelt on foreign policy is chiefly influenced by Burns[2], pp. 381–404. For chronology of events, see Langer and Gleason. Roosevelt on economic-political plan: DM, Chapter 1. Kennedy stresses economics over politics: letter to Walter Lippmann: March 21, 1938, Lippmann papers. Kennedy's worry over sons: quoted in *New York Post*, January 11, 1961, p. 37. Survey of theater audiences: Moffat diary,

January 28, 1938. Kennedy to Borah, April 28, 1938: Borah papers. Byrnes to Kennedy on halting court presentations: April 12, 1938: Byrnes papers. Kennedy pique over Roosevelt Gainesville speech: transcript of telephone conversation between Kennedy and Hull, March 30, 1938, Hull papers and Moffat diary. Kennedy on Chamberlain: letter of March 22, 1938, Hull papers, and DM, Chapter 10. Kennedy's professed closeness to Chamberlain: *The Nation*, December 14, 1940. Kennedy appeal for Roosevelt to support Chamberlain policy: Kennedy to Roosevelt: March 11, 1938, RP. Ickes on Kennedy's "malevolent" hand: Ickes diary, May 1, 1938. For German version of Kennedy meetings with von Dirksen, see *German Documents*. Kennedy to Drew Pearson: undated telegram, Pearson papers. Kennedy to Krock; May 24, 1938, Krock papers. Lippmann to Kennedy: May 4, 1938, Lippmann papers. The quotations from Kennedy's "Private and Confidential" letters are common to letters from Kennedy in the Baruch, Byrnes, Kent, Krock, Lippmann, and Pearson papers. Rumor of Kennedy Harvard degree and his "declination": *NYT*, May 18, 1938, p. 19, and *Boston Globe*, June 22, 1938, p. 5.

Kennedy for President Kennedy as "crown prince": *New York Daily News*, December 10, 1937, p. 22. Kennedy as first Catholic president: Harlan Miller in *Washington Post*, March 15, 1938, p. 15. *Boston Post* editorial: May 29, 1938, p. 6. "Will Kennedy Run for President?": *Liberty*, May 21, 1938, p. 15. Ernest Lindley comment is from interview. Hugh Johnson on Kennedy publicity: *New York World-Telegram*, June 17, 1938, p. 21. Ickes on alleged arrangement between Kennedy and Krock: Ickes diary, July 3, 1938. Kennedy confirms appeal to Sulzberger: Kennedy to Krock, October 10, 1941, Krock papers. Krock confirms Kennedy presidential hopes: Krock, p. 148. C. L. Sulzberger recounted his interview and article about Kennedy in Sulzberger[1], pp. 21–23. Eva Hinton described her husband's duties and compensation to the author. Kennedy fifth in presidential survey: Hadley Cantril (ed.), *Public Opinion* 1935–1946 (Princeton, 1951), p. 81. Kennedy on presidential chances: DM, Chapter 9. Kennedy's arrival in New York: *NYT*, June 21, 1938, p. 6, and James Roosevelt interview. Roosevelt message for Chamberlain: DM, Chapter 10. Kennedy and Roosevelt emerge from Hyde Park meeting: *NYT*, June 22, 1938, p. 4. Early offers exclusive to Walter Trohan: Trohan interview. "Kennedy's 1940 Ambitions Open Roosevelt Rift": *Chicago Tribune*, June 23, 1938, p. 1. Krock reaction to story: Trohan interview. Kennedy discovers source: DM, Chapter 9. Roosevelt recounts his discussions with Kennedy for the Ickeses: Ickes diary, July 3, 1938 and September 5, 1938.

The Path to Munich John D. Rockefeller, Jr., to Kennedy: June 10, 1938, KP. Sources on Kennedy's negotiations with Thomas Lamont are private memorandums of June 27 and 28, 1938, by Arthur Krock, who was present, Krock papers, and Thomas Lamont to Kennedy, June 25, 1938, Lamont papers. Kennedy on James Roosevelt and whiskey: *Baltimore Sun*, June 29, 1938. Neville Chamberlain diary entry: July 1, 1938, quoted in Robert Keith Middlemas, *The Strategy of Appeasement: The British Government and Germany, 1937–1939* (Quadrangle, 1972), pp. 284–285. Kennedy to von Dirksen: *German Documents*, pp. 721–723. American correspondent: De Witt Mackenzie in *Washington Evening Star*, September 15, 1938. A copy of Kennedy's proposed speech draft, August 31, 1938, is in SD file 123, NA. Roosevelt's paraphrase to Morgenthau: Blum, I, p. 518. Kennedy Hearst interview and Roosevelt complaint to Hull: *Boston Evening American*, August 31, 1938, p. 1 and Roosevelt to Hull, September 1, 1938, SD file 123, NA. Roosevelt to Kennedy on "difficult days": August 25, 1938, RP. Roosevelt on "red-headed Irishman": Morgenthau diary, September 1, 1938, Alsop and Kintner on Roosevelt resentment of Kennedy: *Washington Evening Star*, September 19, 1938. Krock to Alsop was reported in *National Issues*, February 29, 1939, p. 22. Kennedy warning to Halifax and Roosevelt reaction: Morgenthau diary, September 1, 1938.

Sir Ronald Lindsay to Foreign Office on Roosevelt's thinking: September 12, 1938, FO 414, PRO. Lindsay on second meeting with Roosevelt: September 20, 1938, FO 371, PRO. Lindbergh's view of Kennedy: *The Wartime Journals of Charles A. Lindbergh* (Harcourt

Brace Jovanovich, 1970), p. 26. Anne Morrow Lindbergh on Kennedy is from her *The Flower and the Nettle: Diaries and Letters of Anne Morrow Lindbergh* (Harcourt Brace Jovanovich, 1976), pp. 262, 529. Chamberlain to Cabinet on fighting Germany: R. J. Minney (ed.), *The Private Papers of Hore-Belisha* (Doubleday, 1961), p. 146. Rose Kennedy's diary entry is quoted in Rose Kennedy, p. 238. Kennedy to Krock: September 26, 1938, Krock papers. Roosevelt appeal for continued negotiation: Hull, pp. 591–592. "War is off": DM, Chapter 16. Kennedy to Lindbergh: Charles Lindbergh, p. 78. Roosevelt congratulation to Chamberlain: September 28, 1938, *FRUS*, I, p. 688. Kennedy to Hull on Roosevelt's role: same date, *FRUS*, I, p. 693, and DM, Chapter 16. Kennedy to Halifax is from E. L. Woodward and Rohan Butler (eds.), *Documents on British Foreign Policy, 1919–1939*, Series III (His Majesty's Stationery Office, London, 1949), September 29, 1938, II, p. 625. Roosevelt telegram on Chamberlain's return: October 5, 1938, quoted in Langer and Gleason, p. 35n. Kennedy's recollection of delivery: *New York World-Telegram*, April 11, 1960. Kennedy to Jan Masaryk: James Laver, *Between the Wars* (Houghton Mifflin, 1961), p. 225.

Brickbats Over the Atlantic Kennedy on exciting month: Kennedy to Byrnes, October 10, 1938, Byrnes papers. Kennedy's Trafalgar Day address was reported in *NYT*, October 20, 1938, p. 10. Heywood Broun's comment appeared in the *Wall Street Journal*, October 28, 1938, p. 2. Krock on difficulty facing Kennedy: *NYT*, October 25, 1938, IV, p. 3. Kennedy "hardly prepared": DM, Chapter 18. Roosevelt "not upset" by Munich: *PL*, IV, p. 818. Roosevelt's address: *PPA*, 1938, pp. 563–564. Kennedy on back-stabbing: Whalen, p. 251. Kennedy to Byrnes is from letters of October 10 and November 10, 1938, Byrnes papers. Boettiger to Kennedy, October 28, 1938, and Kennedy reply, November 25, 1938, are in Boettiger papers. Rublee to Roosevelt on Kennedy and refugees: George Rublee oral history, OHP. Roosevelt on anti-Semitism: DM, Chapter 21. Kennedy on refugees: DM, Chapter 19. *Life* on Kennedy Plan: January 16, 1939. Roosevelt's and Hull's professed ignorance: *NYT*, November 16, 1938, p. 1. Boake Carter on Kennedy's return is from his column in the *New York Daily Mirror*, November 12, 1938. Kennedy on possible firing: quoted by William Gross in letter to Herbert Hoover, January 28, 1939, Hoover papers. Farley to Morgenthau: Morgenthau diary, December 5, 1938. Kennedy's press conference on arrival in New York: *NYT*, December 16, 1938, p. 13. Talk at White House: DM, Chapter 21. Kennedy's memorandum on the effect of the decline of the British Empire, December 19, 1938, is in RP. "Virtual publicity bureau": Henry Ehrlich in *Boston Herald*, March 26, 1939. Lamont to Kennedy on Coughlin: January 26, 1939, Lamont papers. Corcoran on Kennedy presidential campaign: Blum, II, p. 36. Kennedy recollection of Roosevelt's private declaration is from DM, Chapter 21. Boake Carter on Kennedy's departure: *Boston Globe*, April 20, 1939, p. 1. Kennedy to Roosevelt: DM, Chapter 21. Krock inquiry on Princeton degree for Kennedy: Moffat diary, February 15, 1939. Drew Pearson to Robert Allen on possible Kennedy resignation: undated memorandum in Pearson papers. James Roosevelt on his father's decision to leave Kennedy in London: interview.

"The End of Everything" Kennedy on heightened optimism in Britain: Kennedy to Byrnes, February 24, 1939, Byrnes papers. Kennedy's world prophecy: Kennedy to Roosevelt, March 3, 1939, RP. Frank Kent on Roosevelt-Kennedy relations: *Wall Street Journal*, October 28, 1938, p. 2, Kennedy to Hoover on guarantee of Poland: private memorandum by Herbert Hoover after conversation with Kennedy, April 19, 1945, Hoover papers. Kennedy to Hull on Hitler reluctance to fight: transcript of telephone conversation, April 24, 1949, Hull papers. Criticism of Kennedy by Ickes and Frankfurter is from Ickes diaries, April 29 and October 26, 1939. Ickes shows *The Week* article to Roosevelt and Roosevelt's response: Ickes diary, July 2, 1939. J. Edgar Hoover's dispatch of a copy to the White House is noted in an internal memorandum on Joseph Kennedy, June 9, 1948, in FBI files. Kennedy to Welles on Paris dinner and reply: May 4, 1939, in SD file 123, NA. Kennedy complaint to Byrnes on State Department: July 15, 1939, Byrnes papers. Kennedy to Hull on being circumvented: Kennedy to Hull, October 28, 1938, in SD file 841, NA. Queen on U.S. visit: DM, Chapter 16. Smith-Kennedy exchange: November 10 and 25, 1938, KP. Corcoran on visit of king and queen: interview. Kennedy to Roosevelt complaining of being wasted: July 20, 1939, RP. Roosevelt's reply: July 22, 1939, RP. Ickes on Roosevelt's letter to Kennedy: Ickes diary, August 12, 1939. Kennedy to Byrnes on "smart thing for the United States to do": July 15, 1939, Byrnes papers.

Roosevelt asks Kennedy to embolden Chamberlain: quoted by Kennedy to James Forrestal in Walter Millis (ed.), *The Forrestal Diaries* (Viking, 1951), pp. 121–122. Kennedy on peace appeal: DM, Chapter 33. Kennedy to Roosevelt on Henderson report: August 25, 1939, RP. Roosevelt reaction: Ickes diary, August 29, 1939. Kennedy to Eleanor Roosevelt, August 31, 1939, and her reply, September 12, 1939, are in the Eleanor Roosevelt papers. Account of the coming war is based on Joseph Alsop and Robert Kintner, *American White Paper* (Simon and Schuster, 1940); Burns[2], pp. 349–395; Hull, I, pp. 671–682; DM, Chapters 33 and 34; and Moffat diary, September 1939.

Seven / TURNING OF THE LEAVES

Kennedy appeal for Roosevelt to make peace: Kennedy to Hull, September 11, 1939, *FRUS*, I, pp. 421–424. Roosevelt to Farley on Kennedy's message: Farley, pp. 198–199. Roosevelt to Morgenthau on Kennedy as "appeaser": Blum, II, p. 102. Hull's reprimand to Kennedy: September 11, 1939, *FRUS*, I, p. 424. Kennedy on end of days as diplomat: Whalen, p. 274. Kennedy to Krock on advent of war: September 15, 1939, Krock papers. British diplomat perceives emotionalism in Kennedy's views: J. Victor Perowne, January 29, 1940, FO 371, PRO. Kennedy warning to Roosevelt against British designs on America: September 10, 1939, RP. George VI to Kennedy: John Wheeler-Bennett, *King George VI* (Macmillan, 1958), p. 419.

Diplomatic Tug-of-War Kennedy again warns Roosevelt about British: September 30, 1939, RP. Kennedy's warning to Hull: October 2, 1939, *FRUS*, I, p. 500. Roosevelt's response: *PL*, IV, p.,. Kennedy on Churchill: DM, Chapter 36. Kennedy meetings with von Dirksen and von Dirksen's conclusion: *German Documents*, IV, pp. 634–637. *The Week* on Kennedy's embassy as intermediary with Berlin and Ickes transmittal to Roosevelt: Ickes diary, September, 27, 1939. Kennedy resumes appeal to Roosevelt for peace settlement: November 3, 1939, RP. Kennedy meeting with Chamberlain: DM, pp. 483–486. Citations from Whitehall minute books refer to documents located in FO 371, PRO. Balfour on Kennedy assurance of British defeat: September 4, 1939. Cadogan's response: same date. Report on American Embassy dinner: Sir John Balfour, September 20 and 26, 1939. Kennedy "entitled to his opinion": September 21, 1939. Cadogan disagrees: same date. Comments by Victor Perowne and Sir Berkeley Gage: September 26, 1939. Warning to Lord Lothian: October 3, 1939. Report on Hillman talk: Charles Peake, October 12, 1939. Balfour interjection: September 30, 1939. Intelligence officer on Kennedy White House ambitions: Rex Leeper to J. Victor Perowne, October 16, 1939. Perowne on merits in Kennedy talk: September 26, 1939. Churchill on Kennedy comments: quoted by Walter Lippmann in oral history, OHP. Kennedy on effects of Britain's entry into war on American economy: Kennedy to Hull, November 28, 1939, SD file 640, NA. Kennedy to Krock, November 3, 1939, Krock papers. Kennedy dinner with king and queen and desire to rest in Palm Beach: DM, Chapter 37.

Reprise: Kennedy for President Kennedy press conference on return at New York: *NYT*, December 7, 1939, p. 3. Kennedy to friend on third term: Whalen, p. 283. Kennedy third-term endorsement: *NYT*, December 9, 1939, p. 1. Kennedy's day at White House: DM, Chapter 38. Kennedy warns against intervention: *NYT*, December 11, 1939, p. 2. British criticism of speech was quoted in the *New York Herald-Tribune*, December 16, 1939. Cadogan relief: December 14, 1939, FO 371, PRO. Kennedy fear of stomach cancer: Ickes diary, January 27, 1940. Kennedy promise to Roosevelt of return if European crisis flares: January 18, 1940, RP. Burns[2], pp. 408–415, offers an account of the movements that enabled the Sphinx to win a third-term draft. Roosevelt urges Kennedy to enter Massachusetts primary: DM, Chapter 38. The most thorough contemporary accounts of the Kennedy boomlet are in the *Boston Post,* February 12, 13 and 14, 1940, all p. 1. The Kennedy-Bullitt contretemps is recorded in the Ickes diary, March 10, 1940. Kennedy on Bullitt: Kennedy to Rose Kennedy, Schlesinger[4], p. 29.

"I Do Not Enjoy Being a Dummy" Kennedy on his return to London: DM, Chapter 40. Foreign Office man on reasons for Kennedy's return: March 30, 1940, FO 371, PRO. Beaverbrook on Kennedy pessimism: Beaverbrook to Frank Knox, March 4, 1940, Beaverbrook papers. Kennedy on vestige of his official duties: quoted by Robert Murphy in *Diplomat among Warriors* (Doubleday, 1964), p. 38. Kennedy to Krock, April 22, 1940, Krock papers. Kennedy on Welles mission: DM, Chapter 40. Morgenthau to Roosevelt on Kennedy encroachment: Morgenthau diary, May 3, 1940. Kennedy citation of Denmark and Norway as example of British unpreparedness: Hull, I, p. 763. Morgenthau worry over Roosevelt gloom: Morgenthau diary, April 29, 1940. Roosevelt telegram to Kennedy: May 3, 1940, RP. Kennedy congratulatory telephone call to Churchill is in DM. Kennedy on Churchill's reaction when America drawn into war: *Boston Herald,* April 7, 1947, V, p. 19. Kennedy to Roosevelt on Churchill plea for aid: May 14, 1940, *FRUS,* III, pp. 29–30. Kennedy pleads again with Roosevelt for settlement: *FRUS,* 1940, I, p. 233.

Sources for discussion of Kennedy and the Tyler Kent case are interviews with Clare Boothe Luce and Frank C. Waldrop; transcript of trial in Charles B. Parsons collection; interview with Kennedy in *Washington Daily News,* September 5, 1944; and Whalen, pp. 310–320. Kennedy report on Churchill assurance that America will intervene: June 12, 1940, *FRUS,* III, p. 37. Kennedy wire to Roosevelt opposing publication of Reynaud message: June 14, 1940, in SD file 740, NA. Hoover note on Kennedy's version: private memorandum by Herbert Hoover, April 19, 1945, Hoover papers. Neville Chamberlain's diary entry is quoted in Iain MacLeod, *Neville Chamberlain* (Frederick Muller, 1961), p. 279. Roosevelt on chances for Allied victory: Farley, p. 253. Poll on American pessimism: Langer and Gleason, II, p. 479. Kennedy on Donovan mission: Kennedy to Hull, July 12, 1940, in SD file 740, NA. Kennedy on Mowrer: Kennedy to Hull, July 13, 1940, in SD file 841, NA. Roosevelt on Kennedy's objections: Roosevelt to Frank Knox, July 13, 1940, RP. Balfour on Donovan verdict: August 22, 1940, FO 371, PRO. Kennedy's suspicions about Churchill and Halifax comments on Roosevelt reelection: DM, Chapter 41. Kennedy refusal to pressure son to vote for Roosevelt: *Boston Record-American,* January 22, 1964. Kennedy to Farley on son's vote: telegram, July 19, 1940, Farley papers.

Roosevelt to Kennedy on reasons against appointment as Democratic national chairman: quoted in DM, Chapter 48. Foreign Office on possibility of Kennedy replacement: 1939 Personalities, 371, PRO. Kennedy to Moore and Mrs. Luce on call: DM, Chapter 48. Kennedy on encouraging Jack to write on Munich: quoted in George Bilainkin, *Diary of a Diplomatic Correspondent* (George Allen and Unwin, 1942), p. 194. Kennedy reminder of politician's duties as educator: Burns[1], p. 43. Roosevelt to Henry Luce on destroyer deal: Clare Boothe Luce interview. Kennedy on destroyer deal: *FRUS,* 1940, III, pp. 72–73. Kennedy suspicions about circumvention: DM, Chapter 48. Kennedy on annoyance at "being a dummy": Kennedy to Roosevelt, August 27, 1940, in SD file 811, NA. Kennedy to Hull on possible resignation: quoted in DM, Chapter 48. Roosevelt reassurance: *PL,* IV, pp. 1061–1062. Hull reassurance: September 21, 1940, in SD file 123, NA. Kennedy to wife on not fooling himself: DM, Chapter 48. Kennedy to Halifax, DM, Chapter 48. Clare Luce telegram: DM, Chapter 47. Kennedy to Welles and Roosevelt call: DM, Chapter 48. Kennedy cable after Dakar: *FRUS,* 1940, III, pp. 48–49. Willkie to New York audience: *NYT,* October 9, 1940. Clare Boothe Luce reported Kennedy's comments on Roosevelt to the author.

Lord Halifax warned Lord Lothian of Kennedy's "indictment" of Roosevelt on October 10, 1940, copy in FO 371, PRO. Supreme Court huddle: DM, Chapter 52. Roosevelt on Kennedy as troublemaker: Long diary, October 11, 1940. Presidential assistant Edwin Watson transmitted Welles's assurance to Roosevelt: October 25, 1940, RP. Kennedy wire to Welles on displeasure: October 11, 1940, in SD file 123, NA. Kennedy recorded his final meeting with Chamberlain in DM, Chapter 50. He described Chamberlain's letter in a conversation with Herbert Hoover, Hoover private memorandum, May 15, 1945, in Hoover papers. Journalist on Kennedy's departure from London: Bilainkin, p. 242. Roosevelt speech at Philadelphia: *PPA*, 1940, p. 448.

Fateful Return Lyndon Johnson related Roosevelt's telephone conversation with Kennedy to Arthur Krock: Krock, p. 399. Kennedy press conference at La Guardia Field: *NYT*, October 28, 1940, p. 1. Luces waiting in Manhattan: Clare Boothe Luce interview. Roosevelt to Grace Tully on buttering up Kennedy: Grace Tully interview. Rose Kennedy on Roosevelt charm: Schlesinger[4], p. 24. Rose Kennedy to husband on danger of ingratitude: private memorandum by Arthur Krock, December 1, 1940 (excerpt in Krock, pp. 335–336), setting down Kennedy's version of his return from London, Krock papers. General Wood to Kennedy on revealing secret agreements: October 25, 1940, Wood papers. References for the early portion of the evening at the White House are DM, Chapter 51, Schlesinger[4], pp. 35–36, Krock memorandum of December 1, 1940; and James F. Byrnes, *All in One Lifetime* (Harper, 1958), p. 125. John F. Kennedy on Roosevelt's "offer" of 1944 nomination: Stewart Alsop in *Saturday Evening Post*, August 13, 1960, p. 59. William Stephenson on Kennedy transcripts: Stevenson, p. 150. James Roosevelt offered his impression of his father's conversation with Kennedy in an interview. Kennedy agrees to make speech: Krock memorandum, December 1, 1940, Krock papers. Rose Kennedy's overnight stay at White House: Usher's diary, October 28, 1940, in FDRL.

Edward Moore to reporters: *Washington Times-Herald*, October 29, 1940, p. 1. Foreign Office conclusion of Kennedy for Willkie: T. Graham Hutton memorandum, October 18, 1940. FO 371, PRO. *Washington Star* on Kennedy plans: October 29, 1940. Text of Kennedy's third-term endorsement broadcast is in *NYT*, October 30, 1940, p. 1. Telegrams to White House on Kennedy speech, October 29, 1940, RP. *Life* on effectiveness of speech: January 27, 1941. Willkie agreement reported by John Cowles to Kennedy: December 5, 1940, KP. Lindley comment: *Washington Post*, November 1, 1940, p. 11. Morgenthau to Kennedy: Morgenthau diary, October 30, 1940. Jerome Frank comment: Frank to Kennedy, November 1, 1940, Frank papers. Roosevelt to Kennedy: quoted in Krock memorandum, December 1, 1940. Democratic National Committee advertisement: *Chicago Tribune*, November 1, 1940, p. 11. Wood to Kennedy on speaking more frankly: November 4, 1940, Wood papers. Colonel Lee on Kennedy speech: James Leutze (ed.), *The London Journal of General Raymond E. Lee, 1940–1941* (Little, Brown, 1971), p. 115. Wendell Willkie's reaction was reported in the *Chicago Herald-American*, October 30, 1940, p. 1. Clare Boothe Luce's recollection of Kennedy's explanation for his third-term endorsement is from an interview. Willkie on Roosevelt Boston speech: Divine, p. 82. Text of Roosevelt speech is in *NYT*, November 1, 1940, p. 1. It has been wryly noted that the pledge against American boys in foreign wars does not appear in the version of the address in *PPA*. Kennedy on close, vicious fight: Kennedy telegram to Beaverbrook, November 5, 1940, Beaverbrook papers.

The Greatest Cause in the World Description of Washington reception for Roosevelt is from *NYT*, November 6, 1960, p. 1. Long on conversation with Kennedy: Long diary, November 6, 1940. Kennedy talk with Roosevelt: DM, Chapter 52, and Krock memorandum, December 1, 1940. Louis Lyons offers his version of the Kennedy interview story in *Newspaper Story: One Hundred Years of the Boston Globe* (Belknap Press, 1971), pp. 290–292. Text of Lyons article: *Boston Globe*, November 10, 1940, p. 1. Kennedy's reaction on telephone: Dinneen, pp. 84–85. White Committee asks Kennedy repudiation by Roosevelt: William H. Tuttle, Jr., "A Reappraisal of William Allen White's Leadership," *Journal* *of American History*, March 1970, p. 856. Krock to Kennedy on *Globe* interview: November 12, 1940, Krock papers. Kennedy to Krock on White's apology: January 3, 1941, copy in White papers. Frankfurter to Roosevelt: Max Freedman (ed.), *Roosevelt and Frankfurter: Their Correspondence, 1928–1945* (Little, Brown, 1967), p. 553. Laski's article, "Mr. Kennedy and Democracy," appeared in *Harper's*, April 1941, pp. 464–470. Lippmann's column appeared in the *New York Herald-Tribune*, December 5, 1940. Angry letter to White House: November 29, 1940, in RP. Fairbanks to Roosevelt, November 19, 1940, is in RP.

British intelligence report: E. A. Cleugh to Richard Ford, November 22, 1940, PRO. Zanuck on Kennedy motives: confidential memorandum, December 16, 1940, in Alsop papers. Pearson on Kennedy Hollywood talk: *Washington Times-Herald*, November 26, 1940. Marion Davies's version of the conflict between Kennedy and John Boettiger appears in her memoir, *The Times We Had* (Bobbs-Merrill, 1976), pp. 222–224. Boettiger's report to Roosevelt, February 19, 1941, is in the Anna Roosevelt Halsted papers. Hoover's memorandum on his talk with Kennedy, November 22, 1940, is in the Hoover papers. Arthur Schlesinger, Jr., attributes Kennedy's reference probably to an approach through the High Court of Sweden by a Berlin lawyer and Hitler associate to the British minister in Stockholm (Schlesinger[4], p. 36n). Roosevelt to cabinet on recent Kennedy talk and Ickes reaction: Ickes diary, December 1 and 13, 1940. Account of Roosevelt-Kennedy confrontation at Hyde Park is from Lash, p. 287, Gore Vidal in the *New York Review of Books*, November 18, 1971, p. 8, and interviews with James and Franklin Roosevelt, Jr. David Koskoff doubts the occurrence of this meeting on grounds that Kennedy was probably on the West Coast during the weekend the Roosevelts were at Hyde Park (Koskoff, p. 571), but in fact, Kennedy had returned several days earlier in order to speak with Herbert Hoover in New York. Kennedy to Roosevelt on resignation: DM, chapter 52. Kennedy to reporters after resignation announcement: *New York Herald-Tribune*, December 2, 1940, p. 1.

Dorothy Thompson on Kennedy "cause": *New York Herald-Tribune*, December 6, 1940, p. 21. Kennedy to Kintner is reported in Ickes diary, December 13, 1940. Ickes criticism of Kennedy: Ickes diary, same date. *Chicago Daily News* on involvement of Ben Smith and Kennedy in campaign for negotiated peace and Kennnedy's denial: December 4 and 5, 1940. Carroll Binder on Kennedy's involvement and Roosevelt discovery: quote in memorandum to Sir Eric Machtig, February 4, 1941, PRO. Roosevelt on Kennedy as example of "appeasers" problem: Ickes diary, December 21, 1940. Reports on investigation of Kennedy's activities and tax returns: Alsop and Kintner in *Washington Evening Star*, December 5, 1940, and column by Westbrook Pegler, March 30, 1960, in Pegler papers. Ickes on Roosevelt speech against Kennedy "appeasement campaign": Ickes diary, December 1, 1940. Wood offer of America First chairmanship and Kennedy declination: December 11 and 17, 1940, Wood papers. Ludlow on Kennedy: *Washington Times-Herald*, December 20, 1940. Roosevelt "arsenal of democracy" address is in *PPA*, 1940, pp. 633–644. John Boettiger's letter, December 30, 1940, is in Boettiger papers.

Eight / WINTER OF DISCONTENT

1941 State of the Union: *PPA*, 1940, pp. 663–672. *Life* on Roosevelt foreign policy foes: January 20, 1941. Kennedy airplane conversation with Franklin Roosevelt, Jr.: interview with Franklin Roosevelt, Jr. The Englishman also reported the exchange to British intelligence; it appears in J. J. Astor to Brendan Bracken, February 19, 1941, FO 371, PRO. Reporter on "peace-at-any-price broadcast": *Chicago Daily News*, January 17, 1941. British diplomats suggest Kennedy as Irish mediator to Hull: memorandum, January 13, 1941, in Hull papers. Kennedy describes his January 16 meeting with Roosevelt in DM, Chapter 52. Kennedy to Boettiger on faltering relations with president: January 3, 1941, Boettiger papers. Kennedy to White House aide on Wheeler comment and avoidance of Wheeler at hotel: Whalen, p. 356, and James Rowe, Jr., interview.

To Be and Not to Be Text of Kennedy's radio broadcast is in the *Washington Post*, January 19, 1941, p. 5. A recording of excerpts from the address is in JFKL. Dorothy Thompson on speech: *New York Herald-Tribune*, January 22, 1941, p. 17. Telegram from Boston Latin alumnus, January 18, 1941, is in RP. The *New York Herald-Tribune* editorial appeared on January 19, 1941. Wood to Kennedy on speech: January 22, 1941, Wood papers. Internal memorandum on reactions to Kennedy's address is in the America First papers. Kennedy testimony on Lend-Lease: *Hearings Before the Committee on Foreign Affairs*, House of Representatives, 77th Congress, 1st Session, on H.R. 1776 (Government Printing Office, 1941), pp. 221–315. Kennedy version of reason for pulling punches: DM, Chapter 52. Clapper on Kennedy position: clipping in America First papers, January 22, 1941. Coughlin doubts Roosevelt-Kennedy disagreement: *Social Justice*, February 3, 1941, p. 3. Congressman O'Connor on Roosevelt winning over opposition is from a letter to Amos Pinchot, January 2, 1941 in Pinchot papers. Opinions of Fish and Byrnes: *Chicago Tribune*, January 19, 1941, p. 12. Willkie on British attitude toward Kennedy and his jest with the queen are from a transcript of a confidential interview with Joseph Alsop, undated, 1941, Alsop papers. Hopkins sees Kennedy in New York: DM, Chapter 52. *Christian Century* on whispering campaign: January 29, 1941, p. 142. O'Donnell and Fleeson on Hopkins British visit: *New York Daily News*, January 13, 1941. Ickes transmittal of Masaryk story to Roosevelt and Roosevelt response: Ickes diary, January 19, 1941.

Alsop and Kintner on Ben Smith peace campaign: *New York Herald-Tribune*, January 9, 1941. J. Edgar Hoover on alleged Kennedy-Smith-Goering meeting is from a letter to Edwin Watson, May 3, 1941, RP. Kennedy to Herbert Hoover on realizing meaninglessness of Roosevelt promises: Hoover private memorandum, May 15, 1945, Hoover papers. Kennedy speech at Oglethorpe was reprinted in the *Congressional Record*, XXCVII, A2510. Kennedy at Notre Dame was reported in *NYT*, June 2, 1941, p. 20. Article on founding of Harvard Committee Against Military Intervention, undated, is in America First papers. Swearing in of Joseph Kennedy, Jr., and John Roosevelt is from John Roosevelt interview and Hank Searls, *The Lost Prince: Young Joe, The Forgotten Kennedy* (Ballantine reprint, 1977), p. 156. Copy of Hoover's proposed declaration, July 1941, is in Hoover papers. Hoover request for Kennedy's signature and Kennedy demurral: July 1 and 29, 1941, Hoover papers. Kennedy to Hoover on public reaction to foreign policy: July 11, 1941, Hoover papers. Kennedy to Krock on sense of complacency: October 10, 1941, Krock papers.

In the Leper Colony Kennedy Pearl Harbor telegram to Roosevelt: *PL*, IV, p. 1290. Roosevelt's surprise at Kennedy's reticence and Kennedy's attempts to reach the president are noted in Kennedy to Roosevelt, March 4, 1942, RP. Kennedy to Boettiger: January 31, 1942, Boettiger papers. Roosevelt response: *PL*, IV, pp. 1289–1290. Kennedy reply to Roosevelt: March 12, 1942, RP. Bullitt to Ickes on Kennedy "insolence": Ickes diary, March 29, 1942. Roosevelt to Land on job for Kennedy is quoted in Frederic C. Lane, *Ships for Victory: A History of Shipbuilding under the U.S. Maritime Commission in World War II* (Johns Hopkins, 1951), p. 167. Kennedy to Byrnes on breaking ice at White House: March 21, 1942, Byrnes papers. Kennedy after Roosevelt meeting: *NYT*, April 17, 1942, p. 237. Ickes on Kennedy offer and Frank Walker reaction: Ickes diary, March 29 and April 26, 1942. *PM* on pressure for Kennedy: April 21, 1942. Coordinating Committee for Democratic Action position is noted in S. E. McClure to Byrnes, May 2, 1942, Byrnes papers. Clarence Randall to Krock, May 8, 1942, and Krock reply, May 18, 1942, are in Krock papers. National Maritime Union to Roosevelt: April 25, 1942, copy in FBI. Roosevelt on Kennedy talk: PC, April 21, 1942. Joseph Martin on Kennedy in shipping: *NYT*, April 26, 1942, p. 35. *Washington Times-Herald* on Kennedy in war transport: June 15, 1942. Columnist on Kennedy's exile: Bill Cunningham in *Boston Herald*, August 16, 1942. Kennedy to Beaverbrook on exile: August 12, 1942, Beaverbrook papers. Senator Nye's possession of material on Kennedy and James Roosevelt is reported to the White House in letter from J.

Edgar Hoover to Edwin Watson, April 20, 1942, RP. Kennedy to Waldrop on Fitzgerald campaign: September 15, 1942, Waldrop papers.

Other sources on the Fitzgerald campaign of 1942 are Cutler, pp. 295–296; Krock, p. 357; and Kenneth O'Donnell and David Powers, *Johnny, We Hardly Knew Ye* (Little, Brown, 1972), pp. 50–51. Kennedy to Beaverbrook on American sentiment: August 12 and October 1, 1942, Beaverbrook papers. References for Kennedy post-election talk with Roosevelt and Roosevelt report to congressiional leadership are Kennedy to Beaverbrook, December 31, 1942, Beaverbrook papers, and Wallace diary, December 14, 1942. Roosevelt to Byrnes on Kennedy for small business: December 12, 1942, Byrnes papers. Roosevelt to Nelson: December 29, 1942, RP. Roosevelt go-ahead to Byrnes: January 13, 1943, Byrnes papers. Kennedy's reaction to the offer was reported to Roosevelt by Byrnes, January 14, 1943, Byrnes papers. Roosevelt to Krock on Kennedy's "hard-headedness" is from Arthur Krock oral history, JFKL. Kennedy to Kent on his refusal: March 2, 1943, Kent papers. Dr. George Sperti recalled his efforts to bring Kennedy back to government in letters to the author, December 22, 1977, and February 28, 1978. Kennedy on being "fed up" is from letter to Kent of March 2, 1943, Kent papers.

Memorandum on Kennedy's desire to see Roosevelt, March 10, 1943, is in RP. Roosevelt to Kennedy on maté: *PL*, IV, p. 1417. Kennedy on differences with Roosevelt: William J. Duncliffe, *The Life and Times of Joseph P. Kennedy* (Avon, 1964), p. 114. Kennedy to newspaperman on sinking of American ships: Frank Waldrop interview. Frankfurter on Kennedy role in attack on David Niles: Frankfurter diary, May 12, 1943. Kennedy on diplomatic memoir: Blair and Blair, pp. 107–109, and private memorandum by Herbert Hoover, May 15, 1945, Hoover papers. Kennedy on suffering in silence: Kennedy to Beaverbrook, December 31, 1942, Beaverbrook papers. Kennedy declines article for *Reader's Digest:* Lawrence Dennis oral history, OHP. Kennedy to Krock on Pearl Harbor: Arthur Krock oral history, JFKL. Kennedy on Roosevelt promise to Churchill: Dr. George Sperti to author, December 22, 1977. Kennedy in New York restaurant was reported in the *Financial Chronicle* (New York), March 11, 1943. Kennedy's service to the FBI is documented in Edward Soucy to J. Edgar Hoover, September 7, 1943; Miami field office to Hoover, July 1, 1944; and Boston field office memorandum, October 11, 1945, all in FBI. Kennedy to Beaverbrook on growing American conservatism: December 18, 1943, Beaverbrook papers.

Final Reunion Kennedy on next generation: Dinneen, p. 110. Kennedy at cadet ceremony: Searls, p. 171. Byrnes reported the commendation of Kennedy, Jr., and his father's wishes to Roosevelt in a memorandum, March 20, 1944, Byrnes papers. For Kennedy-Douglas friendship, see William O. Douglas, *Go East, Young Man* (Random House, 1974), pp. 200, 281, 317. Rumors on Kennedy as a financier for Douglas campaign: Frankfurter diary, January 11, 1943. Kennedy on probable Roosevelt defeat and on son's return to Beaverbrook: May 24, 1944, Beaverbrook papers. Sources for Joseph Kennedy, Jr.'s explosion and Kennedy, Sr., to family are Searls, p. 242, and Edward Kennedy in EMK, p. 207. Roosevelt to Kennedy on Hartington death: September 20, 1944, RP. Kennedy on war is from a letter to Walter Trohan, June 18, 1948, Trohan papers. Roosevelt on being tired: Gunther, p. 18. "Just doesn't give a damn": Edwin Watson, quoted in Jim Bishop, *FDR's Last Year* (Morrow, 1975), p. 168. Account of the selection of Truman is in Burns[3], pp. 503–506. Boston News Bureau on Kennedy endorsement of Dewey: *NYT*, October 27, 1944, p. 1. Source for Kennedy's final meeting with Roosevelt is private memorandum by Arthur Krock, October 26, 1944, based on Kennedy's recollection immediately after the conversation, Krock papers. Roosevelt's report at luncheon is recorded in the Ickes diary, November 15, 1944. Kennedy discussed his last visit with Roosevelt also with Dorothy Schiff: interview.

References for Kennedy's meeting with Truman are Truman's account in Merle Miller, *Plain Speaking* (Doubleday, 1973), p. 186, and Edward Gallagher oral history, JFKL. James Roosevelt told the author he believed Kennedy contributed to Dewey in 1944. Archivists in the Dewey papers, University of Rochester Library, could find no complete accounting of campaign donations for 1944. Roosevelt Boston speech: *PPA*, 1944–1945, pp. 397–406. Harold Ickes on Kennedy as candidate for lending agencies: Ickes diary, March 4, 1945. Pearson to Kennedy on talk with Henry Wallace and Kennedy reply: March 20 and 24, 1945, Pearson papers. Kennedy statement on death of Roosevelt: *Washington Evening Star*, April 13, 1945. Kennedy to Kathleen: May 1, 1945, quoted in Schlesinger[4], pp. 59–60. Kennedy reminiscences of Roosevelt: Schiff interview.

Epilogue / THE DENOUEMENT

Kennedy on Truman's task: Kennedy to Beaverbrook, May 13, 1946, Beaverbrook papers. Kennedy on knowing Truman well and possible appointment of Jack: Kennedy to Kathleen, May 1, 1945 letter. Hannegan to Truman on Kennedy for RFC and Truman's reply: July 20 and July 27, 1945, Truman papers. Byrnes to Kennedy denying report and Kennedy reply: July 17 and July 19, 1945, Byrnes papers. Kennedy on state socialism: *NYT*, October 7, 1945. Kennedy to Pegler: April 1, 1947, Pegler papers. Kennedy to Hoover: July 26, 1949, Hoover papers. Kennedy declines SEC anniversary invitation: James Landis oral history, OHP.

A New Generation Arthur Schlesinger, Jr., on Roosevelt and Kennedy sons: essay in Kay Halle (ed.), *The Grand Original* (Houghton Mifflin, 1971), p. 282. James Roosevelt on conversations with Joseph Kennedy after the war is from an interview. Franklin Roosevelt, Jr., on friendship with John Kennedy is from interview. Joseph Kennedy on Franklin Roosevelt, Jr., for president: Franklin Roosevelt, Jr., interview. Kennedy on reasons for Mrs. Roosevelt's antipathy is quoted by Gore Vidal in *Esquire*, April 1967, p. 202. Kennedy on meeting at 1956 convention is from transcript of interview with James MacGregor Burns in Professor Burns's possession. Mrs. Roosevelt on Kennedy: Lash, p. 280. Kennedy-Eleanor Roosevelt exchange of letters is in Eleanor Roosevelt papers, December 1958–January 1959. Another reference on their relations is James Landis oral history, OHP. A friend of both, Landis occasionally acted as intermediary. Gore Vidal's account of Mrs. Roosevelt on Joseph Kennedy is in *New York Review of Books*, November 18, 1971. Kennedy on standing for all he was against: Alfred Steinberg, *Sam Johnson's Boy* (Macmillan, 1968), p. 585. John Kennedy on father's support even if Communist candidate is from Schiff interview.

Kennedy to Luce on son as liberal: Henry R. Luce oral history, JFKL. Kennedy to Lippmann on seventieth birthday: September 25, 1959, Lippmann papers. Kennedy to Trohan is from letters of September 10 and October 22, 1960, Trohan papers. Krock on wish to see John Kennedy president: Arthur Krock oral history, JFKL. Kennedy invitation for dinner: August 17, 1960, Krock papers. Kennedy on quitting "dull line" is from private memorandum by Arthur Krock, October 25, 1960, Krock papers. Krock to Kennedy and Kennedy reply: October 20 and 25, 1960, Krock papers. Krock to Farley: January 10, 1961, Krock papers. Krock's final judgment on Kennedy: quoted in Blair and Blair, p. 43.

The Uneasy Alliance This section has been heavily influenced by James MacGregor Burns, *Leadership* (Harper & Row, 1978). Kennedy on power is quoted in Arnold A. Hutschnecker, *The Drive for Power* (Evans, 1974), p. 55. The Roosevelt biographer was Emil Ludwig, *Roosevelt: A Study in Fortune and Power* (Viking, 1938), p. 295. Kennedy on public service: *NYT*, April 18, 1937. Eleanor Roosevelt on husband and people: Joseph P. Lash, *Eleanor Roosevelt: A Friend's Memoir* (Doubleday, 1964), p. 211. Stimson on Roosevelt thought processes is from his diary, December 18, 1940. Kennedy to Roosevelt is from DM, Chapter 32. John Adams on family vs. country is quoted in James Truslow Adams, *The Adams Family* (The Literary Guild, 1930), p. 87. Kennedy on conservatism is in *NYT*, October 6, 1936. Kennedy on president's job: McCarthy, p. 24. Beaverbrook to Kennedy on White House: September 22, 1960, Beaverbrook papers. The New Dealer traded for the pair of murderers was Rexford Tugwell, as noted in his *In Search of Roosevelt* (Harvard,

1973), p. 276. Roosevelt on president's job: *NYT*, November 13, 1932, VIII, p. 1. Tugwell's view of Kennedy's relationship to Roosevelt is from a letter to the author, October 12, 1977. Roosevelt's note accompanying Kennedy's pen may be seen in the December 1937 edition of the "March of Time" newsreel series, housed in NA. Roosevelt to Kennedy on American condition in 1932: DM, Chapter 1. "I can say no to that fellow": McCarthy, p. 64. Kennedy and Roosevelt in West Virginia: *NYT*, April 27, 1960. Schlesinger on dynastic change: Arthur M. Schlesinger, Jr., *A Thousand Days* (Houghton Mifflin, 1965), p. 677. Franklin Roosevelt, Jr., quoted his platform remark on his father's relationship with Joseph Kennedy in interview.

INDEX